EXPLORATION OF TERRESTRIAL PLANETS FROM SPACECRAFT:
Instrumentation, Investigation, Interpretation

THE ELLIS HORWOOD LIBRARY OF SPACE SCIENCE AND SPACE TECHNOLOGY

SERIES IN ASTRONOMY

Series Editor: JOHN MASON
Consultant Editor: PATRICK MOORE

This series aims to coordinate a team of international authors of the highest reputation, integrity and expertise in all aspects of astronomy. It will make a valuable contribution to the existing literature, encompassing all areas of astronomical research. The titles will be illustrated with both black and white and colour photographs, and will include many line drawings and diagrams, with tabular data and extensive bibliographies. Aimed at a wide readership, the books will appeal to the professional astronomer, undergraduate students, the high-flying 'A' level student, and the non-scientist with a keen interest in astronomy.

PLANETARY VOLCANISM: A Study of Volcanic Activity in the Solar System
PETER CATTERMOLE, Department of Geology, Sheffield University, UK
SATELLITE ASTRONOMY: The Principles and Practice of Astronomy from Space
JOHN K. DAVIES, Royal Observatory, Edinburgh, UK
THE ORIGIN OF THE SOLAR SYSTEM: The Capture Theory
JOHN R. DORMAND, Department of Mathematics and Statistics, Teesside Polytechnic, Middlesborough, UK, and MICHAEL M. WOOLFSON, Department of Physics, University of York, UK
THE DUSTY UNIVERSE
ANEURIN EVANS, Department of Physics, University of Keele, UK
SPACE-TIME AND THEORETICAL COSMOLOGY
MICHEL HELLER, Department of Philosophy, University of Cracow, Poland
ASTEROIDS: Their Nature and Utilization
CHARLES T. KOWAL, Space Telescope Institute, Baltimore, Maryland, USA
ELECTRONIC AND COMPUTER-AIDED ASTRONOMY: From Eyes to Electronic Sensors
IAN S. McLEAN, Joint Astronomy Centre, Hilo, Hawaii, USA
URANUS: The Planet, Rings and Satellites
ELLIS D. MINER, Jet Propulsion Laboratory, Pasadena, California, USA
THE PLANET NEPTUNE
PATRICK MOORE, CBE
ACTIVE GALACTIC NUCLEI
IAN ROBSON, Director of Observatories, Lancashire Polytechnic, Preston, UK
ASTRONOMICAL OBSERVATIONS FROM THE ANCIENT ORIENT
RICHARD F. STEPHENSON, Department of Physics, Durham University, Durham, UK
EXPLORATION OF TERRESTRIAL PLANETS FROM SPACECRAFT: Instrumentation, Investigation, Interpretation
YURI A. SURKOV, Chief of the Laboratory of Geochemistry of Planets, Vernandsky Institute of Geochemistry, USSR Academy of Sciences, Moscow, USSR
THE HIDDEN UNIVERSE
ROGER J. TAYLER, Astronomy Centre, University of Sussex, Brighton, UK
AT THE EDGE OF THE UNIVERSE
ALAN WRIGHT, Australian National Radio Astronomy Observatory, Parkes, New South Wales, Australia, and HILARY WRIGHT

EXPLORATION OF TERRESTRIAL PLANETS FROM SPACECRAFT:
Instrumentation, Investigation, Interpretation

Yu. A. SURKOV
Chief of the Laboratory of the Geochemistry of Planets
Vernadsky Institute of Geochemistry and Analytical Chemistry
USSR Academy of Sciences, Moscow

ELLIS HORWOOD
NEW YORK   LONDON   TORONTO   SYDNEY   TOKYO   SINGAPORE

First published in 1990 by
ELLIS HORWOOD LIMITED
Market Cross House, Cooper Street,
Chichester, West Sussex, PO19 1EB, England

A division of
Simon & Schuster International Group

Printed and bound in Great Britain
by Hartnolls, Bodmin

British Library Cataloguing in Publication Data

Surkov, Yu. A.
Exploration of terrestrial planets from spacecraft:
instrumentation, investigation, interpretation
1. Solar system. Planets. Structure and physical properties
I. Title
523.4
ISBN 0–13–297250–6

Library of Congress Cataloging-in-Publication Data

Surkov, Yu. A. (Yuriĭ Aleksandrovich)
[Kosmokhimicheskie issledovaniia planet i sputnikov. English]
Exploration of terrestrial planets from spacecraft:
instrumentation, investigation, interpretation/Yu. A. Surkov.
p. cm. — (The Ellis Horwood library of space science and space
technology. Series in astronomy)
Translation of: Kosmokhimicheskie issledovaniia planet i
sputnikov.
ISBN 0–13–297250–6
1. Planets — Geology.   2. Planets — Surfaces.
3. Cosmochemistry.
I. Title.   II. Series.
QB603.G46S8713 1989
559.9—dc20   89–868536
                                                        CIP

Table of contents

Preface

The development of concepts of the origin, evolution and structure of the bodies in the Solar System, particularly the Earth, has been and remains a most attractive and fascinating branch of science. It is perhaps surprising that the subjects which are of most concern to us in astronomy are those which are the least well understood. We know far less about the origin of our own Solar System than we do about the birth, evolution and death of stars, and rather more about the internal structure of the Sun than we do about that of the planet on which we live — the Earth. The long, hard path of understanding the processes taking place in the Solar System led researchers to accumulate a large amount of unique information and to formulate some general concepts of celestial bodies. However, despite great progress in the development of ground-based facilities (visual observations, optical spectroscopy and radar studies) the possibilities for making further headway in this field remained rather limited.

The 1960s marked the beginning of a new and deeper insight into the history of the Solar System from the moment of its origin to the present. To date, about 70 Soviet and American space vehicles have explored the Solar System from Mercury to Uranus. These spacecraft flew in the vicinity of the planets, flew around them in satellite orbits, penetrated their dense atmospheres, or landed on their surfaces and explored them. As a result of these flights, an enormous volume of fundamentally new scientific information has been accumulated. This has allowed us to make a giant leap in developing concepts of the history of formation and present-day structure of the Solar System bodies.

This achievement has resulted primarily from the development of space vehicles which have brought researchers closer to the objects of their research. At the same time, it is obvious that this success could not be achieved without the development of new methods of analysis and without the creation of adequate onboard scientific instrumentation.

The formulation of scientific objectives, the choice of the means of their solution, the accumulation of experience in designing onboard instrumentation and, finally, the results of space experiments have resulted in a 'natural selection' of the methods which have proved to be most applicable in space research and which provide the greatest amount of useful data.

This book is an attempt to set forth briefly modern concepts of the planets and planetary satellites and to describe in mcre detail the methods, instrumentation and experimental results on the basis of which these concepts have been developed.

The book consists of two parts. In Part 1 the author gives a brief account of the evolutionary path of the Solar System from the earliest stages (the condensation of gas and the accumulation of solid matter) to the formation of planets and the differentiation of their material. The author considers in more detail the geoscientific aspect of the present-day concepts of planets and satellites which are potential objects of study in the near future. New data on the satellites of the giant planets, obtained by Voyagers 1 and 2, are given. The consideration of each celestial body is concluded by a discussion of those problems, at present unsolved, which will benefit most from future scientific exploration.

This section does not consider the historical aspects of theoretical and experimental studies which have led to modern concepts of planets and planetary satellites. Discussion of hypotheses and debatable problems which call for further experimental confirmation is kept to a minimum. This section is rather a reference work and, therefore, can be useful for a broad readership.

Part 2 deals with the methods and instrumentation which have become the most widespread in cosmochemical studies and discusses the results of experiments aimed at determining the composition and properties of extraterrestrial material by space vehicles.

The section dealing with gamma-ray spectrometry considers the results of exploring the Moon, Venus and Mars. This material was partly discussed by the author in his book *Gamma-ray spectrometry in space research* (Atomizdat Publishers, Moscow, 1977). That is why in this section the technical details of some experiments are omitted, while the scientific aspects of the research are expanded. In particular, data on the Moon's gamma-radiation are systematized, new data on Martian gamma-radiation measured by the Mars 5 probe are given, and gas-discharge gas detectors based on compressed xenon, which were not considered earlier, are described.

In the section dealing with X-ray spectrometry, attention is focused on new experiments used for exploring the composition of rocks on Venus by Venera 13 and 14 and VeGa 1 and 2. Earlier experiments in X-ray radiometry from Lunokhod 1 and 2, the Viking 1 and 2 vehicles and from some other spacecraft are discussed. The gas scintillation detector for studying the composition of rocks on the Moon, which has not yet been used, is also described.

One of the sections gives general data on neutronmetry and describes instruments for analysis of the composition of rocks on extraterrestrial bodies according to (n, γ) and (n, n') reactions. These instruments have not so far been used in space exploration.

The next section deals with the method and instrumentation for determining the composition of rocks from the scattering of alpha particles. This technique was used for lunar studies and is recommended in a modified form for Martian studies.

Finally, the last section of Part 2 is devoted to the mass spectrometry of the gaseous and solid phases of extraterrestrial bodies. Particular attention is paid to new mass-spectrometric instrumentation for analysis of the composition of aerosols in Venus's clouds. This instrumentation was designed for the VeGa 1 and 2 spacecraft.

In preparing this book, the author had no intention to review all the onboard scientific instruments used for exploring the bodies of the Solar System. The author's aim is to give data mainly on relatively new experiments and to consider in more detail experiments which have been prepared with his participation.

The book describes the methods and instruments which have already been used or which will be used by space vehicles for exploring the composition, structure and properties of extraterrestrial material with a view to developing the geoscientific aspect of the concepts of planets and satellites. At present this area of research is the most important for understanding the history of the Solar System, and, specifically, the geological history of our planet — the Earth.

The author is grateful to A. T. Basylevsky, F. F. Kirnozov and V. P. Volkov for their comments in reviewing the manuscript and N. I. Kuleshova for assistance in manuscript preparation.

The author also acknowledges the SSED Office of NASA for providing the pictures of planets and satellites taken from American space probes.

Part 1
Modern concepts of planets and satellites

INTRODUCTION

The launching of space vehicles to the Moon, Venus, Mars, Mercury, Jupiter, Saturn and beyond has extended our ideas of the origin and evolution of the Solar System, especially for the period after the formation of planets and their satellites. Studies of meteorites, recent theoretical papers and laboratory research have focused mainly on the protoplanetary period of the Solar System. Finally, ground-based observations of planets, asteroids and comets have widened considerably our knowledge of the Solar System in general.

The availability of numerous information sources has opened up new possibilities for studying the processes in the Solar System; both those which took place in the distant past and those which are still underway.

This book deals solely with the geoscientific aspect of the problem: the study of bodies in the Solar System by space vehicles. Of particular importance here are studies of the nature of matter, the processes and energy sources which contributed to the formation of planets and their satellites and which are still active now. However, the correct understanding, evaluation and interpretation of new data on planets and their satellites requires an examination of the entire evolutionary process of the Solar System from the protosolar nebula to its present state. The understanding of the geoscientific aspect of this history includes:

(1) the development of concepts of the protoplanetary history of the Solar System, i.e. about the origin and physical conditions in the protosolar nebula, about the processes of chemical fractionation, and about condensation and accumulation which resulted in the formation of the bodies of the Solar System;
(2) the forecasting of the average composition of planets and their satellites with a view to getting information on the differentiation of matter in the protoplanetary cloud, and condensation and accretion processes;
(3) the study of processes which changed the appearance and inner structure of planets and their satellites (the differentiation of their matter, tectonic and volcanic activity, meteorite bombardment, etc.);

(4) the study of planetary atmospheres — their origin, composition and physical interaction with the surface of planets — since volatile components emerge as most important in the history of planets and satellites.

Tackling these problems certainly involves not only space- and ground-based facilities, but also laboratory research and theoretical calculations. Special significance is attributed to comparative studies, especially of the Earth, the Moon and meteorites. The Earth, as a highly differentiated body, possessing a core, mantle and crust, whose inner thermal processes are still underway, is a natural laboratory for the study of the endogenous processes occurring on large bodies. The Moon is also of interest since it is the sole studied 'planet' which is devoid of an atmosphere, and subject to the effects of cosmic rays, meteorites and cosmic dust. Besides, the Moon represents the other (earlier) stage in planetary evolution. Finally, an interest in meteorites is aroused because they provide information on the protoplanetary conditions and processes in the Solar System (variations in the chemical composition, the lifetime and frequency of collisions of small bodies, etc.). Therefore, diverse data should be accumulated to help us comprehend the processes of the origin, evolution and modern structure of the bodies in the Solar System.

1.1 Origin and evolution of the Solar System

1.1.1 EARLY HISTORY OF THE SOLAR SYSTEM

Unfortunately, up to now there has been no uniform view on the origin of the Solar System and its evolution in the protoplanetary epoch. To examine this epoch, researchers try to reconstruct the chain of processes going from the present to the time of its origin. The present notion of the origin of the Solar System stems from Schmidt's theory on the cold accumulation of the Earth and planets from the near-Sun gas–dust cloud. This theory was expounded in the 1940s [1]. In the 1950s these ideas were further developed by Urey. On the basis of physicochemical studies of meteorites, Urey came to a conclusion about the accumulation of planets from solid matter [2]. The next steps in this direction were the hypotheses put forward by Cameron [3], Hoyle [4] and Schatzman [5] on the parallel formation of the Sun and the protoplanetary cloud from a single interstellar cloud. Finally, a profound discussion of the problem (especially of the early, protoplanetary period of the Solar System) is found in the papers by Safronov [6], Wood [7], Alfvén and Arrhenius [8, 48], Lewis [9, 10], Grossman [11, 12] and Brahic [49].

At present, most researchers believe that the Sun and planets formed from a single interstellar cloud, although others [8] assume that the cloud was trapped by the magnetic field of the Sun which formed earlier. Due to gravitational forces the cloud turned into a rotating, condensed disc with the central part being hot enough to maintain the first nuclear reactions of the young Sun. Part of the nebula surrounding the Sun was less heated and, probably, emerged as inhomogeneous in the direction from the centre to its outer parts due to varying physical conditions. The cooling of the nebula caused gas condensation in the mixture of solid chemical compounds and minerals which tended to grow, eventually producing solid particles and small bodies. Finally, as a result of the accretion of these solid particles and small bodies, planetary-sized bodies formed. These continued to grow at the expense of the volatiles found in the vicinity of the body which was being formed. This is a simplified view of the possible scenario of the formation of the bodies of the Solar System. However, the actual situation (as we see it now) was much more complicated.

The formation of a star, in this case the Sun, from the interstellar cloud, requires that under certain conditions three difficulties are overcome [13]. First there is the thermal problem, whereby the cloud is too hot. Secondly, there is the magnetic problem: the cloud possesses a magnetic field inherited from the magnetic field of the

Galaxy. When the cloud is compressed, the field, which is closely associated with the gas, contracts with it, and there is a progressive increase in field strength which opposes further contraction. Finally, there is the rotation problem, whereby the cloud is itself slowly rotating, and as the contraction takes place, this rotation speeds up. When the centrifugal force becomes equal to the gravitational force, the contraction of the cloud ceases. Various processes are believed to overcome these three barriers to condensation of the cloud — thermal, magnetic and rotational. To overcome the thermal problem, one may assume the possibility of the radiation pressure of nearby, young stars [4], or the passage of the cloud through a galactic spiral arm [14], leading to a considerable deceleration which strongly compresses it and initiates the self-contraction leading to star-formation. There is also a mechanism by which the excess magnetic field and rotational energy can be dissipated. As it contracts, the cloud ceases to be transparent to ionizing radiation (X-rays, ultraviolet and cosmic rays), the internal ionization disappears and, consequently, the internal magnetic field. Finally, the rotation of the cloud is decreased by the interaction of the rotating cloud with the interstellar magnetic field lines, which are dragged out by the rotation of the cloud, and resist the motion more and more, thereby eventually decreasing the rotational energy [4]. The possibility is also assumed of the cloud's disintegration into fragments; the initial momentum of the cloud then partly turns into the orbital motion of components relative to the centre and partly into rotation of the components themselves [13, 15].

Notwithstanding whether the Sun and planets formed from a single cloud or different clouds, the reverse process is still hotly debated — the differentiation of matter of which the planets formed from the Sun. Apparently planetary matter was not ejected from the Sun [16]. Some researchers seek to explain the partial differentiation of the cloud from the Sun by the effect of the centrifugal force related to the initial momentum [8, 17].

The mass of the protoplanetary cloud which surrounded the Sun, was not less than one-hundredth of the Sun's mass. (The minimum mass is evaluated as an overall planetary mass plus the mass of lost volatiles.) Some other theories suggest a lower limit that is somewhat higher; about one-twentieth of a solar mass. For instance, Safronov [18] assumes the initial mass to be equal to $(0.05–0.1)\,M_s$, where M_s is the Sun's mass. Schatzman [17] takes nearly the same figure. However, Cameron [19] and others take into account that young stars (e.g. TTauri stars) in the initial stage of gravitational contraction, emit a continuous 'stellar wind' which may result in considerable mass loss, and they think that it is more appropriate to put the nebula mass at $2M_s$. The assumption of an initial mass for the solar nebula is crucial for evolving an hypothesis of the origin of planets.

Proceeding from this initial assumption, the majority of modern theories may be sub-divided into two groups: the theories of the minimum and massive solar nebula. The first theory suggests that the protoplanetary cloud from which planets formed was a remnant of the interstellar cloud, a considerable part of which collapsed into a protosun. This diffusive cloud rotated around the protosun in its gravitational field and its dimensions were commensurable with the Solar System. The distribution of matter in it was uneven. The rotation was ordinary but vortices and turbulence also occurred. The basic constituents of the cloud were hydrogen and helium.

The theories of the massive solar nebula (nearly $2M_s$) assume that initially it had no protosun at its centre. The nebula was a huge rotating, gaseous disc. Then part of the mass condensed into the Sun, while the rest remained at a considerable distance. Later on (in the TTauri phase) the Sun ejected some of its material as a 'stellar wind' with an intensity 10^6 times greater than at present. This resulted in the loss of a significant fraction of the mass of the cloud. But there are still other assumptions, e.g. in the Alfvén and Arrhenius model [8] the mass of the primordial cloud is assumed to be very small $(10^{-11}–10^{-12})M_s$, but then it continues to grow, by the addition of trapped interstellar matter.

1.1.2 PHYSICAL CONDITIONS AND CHEMICAL COMPOSITION OF THE SOLAR NEBULA

So far we know little about the physical conditions and chemical composition of the solar nebula. But it is they that controlled the condensation and accumulation processes which resulted in the formation of planets and satellites. Among the data which may shed light on the mass of the solar nebula and its composition, the most important are the mass of the Sun and planets and the present-day composition of the Sun. Additional information is provided by spectral observations of other similar nebulae, which help to provide information about their size, composition and the gas-to-dust ratio. Finally, the isotopic fractionation in meteorites suggests the occurrence of similar fractionation in the Sun's environment as well. It might be caused by nuclear reactions under the effect of the Sun.

The most viable model of the solar nebula is that which can explain the origin of a whole diversity of bodies, from the giant Jupiter, rich in volatiles, to the terrestrial planets and minor bodies, such as comets, asteroids and meteorites. The first demarcation line between the models is the correct choice between the massive nebula with strong turbulence and dynamic instability, and a considerably smaller and quieter nebula, the evolution of which is much slower. Another line is the choice between the relatively cold, dust-rich nebula, in which the rôle of the solar heating is only minor, and, on the other hand, a strongly heated gaseous (vapour-like) nebula. The third line is whether the gas and dust temperatures were similar, i.e. whether thermodynamic equilibrium existed.

In the first two cases the demarcation line is ensured by the choice of the model itself, i.e. the postulation of corresponding initial data. In the latter case it is based, to some extent, on experimental data; for instance, if gas was ionized and had a higher temperature, then reactions proceeded in conditions of thermodynamic disequilibrium and should be dependent on the ionization potential of gaseous components. The data on the analysis of meteorites seem to confirm the existence of ionization [8]. Lindblad [20] has shown that solid particles immersed in ionized gas should radiate strongly in the infrared region and, thus, have a lower temperature. However, having carefully analysed the data available, Anders [21] concluded that there are no grounds to refute a simple equilibrium system.

So far no reliable data on the time characteristics of evolutionary processes are obtained. Cameron and Pine [22] evaluated the lifetime of the nebula by its dissipation, stemming from the inner circulatory processes, and found it ranging from 10^2 years at a distance of 1 AU to 10^4 years at a distance of 10 AU.

The temperature, pressure and density as a function of the distance from the centre were calculated by many workers. In particular, Safronov [6] assumes a temperature of some 100 K at the distance of the inner planets and 30 ± 10 K for the outer planets, while Schatzman [17] allows a temperature of nearly 200 K at the Earth's distance and nearly 50 K at the Uranus–Neptune distance. Ter Haar [23] and others make use of rather similar temperatures.

Ground-based observations indicate that interstellar clouds similar to that from which the solar nebula evolved, contain not only a gas component, but also grains of interstellar dust. Numerous theoretical studies and spectroscopic analyses in ultraviolet and infrared regions prove the existence of graphite, iron, silicate and ice-dust grains. Investigating the ultraviolet region, Hoyle and Wickramasinghe [24], and Wickramasinghe and Nandy [25] came to the conclusion that, judging by the light-absorption characteristics, the interstellar medium should contain a mixture of graphite, iron and silicate grains, having a size range of 10^{-7} to 10^{-8}m. The absorption peak in the infrared region, identified with silicate dust, was detected while investigating a dust cloud in the vicinity of the star Alpha Orionis [26, 27]. According to Girla [28], dust surrounding the stars Zeta Ophiuchi and Sigma Scorpii comprises grains of graphite, moissanite (SiC) and silicate in the ratio of 1:4:5, respectively.

Therefore, the data on the near-star dust prove that it is a refractory fraction of stellar matter, excluding ice particles surrounding a star. It may be assumed that near-star dust reflects the chemical composition of the refractory part of stars to the same degree as solid bodies in the Solar System (meteorites, asteroids, and terrestrial planets) reflect the composition of the Sun's refractory part [29].

1.1.3 GAS CONDENSATION INTO DUST GRAINS

When the interstellar cloud collapsed into a rotating disc and formed a protosun, the remaining part of the cloud which surrounded the young Sun contained both a gaseous component and grains of interstellar dust. Initially this protoplanetary cloud had, evidently, a homogeneous solid phase, although a temperature gradient in the direction from the protosun centre existed. The primitive material of this cloud reflected the processes which contributed to the formation of the primordial interstellar cloud. If the bodies were formed directly from such a protoplanetary cloud, then all of them would have approximately the same composition. However, variations in planetary densities point to essential differences in their chemical composition, and variations in the chemical composition of meteorites investigated in laboratories are indicative of the fact that the matter of the protoplanetary cloud had differentiated prior to the time when solid bodies condensed from it. It is believed that in the early phase of its evolution the solar nebula passed through a high-temperature stage and that the initial grains (embryos) containing iron and silicates (as a result of the contraction and heating of the nebula) partially evaporated and then condensed again when it cooled down. This is also proved by the studies of meteorites which have indicated that these bodies display wide variations of chemical composition and differentiation, and that there are two different condensation products at a time (in particular, in carbonaceous chondrites) — low-temperature, volatile-rich condensates and high-temperature refractory condensates. Finally, the existence of isotopic variations among various meteorites is also indicative of the fact that a significant amount of protosolar (interstellar) dust survived to the present and is found in meteorites. The condensation process, proceeding in gas of solar composition, was studied from a thermodynamic viewpoint in many papers [9–12, 30]. It was assumed that the condensation occurred in a nebula in which the temperature and pressure decreased with increasing distance from the centre. It was suggested that every planet emerged from the material which condensed within a narrow enough temperature interval (e.g. 100 to 200 K for terrestrial planets). Finally, investigations were made of the systems in which the gaseous and condensate phases were in equilibrium. Such calculations became possible only for a small group (not more than 10–15) of the most widespread elements. As a result, condensation curves were obtained for the most likely compounds. Calculations of condensation-equilibrium models were made, employing thermodynamic constants, the occurrence of elements in space, and some assumptions about the most probable chemical compounds for estimating the temperature of the nebula.

Some models are calculated for the low cooling rate so as to maintain the thermodynamic equilibrium of chemical reactions between gases and solid grains. In other models the equilibrium and chemical reactions are limited so that the layers of imbalanced condensates may emerge. Still other models suppose a slow growth of cooler solid grains from high-temperature vapour which has low density and is partially ionized. Not all models use high-temperature condensation; some models assume a low-temperature condensation. Various condensation models differ in their predictions, in particular, in respect of the relationship between iron sulphide, iron and iron oxide for the Earth and Venus; iron sulphide and iron oxide for Mars; iron and silicate for Mercury.

Table 1.1.1 gives the distribution of the major elements of the Sun which was used by Lewis *et al.* [9, 10] in their condensation models. They calculated the stability limits of high-temperature condensates, which may emerge during the cooling of the solar nebula, and proved that the first condensates should comprise groups of poorly volatile scattered elements (Os, Re and Ir). They condense at a temperature much higher than 1679 K — the condensation temperature of Al_2O_3, which is the first condensate of a widespread element. At a temperature of 1500 K the Ti and Ca condense in the form of $CaTiO_3$. Probably, other refractory elements enter into the $CaTiO_3$ solid solution as admixture oxides. A further lowering of the temperature gives rise to the condensation of the Fe–Ni alloy, then the solid component of $MgSiO_3$. Such elements as Fe, Mg, Si and their compounds prevail in all terrestrial planets. Alkaline aluminosilicates form at a temperature 100-200 K lower than for $MgSiO_3$. The condensation of volatile components falls into four reactions: the entry of water into a tremolite amphibole where calcium is one of the principal components; the entry of water into talc and serpentine; the entry of sulphur into forming FeS, and the oxidation of metallic iron to FeO in magnesian silicates.

Table 1.1.2 shows the sequence of reactions taking place during the cooling of matter in the solar nebula [10]. One can see from the table the correlation of the low temperatures of the formation of condensates with the low density and high content of volatile components.

It follows from the relationship between the condensate temperature and density that the density decreases as a result of such processes as iron oxidation, silicate hydration, ice condensation and solid gas-hydrate formation. In the formation of FeS (troilite) at 680 K, some anomaly in the general tendency towards a decrease in the density with the lowering of the condensate temperature is observed. Tremolite forms at the time when the density of the condensate starts dropping quickly due to the Fe oxidation and should be much lower than at the moment of the FeS formation.

Table 1.1.1 — Distribution of elements on the Sun

Element	Distribution (atomic) in relation to Si
H	28000
He	1780
O	16.6
C	10.0
N	2.4
Ne	2.1
Fe	1.06
Si	1.00
Mg	0.85
S	0.46
Ar	0.15
Al	0.071
Ca	0.060
Ni	0.050
Na	0.043

Table 1.1.2 — Condensation sequence of solar material [10]

Reaction	Temperature (K) at 10^2 Pa	Density of condensate ($\times 10^3$ kgm^{-3})
1. Refractory oxides (condensation)	1720	~3.5
2. Metallic iron (condensation)	1460	~7.0
3. $MgSiO_3$ (condensation)	1420	4.4
4. Alkaline aluminosilicates (formation)	1250	4.4
5. FeS (formation)	680	4.46
6. Tremolite (formation)	540	4.3
7. Termination of Fe and FeO oxidation	490	3.85
8. Talc/serpentine (formation)	400	3.2
9. Ice H_2O (condensation)	195	1.7
10. $NH_3 \cdot H_2O$ (formation)	130	1.7
11. $CH_4 \cdot 7H_2O$ (formation)	85	1.6
12. CH_4 (condensation)	40	1.0
13. Ar (condensation)	35	1.0
14. Ne (condensation)	8	1.0
15. H_2 (condensation)	6	0.1
16. He (condensation)	1	0.1

But the entry of sulphur, a rather heavy element, into tremolite maintains the high density of the condensate. In this model great importance is attached to the formation of gas-hydrates ($NH_3 \cdot CH_4$, and $CH_4 \cdot 7H_2O$), which results in the conversion of such gases as NH_3 and CH_4 into a condensed phase at a much higher temperature than when they condense in the free state. It should be noted that in this model the density, the oxidized state, and the content of volatiles are interrelated.

1.1.4   ACCUMULATION OF DUST GRAINS AND GAS INTO PLANETARY BODIES

The process of accumulation of dust grains into large bodies and then, finally, into planetary-sized bodies is one of the least understood in the history of the formation of the Solar System. When did the appropriate conditions in the gas density, temperature and motion of particles appear and which mechanisms contributed to accumulation, especially in the initial stage of the formation of these bodies? Such questions have been debated for many years already.

However, when the bodies had reached adequately large sizes their gravitational fields began trapping solid particles and gas. A relatively small number of such bodies grew at the expense of others and finally emerged as planets. The regularities in the changes of such properties as the masses of planets, their spatial location and rotation velocity may be essential for understanding the features of the primordial system. Even the exception to the rule may be helpful for proving the importance of the time and statistical fluctuations in the accumulation process. Such deviations may include the existence of an asteroid belt; restrained growth of Mars in comparison to neighbouring Jupiter; the anomalous axial tilts of Venus and Uranus; the presence of satellites for some planets and their absence for others.

Our ideas of the processes leading to the agglomeration of grains are mostly speculative due to the high uncertainty in our knowledge of the conditions reigning in the solar nebula.

It is assumed that in the first (early) stage, when dust particles had no significant gravitational field of their own, in the process of deposition they started sticking ('cold welding') together in the central plane of the disc of the solar nebula. In the area of higher temperatures the sticking of melted drops was possible. As a result, solid and liquid particles and gas, concentrated in the nebula's plane, coalesced into larger bodies during a relatively short period of time. In some papers the computer-based mathematical modelling of this process was undertaken. However, the data on the physical and chemical characteristics of the nebula are insufficient for such modelling.

After a swarm of protoplanetary bodies, the so-called planetesimals, formed, the rate and nature of further accumulation determined the principal characteristics of the planets and the regularities of the planetary system as a whole.

One of the important characteristics inherent in a multitude of protoplanetary bodies is their arrangement by size, since it determines the dynamics of this process of accumulation and, consequently, the initial stage of planets (their temperatures and the heterogeneity of their interiors). Thus, for instance, when small planetesimals fall onto the surface of a body, which is forming, the energy distributes in the surface layer and quickly dissipates into outer space. When large planetesimals fall, the energy distributes within a large volume and, hence, much of it remains in the planet's interior which may entail the heating and, consequently, the differentiation of its material.

Many models were constructed to explain the diversity of the planets and the regularities in their arrangement. Most important here are the initial postulates on the distribution of colliding bodies by mass and velocity. Using the model of mutual collisions, some researchers assume the power law of body distribution in masses. Other researchers think that the accretion process does not depend on the initial distribution of bodies by mass. They believe that more important here are the conditions of the collision and crushing of colliding bodies. For example, if relative velocities are much greater than the velocity of the dissipation from planetesimals, then the crushing process would prevail during the collisions. Otherwise planetesimals would act as 'embryos' accumulating the remaining material. Further embryo growth depends on its ability to accumulate material from nearby circular orbits. Here the embryo development may be retarded if a greater body is formed nearby, a planet which attracts remaining material from the immediate environment. The accumulation time of terrestrial planets and giant planets, obtained in different models using various assumptions, lasts 10^5 and 10^8 years; the accumulation time of more distant planets is evidently still greater.

Progress in understanding the condensation process and new data on planets obtained as a result of space flights and ground-based observations brought about the need to critically review the existing models of the formation of bodies in the Solar System. This was done by Kenneth and Goettel [31] who, firstly, critically analysed the initial data — the content of the most widespread elements (Fe, Si, S, Cl, etc.) and heat-generating elements (K, U, Th) on the Sun — and estimated the composition of terrestrial planets. They also made several simplifying suppositions. First, it was assumed that every planet accumulated material in one area, i.e. with a narrow composition range determined by the temperature and pressure in its particular part of the cloud. Second, the possible effects of mixing and fractionation were ignored. Third, it was assumed that planets formed homogeneously with the follow-up differentiation into envelopes. Fourth, it was assumed that the accretion of planets was a slow process. Thus, their primary composition did not vary because of the loss of volatiles induced by the heat generated in the course of the accretion process.

Table 1.1.3 — Composition of terrestrial planets [31]

(percentage by mass)

Component	Mercury		Venus		Earth		Mars	
	Planet in general	Mantle/ core	Planet in general	Mantle/ core	Planet in general	Mantle/ core	Planet in general	Mantle/ core
Mantle								
MgO	12.83	36.89	25.74	37.82	24.25	34.79	23.07	26.20
SiO$_2$	11.67	33.53	36.16	53.13	34.06	48.88	32.41	36.80
Al$_2$O$_3$	5.32	15.30	2.61	3.83	2.46	3.53	2.34	2.65
CaO	4.97	14.28	2.43	3.58	2.29	3.29	2.18	2.48
Na$_2$O	0	0	1.12	1.64	1.05	1.51	1.0	1.14
FeO	0	0	0	0	5.58	8.0	27.06	30.72
Total	34.79	100	68.86	100	69.69	100	88.07	99.99
Core								
Fe	61.75	94.69	30.25	94.69	24.16	79.73	6.09	51.00
Ni	3.46	5.31	1.70	5.31	1.60	5.27	1.52	12.74
S	0	0	0	0	4.54	15.00	4.32	36.25
Total	65.21	100	31.94	100	30.31	100	11.93	100

Table 1.1.3 gives the composition of terrestrial planets estimated by Kenneth and Goettel [31]. It follows from the table that the farther from the Sun a planet formed, the smaller was its core (for Mercury it takes up 65% of the planet's mass, for Mars 12%) and the larger the mantle. The cores of Mercury and Venus, the planets closest to the Sun, are composed of the Fe–Ni melt. The cores of more distant planets (the Earth and Mars) include sulphur in the form of troilite (FeS). The mantles of planets are composed of silicates. Oxidized iron is present only in the mantles of the Earth and Mars. On Mercury and Venus iron is found only in the planets' cores.

This model [31] is attractive because of its simplicity, since estimations took into account only 10 basic elements comprising nearly 99% of the overall planetary mass (as distinct from the more complicated models taking into consideration the multistage evolution of planets and intrinsic fractionation processes). But some inferences, in particular a conclusion on the availability of all iron on Venus in a reduced form and its concentration in the core, conflict with observational data [32].

1.1.5 STRUCTURE OF PLANETS. DIFFERENTIATION OF MATTER

The fact that planets, and first of all terrestrial planets, have envelopes has long been the focus of attention. Until recently, two hypotheses — homogeneous or heterogeneous formation of planets — were debated. Schmidt's viewpoint [1] suggesting homogeneous accretion has been reigning for a long time. Homogeneous accretion supposes the formation of the core not at the time of a planet's formation but later on, as a result of the differentiation of matter due to heating of the planet's interior. The causes of heating might be accretion, radioactive decay, gravitational contraction and others. Supporters of the homogeneous accretion hypothesis explain the formation of the core as a result of the sedimentation of compact matter from the metl to the centre of a planet. But in-depth studies, carried out at a later stage, gave rise to doubts concerning the possibility of melting such a large iron core as, for example, that possessed by Mercury, Venus and the Earth. The heterogeneous accretion concept was adopted by Vinogradov [33] and others. It proceeds from the assumption that planets were built in the same sequence as elements and their compounds condense. In this case the iron core formed at the very beginning as a result of the accretion of condensed iron–nickel drops, since they exhibit poor volatile properties. Then a silicate mantle was deposited on the core. This mantle prevented the core from further reactions with H_2S and H_2O to form sulphides and oxides, then dissipated volatiles, organic compounds, hydrated silicates and rare gases. Heterogeneous accretion is also supported by the fact that a depth stratification on the planets (the Earth, in particular) coincides with the sequence of the condensation of elements and compounds. Besides, this approach enables the explanation of some events which occurred in the early stages of the existence of the Solar System. In heterogeneous accretion models the core could be in a molten state from the very beginning or could melt at a later stage. The heterogeneous accretion hypothesis explains well the fact that the closer a planet is to the Sun, the greater the proportion of the planet that is made up by its refractory fraction, i.e. the Fe–Ni core, because the temperature of accretion is higher. This hypothesis allows one to explain the low density of the Moon, Galilean satellites of Jupiter, Saturn's satellite Titan, and other phenomena.

While speaking about homogeneous and heterogeneous accretion, we must, first of all, keep in mind the difference in the formation of planetary cores. The prevalent formation of the iron–nickel embryo of a planet is associated not only with the sequence of the condensation (since the metallic fraction is most refractory, it gets condensed first), but with the advantages that the accumulation of the metallic fraction has in comparison to the silicate one. Depending on the temperature of the formation of the planets' embryo the colliding particles (melted or solid) were subject to 'cold' or 'hot' welding. However, iron particles at a high enough temperature (but below the Curie point of 1043 K) might be magnetized by the Sun's magnetic field and, thus, ineract more readily than silicate particles. The cross-section of the interaction (trapping) for mutually magnetized particles in nearly 10^4 times greater than their geometrical cross-section [34]. Hence, it is quite probable that heterogeneous accretion might occur, with the initial phase being the formation of the metallic core. In the course of heterogeneous accretion the formation of the metallic core was followed by building of the mantle in the same sequence as elements and compounds were condensed. At first, the primordial mantle was accumulated as a mixture of silicate, metallic and sulphide phases, with the metallic particle content in its deeper part being greater than in the upper part. In later periods hydrated silicates and organic matter were deposited. In the final stage, gravitational trapping of gases from the primordial nebula (H_2O, CO_2 CO, NH_3 and others) occurred. Thus, the primordial mantle of the planet formed and it was not homogeneous.

A planet's crust was built up evidently in later stages as a result of the differentiation of the mantle's material, although there are other opinions seeking to explain that the crust (more precisely, some 'protocrust') was shaped in the late period of accretion [35]. The degree of planetary differentiation was governed by some fundamental characteristics of a planet, such as its size (which determines gravitational contraction and the rate of the loss of heat); chemical composition (the presence of water and other volatiles is of special significance); content of short-lived radioactive nuclei and long-lived radioactive elements (which control the rate of the heat release); and initial thermal state (which is determined mainly by the duration of the accretion process). The rôle of these factors has been studied in many papers. For instance, Lyubimova [36] estimated the energy of the Earth's gravitational contraction. She evaluated it as $(5–9) \times 10^{31}$ J, while Safronov [6] obtained 4.2×10^{31} J.

Since the contribution of the above heat sources was different on various planets, the thermal history of planets was similar only in general; in reality there were differences, which were reflected in their inner structure. The effect of these sources was the heating of the planets' interiors (obviously during the first thousand million years it was at a maximum). The highest temperature was attained in the central part of planets and the lowest near the surface. At depths where the temperature surpassed the melting point of the most readily melted components, they converted into a liquid state. If one takes a planet such as the Earth and the composition of its primary mantle, the lowest melting temperature was displayed by the Fe–FeS eutectic structure which was least dependent on an increase in pressure [29]. The melted eutectic from the boundaries of its lower mantle flowed down (subsided) towards the centre, making up the outer FeS core.

However, the differentiation of the Earth's mantle proceeded not only in the direction of the melting of heavy elements, which subsided towards the centre, forming the outer core, but in the direction of the melting or readily melted, volatile-rich silicate fractions which, being the most lightweight melts, moved, as a result of centrifugal migration, to the outer part of the planet, building up the planetary basaltic crust. The formation of the outer core seemed to occur in an earlier period than the formation of the crust. Therefore, siderophilic and chalcophilic elements migrated down to the core, while lithophilic and and atmophilic elements rose upward to the crust. In the course of the melting and outgassing of the upper mantle, apart from the melting of basaltic magma, a great amount of water and gases dissolved in it was released, which contributed to the formation of the Earth's hydrosphere and atmosphere. Besides this hypothesis there is a viewpoint that the atmosphere and hydrosphere might have emerged directly in the course of the planet's growth [37].)

The differentiation of the Earth's primordial mantle was obviously a heterogeneous process, which is proved by the comparison of the isotopic composition of some elements in crustal rocks with that of mantle rocks and stony meteorites. In particular, this was demonstrated on carbon isotopes by Galimov [38], on lead and strontium isotopes by Hutcheson [48] and others.

Such were the processes of the formation and differentiation of matter in the Earth's interior. As far as other planets are concerned, their differences in initial characteristics and, first of all, size and composition, gave rise to corresponding differences in the structure, primarily in size and composition, of their core, mantle and crust.

1.1.6 ATMOSPHERES OF PLANETS AND SATELLITES

Much material has been amassed nowadays on the atmospheres of planets and satellites, and hypotheses on their origin and evolution have been developed [39–45]. The Moon, Mercury and Jupiter's satellite Io have highly rarefied atmospheres; the Earth, Venus and Mars more massive atmospheres; giant planets highly dense ones. The composition of their atmospheres also differs greatly: inert gases prevail in the atmospheres of the Moon and Mercury, terrestrial planets have nitrogen–oxygen or carbon dioxide atmospheres, and giant planets have hydrogen–helium atmospheres. Such diversity of atmospheres is a reflection of the differences in the evolution of these bodies. The present composition of the atmospheres characterizes only a certain stage in the evolution of planets and does not reflect a relative abundance of these volatiles on planets and satellites. The principal sources of the gases making up the atmosphere are the primordial solar nebula, the solar wind, meteorites, comets and other celestial bodies crossing the orbits of planets. All these sources were most active in the early period of the existence of planets and their satellites.

The primordial solar nebula, made up of gas and dust, had an elemental composition close to that which is at present typical of the outer parts of the Sun. After the planets and their satellites had formed, their gravitational fields caused a concentration of gases from the solar nebula near their surfaces. This atmosphere partly survived and partly got dissipated. The process was controlled by the relationship between the rate of a body's formation, the rate of the nebula's disappearance and the rate of dissipation. For giant planets the solar nebula is practically the only source of atmospheres.

The solar wind is a source of magnetized and ionized gas from the upper part of the Sun's atmosphere. At the Earth's orbit it has a temperature of about 2×10^5 K, a velocity of nearly 500 Kms^{-1}, a density of about 5×10^6 particles m^{-3} and a particle flow of approximately 2×10^4 m^{-2} s^{-1} [45]. Falling on a surface, which is not protected by an atmosphere, charged particles of the solar wind get neutralized, and after a time interval might again drift away or remain, depending on the body's gravitation and kinetic energy, which is governed by the surface temperature. Falling on a body protected by an atmosphere, the particles of the solar wind may remain for a long time in the atmosphere. The magnetic field and ionosphere of a planet or a satellite might be a protective shield in the early stage of the existence of the solar nebula.

The cratered surfaces of the Moon, Mercury and Mars show that a great number of small objects, mainly asteroids and comets, fell on them, as well as on other bodies. Some asteroids contain many volatiles similar to carbonaceous chondrites, and all comets are rich in volatiles. During a collision at high velocities (~ 10 Kms^{-1}) all volatiles are released into the atmosphere of the colliding body. However, colliding bodies are not considered an important source of planetary atmospheres. For instance, if one estimates the cumulative mass of matter which has fallen on the Moon's surface, recalculates it for the Earth's surface and assumes the volatile content of this mass to be identical to that of carbonaceous chondrites (matter most rich in volatiles), then one can evaluate the maximum amount of volatiles brought by colliding bodies to the Earth. Turekian and Clark [46] made such estimations for water and carbon. It was discovered that the amount of these volatiles is three orders of magnitude smaller on the Earth than the water content in the World's oceans and the carbon content in carbonates of sedimentary rocks.

Inner sources are the main suppliers of atmospheric components. Solid and liquid particles of the gas–dust cloud that gave rise to the planets and satellites contained volatiles. Later on, volcanic and tectonic activity resulted in the release of some of the accumulated volatiles. Certain classes of meteorites, which underwent a relatively insignificant thermal and chemical evolution, open up the possibility of judging the chemical composition of matter of which terrestrial planets were shaped. Table 1.1.4, taken from [43] lists the principal chemical compounds found in meteorites which contain elements making up volatiles.

The table also gives the temperature in the solar nebula at which the formation of a chemical compound is thermodynamically possible. It is worth noting that, except for rare gases, volatiles of the atmosphere did not appear in the form in which they were found in primordial matter of the meteorite composition (largely due to the interaction with oxygen). Volatiles of planets and satellites were released into the atmosphere as a consequence of the heating in the course of accretion as a result of the global differentiation of matter caused by the radiogenic warming, and in the process of local volcanism. If one assumes that accretion of terrestrial planets took rather a long period (nearly 10^8 years), then it would not have resulted in the heating, and planets would have formed at low temperatures. In this case such volatiles as H_2O, CO_2 and others would have reacted with minerals, producing corresponding compounds. With such accretion the atmosphere would have appeared at a later stage when the differentiation of matter occurred. In the case of a shorter accretion period (about 10^6 years) the bodies would have been heated to higher temperatures, which would result in the release of gaseous products and formation of the primordial atmosphere.

Table 1.1.4 — Chemical components in meteorites containing volatile-forming elements [43]

Volatile compound	Volatile element	Chemical compounds	Formation temperature (K)
Water	H	Organic compounds, hydrated minerals (water crystalization and hydroxyl groups)	$\lesssim 750$ $\sim 150\text{--}450$
Carbon dioxide	C	Organic compounds	$\lesssim 750$
Methane	C, H	Graphite	
Carbon monoxide	C	Carbonate	
Nitrogen	N	Organic compounds	$\lesssim 750$
Ammonia	N, H	Ammonia salts, nitrides	
Sulphur dioxide	S	Troilite (FeS)	500–700
Hydrogen sulphide	S	Sulphates, free sulphur, organic compounds	$\lesssim 750$
Hydrogen chloride	Cl	Apatite $(Ca_5(PO_4)_3Cl)$, Lawrencite $(FeCl_2)$, organic compounds	$\lesssim 750$
Rare gases	Rare gases	Occluded gases, radioactive elements	

The composition of outgassed volatiles was not constant. Initially it corresponded to the composition that was in a thermodynamic equilibrium with magma, heated to partial melting, from which gaseous products were released. Then the atmosphere cooled down to the temperatures observed on the surface of a body. Here some gaseous components condensed, others became constituents of rocks, and the atmosphere attained a new state of thermodynamic equilibrium corresponding to the surface conditions. The atmospheres of planets and satellites continue their evolution — their chemical composition, physical conditions and the general mass undergo changes. On the one hand, the above-mentioned sources of volatiles are active. On the other hand, the reverse process develops which results in the removal of some components from the atmosphere. The latter is a result of either the escape of gases into outer space due to thermal evaporation and photochemical dissociation and other factors, or the condensation of gases by the cooling surface rocks. Evidently only heavy inertial gases did not take part in the evolution of atmospheres.

To understand the evolution of planetary atmospheres we should know the initial distribution of volatiles. Turekian and Clark [46] evaluated this distribution for the Earth proceeding from the present atmospheric composition and content of volatiles accumulated in the reservoirs of the crust and the mantle. For Venus it may be made to a first approximation proceeding from the composition of the modern atmosphere, assuming that the bulk of volatiles is in the atmosphere. For Mars the distribution of volatiles may be estimated on the basis of the content of rare gases in the atmosphere and assuming that other volatiles should be present in nearly the same ratios as on the Earth. Such estimations made by Pollack and Black [47] are given in Table 1.1.5. For comparison respective data for meteorites and the Sun are also given. It follows from the table that the content of Ar, N_2, and CO_2 on Venus and the Earth is nearly identical, and on Mars is much lower. The highest H_2O content is on the Earth, it is lower on Mars and the lowest on Venus. All these differences are quite explainable if one keeps in mind that the bodies formed in various regions of the primordial cloud where physical conditions differed. The atmosphere of planets and satellites permanently evolved. The present-day composition and density of atmospheres reflect only some stages of development. The principal sources of the modern atmospheres of the Earth, Venus, Mars, Io and Titan is release of their own volatiles from their interiors. The main outgassed components of the Earth, Venus and Mars are water, carbon, chlorine, nitrogen and sulphur; on Io sulphur prevails; on Titan most likely H_2O, NH_3 and CH_4 which were released from ices (on Titan volatiles should take up much of its mass). The principal sources of the modern exospheres of the Moon and Mercury are outgassed radiogeneous gases and trapped components of the solar wind. In the earlier stages the Moon and Mercury had apparently denser atmospheres, including the same components as the Earth's present atmosphere. The highly dense atmospheres of the giant planets originated from the solar nebula.

At present the atmospheres of inner planets and satellites (except for Venus) contain only a small share of the overall amount of outgassed volatiles. Most of them are found in surface and subsurface reservoirs. For instance, on the Earth a great deal of water and CO_2 is found in oceans and sedimentary rocks respectively. On Mars a greater part of H_2O, CO_2 and N_2 are bound in subsurface ice and regolith; CH_4 on Titan and SO_2 on Io are also largely concentrated in surface and subsurface ice depositions. However, such distribution of volatiles between the atmosphere on the one hand, and the hydrosphere and lithosphere on the other hand, is not permanent. The history of planets and satellites bears traces of the equilibrium shifts caused by variations in the eccentricity of orbits and the inclination of the planets' rotational axes, the tidal heating of satellites, changes in solar constant, etc.

If the atmospheres of planets and satellites are in a thermodynamic equilibrium with surface rocks, they reflect not only the physical conditions on the surface and the composition of surface rocks, but also indirectly indicate the crustal composition and the inner structure of planets and satellites.

Table 1.1.5 — Distribution of main atmosphere-forming gases (kg/kg)^a [47]

Object	Primary $^{36}Ar + ^{38}Ar$	N_2	CO_2	H_2O
Venus	$6 \times 10^{-10} - 9 \times 10^{-9}$	$(2.0-2.2) \times 10^{-6}$	$(9.4-9.6) \times 10^{-5}$	$1 \times 10^{-9} - 6 \times 10^{-8}$
Earth	4.6×10^{-11}	2.4×10^{-6}	1.6×10^{-4}	2.8×10^{-4}
Mars	$(1.9-2.5) \times 10^{-13}$	$4 \times 10^{-8} - 4 \times 10^{-7}$	$>3.5 \times 10^{-8}$	$>5 \times 10^{-6}$
Usual chondrites	$3 \times 10^{-12} - 1 \times 10^{-9}$			
Carbonaceous chondrites	$4 \times 10^{-10} - 1 \times 10^{-9}$			
Sun	1×10^{-4}	1.3×10^{-3}	1.3×10^{-2}	9.5×10^{-3}

^{a} The ratio of the gas mass in the outer envelope of a planet to planetary mass.

1.1.7 GENERAL PROBLEMS IN THE STUDY OF THE SOLAR SYSTEM

In this section only some aspects of the processes which contributed to the formation of the bodies of the Solar System will be discussed. Most of the models are hypothetical and only some are experimentally proven. It would be wrong to believe that this cardinal problem in cosmogony — the origin and evolution of planets and satellites — will be resolved within a brief time period. But undoubtedly the coming years (or decades) will see essential advances in understanding the history of the world surrounding us.

Scientific problems to be tackled in the near future will remain the same, and the first steps have already been taken in their solution:

Composition, structure and properties of the solar nebula
How did the solar nebula originate? What were the physical conditions in the nebula — the temperature, pressure, magnetic field, the Sun's effect? What are the dynamics of all these processes in time and space? What is the composition of gases and dust and what chemical and isotopic heterogeneities existed in the nebula?

Gas condensation in the solar nebula
How did gas condensation in solid bodies proceed and what was the sequence of elements and compounds? How did the relationship between gases, liquid and solid particles depend on the radial distance? Was there a thermodynamic equilibrium in the cloud?

Accretion of dust grains in the solar nebula
How did the accretion of dust grains into large objects and, finally, into planetary-sized bodies, proceed? What is the relationship between accretion and condensation? What is the rôle of collisions and magnetic fields in particle accretion? How long did the accretion of planets formed in various regions of the solar nebula last? How can the planets' size and distances from the Sun be explained? What is the origin of planetary satellites?

Structure and evolution of the core, mantle and crust of planets and satellites
What is the inner structure of planets and satellites? What is the size, composition and structure of the core, mantle and crust? How did the core form (as a result of accretion or global differentiation of matter)? What endogenous and exogenous processes contributed to the crust formation? What was the contribution of tectonic, volcanic and climatic conditions to the crust formation? What is the effect of meteorite bombardment? What is the effect of the processes taking place in the mantle and core on the crust formation? In what stage of history and for how long did a large-scale formation of the interior occur? What were the regularities in the inner structure of planets and satellites?

Origin and evolution of the atmospheres of planets and satellites
How and when did the atmospheres form on various bodies? What was the primordial atmosphere on various bodies? What was the rôle of endogenous and exogenous factors in the formation of the atmosphere? How did the atmosphere evolve? What was the relationship between the atmosphere and the surface? What

were the general regularities in the formation of the atmosphere on various bodies? What was the nature of aerosols and their rôle in the heat balance of the atmosphere?

REFERENCES

[1]   O. Yu Schmidt, *The origin of the Earth and planets*. (In Russian.) Moscow, Publishing House of the USSR Academy of Sciences, p. 130 (1962).

[2]   H. C. Urey, *Proc. Nat. Acad. Sci. US*, **41**, 127 (1955).

[3]   A. G. W. Cameron, *Space Sci. Rev.*, **15**, 121 (1973).

[4]   F. Hoyle, *Quart. J. Roy. Astron. Soc.*, **1**, 28 (1960).

[5]   E. Schatzman, *Ann. d'Astrophys.*, **30** 963 (1967).

[6]   V. S. Safronov, *The evolution of the preplanetary cloud and the formation of the Earth and planets*. (In Russian.) Moscow, Nauka, p. 244 (1969).

[7]   J. Wood, *Meteorites and the origin of Planets*, McGraw Hill, New York (1968). Translation into Russian, Moscow, Mir, p. 173 (1971).

[8]   H. Alfvén and G. Arrhenius, *Evolution of the Solar System*, NASA, SP-345 (1976).

[9]   J. S. Lewis, *Ann. Rev. Phys. Chem.*, **24**, 339 (1973).

[10] J. S. Lewis, *Icarus*, **16**, 241 (1972).

[11] L. Grossman, In *Cosmochemistry of the Moon and planets*, Moscow, Nauka, p. 89 (1975).

[12] L. Grossman, *Geochim. et Cosmochim. Acta*, **36**, 597 (1972).

[13] H. Reeves, In *The origin of the Solar System*, S. F. Dermott (ed.), Chichester, Wiley, pp 1-17 (1978).

[14] G. B. Field, *Astrophys. J.* **165**, 29-40 (1971).

[15] W. H. MCrea, *Proc. Roy. Soc.*, **A256**, 245 (1960).

[16] L. Spitzer, *Diffuse Matter In Space*, Interscience, New York, p. 48 (1968)

[17] D. A. F. Schatzman, In *The origin of the Solar System*, S. F. Dermott (ed.), Chichester, Wiley, p. 118 (1978).

[18] V. S. Safronov, In *Cosmochemistry of the Moon and planets*. (In Russian.) Moscow, Nauka, p. 624 (1975).

[19] A. G. W. Cameron, In *The origin of the Solar System*, S. F. Dermott (ed.), Chichester, Wiley, pp. 49-73 (1978).

[20] B. Lindblad, *Nature*, **135**, 133 (1935).

[21] E. Anders, *Space Sci. Rev.*, **3**, 583 (1964).

[22] A. G. W. Cameron and M. R. Pine, *Icarus*, **18**, 377 (1973).

[23] D. Ter Haar, *Ann. Rev. Astron. Astrophys.*, **5**, 267-278 (1967). Chichester, Wiley, p. 107 (1978).

[24] F. Hoyle and N. C. Wickramasinghe, *Nature*, **233**, 459 (1969).

[25] N. C. Wickramasinghe and K. Nandy, *Nature*, **227**, 51 (1970).

[26] F. J. Low and K. S. Krishna-Swamy, *Nature*, **227**, 1333 (1970).

[27] N. J. Woolf and E. P. Ney, *Astrophys. J.*, **155**, 181 (1969).

[28] D. P. Girla, *Nature*, **229**, 237 (1971).

[29] G. V. Voitkevich, *The fundamentals of the theory of the Earth's origin*. (In Russian.) Moscow, Nedra Publishers, p. 135 (1979).

[30] J. W. Larimer, *Geochim. et Cosmochim. Acta*, **31**, 1215 (1967).

[31] A. Kenneth and K. A. Goettel, NASA, TM X-3511, p. 47 (1977).

[32] V. P. Volkov, *Chemistry of the atmosphere and surface of Venus*. (In Russian.) Moscow, Nauka, p. 208 (1983).

[33] A. P. VInogradov, *Geochimia*, **11**, 1283. (In Russian.) (1971).

[34] P. G. Harris and D. C. Tozer, *Nature,* **215**, 1449 (1967).

[35] K. P. Florensky, A. T. Basilevsky and G. A. Burba, *An outline of comparative planetology*. (In Russian.) Moscow, Nauka, p. 326 (1981).

[36] Ye. A. Lyubimova, *The thermics of the Earth and the Moon*. (In Russian.) Moscow, Nauka, p. 277 (1968).

[37] A. P. Vinogradov, *Vestnik MGU, Geol.,* **4**, 3. (In Russian.) (1969).

[38] E. M. Galimov, *Geochemistry of stable carbon isotopes*. (In Russian.) Moscow, Nedra, p. 224 (1968).

[39] K. Ya. Kondratyev, *Meteorology of the planetary atmospheres*. (In Russian.) Leningrad, Hydrometeoizdat, p. 293 (1977).

[40] Ya. K. Kondratyev, *Comparative meteorology of planets*. (In Russian.) Leningrad, Hydrometeoizdat, p. 48 (1975).

[41] A. D. Kuzmin and M. Ya. Marov, *The physics of the planet Venus*. (In Russian.) Moscow, Nauka, p. 408 (1974).

[42] D. M. Hunten and T. M. Donahue, *Ann. Rev. Earth. Sci.,* **4**, 265 (1976).

[43] J. B. Pollack and Y. L. Young, *Ann. Rev. Earth and Planet. Sci.,* **8**, 425 (1980). (1980).

[44] D. E. Shemansky and A. L. Broadfoot, *Rev. Geophys. and Space Phys.,* **15**, 491 (1977).

[45] J. C. G. Walker, *Evolution of the atmosphere*, Macmillan, New York, p. 195 (1977).

[46] K. K. Turekian and S. P. Clark, *J. Atmos. Sci.,* **32**, 1257 (1975).

[47] J. B. Pollack and D. C. Black, *Science,* **205**, 36 (1979).

[48] H. Alfvén and G. Arrhenius, *Structure and evolutionary history of the Solar System*. D. Reidel, Boston (1975).

[49] A. Brahic (ed.), *Formation of planetary systems*, CNES, France (1982).

1.2 Mercury

1.2.1 GENERAL CHARACTERISTICS

Mercury is the planet closest to the Sun. It is discernible from the Earth with difficulty since its angular elongation from the Sun is never more than 28°. Its exploration by space vehicles (except for orbital spacecraft) is also hampered by the rigorous climatic conditions prevailing on its surface. At noon the temperature at the subsolar point rises to 427°C and then drops to −173°C at midnight. This is why it remains the least-explored planet in the terrestrial group. Mercury is practically devoid of an atmosphere. The upper limit of pressure is put at 10^{-7} Pa. A very weak (about 10^{-10} Pa) helium atmosphere has been discovered near the planet [1]. It was suggested that it might have emerged as a result of the decay of the natural radioactive elements present in the rocks or due to the trapping of the solar wind. Table 1.2.1 gives Mercury's principal physical characteristics.

Table 1.2.1 — Mercury's principal characteristics

Distance to the Sun	0.307–0.467 AU	Surface pressure	$\sim 10^{-7}$ Pa
Radius	2439 km	Surface temperature	−173, +427°C
Mass	3.302×10^{23} kg	Albedo	0.125
	$5.45 \times 10^3 \pm 50$ Kg m^{-3}	Magnetic dipole field strength	350 nT
Acceleration due to gravity at surface	3.7 ms$_{-2}$	Axial revolution period	58.65 days

At present the principal characteristics of Mercury are reliably specified. It has a radius equal to 0.382 of the Earth's radius (2439 km). Its mass is 0.05527 of the Earth's mass (3.30×10^{23} kg), and the mean density is nearly the same as of the Earth ($\rho\pi = 5.45 \times 10^3$ kg m$_{-3}$, $\rho E = 5.51 \times 10^3$Kg m^{-3}). The fact that, despite being small in size, Mercury has the same density as the Earth is indicative of a high content of heavy elements within it. It is suggested [2] that nearly 65% of Mercury is taken up by the iron core and 35% by the silicate phase (the mantle and the crust). Such an idea of Mercury was proposed as a consequence of the cosmochemical models of building

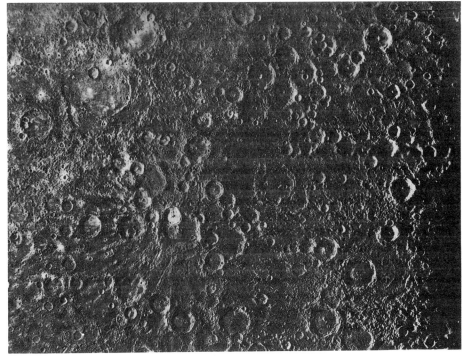

Fig. 1.2.1 — Surface of Mercury. (a) picture taken from Mariner 10 at a distance of several hundred kilometres; (b) mosaic of the Kuiper crater region (longitude 032°, latitude −11°), diameter 60Km compiled from pictures taken from Mariner 10.

the bodies of the Solar System. The density of the terrestrial planets is known to be inversely proportional to their distance from the Sun. In this row Mercury is marginal not only in its position, but evidently also in its properties. Since iron exhibits high thermal and electrical conductivities and high density, it is quite probable that Mercury had a history differing from the histories of other terrestrial planets. In this context it is of special interest.

Up to 1974 Mercury had been studied only through ground-based observations. In 1974 it was first studied from the spacecraft Mariner 10 — its surface was photographed (Fig. 1.2.1), the magnetic field measured, the atmosphere and thermal properties of the surface investigated.

These studies extended essentially our knowledge of Mercury, although in general we still know little about it — obviously not more than what we knew of the Moon prior to the flights of spacecraft to it [3].

Mariner 10 discovered Mercury's magnetic field and this was most important, since until recently it was assumed that the planet's slow rotation and its intensive irradiation by the solar wind lead to the lack of an appreciable magnetic field (similar to the Moon). When Mariner 10 approached Mercury, it detected a magnetosphere with protons and electrons in the area of the solar wind–planet interaction [4]. It was established that Mercury has its own dipole magnetic field one hundred times weaker than the Earth's field. [5]. The maximum intensity of the magnetic field was estimated at ~ 350 nT, i.e., some 20 times more than the interplanetary magnetic field near Mercury's orbit. But the generation mechanism of this field still remains obscure. Is this residual magnetization of the recent work of an inner 'dynamo'? In any case, however, it proves the existence of a large metallic core in the planet. Judging by the high density, Mercury evidently has twice as large an iron concentration as any other planet.

The discovery of the magnetic field and the proving of the existence of volcanism (from pictures of the surface) lead to the conclusion about the planet's differentiation. If it is so, then much of iron is concentrated in the core. Hence, the core takes 50% of the planet's volume, and the core's radius is 70–80% of the planet's radius. In view of its high density, the acceleration due to gravity at the planet's surface (3.7 m s^{-2}) is very nearly the same as on the surface of Mars, although Mercury is much the smaller of the two bodies.

The photometric, polarimetric and thermal properties of the Mercurian surface obtained through ground-based observations show its surface to be covered with a layer of dark porous fine-grained rock resembling lunar regolith [6]. Measurements made from Mariner 10 by the infrared radiometer also testify to the existence of a regolith-like layer on the planet. Besides, the spatial variations in the thermophysical properties of this surface layer point to the existence of vast regions with denser rocks, possibly outcrops of bedrock [7]. Radar studies of the high-altitude profiles of the surface in equatorial regions of the planet has revealed a surface studded with craters, whose topography bears resemblance to the Moon [8]. This came as a surprise because before the mission of Mariner 10, it was believed that the density of the craters on the Mercurian surface should be much smaller than on the Moon or Mars, since it is located much farther from the asteroid belt.

1.2.2 GEOLOGICAL FEATURES OF THE MERCURIAN SURFACE

The surfaces of Mercury and the Moon are very much alike. Highlands and maria are discernible on the Mercurian surface with highlands covering the greater part of the planet. Intercrater plains studded with small craters, being the most ancient parts of the surface, are encountered in the highlands. Most continents are covered with overlapping craters of various sizes. The inner parts of large ancient craters are plains, but younger craters on the continents are also destroyed. In appearance they resemble young lunar craters [9].

Younger regions differ from continental areas in the character of the surface. These take the form of extended plains with a smooth surface, although broken in places by scarps, fissures and ridges. Mare plains make up 15% of the part of the surface photographed from Mariner 10. The largest of these is the circular Caloris basin some 1300 km in diameter. It resembles the Mare Imbrium on the Moon. The differences in the reflectivity of the continental and mare regions on Mercury are not so obvious as on the Moon. Mercury's mare plains may be distinguished from the continents only by their slightly darker and reddish colour.

Material making up the mare basins is evidently of a volcanic origin (basaltic lavas) similar to the lunar mare depressions. The volcanic nature of the Mercurian basins is manifested in their geological structure. Meandering scarps resembling the frontal scarps of the lava flows in lunar maria are traced in some places. However, unlike the Moon and the Earth where the height of these scarps is only some tens of metres, on Mercury's plains their height reaches 200 to 500 m [10]. The reason for this lies, obviously, in the greater viscosity of lavas on Mercury.

At the same time there are structures on Mercury which are not typical of the Moon. These are a system of extended scarps in the form of curved arc-shaped or sometimes meandering lines stretching for hundreds of kilometres. The height of the scarps may vary from several hundreds of metres to three kilometres. The Mercurian crust, obviously, warps, thus giving rise to folding. The probable reason for this is the phase conversion of part of the large metallic core from the liquid into solid state which results in the diminished volume and compression of the silicate envelope [10]. The newly discovered scarp is an example of such a geological structure.

There is one more difference between Mercury and the Moon. Mercury's cratered surface is divided by rather smooth intercrater areas or plains, while on the Moon craters in the highlands are often overlapping each other or densely located. Most of these intercrater plains existed prior to the formation of many large craters [10–12]. The difference in cratered regions of the Moon and Mercury may be attributed to different values of the acceleration due to gravity [13]. The ballistic scattering of material from the primordial craters on Mercury is less pronounced than on the Moon, and, consequently, the coverage area (depending on the velocity of ejecta) is 5 to 12 times smaller for craters of the same size. As a result, the ejecta blankets and secondary craters on Mercury encircle the primordial craters more closely than on the Moon. Consequently more ancient regions on the Mercurian surface may be preserved better than on the Moon [13].

The differences in the gravitational fields of the Moon and Mercury evidently also explain the differences in shape (geometry) of commensurable craters. In both cases small craters are cup-shaped, but in larger craters central peaks appear, and terraces on their inner slopes (walls) are formed. In large craters the central peak becomes a complicated structure turning into an inner ring mountain located concentrically with the crater's caldera. This is observed on Mercury and the Moon alike, but on Mercury this process is underway in smaller craters due to the stronger gravitational field [13].

Many researchers [13–16] have studied the morphology of Mercurian craters. Some authors interpreted the morphological features of craters, employing data on lunar craters as the most properly studied. The differences in crater morphology on various planets may in general be attributed to the differences in the acceleration due to gravity, the cosmic velocity of the impacting bodies, the properties of the falling bodies, planets' surface, etc. But for a single planet all these properties are identical, except for the features of the surface. Cintala *et al.* [14] systematized lunar craters and established that a crater's morphology is dependent on the physical properties of the rock in which the crater formed. An insignificant difference was revealed between the morphology of craters on smooth surfaces and in Mercury's cratered regions. This proves that the physical properties of rocks in these morphologically different regions are similar or identical.

The morphology of craters on lunar maria, Mercury's smooth surfaces (in basins) and in crater-studded regions exhibited similar features. At the same time a dissimilarity between lunar continents and Mercury's cratered regions was discovered and this led Cintala *et al.* [14] to three major conclusions.

(1) The similarity of the craters' morphology on lunar maria and Mercurian smooth plains proves that the strength of the gravitational field is not a dominating factor in crater formation.
(2) The similarity between lunar maria and the smooth Mercurian plains points to their volcanic origin.
(3) The great difference in the morphology of craters on lunar continents and in Mercury's cratered regions is indicative of their dissimilarity in physical properties. (The regolith covering lunar highlands is perhaps not widespread in Mercury's cratered regions.)

Irrespective of the mechanism of the formation of scarps, their presence in large well-preserved craters helps to roughly rank them in age and exclude the possibility of the intensive melting of the planet or the displacement of tectonic plates from the time when this heavily cratered basement emerged.

Apart from cratered regions and basins, other geological structures are also found on Mercury. One of these is a system of linear hills and narrow valleys which extend for 300 km and more, traversing in places the heavily cratered or intercrater areas of the surface. They may be as wide as 10 km. A valley stretching for over 1000 km from the north-east (the Caloris Montes region) to the Shakespeare crater is an illustration of the above. Such fissures in the crust may appear in the course of the formation of large basins of impact origin.

In one of the regions on Mercury's surface, unusual small-scale structures are detected. This region is called 'hilly' since numerous hills with a height ranging from several hundred metres to 2 km and a base 5–10 km in diameter are found here. Such regions are known to exist in two places on the Moon. In all three cases these regions are located in places opposite to large young mare basins. On the Moon these regions are antipodal to Mare Imbrium and Mare Orientale, while on Mercury the region is antipodal to the Caloris basin. It was suggested [17] that seismic waves, generated as a result of meteorite impacts in the course of the formation of these maria, focus at opposite points of the surface, transforming it in some way.

Five periods may be distinguished in the geological history of Mercury [11, 18]. The first period covers the time interval from the early stage of the existence of the Solar System (the condensation of the gas cloud into solid grains and the accumulation of solid material into Mercury's basic mass) to the differentiation of matter and the formation of the planet's primordial crust. Apparently, even in this earliest formation period Mercury did not have a dense atmosphere. Otherwise old craters destroyed through weathering, as on Mars, would have been preserved.

The second period is marked by intensive bombardment of its surface with large bodies with the resultant emergence of heavily cratered regions on the surface and large mare basins. The period terminated with the formation of the giant Caloris basin. Whether this period was a final stage in the Mercurian accumulation or whether it was a later event of bombardment, not related to the first period of accretion, still remains unclear. Intercrater plains evidently represent the more ancient part of the surface, the formation of which dates back to the first period [19].

The third period (evidently short enough) started after the formation of the Caloris basin and lasted to the beginning of volcanic activity. This was the period of the formation of Mercury's surface as a result of the fall of smaller meteoritic bodies.

The fourth period, which began some 4000 million years ago, is characterized by intensive volcanic activity which gave rise to the formation of basins bearing a resemblance to lunar maria. It is assumed, however, that large smooth basins, such as the Suisei, Odin and Tir plains, surrounding the giant Caloris basin, emerged from the melted material ejected from the Caloris basin. If smooth basins on Mercury are similar to lunar maria, then they formed from 3000 to 4000 million years ago. But if these basins are of an impact origin, they were formed some 4000 million years ago.

The fifth period started approximately 3000 million years ago and has lasted to the present day. Mercury's surface in that period has undergone only insignificant changes. Impacts of small meteorites and the fall of cosmic dust resulted in the formation of regolith on the planet's surface.

Although Mercury bears most resemblance to the Moon, it is also essentially dissimilar from it. On the one hand, it is known that Mercury and the Moon are similar in the reflectivity of the surface within the range of visible and radio waves, in the formation of the cratered surface, the regolith cover and other features. On the other hand, greater density, pointing to a high content of heavy elements, and the discovery of a magnetic field, make Mercury and the Moon dissimilar to some extent.

Mercury's similarity to other bodies in the Solar System becomes still more significant for understanding the evolution of terrestrial planets. Now it is clear that Mercury has some similar features not only with the Moon, but also with Mars and the Earth. This allows one to think that all these bodies developed along a common evolutionary path, and this means that in the early period the Earth was also subject to the heavy bombardment with large cosmic bodies which shaped its surface in a similar manner to that of the Moon, Mercury and Mars.

1.2.3 COMPOSITION AND STRUCTURE OF MERCURY

The evolution of any planetary body is governed by its thermal régime. This relates, in particular, to the differentiation of matter, volcanism, tectonic activity and even the magnetic field. Any estimations of the thermal evolution of planets may be considered only as approximate, since they proceed from numerous assumptions and unproved initial data. As initial conditions, assumptions are made here on the sources of heat, the mechanism of the heat transfer, specific heat, the density, the melting temperature, the dependence of these parameters on the temperature and pressure, etc. In most cases the validity of these assumptions cannot be checked through experimentation. Some uncertainty also remains about the planet's initial heating through accretion, the rôle of such sources as tidal fluctuations, induced electric currents, the radioactive decay of elements, etc., in the thermal regime.

Kozlovskaya [20] proposed one of the first models of the Mercurian composition. She calculated models of the planet based on various sizes of iron ore. It was assumed that the silicate parts of Mercury and the Earth are similar. Estimations have shown that the iron content in Mercury's core and mantle makes up 54–60%. The thermal history was calculated by Mayeva [21] on the basis of the homogeneous model of Mercury with a 58% content of iron and 42% silicates. The initial temperature was assumed to be about 1000 K, and the content of radioactive elements to be the same as in chondrites. Consequently, it was calculated that the temperature inside Mercury did not rise higher than 2300 K and the interior did not melt at all. Hence, Mercury should not have a core. But it has already been mentioned that there is some indirect evidence for the existence of the core – the availability of the inner magnetic field [5], volcanism [15], and the probable presence of uranium and thorium.

Sigfried and Solomon [22] also calculated Mercury's thermal history. But they proceeded from a higher initial temperature — approximately 1400 K. The accretion time was assumed to be nearly 10^5 years. According to their model, Mercury should have a core the radius of which makes up approximately 75% of the planet's radius, and the mass of which is 66% of the planet's mass. The iron content in Mercury was taken to be nearly the same (60%) as in [21]. Proceeding from the lack of heat sources in the core and the above initial data, the authors of [22] estimated that the differentiation process on Mercury was completed 3000 million years ago. There are some objections to this figure since in this case Mercury's core should be solid at present and then no magnetic field should exist. In this context Siegfried and Solomon revised their theory and made new calculations, taking into account adiabatic compression as an additional inner source, and changes in the content of natural radioactive elements on Mercury. In their new model the formation of the core came to an end only 1800 million years ago.

At last Toksöz [23, 24] calculated a thermal model for Mercury. He also assumed the initial temperature to be 1400 K, but a shorter accretion period, of about 10^3 years. He suggested the existence of a thermal source (potassium) in the planet's core, which maintains at present the core in a melted state. According to this model, 2000 million years ago Mercury had a lithosphere which was 200 km thick; at present it is 500 km thick. Such a thick lithosphere results in the low level of tectonic activity. The model might explain Mercury's present state. However, the potassium content in the core assumed by him has no convincing proof [25].

The headway made in understanding the condensation and accretion processes enabled several attempts to estimate the composition of terrestrial planets. Such estimates are only approximate since they are based on numerous assumptions. Table 1.2.2 gives Mercury's composition calculated by Kenneth and Goettel [3]. They calculated the content of the most widespread elements constituting over 99% (together with oxygen) of the material in the protoplanetary nebula from which the planets emerged. The table also includes the content of natural radioactive elements determining the thermal history of the planet.

Table 1.2.2 — Mercury's composition (percentage by mass) [3]

Components	Whole planet	Mantle	Core
MgO	12.83	36.89	—
SiO_2	11.67	33.53	—
Al_2O_3	5.32	15.30	—
CaO	4.97	14.28	—
Na_2O	—	—	—
FeO	—	—	—
Fe	61.75	—	94.69
Ni	3.46	—	5.31
S	—	—	—
K	—	—	—
U	77×10^{-9}	220×10^{-9}	—
Th	165×10^{-9}	490×10^{-9}	—

The qualitative model of Mercury's composition was calculated proceeding from the following assumptions:

(1) condensation goes on under a chemical equilibrium (the initial temperature, pressure and condensed phases were taken from [26, 27];
(2) the initial ratio of elements is as in the Sun [28], except for the Fe/Si ratio assumed as 90 and S/Si, assumed as 0.25;
(3) simplified assumptions on the accretion were made. It was assumed that the accretion of the material took place in one region of the nebula (i.e. a narrow region in terms of composition); the possible effects of mixing or fractionation in the cloud were ignored; the planet's homogenous accretion with the subsequent complete differentiation and a relatively slow accretion were assumed [29].

It follows from Table 1.2.2 that Mercury has a Fe–Ni core, making up approximately two-thirds of the whole planetary mass. The mantle is enriched with refractory Mg, Si, Al and Ca condensates. Forsterite ($Mg_2 SiO_4$), obviously makes up the basis of the Mg–Si phase. In this simple model Mercury is practically devoid of FeO, Na, K, S and H_2O. The U and Th content here is more than on the Sun due to the incomplete Mg and SiO_2 condensation. But notwithstanding the U and Th enrichment the overall amount of heat released per unit of the planet's mass is smaller than on any other terrestrial planet due to the absence of potassium.

Mercury's composition given in Table 1.2.2 agrees well with the data on the spectral reflection of Mercury's surface obtained by Adams and MacCord [30], which proves the lack of iron pyroxene, the nearly complete absence (about 6%) of FeO and the presence of the anorthositic crust on the planet.

Mercury's composition as estimated by Kenneth and Goettel [3] is based only a simplified model, which may be made more accurate or corrected in keeping with other initial data. In particular, the fractionation process in the cloud could lead to the condensation of most of the silicate fractions on Mercury in the peripheral part of the cloud. The result would be the addition of enstatite ($MgSiO_3$), Na and K to Mercury and, correspondingly, the proportional decrease in $MgSiO_4$, Al_2O_3, CaO, U and Th. But even with such a small potassium increment the overall amount of heat released by Mercury would still remain lower than in other planets. Evidently, a relatively low generation of radiogenic heat and the small size of the planet are the causes of the apparent lack of global tectonic activity on Mercury.

1.2.4 ATMOSPHERE AND VOLATILE COMPONENTS OF MERCURY

The present notions about the protoplanetary cloud suggest that its temperature dropped and its composition changed with increasing distance from the Sun. The radiation pressure of the bright protosun caused the migration of light volatiles to the periphery of the protoplanetary cloud. There were no light gases (H, He) in the region of Mercury's formation. Therefore, they could not become the constituents of the planet. Heavier, but volatile components (S, Cl, K, H_2O, etc.) were not found in Mercury either since this planet condensed at a relatively high temperature (around 1400 K). This explains the lack of a significant atmosphere on Mercury at present, and apparently in the past. The emergence of CO_2 as a result of the reactions of carbon-bearing metals (carbides) with FeO traces in silicates is possible, in principle. However, the low gravitational acceleration on the surface and high temperatures are conducive to the quick dissipation of gases on Mercury [31].

As mentioned above, Mercury's atmosphere was studied by the ultraviolet spectrometer mounted on Mariner 10. The results obtained allow one to speak about the presence of only highly insignificant amounts of helium, the origin of which is still obscure. There are three probable sources of the helium:

(1) it was trapped in small quantities in the course of accretion;
(2) it was formed as a result of the decay of natural radioactive elements and was released from the lithosphere;
(3) it was carried with the solar wind.

Mariner 10 did not detect argon which may be attributed to the lack of potassium on Mercury. This fact is in accord with the models of the Mercurian composition calculated in [3, 32, 33].

Neon was not registered either, as its predicted amount is below the sensitivity threshold of instrumentation. No other volatiles were registered.

Making use of the upper limits in the H_2O, CO_2 and CO distribution in the Mercurian atmosphere and the estimates of their lifetime, Kumar [34] concluded that the present outgassing rate of H_2O and CO_2 is at least four orders of magnitude less than on the Earth. This dramatic difference may be accounted for by the great thickness of the Mercurian lithosphere at present and by the shortage of volatiles on Mercury.

It follows from the models of thermal history [23, 24, 35] that intensive outgassing of the atmosphere occurred in the early stage of Mercury's evolution in the period of accretion, global differentiation and somewhat later basaltic volcanism. Many volatiles, evidently, were released during the first hundred million years. Perhaps Mercury had some atmosphere which might leave traces by its interaction with rocks and minerals. Mercury's atmosphere might have existed for long. If the magnetic field was formed during the emergence of the atmosphere or prior to it, then it could have prevented the blowing out of the atmosphere by the solar wind. And vice versa: if there was no magnetic field, the closeness to the Sun might create unfavourable conditions for the maintenance of the primary atmosphere. Further on, this atmosphere was lost as a result of thermal evaporation, photodissociation and photochemical losses. Mercury's present atmosphere is maintained largely by the solar wind. Under conventional conditions the solar wind is deviated by the magnetic field of Mercury to some 1500 km from the surface. But some part of it still intrudes into the planet's exosphere, and in periods of enhanced solar activity it even reaches the surface [36].

1.2.5 GENERAL PROBLEMS OF EXPLORING MERCURY

It was said already that the present notions about Mercury are very limited. The data, obtained by ground-based methods and by space vehicles, are obviously inadequate for understanding Mercury's history and structure. Therefore, in the coming years Mercurian studies will be aimed at securing fundamental data which may be used as a basis for improving our knowledge of the composition, structure and history of Mercury's formation.

The most important objectives in Mercurian exploration are given in [37]:

Investigations of the rock composition of Mercury's surface

What is the composition of the most widespread rocks? Are there traces of volatiles? What is the amount of natural radioactive elements, and how are they distributed over the surface and in depth?

The refractory rock composition proves the validity of modern theoretical models of Mercury and of the general notions about the differentiation of material in the protoplanetary cloud.

The specification of the nature of the planet's magnetic field

What is the source of the magnetic field (inner, outer or relic)? How did the field change in size and direction during the planet's existence? Are there presently any large magnetic anomalies on the surface? Are there traces of palaeomagnetism?

Studying Mercury's magnetic field and its comparison with the magnetic fields of other planets allows one to approach the solution of the most important problem — the rôle of the magnetic field in the history of planets, and, most of all, the Earth.

Investigation of the volcanic and tectonic processes taking place on the planet

What is the contribution of volcanism and tectonic processes to the shaping of Mercury's surface? When did the volcanic activity on the planet take place and when did it come to an end? What are the specific features of volcanism on Mercury in comparison to the other bodies? Are there any traces of tectonic activity on the surface? What is the difference between the lava basins on Mercury and the Moon?

The comparison of volcanism and tectonics on Mercury and other planets helps us to extend our knowledge of the early stage of the evolution of planets and, above all, the Earth.

Investigation of the planet's regolith cover

How is the regolith cover distributed over the surface? What is its thickness? What are the differences of the regolith composition in different regions? How does the regolith composition differ from underlying rocks?

What were the temporal variations in the intensity and spectral composition of cosmic rays which irradiated the regolith? How did the intensity of the fall of cosmic dust change? What is the radiation age of the surface regolith layer?

Studies of these problems will help us to understand the processes which took place on the surface and to examine the chronology of the events which occurred on the surface in the distant past and in recent time, to study the history of cosmic rays and cosmic dust.

Exploration of the relief

What are the specific features of the geological structure of Mercury's surface? How do they differ from those of the Moon? What is the age of the largest geological structures? What is the chronology of the events which contributed to the shaping of the planet's surface? Are there traces of modern volcanism and tectonics? When was the formation of the relief completed? What is the correlation between the exogenous and endogenous processes in shaping Mercury's surface?

The solution of these problems will represent an important advance in understanding the history of the shaping of the planet's surface and crust.

Studies of the magnetosphere

What is the nature of Mercury's magnetosphere? What are the specific features of the magnetosphere? What is the effect of the Sun's magnetosphere on it? To what extent does it protect the surface from the solar wind and solar flares?

The answers to these questions will be helpful for comprehending the rôle of magnetospheres in the history of planets and particularly the Earth, the planet which gave rise to life.

REFERENCES

[1] A. L. Broadfoot, S. Kumar, and M. J. S. Belton, *Science,* **85**, 166, (1974).
[2] J. S. Lewis, *Icarus*, **16**, 241 (1972).
[3] A. Kenneth and K. A. Goettel, NASA, *TM X-3511*, p. 47 (1977).
[4] K. W. Ogilvie, J. D. Scudder, and R. E. Hartle, *Science,* **185**, 145 (1974).
[5] N. F. Ness, K. W. Behannon, and R. P. Lepping, *Nature,* **255**, 204 (1975).
[6] T. Gehrels, NASA, *SP-267*, p. 95 (1971).
[7] S. C. Chase, E. D. Miner, and D. Morrison, *Science,* **185**, 142 (1974).
[8] S. Zohar and R. M. Goldstain, *Astron. J.,* **79**, 85 (1974).
[9] M. S. Davies, S. E. Dwornik, D. E. Gault, R. G. Strom. *Atlas of Mercury*, NASA (1978).

[10] B. S. Murrey, R. G. Storm, and N. J. Trask, *J. Geophys. Res.*, **80**, 2508 (1975).

[11] H. T. Howard, G. L. Tyler, and P. B. Esposito, *Science,* **185**, 169 (1974).

[12] N. J. Trask and J. E. Guest, *J. Geophys. Res.*, **80**, 2461 (1975).

[13] D. E. Gault, J. E. Guest, and J. B. Murrey, *J. Geophys. Res.*, **80**, 2444 (1975).

[14] M. J. Cintala, C. A. Wood, and L. W. Head, In *Proc. 8th Lunar and Planet. Sci. Conf.*, New York, Pergamon Press, **3**, 3409 (1977).

[15] M. C. Malin, In *Proc. 9th Lunar and Planet. Sci. Conf.*, New York, Pergamon Press, **3**, 3395 (1978).

[16] J. A. Wood, J. W. Head, and M. J. Cintala, In *Proc. 8th Lunar and Planet. Sci. Conf.*, New York, Pergamon Press, **3** 3503 (1977).

[17] P. H. Schultz and D. E. Gault, *Moon*, **12**, 159 (1975).

[18] B. C. Murrey, *Sci. Amer.*, **233**, 58 (1975).

[19] J. E. Guest, and D. E. Gault, *Geophys. Res. Lett.*, **3**, 121 (1976).

[20] S. V. Kozlovskaya, In *Physics of the Moon and planets.* (In Russian.) Moscow, Nauka, p. 228 (1972).

[21] S. V. Mayeva, In *Physics of the Moon and planets.* (In Russian.) Moscow, Nauka, p. 223 (1972).

[22] R. W. Sigfried and S. C. Solomon, *Icarus*, **23**, 192 (1974).

[23] M. N. Toksöz and D. H. Johnston. In *Cosmochemistry of the Moon and planets.* (In Russian.) Moscow, Nauka, p. 210 (1974).

[24] M. N. Toksöz, A. T. Hsui, and D. H. Johnston, *Moon and Planet*, **18**, 281 (1978).

[25] A. G. W. Cameron, *Icarus*, **18**, 407 (1973).

[26] L. Grossman, *Geochim. et Cosmochim. Acta*, **36**, 597 (1972).

[27] J. S. Lewis, *Icarus*, **15**, 174 (1971).

[28] A. K. Baird, P. Toulmin III, and B. C. Clark. *Science,* **194**, 81 (1976).

[29] K. A. Goettel and S. S. Barshay, In *The origin of the Solar System*, S. F. Dermott (ed.), Chichester, Wiley, pp. 611-627, (1978).

[30] J. B. Adams and T. B. McCord. *Conference on comparison of Mercury and the Moon*, Houston, LPI, p. 112 (1976).

[31] S. J. Rasool, S. H. Gross, and W. E. McCowern. *Space Sci. Rev.*, **5**, 565 (1966).

[32] J. S. Lewis, *Ann. Rev. Phys. Chem.*, **24**, 339 (1973).

[33] A. E. Ringwood. *Geochim. et Cosmochim. Acta,* **30**, 41 (1966).

[34] S. Kumar, D. M. Hunten, and A. L. Broadfoot. *Planet and Space Sci.* **26**, 1063 (1978).

[35] V. N. Zharkov and V. P. Trubitsin, In *The physics of planetary interiors.* (In Russian.) Moscow, Nauka, p. 448 (1980).

[36] S. Kumar, *Icarus*, **37**, 207 (1976).

[37] *An outline of planetary geoscience*, NASA, TM-X-58202 (1977).

1.3 Venus

1.3.1 GENERAL CHARACTERISTICS

During the Space Age, Venus has been a major focus of attention. Nineteen Soviet and six American spacecraft have been launched to carry out intensive investigations of this planet. All previous data, obtained by ground-based methods, failed to provide a notion about the nature and thickness of Venus' clouds, the composition and structure of its atmosphere, the character of surface rocks and especially the planet's inner structure. Thus, what we have found out by penetrating the dense clouds has, in effect, been a new 'discovery' of the planet. These studies contributed to the development of certain ideas about the history of the shaping and modern structure of Venus. The principal results obtained have been discussed in numerous review papers [1–7].

Venus has a nearly circular orbit with a mean distance from the Sun of 108 million km. The inclination angle between the orbit and the plane of the ecliptic is 3.4°. According to verified data, Venus' mass is 4.87×10^{24} kg (or 0.815 of the Earth's mass), radius 6052 km, the rotation period (retrograde) 243.09 terrestrial days, mean density 5.24×10^3 kg m^{-3}, a difference in the equatorial axes of 1.1 ± 0.4 km, a shift of the centre of the mass in relation to the centre of the figure 1.5 ± 0.3 km, acceleration due to gravity at the surface 8.9 m s^{-2}, dipole magnetic field at the surface 30 nT, the relief of the surface (the value of topographical variations) $\Delta H = 13$ km, and density of top rocks $1.2 - 2.7 \times 10^3$ kg m^{-3}. Space flights have greatly extended our knowledge of Venus' atmosphere, the mass of which is 5×10^{20} kg, as well as the physical and climatic conditions on the planet's surface.

Taking the cosmochemical aspect of Venusian studies, it is seen that its atmosphere has become an important source of information. It determines the character of Venus, the physical conditions on its surface and the planet's thermal balance. The mass of Venus' atmosphere is approximately 100 times as large as the mass of the Earth's atmosphere, and the density of the atmosphere at the surface is 70 times higher. Table 1.3.1 gives the results of measurements of the atmosphere at Venus' surface made by Soviet spacecraft.

Table 1.3.1 — Physical characteristics of Venus' atmosphere near the surface

Station	Temperature (°C)	Pressure (10^5Pa)	Landing coordinates		Mean uplift relative to $R = 6052$ km
			Latitude	Longitude	
Venera 4 (1967)	—	—	19°	38°	—
Venera 5 (1969)	—	—	−3°	18°	—
Venera 6 (1969)	—	—	−5°	23°	—
Venera 7 (1970)	474 ± 20	92 ± 15	−5°	351°	—
Venera 8 (1972)	470 ± 8	93 ± 1.5	−10°	335°	1.0
Venera 9 (1975)	455 ± 5	85 ± 3	32°	291°	2.1
Venera 10 (1975)	464 ± 3	91 ± 3	16°	291°	1.5
Venera 11 (1978)	461 ± 5	91 ± 3	−14°	299°	1.2
Venera 12 (1978)	462 ± 5	92 ± 3	−7°	294°	1.3
Venera 13 (1981)	462 ± 5	88.7 ± 3	−7°	303°11′	1.4
Venera 14 (1981)	465 ± 5	94.7 ± 3	−13°15′	310°09′	1.0
VeGa 1 (1984)	460 ± 5	93.4 ± 3	7°11′	177°48′	0.4
VeGa 2 (1984)	452 ± 5	86 ± 3	−6°27′	181°5′	1.8

It is quite obvious that higher temperatures and pressures should be found in the lower-lying areas of the surface. This is well corroborated by the radar map of Venus' surface obtained by the Pioneer Venus Orbiter spacecraft (Fig. 1.3.1 which is reproduced in the colour section facing page 46). Passing from the night side to the day side the temperature remains unchanged. The decrease in the temperature while passing from the equator to the poles is also insignificant.

1.3.2 COMPOSITION AND STRUCTURE OF THE ATMOSPHERE

We shall deal mainly with the lower atmosphere, i.e. the area below the homopause, where the atmosphere is well-mixed both vertically and horizontally. Table 1.3.2 gives data available on the content of principal components and admixtures in Venus' atmosphere.

Table 1.3.2 — Composition of Venus' atmosphere[a]

Atmospheric components	Veneras 4–10 [8–10]	Veneras 11, 12 [17]	[12]	Pioneer–Venus ·[18]	[15]
CO_2	97 ± 3	—	—	—	—
N_2	2–3	4.5 ± 0.5	2.5 ± 0.3	4.0 ± 0.2	3.4 ± 4.6
H_2O	1000–5000	–	700 ± 300	<1000	1350–5200
Ar	100–200	110 ± 20	—	70^{+50}_{-25}	67.2 ± 2.3
Ne	—	12^{+5}_{-3}	—	10 ± 7	4.3 – 10.6
Kr	—	0.5–0.8	0.7 ± 0.3	<0.2	—
O_2	—	—	18 ± 4	<30	16.0–43.6
SO_2	—	—	130 ± 35	<300	185 ± 43
CO	—	—	28 ± 17	—	20 ± 3

Atmospheric components	Ground-based observations [19]	[20]	[21]
H_2SO_4	10	—	—
CO	—	50	—
HCl	—	0.4–0.6	—
HF	—	0.01	—
O_2	—	—	1

[a] The content of CO_2 and N_2 is given as a percentage, while the rest is in millionths by volume.

The table shows that the atmosphere comprises chiefly CO_2 (about 97%) and N_2 (from 2 to 3%) [8–11]. The other components enter the atmosphere as minor admixtures. They are measured directly in the lower atmosphere of Venus employing gas analysers, mass spectrometers and gas chromatographs mounted on the atmospheric sondes. The most comprehensive measurements were made during the flights of Soviet Veneras 11 and 12 and American Pioneer–Venus spaceprobes [12–15]. The data obtained by ground-based spectrometers refer mainly to the over-cloud layer located at a height of not less than 60–70 km from the planet's surface.

The composition of the over-cloud atmosphere, the cloud layer and the sub-cloud atmosphere may differ mainly in gases which undergo phase conversions; are condensed, forming the aerosol particles of the clouds; or participate in photochemical processes. Thus, for instance, if Venus' clouds consist of an aqueous solution of sulphuric acid, then the H_2O content should vary from millionths above the clouds to 1–2% in the clouds [5]. On the other hand such components as CO and O_2, which emerge as a result of the photochemical dissolution of CO_2, should be found in greater quantities in the upper atmosphere (above the clouds). The apparently smaller amount of O_2 in comparison to CO in the upper atmosphere of Venus indicates that O_2 plays the more active rôle in forming the clouds and the oxidation of hot surface rocks. Other components may also be met in Venus' atmosphere — hydrogen formed during the photodissociation of H_2O and HCl, and inert gases which may be residual gases of the solar nebula or those accommodated

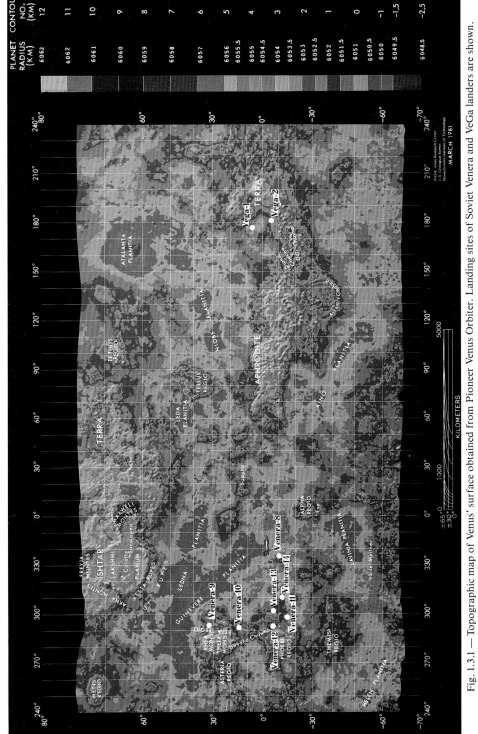

Fig. 1.3.1 — Topographic map of Venus' surface obtained from Pioneer Venus Orbiter. Landing sites of Soviet Venera and VeGa landers are shown.

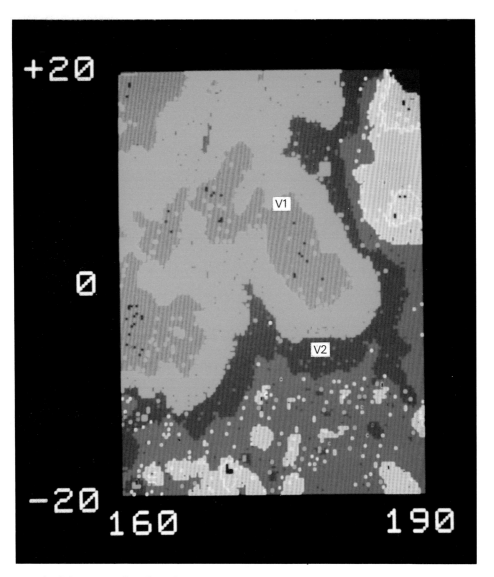

Fig. 2.2.17 — Landing sites of the VeGas 1 and 2 on Venus' surface. Topography at 500 m intervals. Mercator protection at 0.25° (approximately 30 km) resolution. Blue 0−1 km); green (1−2 km); yellow (2−3 km); red (3−4 km). [169]

from implantation by the solar wind during the geological history of the planet.

The composition and structure of Venus' clouds were studied in all space experiments involving Veneras 8 to 14, as well as research within the framework of the Pioneer–Venus project. Extensive material on the physical properties and structure of the cloud cover was obtained. However, the problem of the chemical composition of its condensates is still not quite clear.

At present the whole set of indirect data on the nature of the clouds (polarimetric measurements, the character of the infrared spectrum, the physicochemical properties of the H_2SO_4–H_2O system) indicates that the principal component of the cloud layer (75–85%) is aerosols of sulphuric acid. In addition, sulphur particles in clouds were detected in X-ray fluorescence analyses onboard Veneras 12 and 14 [22, 23] and in mass-spectrometric analyses of tropospheric gases by the large probe of Pioneer Venus [14].

Aerosols of H_2SO_4 apparently form during photochemical oxidation at a height of 60 km and above. Atomic oxygen, produced during the photodissociation of CO_2 or SO_2 at an altitude of 60–80 km, ensures oxidation of SO_2 to SO_3 with its subsequent hydration and formation of H_2SO_4 droplets. At an altitude of 48–49 km and at a temperature of 90–100°C the aerosol H_2SO_4 is subject to thermal disintegration with the formation of gaseous SO_3 again, while the SO_2 regeneration is ensured by thermochemical reactions as follows:

$$SO_3 + CO \rightleftarrows SO_2 + CO_2$$

These are the cyclical processes of the formation and decay of sulphuric acid aerosol, making up a short atmospheric cycle of sulphur [24]. Cloud formation from H_2SO_4 agrees both with theoretical vertical profiles of SO_2, H_2O and CO concentrations and also with the experimental data on the content of these gases in the troposphere (Fig. 1.3.2). Apart from this, theoretical evaluations [24] have shown that condensates of elementary sulphur shaped as drops and crystals are also probable components of Venus' cloud layer. Sulphur plays the same rôle in Venus' meteorology as does water on the Earth.

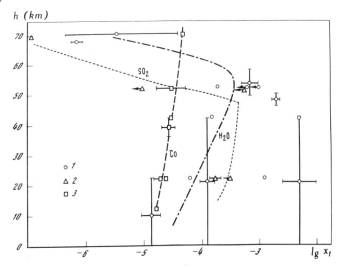

Fig. 1.3.2—Model of the Venusian atmosphere according to Volkov [24]. 1, H_2O; 2, SO_2; 3, CO.

More profound analysis of the geochemical model of Venus' troposphere, and the rôle of microcomponents in particular, is given in [24–26].

Experiments on board Veneras 12 and 14 helped to detect not only sulphur, but also chlorine in Venus' clouds [27, 23], but the form of the chlorine encountered has not yet been identified.

Measurements made on board Veneras 9 and 10 with a nephelometer [28] point to the clouds' complicated structure. In general the cloud density has turned out to be insignificant, more resembling the Earth's mist or haze. The highest density of the clouds was observed at an altitude of 50–60 km (the number of particles at this altitude reaches some 1.5×10^9 m^{-3}, and mass concentration nearly 5 kg m^{-3}. At altitudes of 49–32 km the particle density is much smaller; still lower, at the 18 km level, very mild clouds consisting of particles with a high light-refractive capacity are observed. Below the 18 km level, clouds are evidently non-existent. Nephelometric measurements were also carried out on board Veneras 11, 13, 14 [29, 30] and Pioneer Venus [31].

Despite the low cloud density on Venus only a minor portion of solar energy reaches the planet's surface. Data [32] obtained on board Veneras 8, 9 and 10 show that this energy makes up one per cent of the overall energy falling on the planet. A considerable portion of solar heat is absorbed at altitudes of over 50 km. But even this small portion of solar energy which reaches the lower atmosphere is sufficient to maintain high temperatures in the lower atmosphere. This is favoured to a considerable extent by the so-called 'greenhouse effect' to which Sagan [33] has drawn scientists' attention. This mechanism is considered in more detail in [34 and 35]. Its essence lies in the presence of conditions on the planet such that solar heat penetrates the atmosphere, heating its lower layers and the planet's surface, whereas the heat flow from the surface is to a great extent absorbed by the atmosphere. Unfortunately, we are still not very well versed in the nature of the basic absorbers of infrared radiation in the atmosphere and the conditions of vertical heat transfer. Thus, the thermal régime mechanism proper needs further improvement.

1.3.3 ORIGIN AND EVOLUTION OF THE ATMOSPHERE

Venus' atmosphere, so different at first glance from the Earth's atmosphere, gives grounds to assume some other mechanism of its formation. However, a deeper analysis of the data available (although still insufficient) suggests the idea about the same nature of both Venus' and the Earth's atmospheres.

It was already mentioned that the modern views on the origin of the Solar System proceed from the accretion of planets from the primordial solar nebula. Therefore, if Venus actually had some atmosphere in the early stages, its composition was similar to the volatile component of the environment. From the time of its emergence up to now, Venus' atmosphere has been undergoing continuous evolution — a change in its composition, structure and mass. On the one hand, the atmosphere took in volatiles released in the course of the outgassing of the planet's interior or trapped by the solar wind, or which were produced as a result of the random collisions with comets. On the other hand, a thermal dissipation of mainly light volatiles took place. Venus' primordial atmosphere might contain hydrogen, helium and, to a lesser degree, neon. The comparison of the distribution of inert gases in the Earth's atmosphere and on the Sun (in particular helium) shows that only a small share of this primordial atmosphere survives in the Earth's present atmosphere. Hydrogen and helium of the Venusian atmosphere also volatilized under the influence of sufficiently high kinetic energy. Water losses in the atmosphere might also occur due to photodissociation. But was there as much water on Venus as on the Earth?

The Earth's surface is known to be covered by a nearly 3 km water layer. If all this water were to be evaporated, the pressure of water vapour on the Earth's surface would be about 3×10^6 kg m^{-2}, but on Venus the amount of water does not appear to exceed 1% of this value [36]. Numerous attempts have been made to explain this difference. Here are some of the explanations proposed.

(1) In Lewis' opinion [37], the lack of water in Venus' primordial matter may be attributed to the lack of volatiles, and water in particular, in the solar nebula where Venus formed.

   During the Earth's accretion, water, apparently, became its constituent as hydrated minerals, such as serpentine, tremolite and others. These minerals might get condensed at temperatures lower than the temperature at which Venus accreted from the primordial solar nebula. At the high temperature of Venus' condensation (550 K according to Lewis [37]) any appreciable amounts of hydrated minerals cannot be expected in its composition. Thus, on the Earth and more so on Mars, which condensed at relatively low temperatures, water is available in greater quantities, while on Venus it is almost nonexistent. If this explanation is valid, it imposes certain constraints on the temperature of its formation and convincingly proves the heterogeneity of the primordial solar nebula from which the bodies of the Solar System emerged [37, 38]. However, this explanation stumbles over the difficulties pointed out by Ringwood and Anderson [39].

(2) Sagan [40], Dayhoff *et al.* [41], Rasool and de Bergh [42] and others think that water released as a result of the outgassing of Venus' interior was lost. To explain this assumption they relied on the photodissociation of water in the upper atmosphere induced by the ultraviolet radiation of the Sun. (As is known, water dissociates into hydrogen and oxygen.) Not everything was satisfactory with this idea either. In particular, oxygen released in the process of photodissociation overcomes the planet's gravitational field and disperses into outer space. (The higher D/H ratio in comparison with the Earth, found for water on Venus by Hoffman *et al.* [43], supports this idea). The oxygen released becomes a still more effective absorbent of ultraviolet radiation than water. Hence, water dissociation may give rise to an effective oxygen protection against the ultraviolet, which should reduce the rate of water dissociation. This explanation of the planet's water loss might be much more convincing if some mechanism of binding great amounts of oxygen in the lithosphere is proposed. So far, it has turned out impossible to overcome these difficulties [44, 45].

One more specific feature of Venus' atmosphere is the abundance of carbon dioxide. How can this be explained? Moroz and Mukhin [46] offer two explanations:

(1) the initial release of a small amount of water and a resultant quick development of the greenhouse effect which ultimately gave rise to the intensive release of carbon dioxide into the atmosphere;
(2) the formation, in the early stage of Venus' existence, of polar caps consisting of solid carbon dioxide which later on was exceptionally quickly released in no more than 10^6 years.

Hypothesis (1) seems to be more viable if we proceed from condensation models [37, 38, 47]. But here some ambiguity still remains if one keeps in mind that at the time of the planet's formation the solar constant was 40% less and, consequently, the temperature was conducive to the condensation of some water.

If one sticks to hypothesis (2), then it needs to be explained where water, which was initially present in the polar caps on Venus, disappeared. Some proof in favour of this hypothesis is the enrichment of hydrogen with deuterium on Venus [48].

In [46] attention was drawn to the possibility of CO_2 and H_2O condensation in polar regions during the early stage of planet's existence. On Venus, whose axis of rotation is nearly perpendicular to the plane of the ecliptic, the temperatures should be extremely low in view of the thin atmosphere in polar regions. Thus, for instance, T_p (polar temperature) = 160 K for the present solar constant, while T_p = 141 K for the solar constant corresponding to the time of primordial Venus (i.e. 40% less). At T_p = 141 K a rather effective trap for CO_2 and H_2O might exist at the poles, and at T_p = 160 K a trap equally effective for H_2O, but of low effectiveness for CO_2.

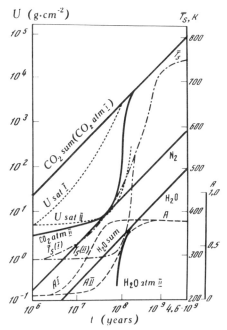

Fig. 1.3.3 — Model of the evolution and climate of Venus' atmosphere calculated by Moroz and Mukhin [46]. T_s — average temperature of the surface; U — amount of volatiles released in the course of the outgassing process. U_{sat} — level of saturation of the planetary surface. Version I presupposes the initial accumulation of CO_2 condensate in polar regions. Version II presupposes no accumulation.

Fig. 1.3.3 shows the Venus evolution scheme corresponding to hypothesis (1). The x-axis is time, t (measured from the conventional moment of the termination of accretion) the y-axis is the amount of volatiles, U, released in the course of the outgassing, the mean temperature of the surface, T_s, and albedo, A. Alternative I assumes the initial accumulation of CO_2 condensate in polar regions, alternative II is without accumulation. U_{sat} is the level of the saturation of the atmosphere with moisture. While estimating T_s a simple convection model was used; the tropopause is at a level where the temperature equals that of effective temperature. Over the tropopause a value of $U = 10^3$ kg m^{-2} is found; below the tropopause the adiabatic gradient is observed.

It follows from Fig. 1.3.3 that if carbon dioxide polar caps did appear on Venus, they survived for not more than 10^8 years. The temperature on Venus' surface exceeded 600 K even more than 4000 million years ago.

Moroz and Mukhin [46] believe that the physical conditions on Venus may be explained most easily if one assumes that it formed with a great water deficiency. While evolving, Venus never had water on the surface and there was no chemical binding of CO_2 by rock. Consequently carbon dioxide remained wholly in the atmosphere whose temperature was always high. Hoffman *et al.* [36] came to the same conclusion, analysing present-day data on Venus' atmosphere. They believe that the present dissimilarity in Venus' and the Earth's atmospheres, disregarding the probable similarity of their original nature, may be explained by the following sequence of events in the history of development of the planets: lack of water on Venus due to a high condensation temperature; the development of the greenhouse effect only on Venus; the development of life only on the Earth; the difference in the interaction of atmospheres and lithospheres on both planets, which brought about the differences in the present-day atmospheres.

1.3.4 THE NATURE AND HISTORY OF THE SURFACE AND THE CRUST

The planet's surface

The present-day notions about Venus' surface are based on relatively scarce data, among which there are radar studies of relief, telephotometric panoramic views of the surface, the chemical composition and the physicochemical features obtained from spacecraft, the composition and properties of the planet's atmosphere.

Modern radiotelescopes usually operate within wavelengths of 1 mm to 30–60 m where the Earth's atmosphere is 'transparent' (shorter wavelengths are absorbed by oxygen and water vapour, longer wavelengths cannot pass through the ionosphere). The intensity of a reflected signal is used a basis for compiling a radar map of the planet's surface. These measurements, together with measurements of the polarization of a reflected signal, allow the determination of electric and magnetic permeability, density, the relief of the surface, etc. Since Venus' revolution period (243.09 days) is close to the resonance period of the Earth–Venus system, which is equivalent to 243.16 terrestrial days, then at each inferior conjunction Venus faces the Earth with the same hemisphere. Therefore, the map of radar measurements is plotted within longitudes from 0° to –80° and latitudes from –50° to +40°. The best resolution is obtained in the equatorial regions.

The first radar studies of Venus were undertaken nearly 20 years ago [49, 50, 51].

Great differences in the reflectivity of various regions on Venus' surface were revealed. Radio-bright and radio-dark regions on the surface point, firstly, to differences in topography and small-dispersed roughnesses and, to a lesser extent, to physical properties of the surface. Recent years have seen a mounting interest in radar studies of Venus [52–57]. Radar images and altimetric cross-sections of some surface regions were obtained. The radar systems used gave an elevation accuracy of 100m, with a horizontal resolution of 10 km near the equator and 100 km near poles. This method, with more or less acceptable resolution, was used to study the equatorial part of the planet within latitudes ± 40°.

The high-resolution images of some small regions made it possible to identify large structures resembling craters, canyons and valleys. The diameters of the craters identified varied from 35 to 160 km. Most of them are, apparently, not deep. For instance, a crater 160 km in diameter had a depth of only 500 m, which is almost an order of magnitude less than the depth of craters having similar diameters on the Moon. If these structures and lunar craters have the same nature they should have appeared in the early stages of Venus' evolution and their existence proves that the processes which modified Venus' surface were not so effective as on the Earth.

A very intriguing structure was discovered. Known as Diana Chasma, it is a giant trough-like depression up to 1400 km long, 150 km wide and 2 km deep. Saunders and Malin [57] believe that it resembles Valles Marineris on Mars and the East African Rift Valley on the Earth. Such structures are indicative of the intensive tectonic activity on Venus in the past and at present.

Therefore, radar images, on the one hand, show the existence of ancient regions which evidently have changed only slightly since the emergence of these craters which are of impact origin, and on the other hand, give some proof that Venus is a geologically active planet forming various geological structures. The diversity of Venusian structures is evidently not less than those on the Earth. So far these contradictory facts cannot be explained convincingly enough due to insufficient factual material.

One more aspect of events remains unclear. The abundance of the impact structures points to the preservation of regions and, consequently, to much slower crust erosion than on the Earth. At the same time, the lack of regions with multicircular basins and deep craters is still not understood. This should prove that they were never shaped, were destroyed in the course of the endogenous evolution of the crust, or were destroyed and covered with sediments as a result of weathering and erosion.

Altimetry and radar images obtained by the Pioneer Venus Orbiter were the next step in comprehending the global characteristics of the relief, the regional morphology, and the chronology of the formation of Venus' surface, which led to some conclusions on the history of the crust and the planet. The resolution of the images from Pioneer Venus was approximately the same as for those obtained by ground-based methods, but the coverage was much greater. The resolution is nearly 20–30 times poorer than that which was used previously for compiling the map of the Moon on the basis of telescopic observations.

Analysing the results of the radar (ground-based and orbital) studies of Venus, Masursky [58] summarizes the whole diversity of the relief by three principal types of terrain: (1) upland rolling plains taking up some 65% of the surface area; (2) high-mountain regions covering some 8% of the surface, and (3) smooth lowlands extending over a quarter (27%) of the whole territory photographed from Pioneer Venus. The location of these provinces is seen on the map of Venus' surface (Fig. 1.3.1 which is reproduced in the colour section facing page 46).

Upland rolling plains lie 0.5–2 km above the planet's mean radius of 6052 km. other terrestrial planets. These plains are Venus' ancient cratered regions.

Two high-mountain massifs (Ishtar Terra and Aphrodite Terra), taking up about 10% of the planet's surface, lie at an altitude of 2–11 km above the mean level. They may include upland parts of the low-density crust covered with lava and crowned with large volcanic structures. The volcanic and tectonic features are more pronounced on Aphrodite Terra than on Ishtar Terra; the washed-out appearance of structures on Ishtar Terra may be indicative of its great age. High-mountain regions on Venus show a greater similarity to terrestrial than Martian equivalents since they were, most likely, isostatically compensated. The third high-mountain region forms a vivid sequence of random (irregular) volcanic structures which, according to Veneras 9 and 10, have a 'basaltic' composition and extend along the intermittent fault zones in the Beta Regio area. The radar brightness of ray-like structures, resembling slightly changed lava flows, seems to indicate that Beta Regio is a geologically recent formation.

Lowlands are widespread regions. They are located 0.5–1.5 km below the average level of the planet's surface. These surface areas exhibit a low crater density. They may be covered with lava flows similar to terrestrial and lunar low-lying regions.

If the crust was initially distributed evenly, the formation of low-lying regions with mostly a thin crust and high-mountain regions with a thicker crust may stem from the very early widespread mantle convection. The differences in crater density and the preservation of the geological–morphological forms of more elevated regions show that volcanic and tectonic activity on Venus was a prolonged process. These low-lying regions may be somewhat younger than Beta Regio.

The abundance of highlands and lowlands on Venus resembles the topography of the Moon and Mars. But highlands are nearly compensated for isostatically and, thus, bear resemblance to those on the Earth. The tectonic destruction of the crust, similar to that which attended tectonic dislocations of plates on the Earth, is traceable only in some localities. No proof of global plate tectonics on Venus was discovered.

Masursky [58] gives the following probable sequence of geological events on Venus:

(1) The formation of the primordial crust which most likely was homogeneous, the intensive meteorite bombardment of the crust and the shaping of heavily cratered surface regions.

(2) The reformation of the crust, obviously as a result of the convection of the mantle, with the emergence of the thinner crust in low-lying areas and the thicker crust in highland areas.

(3) The development of high-mountain regions by the uplifting and outflowing of localized mantle streams or convective centres which arise from local heterogeneities in the mantle of Ishtar Terra. This high-mountain region formed

as a result of the uplift of the plateau and the formation of the Maxwell Mountains.

(4) The filling of low-lying regions and craters in upland circular plains with lavas, perhaps of a basaltic composition, or fine grained material, or both.

(5) The formation of a shield in the Beta Regio area and mountain ridges along the fault zone which broke the present-day surface of the shield.

(6) The intermittent tectonic activity with concomitant volcanic eruptions; the ruptures (dislocations) are concentrated east of Aphrodite Terra and Ishtar Terra and stretch southward and south-westward from Beta Regio.

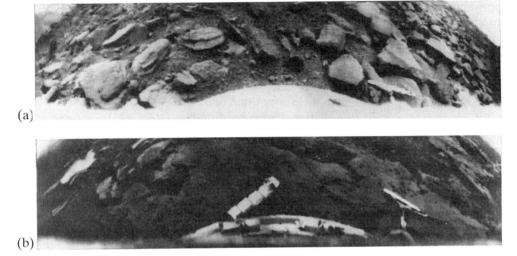

(a)

(b)

Fig. 1.3.4 — Panoramic images of the Venusian surface taken by Venera 9 (a) and Venera 10 (b).

In 1975 Veneras 9 and 10 supplied the first panoramic views of Venus' surface (Fig. 1.3.4). They are described in papers by Florensky *et al.* [59-63]. The space probes landed at a distance of 2000 km from each other. The landscape at the two landing sites was different. A region of débris which might have formed from an eruption or collapse was seen at the Venera 9 landing site. If it was an eruption, then a crater should be somewhere nearby. Large rock fragments lie on fine-grained material which resembles the halo of material surrounding the Arizona meteor crater on Earth [58]. It should be noted that, in view of the high density of Venus' atmosphere, the fine-grained fraction should settle down in the vicinity of a crater, while only large fragments may fly far away. Most fragments of the panoramic view from Venera 9 exhibit an angular shape, fresh and sharp edges confirming that they were either of a recent origin, or that the erosion processes on Venus proceed rather slowly. Some fragments exhibit a stratified structure. Other fragments are round in shape. This roundness, in view of the lack of water, may be attributed to several processes [58]: (1) etching by the corrosive atmosphere; (2) caking; (3) aeolian processes — the most probable supposition. The wind velocity of 0.4–1.3 m s^{-1} on the surface and the availability of fine-grained material on both panoramic views speak in favour of aeolian erosion.

Eroded parent rocks are visible on the Venera 10 panoramic view. Dark spots on rocks are obviously cavities and exposed surface blisters. The photograph also shows fine-grained material with low albedo of an impact or aeolian origin. Both panoramic views have shown landscapes evidently typical of planets with atmospheres (Venus, the Earth and Mars) unlike the landscapes of bodies devoid of atmospheres (the Moon and Mercury).

In 1982, Veneras 13 and 14 transmitted images of Venus' surface at their landing sites. Veneras 9 and 10 provided only black-and-white photographs with a semicircular view, while Veneras 13 and 14 sent back both black-and-white and colour (synthesized from photographing through filters) pictures with a nearly circular view of the surface. The angular resolution of the television cameras installed on Veneras 13 and 14 was 11 arc minutes, two times better than the cameras carried by Veneras 9 and 10. Such resolution may be helpful in revealing surface details 4–5 mm in size in the nearest zone. Fig 1.3.5 shows panoramic views from Venera 13 and 14.

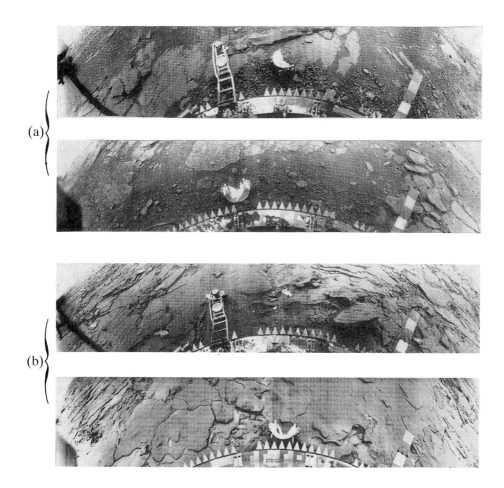

Fig. 1.3.5 — Panoramic pictures of the Venusian surface taken by Venera 13 (a) and Venera 14 (b).

The panoramic view from the Venera 13 landing site shows that it surveyed rocks of a stony desert. No high outcrops of parent rocks are seen on the surface. Their appearance bears indications of deep chemical weathering. On some blocks flattened projections are seen pointing to a layered rock structure. In depressions among parent rock outcrops a darker surface of fine-grained soil is discernible. Soil is loose and apart from the fine-grained component it contains angular stone lumps up to 5 cm in size. From its appearance, the fine-grained material should contain a great number of small-sized particles, smaller than the resolution of the telephotometer (several millimetres), i.e. it is most likely that even the dust fraction is present there. Evaluations of mechanical properties obtained (in particular, bearing strength) are indicative of low stability associated with loose, poorly cemented highly porous material.

Veneras 9 and 10 launched earlier landed several thousand kilometres east and north-east of the Venera 13 landing site, but in an area with the same structural–morphological type of surface.

Comparison of the panoramic views sent back from Veneras 9 and 10 (Fig. 1.3.4) and Venera 13 (Fig. 1.3.5) shows that the appearance of the surface is almost identical everywhere, which points to the fact that the relief and appearance of rocks are typical of this structural–morphological type of Venus' surface.

A panoramic view of the Venera 14 landing site differs somewhat from that of Venera 13, since the former did not bear indications of the accumulation of fine-grained dark material. Both panoramas show that the landing sites are on a flat rocky plain composed of rocks displaying well-defined layering or horizontal stratification. Layers here differ in their photographic tone, and consequently by their composition or granularity. Their multitude, thinness and consistently layered structure are also visible. Layered rocks around Venera 14 resemble terrestrial rocks of a sedimentary type, being products of a sedimentation process in an undisturbed, non-turbulent medium. On the Earth such a medium is water, while on Venus, where there is no water, such a medium may be the dense atmosphere. Therefore, there should exist mechanisms for the uplift of fine-grained material into the atmosphere, which ought to be planet wide, since bedrock is visible on all panoramic views of the landing sites of Veneras 9, 10, 13 and 14, which are several thousand kilometres apart. Volcanic eruptions seem to be the process on Venus which causes the loose material to be uplifted into the atmosphere.

Veneras 15 and 16 photographed at high resolution (approximately 2 to 4 Km) the northern polar region of Venus — about 25 per cent of the surface. The pictures obtained enabled the identification of many new geological structures which escaped observations in previous radar studies from Pioneer Venus. Fig. 1.3.6 shows radar images of several areas obtained from Veneras 15 and 16. The photographs are described in [64].

Physical characteristics of rocks

So far we do not have enough data to give a complete picture of rock composition on Venus. But even the data we have at our disposal impose certain limitations on probable physical properties and conditions conducive to the formation of Venusian rocks.

As a result of the radar studies, Krupenio *et al.* [65, 66] has estimated the dielectric constant for the surface layer of Venus' rocks. The analysis of data has shown that

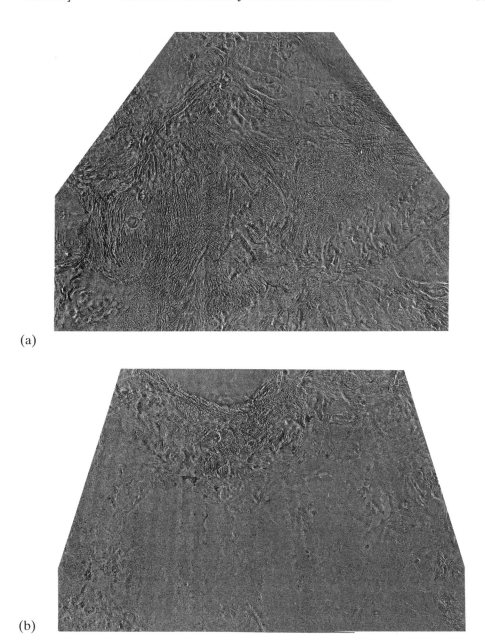

(a)

(b)

Fig 1.3.6 — Photomosaics of radar images of the surface of Venus acquired by Veneras 15 and 16. (a) The highland region at the eastern side of Ishtar Terra (size of region shown is 1500 × 2000 Km). The huge volcanic mountain Maxwell Montes, with its summit crater Cleopatra Patera, is shown at lower left. The area to the east of Maxwell Montes is grooved and is called 'parquet' terrain. (b) The lowland plains of Sedna Planitia, which lie to the south-west of the giant cliffs Vesta Rupes and Ut Rupes, marking the southern flank of Ishtar Terra (size of region shown is 1500 × 2000 Km).

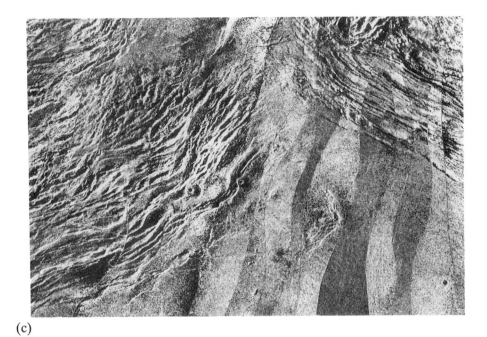

(c)

(d)

Fig. 1.3.6 — Detailed radar images of Venus' surface obtained by Veneras 15 and 16. (c) A
system of parallel ridges in the highland region near AKna Montes and Freyja Montes, formed
in the zone of tectonic compression at the north-western edge of LaKshmi Planum, the vast,
smooth plateau forming the western part of Ishtar Terra (size of region shown is 500 × 700 Km).
(d) One of several unusual elliptical structures, 300 to 500 Km in diameter, known as
Nightingale Corona, formed as a joint effect of volcanic and tectonic processes, in the higher
upland region of Tethus Regio (size of region shown 600 × 900 Km).

there exists a thin (about 0.5 m thick) layer with a low dielectric constant and a mean density of 1.2 to 1.9×10^3 kg m^{-3} which covers the thick layer of rocks possessing a higher dielectric constant and a density varying from 2.2 to 2.7×10^3 kg m^{-3}. The density of the surface layer is evidently typical of loose porous material. The density of underlying Venusian rocks is somewhat lower than the density of crystalline rocks in the Earth's crust. However, the error of these estimations is great due to the dependence of the dielectric constant on the chosen model of the atmosphere.

The Venera 10 lander was used for the first time for the direct determination of rock density [67–69]. This experiment has shown that the outcropping of rocks to the surface (see the panoramic view from Venera 10) has a high density ranging from 2.7 to 2.9×10^3 kg m^{-3}, which corresponds on the Earth to the denser basalts having low porosity. Similar rocks on the Earth might have originated in conditions of the slow cooling of basaltic lavas with insignificant gas release. Information about the physical and mechanical properties of Venusian rocks was obtained from television pictures; from the analysis of the probe–soil collision during the landing and the collision of the body of the sensor of the densitometer with the rocks to be studied; and from the studies of the location of stones by examining some features inherent in the mechanism of rock transfer by the wind, etc. For instance, analysis of the collision of the sensor of the densitometer with rocks led Kemurdzan *et al.* [70] to the conclusion that stones visible at the landing site of the lander may be referred to rock or semi-rock soil the strength of which is measured in millions of kilogrammes per square metre. Rock fragments discernible on the Venera 9 panorama evidently exhibit lower strength, which is confirmed by their layered structure and the shearing of part of the rock fragments. Venera 10 landed on strong rocks; this is proved by their high density and lack of deformation in the place where the densitometer sensor was located.

Information on physical and mechanical properties was obtained from experiments carried out by Veneras 13 and 14 [126]: (1) measurements of rock strength and electrical resistance by a dynamic penetrometer, (2) determination of rock strength by overloads endured by the vehicle at landing, (3) evaluation of mechanical characteristics by the drilling of rocks for sampling, and (4) analysis of television images of landing sites.

Bearing strength was one of the rock mechanical properties determined and its measurement from Venera 13 gave $2.6–10 \times 10^4$ kg m^{-2}, and from Venera 14, $6.5–25 \times 10^5$ kg m^{-2}. These values were compared with the results of model experiments on most widespread terrestrial rocks. It turned out that the terrestrial analogue for the Venera 13 landing site by bearing strength was the cohesive products of chemical and wind erosion of rocks, and for Venera 14 volcanic tuffs (pyroclastic rocks), pumice and fissured rocks. Consequently, on the basis of terrestrial analogues, it was concluded that soil at the landing sites of both probes may be relegated to volcanic-sedimentary rocks.

General rock characteristics obtained from the direct experiment of determining physical and mechanical properties were corroborated by studies of the impact dynamics of the Venera 13 and 14 landers. Modelling of impact dynamics has shown that the rock analogue for the Venera 14 landing site was foam concrete, and for the Venera 13 landing site compact sand, although the absolute value of the rock-bearing strength for Venera 14 turned out to be essentially smaller than that measured by the penetrometer. In this experiment the bearing strength for Venera 13 was 4–5×10^4 kg m^{-2}. These values were obtained by assuming that the whole area of the shock-proof torus of the landing module contacted the planet's surface. If the contact area were actually smaller, the values of the bearing strength would increase.

While determining the methods of sampling and drilling régimes or rocks with various strengths, the information characteristics of the sampler were studied, which enabled the acquisition of data on the physical and mechanical properties of rocks at the landing sites of Veneras 13 and 14. These corresponded to the characteristics of weathered porous basalts or compacted ashy material (e.g. volcanic tuff), which does not contradict the data provided by the penetrometer and the results of the analysis of impact overloads during the probes' landing.

Table 1.3.3 — Physical properties of Venus' rocks measured at Venera 13 and 14 landing sites and their terrestrial analogues

Experiment	Venera 13	Venera 14
Measurements of physical properties by penetrometer [70]	Bearing strength 2.6–10 $\times$ 10^4 kg m^{-2}. Heavy clays, compacted fine sand	Bearing strength 6.5–25 10^5 kg m^{-2}. Volcanic tuffs, fissured mountain rocks
Studies of impact dynamics of the landing module [123]	Bearing strength 4.0–5.0 10^4 kg m^{-2}. Foam concrete	Bearing strength of a 5 cm layer 2 $\times$ 10^4 kg m^{-2}; deeper 4.0–5.0 $\times$ 10^4 kg m^{-2}. Compacted sand; deeper, foam concrete
Analysis of the sampler's operation régimes [74]	Compacted ashy material of the volcanic tuff type	Compacted ashy material of the volcanic tuff type
Analysis of television panoramas	Volcanogenic-layered rock covered in places with loose soil	Volcanogenic layered rocks of a sedimentary type

Table 1.3.3 sums up the data on the physical characteristics of Venusian rocks provided by experiments on Veneras 13 and 14. Analysis of these data has indicated that at the landing sites of Veneras 13 and 14 rocks displayed similar physical properties. Thus, volcanogenic rocks whose structure resembles sedimentary rocks and whose physical properties correspond to loose products of chemical and wind erosion of parent rocks were studied in both regions.

Finally the values for electrical conductivity of Venus' rocks were obtained. At Venera 13 and 14 landing sites they turned out to be anomalously high in comparison with basalt-type rocks at a temperature close to that of Venus' atmosphere. This fact is not yet explained. At the VeGa 2 landing site, a very low soil-specific conductivity (about 10^6 Ω^{-1} m^{-1}) was discovered. This value is close to that of crystalline rocks in the Earth's crust.

1.3.5 CHEMICAL AND MINERAL ROCK COMPOSITION

So far little is known about the chemical and mineral rock composition on Venus. The notions about the chemical composition of the ,rocks rest mainly on the measurements of the content of natural radioactive elements and the determination of the main rock-forming elements at the landing sites of the Venera and VeGa spacecraft. As far as the mineral composition is concerned, we have only some thermodynamic calculations [24,25], making use of the data on the composition of the surface rock and atmosphere and assuming an equilibrium between the atmosphere and the planet's surface. But this information in totality gives grounds for drawing some conclusions about the nature of Venus' rocks and the conditions of their formation.

uranium, thorium and potassium content by the gamma-spectrometric method at the landing sites of Veneras 8, 9 and 10 [71–73, 76].

The content of uranium, thorium and potassium, measured for the first time in 1972 by Venera 8, turned out to be rather high. This case as a surprise because on Earth the highly radioactive magmatic rocks are encountered only in the continental crust, on the Moon only selective fragments of granophyric rocks have been registered, while on Mars they seem not to be widespread [77].

To verify how representative the rocks with high U, Th and K content were, similar experiments were carried out by Veneras 9 and 10 and VeGas 1 and 2 in other areas of the Venusian surface. The content of natural radioactive elements turned out to be lower than at the Venera 8 landing site. It corresponds, to a greater extent, to the basic rocks in the Earth's crust. The data on the radioactive element content in Venus' rocks are presented in Table 1.3.4.

Table 1.3.4 — U, Th and K content in Venus' rocks

Rocks at landing sites	Content		
	Potassium (%)	Uranium (10^{-4}%)	Thorium (10^{-4}%)
Venera 8 (1972)	4.0 ± 1.2	2.2 ± 0.7	6.5 ± 0.2
Venera 9 (1975)	0.47 ± 0.08	0.60 ± 0.16	3.65 ± 0.42
Venera 10 (1975)	0.30 ± 0.16	0.46 ± 0.26	0.70 ± 0.34
VeGa 1 (1984)	0.45 ± 0.22	0.63 ± 0.47	1.5 ± 1.2
VeGa 2 (1984)	0.40 ± 0.20	0.69 ± 0.38	2.0 ± 1.0

The comparison of the U, Th and K contents measured in different regions of Venus with their terrestrial analogues enables some assumptions to be made about the probable petrological models of the rock formation on Venus [63, 78, 79].

Following the most obvious version, rocks at the landing sites of Veneras 9 and 10 and VeGas 1 and 2 are predominantly effusive basic rocks. Their origin is quite independent of the rock-forming process which could take place at the Venera 8 landing site. Analysis of the data characterizing rock at the Venera 8 landing site has indicated that it corresponds to alkaline rocks — syenites which are not widespread in the Earth's crust.

The K/U ratio used in studies of Venusian rocks turned out to be very close to that typical of most magmatic rocks on the Earth (about 10^4). This may be proof that processes causing changes in the chemical composition of primordial matter were, evidently, similar to terrestrial processes.

The most important contribution to extending our notion about Venusian rocks was made by experiments determining the rocks' chemical composition from Veneras 13 and 14 [79–82] and VeGa 2 [64, 129]. The data obtained are summarized in Table 1.3.5 from which it is evident that the sum of the elements given is somewhat smaller than 100%. This is probably explained by the lack of Na, which could not be measured due to the low energy of its fluorescent radiation.

Table 1.3.5 — Chemical composition of Venus rocks (percentage by mass)

Oxide	Venera 13	Venera 14	VeGa 2
MgO	11.4 ± 6.2	8.1 ± 3.3	11.5 ± 3.7
Al_2O_3	15.8 ± 3.0	17.9 ± 2.6	16.0 ± 1.8
SiO_2	45.1 ± 3.0	48.7 ± 3.6	45.6 ± 3.2
K_2O	4.0 ± 0.63	0.2 ± 0.07	0.1 ± 0.08
CaO	7.1 ± 0.96	10.3 ± 1.2	7.5 ± 0.7
TiO_2	1.59 ± 0.45	1.25 ± 0.41	0.2 ± 0.1
MnO	0.2 ± 0.1	0.16 ± 0.08	0.14 ± 0.12
Fe_2O_3	9.3 ± 2.2	8.8 ± 1.8	7.74 ± 1.1
SO_3	1.62 ± 1.0	0.88 ± 0.77	4.7 ± 1.5
Cl	<0.3	<0.4	<0.3
Total	~96	~96	~93

However, the amount of Na_2O can be evaluated, if one knows the content of K, Mg and Fe oxides [83]. Such evaluations give the Na_2O content as 2.0 ± 0.5% for the Venera 13 landing site, 2.4 ± 0.4% for the Venera 14 landing site and 2.0 ± 0.5 for the VeGa 2 landing site. The remaining missing part is obviously due to an error in determining the content of the main rock-forming elements.

The authors [79–82] believe that the chemical and mineral composition of rocks at the Venera 13 landing site corresponds to poorly differentiated rocks of the nepheline–syenite type. The content of SiO_2 in the rock is low, but the content of MgO and K_2O is very high. According to the data from gamma-spectrometry, the K_2O content was similar (about 4%) in rocks at the Venera 8 landing site 3000 km east of the Venera 13 landing site, but in an area of the same structural–morphological type of surface. This shows that on Venus' cratered ancient rolling plains nepheline and syenite are apparently widespread.

The data on the chemical and mineral compositions of rocks obtained from Venera 14, as well as the ratios of petrogenic components, clearly show the similarity of Venusian rock to the Earth's oceanic tholeiitic basalts of the Meso-Cenozoic age. However, the Earth's tholeiitic basalts form in the course of the outpouring of viscous magmas, while on Venus, apparently because of the great gas saturation of basaltic melts, the erruptions are of an explosive character. This leads to the formation of rocks of the sedimentary type.

The VeGa 2 landing site lies in the north-eastern part of Aphrodite Terra. This is a region of high mountains in which one would expect the rock to differ in composition from the rocks on flat lowlands and on upland rolling plains. As will be evident from Table 1.3.5, the composition of the rock at the VeGa 2 site has proved to be similar to the Earth's crust gabbroic minerals and close to lunar rocks of the anorthosite–norite–troctolite (ANT) type.

Thus, there is the idea of the types of magmatic rocks lying within the limits of the main structural and morphological types of the Venusian surface which correspond to different tectonic and magmatic stages of its development.

It was pointed out [79] that studies of the Moon and other planets led to the identification of two types of primordial crust — the feldspar and the basaltic. The general planetary continental crust of the feldspar composition formed evidently in the final stages of accretion (i.e. 4000 to 4500 million years ago), whereas basaltic melts which cover the continental crust formed somewhat later (3600 to 3800 million years ago). Attention should be paid to the fact that the preservation of the primordial 'continental' crust steadily decreases with the increase in a body's size. Thus, for instance, on the Moon it covers no less than 80% of the whole surface, on Mars some 50%, on Venus no more than 10%. This leads one to the idea about the possibility of the existence of a similar primordial crust on the Earth in the earliest stage of its existence.

Whereas experiments conducted on Venus have provided us with certain notions about the chemical composition of rocks, no experiments have so far been carried out to ascertain their mineral composition. The difficulties involved in obtaining any experimental data on the mineral composition of Venusian rocks gave an impetus for many thermodynamic calculations [84–88]. However, the results of the calculations are based on studying some particular reactions of carbonation and hydration, disregarding their mutual effect. More correct evaluations of the expected mineral composition and trends in the changes of Venusian rocks during their interaction with the atmosphere are presented in [24, 25].

A 16-component model has been made of the physicochemical system of Venus' atmosphere and surface rocks, assuming the existence of a chemical equilibrium at the interface. The mean composition of terrestrial magmatic rocks was taken as an initial matrix, and an analysis is made from Venera spaceprobes and the large probe of Pioneer Venus for the characteristics of the atmosphere. The results of calculations show the eventual composition of the solid phase following 'chemical weathering' to an equilibrium state (Table 1.3.6).

The products of the weathering of basic and acid rocks is determined, apparently, by the sulphide–sulphate solid-phase buffer (pyrite–anhydrite–magnetite). This buffer is responsible for the low partial pressure of oxygen in the near-surface layer of the trophosphere ($P_{0_2} \approx 10^{-26}$ Pa). Depending on the hypsometric level of the surface (there are changes in pressure by several dozens of atmospheres and in temperature by several dozens of degrees), the forms of available sulphur in minerals vary: pyrite is the most stable in high-mountain areas, and anhydrite in lowlands.

The maximum water-vapour content necessary for the stable existence of water-bearing silicates (tremolite) is 300 p.p.m., which is 10 times higher than the vapour concentration in the near-surface atmosphere according to spectrometric data from Veneras 13 and 14 [89]. Therefore, under modern conditions, surface rock hydration on Venus is hardly possible.

Calculations of multisystems have shown that carbonates (calcite and dolomite) on Venus' surface can exhibit stability only in products of the transformation of ultra-

Table 1.3.6 — Mineral composition of Venusian rocks according to thermodynamic calculations (percentage by mass) [92]

Mineral	Venera 13	Venera 14	VeGa 2
Clinoenstatite, $MgSiO_3$	28.1	18.0	40.1
Diopside $CaMgSi_2O_6$	1.1	5.0	6.8
Anorthite $CaAl_2Si_2O_8$	22.7	37.9	23.8
Albite $NaAlSi_3O_8$	—	19.8	—
Microcline $KAlSi_3O_8$	18.7	1.2	0.7
Quartz SiO_2	—	3.4	4.2
Nepheline $(Na, K) AlSiO_4$	12.2	—	—
Magnetite Fe_3O_4	10.1	9.5	3.5
Sphene $CaTi(SiO_4)O$	4.0	3.1	—
Pyrite FeS_2	—	—	0.1
Anhydrite $CaSO_4$	2.8	1.3	6.9
Fluorine-apatite $Ca_{10}(PO_4)_6F_2$	0.1	0.1	—
Marialite $3NaAlSi_3O_8 \cdot NaCl$	—	0.5	1.7
Andalusite $Al_2SiO_4(O)$	—	—	12.0

alkaline rocks similar to terrestrial pantellerites and leucitites. If they are as rare on Venus as on the Earth (less than 0.1%), the chemical mechanism of the buffering of CO_2 partial pressure is not realized according to the reaction of a wollastonite equilibrium. Chlorine and fluorine may be bound in minerals of surface rocks as small quantities of apatites and scapolites (marialites). Iron silicates, apparently, oxidize with the formation of magnetite.

The recently published calculations of the mineral composition of Venusian rocks [91, 92] (Table 1.3.6) relied upon the elemental composition obtained through X-ray fluorescence analysis from Veneras 13 and 14 [81, 82] and, on the whole, confirmed the earlier suggested trend in the development of chemical weathering.

Therefore, judging by the results of the theoretical studies of the lithosphere–atmosphere interaction on Venus, the dominant feature of exogenous processes is the sulphur (and chlorine?) accumulation in the form of pyrites, anhydrites, scapolites and apatites [24, 26, 75, 92]. Here the hydration–dehydration and carbonation–decarbonation processes are either greatly inhibited or eliminated completely.

However, while Khodakovsky *et al.* [75] used a formal approach, assuming an equilibrium between the present-day atmosphere and the planet's surface, Ringwood and Anderson [39] proceeded from the data on the cosmochemistry of the solar nebula and the present-day physical characteristics of the planet — its mass, size and density. Ringwood and Anderson, as well as Sagan [40], Dayhoff *et al.* [41], Ingersoll [93], and Khodakovsky *et al.* [75] concede that water on Venus was spent on oxidizing FeO to Fe_2O_3. Of great interest is the mechanism responsible for the present lack of water on Venus. Ringwood and Anderson proceeded from the supposition that water was present on Venus in the period of its accretion. They believe, as many other geochemists do, that at the very beginning carbon was accreted as polymerized hydrocarbons (as it is discovered in carbonaceous chondrites). Walker *et al.* [94] have shown that while oxidizing inside the planet, hydrocarbons must release some comparable amounts of CO_2 and H_2O, i.e.

$$CH_2 + 3Fe_3O_4 \rightarrow CO_2 + H_2O + 9FeO.$$

Further on, two water consumption mechanisms are possible: water may become dissociated into oxygen and hydrogen under the effect of ultraviolet radiation, then hydrogen volatilitizes and oxygen is consumed by iron oxidation [40, 48, 93].

$$4FeO + O_2 \rightarrow 2Fe_2O_3$$

Or the other mechanism is at work, which is provided by the availability of sulphuric acid in Venus' clouds. Probably, there exists a complicated path which leads to the following simplified equation valid for high temperatures at Venus' surface [95]:

$$2FeS + 11H_2O = Fe_2O_3 + 2H_2SO_4 + 9H_2 \uparrow$$

On the Earth, FeS is the first sulphur component of basaltic lavas emerging to the surface. Primitive tholeiitic basalts contain 0.08–0.15% of primary structure and 0.025–0.5% of primary water [96, 97]. If a similar S/H_2O ratio is valid for Venusian basic rocks, then the sulphur amount would be enough to turn all water into sulphuric acid. Then much of the H_2SO_4 will react with surface rocks, forming $MgSO_4$ and $CaSO_4$. Consequently, the lack of large water quantities at present is outbalanced by the availability of magnesium and calcium sulphates in Venus' rocks.

1.3.6 ENDOGENOUS PROCESSES; DIFFERENTIATION OF MATTER

The following features may be indicative of matter differentiation on Venus: (1) the character of the surface, (2) the planet's configuration, (3) the mean density, (4) the content of natural radioactive elements, (5) the composition of the atmosphere. Let us discuss these features within the context of the present problem.

The character of the surface

A comparison of the two best-studied celestial bodies (the Earth and the Moon) has shown that they exhibit bimodal topography; i.e. seas and continents on the Earth, and maria and highlands on the Moon. In both cases 'continental' areas are covered with a thick crust containing silicate rocks of lower density, while 'seas' have a thinner crust consisting mostly of denser basaltic rocks. Such a bimodal pattern is observed also on Mars [98] and, apparently, on Mercury [99], although in the latter case the contrasts are less pronounced. Clearly, the similarity in the appearance of the bodies implies a similarity in their histories. Contradictory evaluations of the age of structural formations on Venus' surface prevent us so far from coming to a single conclusion on the history of its crust formation. In all probability these structures on Venus' surface emerged in the early stage of its existence, as on other bodies of the Solar System. Great variations in height (±3 km) within extended sections of the surface suggested differences in the crystal pressure up to 5×10^7 Pa [100] which would be difficult to explain in the context of the homogeneous structure of the interior. This topographic difference may be either compensated for isostatically or it emerged long ago. Finally, the detection of features pointing to tectonic and volcanic activity on Venus in later time also speaks in favour of geological activity on the planet.

The configuration of the planet

This does not correspond to the homogeneous sphere which is to be expected in a geologically inactive body of such a size in at least two ways. Firstly, radio observations of Venus have disclosed a shift of the centre of mass in relation to the geometrical centre by 1.5 ± 0.3 km [101]. The most fitting explanation here may be a difference in the differentiated crust thickness, since any heterogeneity deeper within the planet would lead to unreasonably great stresses. A difference in the crust thickness of some 30 km would be enough to explain this shift. Secondly, a difference in the equatorial axes of the order of 1.1 ± 0.4 km is observed [101]. Apparently, this anomaly was partially compensated for by an isostatic equilibrium, and that which is observed might be accounted for chiefly by the inner convection, if it is manifested there on the same scale as the Earth.

The density

Using the calculations of Kovach and Anderson [102] for the Earth, Ringwood and Anderson [39] have found that if Venus were identical to the Earth in composition and structure, if it had the same mass ratio of the core to the mantle and the crust, and if it possessed the same inner temperatures at corresponding pressures, then Venus' mean density would be 5.34×10^3 kg m^{-3}, instead of the 5.24×10^3 kg m^{-3} observed. Consequently, its actual mean density is 1.7% smaller than the density of the model based on similarity to the Earth. So far there is no single opinion on how to explain this disparity. Some of the explanations proposed contradict each other, although there are good arguments on both sides.

Thus, for instance, Lewis [103, 104] proceeds from the fact that Venus was accreted at higher mean temperatures since it was closer to the nebula's centre. But then it should be reduced to a greater extent than the Earth. He concedes that almost no FeO can be present in Venus' mantle, and most of the iron must be contained in the core. But Venus' core must be relatively larger than the Earth's core. As Venus' accretion went on at higher temperatures, no sulphur or potassium can be available in such quantities as on the Earth. Therefore, the observed density of Venus turns out to be lower than the estimations on the basis of the Earth model. However, most recent data obtained from Veneras 13 and 14 point to the presence of sulphur in clouds, as well as sulphur, potassium and iron in rocks, which does not support Lewis's position.

Ringwood *et al.* [39, 105, 106] explain Venus' density quite differently. They assume that, in view of the smaller mass and consequently lower mean temperature of accretion than the Earth, Venus is much more heavily oxidized. The FeO/ (FeO + MgO) ratio is equal to 0.24 for Venus, while for the Earth it is 0.12. Hence, Venus' core is smaller (about 23%) in proportion to the whole planet than the Earth's core (about 32.5%). The authors use this to explain the differences in density and similarity of K/U ratios and the identical content of CO_2 on the planets. But in this reasoning many ideas are not indisputable. It is important here that many explanations, and the above-mentioned in particular, assume the interior differentiation of Venus and the existence of the crust, the mantle and the core similar to the Earth's envelopes.

The content of U, Th and K

The content of these elements in Venus' crust is, clearly, the most reliable proof of Venus' differentiation. It was mentioned earlier that the concentrations and the relative amounts of these elements in Venus' crust are close to those in the Earth's crust. Consequently, it may be assumed that the mean content of these elements in primordial matter on the Earth and Venus was nearly the same. But opinions diverge as far as the potassium content in the primordial matter of these planets is concerned. There are some indirect data proving that the potassium content in the Earth's mantle is approximately five times smaller than in chondrites, which are believed to have the composition of the solar nebula [107, 108]. The temperature of condensation of potassium in the solar nebula was about 730°C as compared to 430°C for sulphur [109]. Therefore, if the temperature of the Earth's condensation was such that the whole or a greater part of the sulphur component was condensed, then obviously, the whole potassium component would have condensed too. Thus, Lewis [37] believes that the amount of potassium on the Earth should be the same as in chondrites, but it is in the sulphide phase of the core consisting of the Fe–FeS melt. Besides, it follows from some papers [110, 111] that not more than 1% passes over from the silicate phase into the Fe–FeS melt. Consequently, a potassium deficiency is found on the Earth (and even more so on Venus) as compared with chondrites. However, no matter which amount of potassium was present in primordial material of Venus (that found in chondrites or five times more), the measured quantities of potassium in Venus' crust prove that the crust is enriched with it to a much greater extent than the mantle.

Venus' atmosphere

As can be seen from the above, this is secondary and was built up as a result of the outgassing of the planet's interior. This suggests certain thermal activity on Venus. Since the surface temperature is high, the partial pressure of such volatiles as HCl, CO, HF, H_2O, Hg and sulphur compounds is adequate for them to pass from rocks into the atmosphere. Knowing the content of these components in the atmosphere, and assuming that the atmosphere is in equilibrium with surface rocks, it is possible to evaluate the weathering rate of surface rocks and the rate of the volcanic and tectonic processes which contribute to the renovation of surface rocks. Volcanic processes also release gases directly from the interior into the atmosphere. But if no renovation of surface rocks occurs, the atmosphere will not be in equilibrium with deep-seated rocks, but only with the thinnest surface layer of matter.

Also, the nearly complete absence of oxygen and the low water content in the atmosphere indicate that Venus' lithosphere must be rather dry.

However, such unbalanced processes as volcanic activity or the lack of mechanisms producing fresh surface rocks may give rise to a unbalanced atmosphere (at least as far as some components are concerned), which does not react with the surface, and all gases released into the atmosphere remain there.

A good indicator of the intensity of the release of gases into the atmosphere (apart from the above-mentioned active gases) is ^{40}Ar formed during the decay of ^{40}K. Its presence in Venus' atmosphere is also proof of the planet's differentiation.

Therefore, the above data on the character of the surface, the planet's configuration, its density, the content of natural radioactive elements, and, finally, the composition of the atmosphere leave no doubts that Venus had an active thermal history resulting in the differentiation of its matter.

1.3.7 VENUS' INNER STRUCTURE

In view of the shortage of factual material on the planet's interior, many aspects of its history and structure remain obscure. However, some notions about them may be obtained from studies of the general condensation models of the formation of planets and from the comparison of Venus with the Earth. Let us try to explain what factors, no matter how insignificant they seem at first sight, could lead to the planets' dissimilarity in outer appearance. Such factors are:

(1) Venus' condensation zone is closer to the Sun than the Earth's condensation zone;
(2) Venus is smaller in size than the Earth.

Let us discuss the implications of these differences.

Many attempts have been made to explain the inner structure of Venus proceeding from various models. Of particular interest are at least two highly differing models of Venus, that of Lewis [37, 103] and that of Ringwood [105, 106] which, to some extent, agree with the factual data on Venus obtained over the past few years. years.

Both models assume an identical relative content of basic elements (Fe, Si, Mg, Al and Ca) on the Earth and on Venus.

According to the condensation model of Lewis [37] and Grossman and Larimer [38] the mean temperature of the solar nebula in the condensation zone of Venus was around 750 K, and that of the Earth around 430 K. The Earth included such volatiles as H_2O, sulphur (FeS) and potassium, whose condensation temperatures (at an atmospheric pressure) are 100, 430 and 774°C, respectively. Lewis admits that sulphur and potassium, whose content in the Earth's crust is small as compared to their content in chondrites, are concentrated in the Earth's core. (It is worth noting that many papers studying potassium solubility in the Fe–FeS melt of the Earth's core provide highly contradictory conclusions, which either confirm [112–114] or disprove [110, 111] the model.) There must be a deficiency of these volatiles on Venus due to a higher condensation temperature. Therefore, Venus' core must contain the Fe–Ni melt, and there is almost no water, a small amount of sulphur, and a minute quantity of potassium in the crust as compared to chondrites or the Earth. Lewis explains the lower density of Venus (5.24×10^3 kg m^{-3}) by the deficiency of these elements, mainly sulphur. The sulphur deficit fails to fully compensate for this difference, and the author adds a second factor, assuming that Venus is more reduced due to a higher condensation temperature; i.e. its mantle almost lacks FeO, while Venus' core contains proportionally more iron than the Earth. The present atmosphere of Venus easily fits into this hypothesis. As mentioned above, the planet's water deficit gave rise to high temperatures at its surface and to a high CO_2 content in the atmosphere [46]. But the publication of data on the presence of sulphur in the atmosphere [24, 36, 115–118, 126] and potassium and sulphur in Venusian rocks [16, 69, 72, 79, 82, 119] puts one on alert and calls for the introduction of some corrections into the present model.

Ringwood and Anderson [39] have constructed their model relying on other assumptions. They stress not the difference in condensation temperatures but the difference in the conditions of local accretion controlled by the planet's mass. They think that Venus, possessing a smaller mass than the Earth, had lower accretion energy and, thus, was subject to heating to a lesser extent. Consequently, Venus accreted not at higher but at lower temperatures than the Earth. Thus, it must contain the same volatiles, in particular water, sulphur and potassium, and in nearly the same proportion as the Earth.

It was established in the above discussion that Venus is a differentiated planet. Many data show that igneous rocks, the composition of which is already known, can be found on its surface. The data on the content of natural radioactive elements and basic rock-forming elements prove the similarity of Venusian rocks to the basic rocks of the Earth's crust. But the content of volatiles in them still remains the most intriguing unknown factor. If one admits a high initial temperature of Venus' condensation, its core must consist of the Fe–Ni melt. The fact that on Venus' surface there are ancient regions formed at the very beginning of the planet's existence (during the intensive fall of large bodies on the surface), and perhaps even in the final stage of Venus' accretion, proves that its inner structure, and the core in particular, were shaped in the early stage.

Toksöz and Johnson [120] created a thermal model of Venus based on Lewis's cosmochemical model of the solar nebula [103]. They excluded volatiles, and sulphur in particular (which resulted in the high initial temperature of the formation of the core), assumed a short period of accretion of approximately 25000 years and made use of terrestrial amounts of natural radioactive elements. Their calculations have shown that at present Venus has a lithosphere about 100 km thick, a partially melted upper mantle, a solid lower mantle and a melted core approximately 2900 km in radius. However, this model must apparently be somehow modified, taking into account new experimental data revealing small quantities of sulphur on Venus [64, 81, 82, 129] and some theoretical estimations proving a longer accretion period [121].

Therefore, as far as endogenous processes are concerned, the histories of Venus and the Earth are similar. Venus is also a differentiated planet, possessing a crust, mantle and core. The differentiation of its material is evidently not terminated yet. Its interior and surface are still being shaped. Only the closer location of Venus to the Sun and its somewhat smaller size in comparison to the Earth have led to such great differences in their outer appearance.

1.3.8 GENERAL PROBLEMS OF THE EXPLORATION OF VENUS

Although greater progress has been made in the exploration of Venus than in studying other planets, in the near future the interest in Venus will not diminish. In the first place, this is due to the fact that it is a natural body which has a size, mass and location in the Solar System close to those of the Earth. That is why exploring that planet helps us better to understand the history of the development of the Earth; in particular, such processes as the differentiation of material, tectonics, volcanism, etc.

However, Venus is of particular interest not only due to its similarity, but also due to its fundamental differences from the Earth in some characteristics (the presence of a unique atmosphere, slow retrograde rotation, etc.).

Venusian studies are also helped by the fact that it approaches the Earth more frequently and is closer to the Earth than other planets.

The major scientific problems in exploring Venus are the development of our ideas of the history of Venus' formation (its comparison with the history of the Earth); the determination of the degree of differentiation of its material (the composition and size of the core, mantle and crust) and when this came to an end; studies of volcanic activity in the past and at present; studies of the history of magnetism and the modern (weak) magnetic field; and the elucidation of the causes of Venus' retrograde rotation.

It is also important to answer the following questions. What is the nature of the greenhouse effect of the planetary atmosphere? Was there water on the planet in the past? Was there a nitrogenous atmosphere in the past? What is the nature of the clouds (composition, structure, dependence on the latitude and season)? What is the difference between Venus and the Earth in content of natural radioactive elements (uranium, thorium and potassium) and volatiles (sulphur, water, etc.)?

REFERENCES

[1] D. M. Hunten, L. Colin, T. M. Donahue and V. I. Moroz (ed.) *Venus,* The University of Arizona Press, p. 1143 (1983).

[2] L. V. K. Ksanfomality, *Planet Venus.* (In Russian.) Moscow, Nauka, p. 376 (1985).

[3] A. D. Kuzmin and M. Ya. Marov, *The physics of the planet Venus.* (In Russian.) Moscow, Nauka, p. 408 (1974).

[4] M. V. Keldysh (ed.), *The first panoramas of Venus' surface.* (In Russian.) Moscow, Nauka, p. 132 (1979).

[5] D. M. Hunten, G. E. McGill and A. F. Nag, *Space Sci. Rev.,* **20**, 265 (1977).

[6] M. V. Keldysh, *Icarus,* **30**, 605 (1977).

[7] Special issue of 'Venus exploration', *Space Sci. Rev.,* **20**, 249 (1977).

[8] A. P. Vinogradov, Yu. A. Surkov and K. P. Florensky, *Dokl. AN SSSR,* **179**, 37 (In Russian.) (1968).

[9] A. P. Vinogradov, Yu. A. Surkov and B. N. Andreichikov, *Kosmich. Issled.,* **8**, 578 (In Russian.) (1970).

[10] Yu. A. Surkov, B. M. Andreichikov and O. M. Kalinkina, *Geokhimiya,* **10**, 1435 (In Russian.) (1973).

[11] A. P. Vinogradov, Yu. A. Surkov and K. P. Florensky, *J. Atmos. Sci.,* **25**, 535 (1968).

[12] B. G. Gelman, V. P. Zolotukhin and N. I. Lamonov, *Kosmich. Issled.,* **17**, 708 (In Russian.) (1979).

[13] V. A. Krasnopolsky and V. A. Parshev, *Kosmich. Issled.,* **17**, 763 (In Russian.) (1979).

[14] J. H. Hoffman, V. I. Oyama and U. Von Zahn, *J. Geophys, Res.,* **85**, 7871 (1980).

[15] V. I. Oyama, *J. Geophys. Res.,* **85**, 7891 (1980).

[16] Yu. A. Surkov, In *Proc. 8th Lunar and Planet. Sci. Conf.,* New York, Pergamon Press, p. 2665 (1977).

[17] V. G. Istomin, K. V. Grechnev and L. N. Ozerov, *Kosmich. Issled.*, **8**, 16 (In Russian.) (1975).

[18] J. H. Hoffman, R. R. Hodges and W. W. Wright, *IEEE Trans. Geosci. Electron*, **GE-18**, 80 (1980).

[19] W. B. Rossow and C. Sagan, *J. Atmos. Sci.*, **32**, 1164 (1975).

[20] L. D. C. Young, *Icarus*, **17**, 632 (1972).

[21] W. A. Traub and N. P. Carleton, *J Atmos. Sci.*, **32**, 1045 (1975).

[22] Yu. A. Surkov, F. F. Kirnozov and V. K. Khristianov, *Kosmich. Issled.*, **14**, 697 (In Russian.) (1976).

[23] Yu. A. Surkov, F. F. Kirnozov and V. N. Glazov, *Letters to Astron. J.*, **8**, 700 (In Russian.) (1982).

[24] V. P. Volkov, *The chemistry of Venus' atmosphere and surface rock.* (In Russian.) Moscow, Nauka, p. 208 (1983).

[25] U. von Zahn, S. Kumar, H. Niemann and R. Prin, In *Venus,* D. M. Hunte (ed.), The University of Arizona Press, p. 299 (1983).

[26] V. L. Barsukov, I. L. Khodakovsky and V. P. Volkov, In *Lunar and planetary science,* Houston, LPI, **12**, 43 (1981).

[27] Yu. A. Surkov, Paper presented at the 22nd COSPAR meeting, Bangalore, India (1979).

[28] M. Ya. Marov, V. N. Lebedev and V. E. Lystsev, Report presented to the 19th COSPAR meeting, USA (1976).

[29] M. Ya. Marov, *Astron. Vestnik,* **13**, 3 (In Russian.) (1979).

[30] M. Ya. Marov, B. V. Bivshev and B. P. Baranov, *Kosmich. Issled.*, **21**, 269 (In Russian.) (1983).

[31] R. G. Knollenberg and D. M. Hunten, *Science,* **203**, 792 (1979).

[32] B. D. Mochkin, V. N. Economov and V. S. Avduevsky, *J. Atmos. Sci.*, **30**, 1215 (1973).

[33] C. Sagan, *Icarus*, **1**, 151 (1962).

[34] V. I. Moroz, *Advances in Phys. Sci.*, **104**, 255 (In Russian.) (1971).

[35] J. B. Pollack and K. Young, *J. Atmos. Sci.*, **32**, 1025 (1975).

[36] J. H. Hoffman, R. R. Hodger and F. S. Johnson, In *Proc. 4th Lunar and Planet. Sci. Conf.,* New York, Pergamon Press, **3**, 2865 (1973).

[37] J. S. Lewis, *Earth and Planet Sci. Lett.*, **15**, 286 (1972).

[38] L. Grossman, J. W. Larimer, *Rev. Geophys. and Space Phys.*, **12**, 71 (1974).

[39] A. E. Ringwood and D. L. Anderson, *Icarus*, **30**, 243 (1977).

[40] C. Sagan, In *International dictionary of geophysics,* S. K. Runcorn (ed.), New York, Pergamon Press, p. 97 (1967).

[41] M. O. Dayhoff, R. Eck, E. Lippincott and C. Sagan, *Science,* **155**, 556 (1967).

[42] S. J. Rasool and C. de Bergh, *Nature,* **226**, 1037 (1970).

[43] J. H. Hoffman, R. R. Hodges and T. M. Donaghue, *J. Geophys. Res.*, **85**, 7882 (1980).

[44] M. B. McElroy and D. M. Hunten, *J. Geophys. Res.*, **74**, 1720 (1969).

[45] G. C. G. Walker, *J. Atmos. Sci.*, **32**, 1248 (1975).

[46] V. I. Moroz and L. M. Mukhin, *Kosmich. Issled.*, **15**, 901 (In Russian.) (1977).

[47] N. D. Holland, In *Origin and evolution of the atmosphere of the Earth and Venus,* Ed. P. Brancazio, A. G. W. Cameron (eds), New York, Wiley, p. 86 (1964).

[48] T. N. Donahue, J. H. Hoffman and R. R. Hadger, *Science*, **216**, 630 (1982).

[49] R. M. Goldstein, *Radio Sci.*, **69d**, 1623 (1965).

[50] A. E. E. Rogers and R. P. Ongalls, *Science*, **165**, 797 (1969).

[51] S. Zohar and R. M. Goldstein, *Nature*, **219**, 357 (1968).

[52] D. B. Campbell, R. F. Jurgens and R. B. Dyce, *Science*, **170**, 1090 (1970).

[53] D. B. Campbell, R. B. Dyce and G. H. Pettengill, *Science*, **193**, 1123 (1976).

[54] R. M. Goldstein, *Icarus*, **23**, 1 (1974).

[55] R. M. Goldstein and H. C. Ramsey, *Trans. Amer. Geophys. Union*, **56**, 388 (1975).

[56] M. C. Malin and R. S. Saunders, *Science*,**196**, 987 (1977).

[57] R. S. Saunders and M. C. Malin, *Geophys. Res. Lett.*, **4**, 547 (1977).

[58] H. Masursky, W. M. Kaula and G. E. McGill, *Space Sci. Rev.*, **20**, 431 (1977).

[59] A. P. Vinogradov, K. P. Florensky and A. T. Bazilevsky, *Dokl. AN SSSR*, **228**, 570 (In Russian.) (1976).

[60] K. P. Florensky, A. T. Bazilevsky and V. V. Zasetsky, *Priroda*, **8**, 12 (In Russian.) (1976).

[61] K. P. Florensky, A. T. Bazilevsky and G. A. Burba, An outline of comparative planetology. (In Russian.) Moscow, Nauka, p. 326 (1981).

[62] K. P. Florensky, L. B. Ronca and A. T. Basilevsky, *Data Science*, **196**, 869 (1977).

[63] K. P. Florensky, A. T. Basilevsky and G. A. Burba, In *Proc. 8th Lunar sci. Conf.*, Pergamon Press, New York, p. 2655 (1977).

[64] Yu. A. Surkov, L. P. Moskalyeva and O. P. Shcheglov, *Astron. Vestkin*, **4**, 275 (In Russian.) (1985).

[65] N. N. Krupenio (In Russian.) Preprint of the Institute of Space Research of the USSR Academy of Sciences, Pr-212, (1975).

[66] N. N. Krupenio, *Icarus*, **17**, 692 (1972).

[67] Yu. A. Surkov and V. F. Ivanova (In Russian.) Geokhimiya, **4**, 506 (1977).

[68] Yu. A. Surkov, F. F. Kirnozov and V. K. Khristianov, *Space Res.*, **17**, 651 (1977).

[69] Yu. A. Surkov, L. P., Moskalyeva and A. T. Basilevsky, In *Proc. 11th Lunar and Planet. Sci. Conf.*, New York, Pergamon Press, p. 669 (1980).

[70] A. L. Kemurdzan, P. N. Brodsky and V. V. Gromov, *Kosmich. Issled.*, **21**, 323 (In Russian.) (1983).

[71] Yu. A. Surkov, F. F. Kirnozov and O. P. Sobornov, *Kosmich. Issled.*, **11**, 781 (In Russian.) (1973).

[72] Yu. A. Surkov, F. F. Kirnozov and V. N. Glazov, *Kosmich. Issled.*, **14**, 704 (In Russian.) (1976).

[73] Yu. A. Surkov, *Proc. 8th Lunar and Planet. Sci. Conf.*, New York, Pergamon Press, 2665 (1977).

[74] I. V. Barmin and A. A. Shevchenko (In Russian.) *Kosmich Issled.*, **21**, 171 (1983).

[75] I. L. Khodakovsky, V. P. Volkov and Yu. A. Sidorov, *Geokhimiya*, **12**, 1747 (In Russian.) (1979).

[76] Yu. A. Surkov, *Gamma-spectrometry in space research*, (In Russian.) Moscow, Atomizdat, p. 209 (1977).

[77] Yu. A. Surkov and G. A. Fedoseyev, In *Soviet advances in space exploration: The second decade.* (In Russian.) Moscow, Nauka, p. 313 (1978).

[78] K. P. Florensky, L. B. Ronca and A. T. Basilevsky, *Soc. Amer. Bull.*, **38**, 11 (1977).

[79] V. L. Barsukov, Yu. A. Surkov and L. P. Moskalyeva (In Russian.) *Geokhimiya*, **7**, 899 (1982).

[80] Yu. A. Surkov, O. P. Shcheglov and L. P. Moskalyeva, *Analitich. Khimiya*, **37**, 1349 (In Russian.) (1982).

[81] Yu. A. Surkov, L. P. Moskalyeva and O. P. Shcheglov, *Kosmich. Issled.*, **21**, 308 (In Russian.) (1983).

[82] Yu. A. Surkov, O. P. Shcheglov and L. P. Moskalyeva, *Anal. Chem.*, **54**, 957A (1982).

[83] V. S. Sobolev, *Dokl. AN SSSR*, **194**, 922 (In Russian.) (1970).

[84] I. K. Karpov, A. L. Kiselyov and A. F. Letnikov, *The simulation of natural mineral formation on a computer* (In Russian.) Moscow, Nedra, p. 256 (1976).

[85] J. S. Lewis, *Earth and Planet. Sci. Lett.*, **10**, 73 (1970).

[86] P. F. Mueller, *Science*, **141**, 1046 (1963).

[87] P. F. Mueller, *Icarus*, **3**, 285 (1964).

[88] V. A. Krasnopolsky, *Photochemistry of the atmospheres of Mars and Venus* (In Russian.) Moscow, Nauka (1982).

[89] V. I. Moroz, B. E. Moshkin and A. P. Economov, *Kosmich. Issled.*, **21**, 246 (In Russian.) (1983).

[90] Yu. A. Surkov, V. F. Ivanova and A. N. Pudov, *Pisma Astron. Zh.*, **12**, 110 (In Russian.) (1986).

[91] V. L. Barsukov, I. L. Khodakovsky and V. P. Volkov, In *4th Lunar and Planet. Sci. Conf.*, Houston, **1**, 19 (1983).

[92] V. L. Barsukov, V. P. Volkov and I. L. Khodakovsky, *J. Geophys. Res.*, **87**, A3 (1982).

[93] A. P. Ingersoll, *J. Atmos. Sci.*, **26**, 1191 (1969).

[94] J. C. Walker, K. Turecian and D. Hunter, *J. Geophys. Res.*, **75**, 3558 (1970).

[95] R. G. Prinn, *J. Atmos. Sci.*, **32**, 1237 (1975).

[96] D. L. Anderson, C. Sammis and T. Jordan, *Science*, **171**, 1103, 1971.

[97] J. R. Moore and B. Fabbi, *Contrib. Miner and Petrol.*, **33**, 118 (1971).

[98] H. Masursky, *J. Geophys. Res.*, **78**, 4009 (1973).

[99] B. C. Murrey, R. G. Strom and N. J. Trask, *J. Geophys. Res.*, **80**, 2508 (1975).

[100] D. B. Campbell, R. B. Dyce and R. F. Ingalls, *Science*, **175**, 514 (1972).

[101] W. B. Smith, R. P. Ingalls and I. I. Shapiro, *Radio Sci.*, **5**, 411 (1970).

[102] R. Kovach and D. L. Anderson, *J. Geophys. Res.*, **70**, 2873 (1965).

[103] J. S. Lewis, Ann. Rev. Phys. Chem., **24**, 339 (1973).

[104] J. S. Lewis, *Science*, **84**, 440 (1974).

[105] A. E. Ringwood, *Geochim. et Cosmochim. Acta.*, **15**, 257 (1959).

[106] A. E. Ringwood, *Geochim. et Cosmochim. Acta.*, **30**, 41 (1966).

[107] S. P. P. Clark and A. E. Ringwood, *Rev. Geophys.*, **2**, 35 (1964).

[108] G. J. Wasserburg, G. J. F. MacDonald and F. Hoyle, *Science*, **143**, 465 (1964).

[109] L. Grossman, *Geochim. et Cosmochim. Acta.*, **36**, 597 (1972).

[110] I. Ganduly and G. C. Kennedy, *Earth and Planet. Sci. Lett.*, **35**, 411 (1977).

[111] V. M. Oversby and A. E. Ringwood, *Earth and Planet. Sci. Lett.*, **14**, 345 (1972).

[112] K. A. Goettel and J. S. Lewis, *Earth and Planet. Sci. Lett.*, **18**, 148 (1973).

[113] T. Hall and V. R. Murthy, *Earth and Planet. Sci. Lett.*, **11**, 239 (1971).

[114] J. S. Lewis, *Earth and Planet. Sci. Lett.*, **11**, 30 (1971).

[115] R. G. Knollenberg, J. Hansen and B. Ragent, *Space Sci. Rev.*, **20**, 329 (1977).

[116] J. B. Pollack, E. F. Erickson and D. Goorvich, *J. Atmos. Sci.*, **32**, 1140 (1975).

[117] G. T. Sill, Sulfuric acid in the Venus clouds. *Commun. Lunar and Planet. Lab.*, **171**, 191 (1972).

[118] A. T. Young, *Icarus*, **18**, 564 (1973), *J. Atmos. Sci.*, **32**, 1125 (1975).

[119] Yu. A. Surkov, F. F. Kirnozov and V. N. Glasov, *Space and Res.*, **17**, 659 (1977).

[120] M. N. Toksöz and D. H. Johnson, The evolution of the Moon and terrestrial Planets. In *Cosmochemistry of the Moon and Planets*. (In Russian.) Moscow, Nauka, p. 210 (1975).

[121] V. S. Safronov. In *Cosmochemistry of the Moon and Planets*. (In Russian.) Moscow, Nauka, p. 624 (1975).

[122] V. L. Barsukov, A. T. Basilevsky and R. O. Kuzmin, *Geokhimiya*, **12**, 1811 (In Russian.) (1984).

[123] V. S. Avduevsky and Yu. G. Zaharov, *Kosmich. Issled.*, **21**, 331 (In Russian.) (1983).

[124] G. H. Pettengill, E. Eliason, P. G. Ford, G. B. Loriot, H. Masursky and G. E. McGill, *J. Geophys. Res.*, **85**, 8261 (1980).

[125] D. L. Bingschadler, J. W. Head and J. B. Garvin, *Abstract 17th Lunar and Planet Sci. Conf.* p. 52, (1986).

[126] L. M. Mukhin, B. G. Gelman and N. I. Lamonov, *Kosmich. Issled.*, **21**, 225 (In Russian.) (1983).

[127] Yu. A. Surkov, F. F. Kirnozov and O. P. Sobornov, *Pisma v Astron. Zh.*, **12**, 114 (In Russina.) (1986).

[128] Yu. A. Surkov, F. F. Kirnozov and V. N. Glazov, *Abstract 17th Lunar and Planet Sci. Conf.*, p. 847 (1986).

[129] Yu. A. Surkov, L. P. Moskalyeva and V. P. Kharyukova, *Abstract 17th Lunar and Planet Sci. Conf.* p. 849 (1986).

1.4 Mars

1.4.1 GENERAL CHARACTERISTICS

Of all the planets in the Solar System, Mars has always attracted the greatest attention because it is closest in climatic conditions to the Earth (at least this was believed until recently on the basis of ground-based observations), and this gave rise to the possibility of the existence of life-forms on the planet. An interest in Mars was also aroused because, being practically devoid of any significant cloud cover, it renders itself more easily to observation.

Mars is much smaller than the Earth in size, mass and density. It is formed as a slightly oblate sphere having a mean equatorial radius about half that of the Earth – approximately 3400 km. Mars' mass (6.42×10^{23} kg) is nearly 10 times smaller than the Earth's mass, while its average density is about 3.93×10^3 kg m^{-3}; the mean density of the Earth is 5.52×10^3 kg m^{-3}.

Mars has nearly the same rotation period as the Earth (its day is 24 hours 37 minutes 23 seconds) and the inclination of the rotation axis to the orbital plane ($25°\ 12'$) is also close to that of the Earth ($23°\ 26'$). As a result, on Mars, as on the Earth, there is a change of seasons.

Over the past two decades our knowledge of the planet has improved greatly as a result of the flights to Mars of Soviet and American spacecraft Mars 2, 3, 4, 5, 6 and 7*, Mariners 4, 6, 7 and 9, and Vikings 1 and 2. The scientific results of these investigations are discussed in detail in [1–4]. In this section we shall deal solely with the geological and morphological aspects of these investigations.

1.4.2 SPECIFIC FEATURES OF THE GEOLOGICAL STRUCTURE OF THE SURFACE

Photographs of the surface of Mars taken by phototelevision devices installed aboard Soviet and American space probes gave us not only a general panorama of the Martian surface, but the chance to study small features of its relief.

Martian topography has nearly the same range in height as the Earth; there is a difference of typically 12 to 14 km between the top of highlands and the bottom of lowlands. An exception is the giant shield volcano Olympus Mons which is over 550 km across at its base and stands approximately 25 km high above Mars' datum.** There are several other volcanic mountains located in the same region that are only

*N.B. Mars 4 and 7 failed to reach orbit and missed Mars.

** The 'zero' contour or Mars' datum is defined as the 6.1×10^2 Pa atmospheric pressure level.

slightly lower than Olympus Mons, rising to about 20 km in altitude. The geological interpretation of the images revealed four types of terrain: ancient territories studded with craters, younger volcanic plains, large volcanic structures and extensive sedimentary deposits [5].

Large-scale pictures of the surface of Mars at Mare Erythraeum south-east of the Coprates rift system (the southern near-equatorial zone) obtained from Mars 5 (Fig. 1.4.1) convincingly prove the presence of impact-explosion, slope, aeolian and tectonic processes on the Martian surface. Many scientists associate the valley formation on Mars with the water-erosion mechanism which operated in the past during the warm interglacial fluvial period. But the possibility of the formation of valleys through, for instance, aeolian action in frozen rock zones along tectonic faults should not be ruled out [6].

Fig. 1.4.1 — Martian surface in the region of Uzboi Vallis and Nirgal Vallis. Picture was taken from Mars 5 at a distance of 1800 km (surface area is 850 × 850 km).

In polar regions (Fig. 1.4.2) vast areas of layered deposits, sand dunes and ice-free sections have been discovered. This confirms the planet's complicated climatic

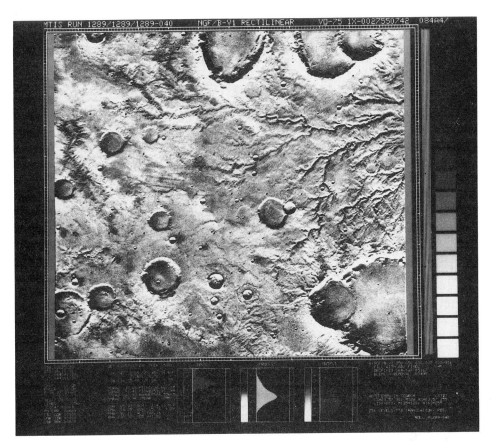

Fig. 1.4.2 — In the polar regions, there are layered deposits, ice-free regions and dune fields.
Picture was taken from Viking 1 at a distance of 5200 km (surface area is 230 × 250 km).

history. Analysis of surface temperatures has shown that the northern polar cap, unlike the southern one, is apparently composed only of aqueous ice with soil inclusions, since the summer temperature at the north pole (205 K), unlike that at the south pole (125 K), is higher than the condensation temperature of CO_2 and clathrate compounds (condensation temperatures of CO_2 and $CO_2 \cdot 6H_2O$ are 148 K and 153 K respectively, at the mean atmospheric pressure of about 6.1×10^2 Pa). It is highly probable that a thick cryolithosphere acting as a kind of a screen and a condenser for volatiles released from the interior of Mars exists on the planet. According to calculations [7] some 10% of the possible overall water content in the outer envelopes of Mars can be found in the cryolithosphere. This considerably exceeds the amount of water lost in the course of the hydrogen dissipation or trapped in polar regions (fractions of one per cent).

Craters are observed on the surface in which frost deposits turn into water vapour with the sunrise and into ice clouds after sunset. This was observed in the vicinity of the northern polar cap where the minimum summer temperature is not sufficient to freeze out CO_2.

In images taken by the Viking probes, traces of water flows are seen. Water appeared near to impact craters as a result of the heat released and the thawing of subsurface ice. The permafrost layer containing ice should apparently be kilometres thick. Water should be also found in minerals, rocks and fine-grained soil.

In the areas studied there were traces of extensive crater formation, fluvial activity, volcanism, erosion and glaciation. The crater density on the Martian surface varies from one-tenth up to nearly equal to that of the Moon. However, the morphology of craters on Mars is much more diversified than on the Moon or Mercury. The existence of numerous small craters proves that wind erosion (aeolian processes) plays a secondary rôle in forming the Martian landscape. A great part of the surface is old. The floor of the vast equatorial canyon system, the Tharsis region and the polar regions are the younger formations (there are fewer craters there). As mentioned above in polar regions (Fig. 1.4.2) there are vast areas of layered deposits, sand dunes and ice-free regions.

The landing sites of Viking 1 (Chryse Planitia, 22.4 ° N, 47.5° W) and Viking 2 (Utopia Planitia, 47.89°N, 225.86°W) are located at a distance of 7400 km from each other. The Chryse basin is a flat low-lying area into which several ancient rivers flow. Since no traces of an ancient ocean can be detected, the question of the source and flow of the liquid that formed this region is still debated. To the north, the Utopia region borders on the volcanic area which undoubtedly was involved in forming its surface cover.

Flat localities were chosen for the landing of the spacecraft. Therefore, small-scale details visible on panoramic pictures may not be typical of the whole of Mars. At first sight both landing sites (Fig. 1.4.3.) have similar landscapes, with a large number of stones scattered over the reddish-brown surface. However, they differ in detail. The Chryse region exhibits greater geological diversity than the Utopia region: mottled and unmottled rocks of light and dark colouring, widespread dunes, with outcrops of underlying (parent) rocks of a layered structure or protruding as dikes. In contrast, the Utopia region is smoother and more monochromatic, covered largely with angular dark blocks with inclusions of mottled fine-grained rock fragments. In both regions (particularly in Utopia) the uppermost rock layer is composed of fine-grained material which should be cemented in a layer 1–2 cm thick and whose mechanical strength varies within a wide range. Unlike Utopia, outcrops of parent rocks and rather sharply pronounced glacier drifts are visible in the Chryse region. While stones in the Chryse regions differ in albedo, shape and texture, in the Utopia region they have identical albedo and vesicular texture. Although aeolian activity is better seen in landscapes of the Utopia region, signs of the effect of winds are more pronounced on the surface of the volcanoes in the Chryse region. A specific feature of the topography of the Utopia region is the presence of polygonal depressions an average of 1 m wide and 15 cm deep.

As mentioned above, the Viking landing sites were 7400 km apart. But the rock composition at the two sites turned out to be nearly identical, which suggests that a considerable part of the Martian surface is covered with crushed material transferred by strong Martian winds over the surface. How thick is this dust cover? Anders and Owen [8] evaluated the thickness as approximately 70 m, proceeding from the measured sulphur and chlorine content of Mars (3.5% and 0.75%, respectively) and from the measured density of the dust layer (1.65×10^3 kg m^{-3}), and taking into account the estimated content of these elements in the Martian crust.

(a)

(b)

Fig. 1.4.3 — Panoramas of the Martian surface at the landing sites of Viking 1 in Chryse Planitia (a), and Viking 2 in Utopia Planitia (b).

1.4.3 COMPOSITION AND PROPERTIES OF THE SURFACE ROCK

The physical and mechanical properties of the Martian top layer were studied from Vikings 1 and 2. The data obtained are listed in Table 1.4.1 [9].

Table 1.4.1 — Physico-mechanical properties of Martian rocks

Rock properties	Viking 1		Viking 2
	Sandy surface	Stone surface	
1. Density ($\times 10^3$ kg m^{-3})			
soil	1.0–1.6	1.2–1.6	1.1–1.5
rocks	—	2.9	2.6
2. Particle size			
(% > 2 cm)	0	25	20
Consolidated soil and			
fine-grained dust (%)	100	75	80
3. Soil cohesion (Nm^{-2})	10–10^2	10–10^4	10–10^3
Soil cohesion (Nm^{-2})	—	>10^4	>10^4
4. Angle of internal			
friction (degrees)	30–45	30–45	30–45
5. Stability (Nm^{-2})	3 × 10^5	6 × 10^6	6 × 10^6
6. Adhesion (Nm^{-2})	1 × 10^2	—	—
7. Slip coefficient	0.3–0.5	0.3–0.5	—

It is seen that the Martian surface is covered largely with fine-grained loose rocks. The density of these rocks is much higher than the density of the regolith covering the lunar surface. The presence of an atmosphere on Mars makes rocks less cohesive than on the Moon. Parent crystalline rocks exhibit features close to the igneous rocks of the Earth's crust.

The year of 1974 saw the first experiment in gamma-ray studies of Mars (10–12). Several measurements of gamma-radiation at Mare Erythraeum were carried out from Mars' orbit by the spacecraft Mars 5. Estimates based on the intensity and spectral analysis of gamma-radiation within the energy range 0.4–10 MeV have shown that for a vast region in Mars' southern hemisphere covering an area of about 4×10^5 km^2, the U, Th and K content of the rocks corresponds to basic igneous rocks on the Earth. But radioactivity was not similar everywhere in the region explored, and this may be associated with differences in rocks making up the surface layer. All differences in the relief forms and rock types here may be in general reduced to two principal types of rocks: ancient continental formations and younger volcanic formations. Other formations found in the explored territory constitute only an insignificant area. Continental formations on Mars usually have a great number of large craters, which makes them similar to the highlands. Volcanic formations are represented by the Tharsis upland, including the Arsia Mons, Pavonis Mons and Ascraeus Mons shield volcanoes, and plains confined to the bottom of depressions (e.g. Argyre Planitia). The former bear some resemblance in morphology to areas of shield basaltic volcanism here on the Earth. The latter are similar to basaltic plains in the lunar maria.

Table 1.4.2 — Thorium and uranium content in various rock types on planets and the Moon

Planet	Rock type	Th	U	Th/U	Reference
Mars	Young volcanic rocks	5.0	1.1	4.5	[11][a]
	Ancient continental rocks	0.3	0.2	4.5	
Venus	Areas of shield basaltic volcanism	0.7	0.5	1.4	[14][a]
	Ancient crust	6.5	2.2	3.0	
Earth	Ultrabasic rocks	0.08	0.03	2.7	
	Tholeiitic basalts of oceans	0.18	0.1	1.8	
	Alkaline olivine basalts	3.9	1.0	3.9	[15, 16][b]
	Geosynclinal basalts	2.4	0.7	3.9	
	Platform plateau-basalts	2.5	0.8	3.1	
	Granites, granodiorites, granite gneisses	15.6	3.9	4.0	
Moon	*Analysis of lunar samples brought to the Earth*				
	ANT-type rocks	1.13	0.73	1.55	
	KREEP matter	9.3	2.8	3.4	
	Ti-high and K-high mare basalts	3.98	0.68	5.8	[17][c]
	Mare basalts with a moderate Ti and K content	1.18	0.64	1.9	
	Mare basalts with a moderate Ti content and a moderate K content	0.61	0.16	3.9	
	Orbital gamma-ray spectrometry				
	Continental formation in the equatorial zone	0.4–1.4	—	—	[18]
	Mare basalts	1.2–8.4	—	—	

a Data of orbital gamma-ray spectrometry
b Analysis of terrestrial rocks
c Analysis of lunar samples brought to the Earth

The content of natural radioactive elements in the ancient continental and young volcanic formations on the Martian surface are listed in Table 1.4.2 [12]. For the sake of comparison the corresponding content in rocks on the Earth, Venus and the Moon are also given. It follows from this table that the thorium and uranium content in volcanic rocks of the explored Martian territory is close to basalts typical of many geological formations, such as alkaline olivine basalts, platform plateau-basalts and geosynclinal basalts of the Earth, lunar basalts with a high potassium content and evidently to rock of shield basalt volcanism on Venus. Tholeiitic basalts of the Earth's oceans and mare basalts with a high titanium content and a moderate potassium content on the Moon show essentially lower thorium and uranium contents and have no analogues among the studied volcanites on Mars.

These estimations have revealed that continental formations on Mars have a lower thorium and uranium content than explored mare volcanites, and differ essentially from the matter of granite continents on the Earth and KREEP matter (radioactive basalts) on the Moon, in which higher levels of these elements are typical. As compared to the widespread rocks of the ANT (anorthosite-norite-troctolite) group on lunar continents, the continental formations on Mars have no significant deviations in the thorium content, but the uranium content is somewhat smaller.

Comparison of reflection spectra of the Martian rock with spectra of terrestrial igneous rocks has revealed that the typical rock of Mars resembles crushed igneous terrestrial rock of basic composition (with a SiO_2 content from 45 to 65%), and with small admixtures of colouring material — goethite $Fe_2 O_3 \cdot H_2O$ [13]. The soil in lighter-coloured Martian regions (continental by analogy with the Moon) consists of more acid rocks than in dark (marine) regions.

Table 1.4.3 — Content of elements in Martian rocks as measured by Vikings 1 and 2

Element	Viking 1			Viking 2
	Sample 1	Sample 2	Sample 3	
Percentage of rock				
Mg	5.0 ± 2.5	—	5.2	—
Al	3.0 ± 0.9	—	2.9	—
Si	20.9 ± 2.5	20.8	20.5	30.0
S	3.1 ± 0.5	3.8	3.8	2.6
Cl	0.7 ± 0.3	0.8	0.9	0.6
K	<0.25	0	0	0
Ca	4.0 ± 0.8	3.8	0	3.6
Ti	0.5 ± 0.3	0	0	0.61
Fe	12.7 ± 2.0	12.6	13.1	14.2
O	50.1 ± 4.3	49.7	—	50.4
Parts per million of rock				
Pb	≤30	—	—	≤30
Sr	60 ± 30	—	—	100 ± 40
Y	70 ± 30	—	—	50 ± 30
Zr	≤30	—	—	30 ± 20

Table 1.4.3 gives results of a chemical analysis of four samples of the Martian fine fraction taken by Vikings 1 and 2 [19, 20]. The content of Martian samples, taken in different regions of the surface, is similar, because all samples have a high iron content, a medium content of magnesium, calcium and sulphur, a low aluminium content and evidently a very low content of alkalines and admixtures. This content is best interpreted as a weathering product of mafic igneous rocks. The mineralogical model obtained from the studies of computer mixtures and prepared laboratory analogues supposes that the Martian fine fraction may be close to a mixture of about 80% of iron-rich aluminosilicates, some 10% of magnesium sulphate (kieserite), some 5% of calcium carbonate (calcite) and nearly 5% of iron oxides (haematite, magnetite, goethite). The mafic nature of the given fine fraction, widespread everywhere, and its probable primary rocks may testify against large-scale planetary differentiation, similar to that on the Earth.

similar to that on the Earth.

The total amount of oxides in Martian rocks, calculated on the basis of Table 1.4.3, is 92–93%, which presupposes the presence of carbonates, nitrates and lightweight elements (e.g. Na). Mass-spectrometry data obtained from Vikings 1 and 2 have shown (qualitatively) the availability of water. The high sulphur content suggests the presence of sulphates, although other sulphur compounds cannot be excluded.

Iron in Martian rocks is evidently present in a highly oxidized form (from red to yellow in colour), covering the surface grains by a very thin and intermittent layer. Iron should also be present in the magnetic fraction, taking up at least 3% by mass (most likely in the form of magnetite). The bulk of iron is evidently present in a silicate form.

The sulphur content in Martian regolith is one or two orders of magnitude higher than in terrestrial and lunar rocks, but close to chondritic meteorites. Perhaps sulphur is a constituent in Na, Mg, Ca and Fe sulphates or sulphides, but not of pyrite.

The potassium content in Martian regolith is low (less than 0.25%), i.e. at least five to eight times lower than in the Earth's crust (1.25–2.1%). Mass-spectrometric measurements in the Martian atmosphere [21] gave approximately 1.6% of argon in relation to CO_2. This is equivalent to an amount of 2.5 kg m^{-2} for the mean partial pressure at the surface (about 6×10^2 Pa), or a total amount in the atmosphere of 3.7×10^{14} kg, i.e. nearly 0.6% of the ^{40}Ar available in the Earth's atmosphere. Taking into account the difference in the mass of the planet, it might be assumed that the degree of outgassing on Mars is 20 times lower than on the Earth. However, if the potassium content in the Martian crust is as low as in the regolith, then the degree of outgassing on Mars will be only three to four times lower than on the Earth.

It is necessary to know the rôle of S, Na and CO_2 to determine the mineral composition and the type of regolith at Viking landing sites. To construct a model of the rock (to fill up the 8% unaccounted for by oxides) the experimenters [20] assume the availability of 0.4% of Na, in NaCl, 4.4% of CO_2 in $CaCO_3$ and 3.2% of H_2O as a structural constituent.

The investigations of regolith content lead one to the conclusion that on Mars' surface mafic parent material is widespread. The interaction of this material with water resulted in the formation of iron-rich aluminosilicates.

1.4.4 MANTLE AND CORE MATTER

The chemical composition of Mars and even of its crust is not known. However, attempts have been made to estimate it, proceeding from the meagre data available on the composition of the atmosphere and the surface. In principal, the composition of terrestrial planets may be roughly estimated, knowing the correlation of only some key elements. Such calculations for the Earth, the Moon and the eucrite parent body have been made in [8, 22]. Proceeding from the content of U, Fe, K and Ti or ^{36}Ar, Morgan and Anders [22] have estimated the distribution of 83 elements on Mars. The values of 0.028 p.p.m. for U and 62 p.p.m. for K were taken on the basis of the ratio K/U = 2200 from orbital gamma-ray measurements. 26.72% for Fe from geophysical data and 0.0014 p.p.m. for Ti from the ^{36}Ar and ^{40}Ar content measured by Vikings 1 and 2.

Table 1.4.4 — Composition of the Martian mantle (percentage by mass)

Oxides	Mars		Earth
	[22]	[23]	[24]
SiO_2	41.60	40.04	45.16
TiO_2	0.33	0.63	0.71
Al_2O_3	6.39	3.14	3.54
Cr_2O_3	0.65	0.38	0.43
Fe_2O_3	—	0.41	0.46
FeO	15.85	18.48	8.04
MnO	0.15	0.12	0.14
NiO	—	0.18	0.20
MgO	29.78	33.22	37.47
CaO	5.15	2.73	3.08
Na_2O	0.10	0.51	0.57
K_2O	0.01	0.12	0.13
P_2O_5	—	0.05	0.06
$Mg/(Mg + Fe)$	0.77	0.67	0.89

Table 1.4.4 gives the chemical composition of the Martian mantle estimated by Morgan and Anders [22] and by McGetchin and Smith [23]. For comparison, a model of the Earth's mantle, calculated by Green and Ringwood [24], is given. The composition [22] in Table 1.4.4 is much richer in refractory elements (Ca and Al) and more depleted in alkaline elements (K and Na) than the composition which is given by the higher content of U and lower ratio of K/U adopted in model [23]. The absence of such components as NiO and Fe_2O_3 in the model [22] is in the author's opinion quite doubtful since the high FeO content in the Martian mantle and the oxidizing effect of material enriched with volatiles in the final stage of accretion may ensure the availability of considerable amounts of NiO and Fe_2O_3. The high ratio of Mg/(Mg + Fe), 0.77, is indicative of an essentially less oxidized planet, which has been shown in some other papers (e.g. 0.67 [23], 0.5 [25], 0.68 [26]. In some papers an attempt has been made to evaluate the mineral composition of Mars. These evaluations are very rough as they are based on many assumptions (the content of U, S and other elements, the density of the core and mantle, the character of chemical processes taking place in the interior, etc.). Table 1.4.5 shows the mineral composition of Mars calculated by Morgan and Anders [22] who estimated two alternatives, proceeding from different uranium contents: 0.028 p.p.m. and 0.046 p.p.m. The alternative with a lower uranium content is preferred. In accordance with experiments [27] the authors suggested that a composition similar to that in Table 1.4.4 (depleted in sulphur and enriched with aluminium) is formed by spinels and not oxides in the stable phase at a pressure of at least approximately 3×10^9 Pa (corresponding to the upper mantle up to 250 km deep). Therefore, Table 1.4.5 gives the mineral composition for two phases.

Table 1.4.5 — Mineral composition of Mars (percentage by mass) [22]

Minerals, metals	0.028 p.p.m U		0.046 p.p.m U	
	Oxides	Oxides→spinel	Oxides	Oxides→spinel
Mantle (81%)				
Chromite	0.68	0.68	0.64	0.64
Ilmenite	0.44	0.44	0.72	0.72
Pyroxene	0.72	0.72	1.14	1.14
Diopside	15.12 ⎱ 19.52	15.12 ⎱ 19.52	24.94 ⎱ 32.07	24.94 ⎱ 32.07
Hedenbergite	4.40 ⎰	4.40 ⎰	7.13 ⎰	7.13 ⎰
Pyrope	20.03 ⎱ 25.84	16.75 ⎱ 21.62	33.05 ⎱ 42.49	0.90 ⎱ 1.15
Almandite	5.81 ⎰	4.87 ⎰	9.44 ⎰	0.25 ⎰
Forsterite	39.33 ⎱ 50.72	43.02 ⎱ 55.48	1.78 ⎱ 2.29	37.95 ⎱ 48.79
Phaelite	11.40 ⎰	32.46 ⎰	0.51 ⎰	10.84 ⎰
Pyroclase	1.64 ⎱ 2.11		16.08 ⎱ 20.67	
Wastite	0.47 ⎰		4.59 ⎰	
Spinel		1.23 ⎱ 1.58		12.06 ⎱ 15.51
Harzinite		0.35 ⎰		3.45 ⎰
Density ($\times 10^3$ kg m^{-3})	3.542	3.526	3.65	3.49
Core (19%)				
Metal $\left\{\begin{array}{l}\text{Fe}\\\text{Ni}\\\text{Co}\end{array}\right.$	82.02 ⎱ 7.99 ⎰ 90.38 0.37		75.85 ⎱ 7.60 ⎰ 84.27 0.35	
Troilite $\left\{\begin{array}{l}\text{Fe}\\\text{S}\end{array}\right.$	6.11 ⎱ 9.62 3.51 ⎰		9.99 ⎱ 15.73 5.74 ⎰	
Density ($\times 10^3$ kg m^{-3})	7.46			

Mars has a relatively small core (around 12% of the planet's mass). The core is probably solid. This is proved also by the virtual absence of a magnetic field. It follows from Table 1.4.5 that the Martian core consists of about 90% metals and about 10% troilite, but the content of sulphur in the core is still debatable. In the model of [22] a low sulphur content (about 3.5%) in the core is adopted, while in other papers [28, 29] a much higher sulphur content is assumed.

The mafic nature of soil and underlying rock samples studied by Viking 1 and 2 imposes certain constraints on the scale of planetary differentiation. By the intensity of volcanism, Mars apparently takes an intermediate position between the Moon and the Earth. At present it is not so active as the Earth, but not so cooled down as the Moon. Estimations have shown that the thermal flow on Mars' surface also lies between the corresponding values for the Moon and the Earth, i.e. approximately 0.04 J m^{-2} s^{-1} [30].

Proceeding from the thermal model of Mars, developed by Toksöz and Johnson [31], with a mean uranium concentration of nearly 0.03 p.p.m., a solid 200 m lithosphere should form, the thickness of which is in agreement with the depth needed, according to hydrostatic laws, for uplift of magma to the top of such volcanoes as Olympus Mons.

1.4.5 ATMOSPHERE AND VOLATILE COMPONENTS ON MARS

Mars is known to have a rarefied atmosphere. The atmospheric pressure on its surface is about 6×10^2 Pa. The chemical composition of the Martian atmosphere is given in Table 1.4.6 [21] which shows that the basic components there are CO_2, N_2, Ar and O_2, i.e. the same as in the Earth's atmosphere. But the relative amounts of atmospheric components differs from the Earth, which may be explained by several factors: (1) the lower temperature on the surface at which most active components may be bound in rocks, (2) the lower initial contribution of volatiles (probably due to the small size of the planet, (3) the incomplete outgassing of the interior, (4) the loss of volatiles in the course of the evolution of the planet.

Table 1.4.6 — Chemical composition of the Martian atmosphere [21]

Component	Content (%)	Component	Content (p.p.m.)
CO_2	95	CH_4	120
N_2	2–3	Ne	20
Ar	1–2	Kr	0.3
O_2	0.1–0.4	Xe	1.5
CO	<0.1		
Water vapour, H_2O	<0.1		

(p.p.m. = parts per million)

The differences in the isotopic composition of the atmospheric components of Mars and the Earth given in Table 1.4.7 [21] may be attributed to the above factors and particularly to (2) and (3). The depletion of the Martian atmosphere in cosmogenic nuclides ^{36}Ar and ^{38}Ar with respect to the radiogenic nuclide ^{40}Ar is particularly obvious.

Table 1.4.7 — Isotopic composition of the Martian atmosphere [21]

Isotopic ratio	Mars	Earth	Enrichment on Mars (%)
$^{13}C/^{12}C$	0.0118 ± 0.0012	0.0112	+10
$^{15}N/^{14}N$	$0.0050 - 0.0064$	0.00368	+36–74
$^{18}O/^{16}O$	0.00189 ± 0.0002	0.00204	−10
$^{36}Ar/^{38}Ar$	4–5	5.3	—
$^{36}Ar/^{40}Ar$	0.000036 ± 0.0006	0.00301	740 times

The Martian atmosphere is rather dry. The water vapour content there varies from 8 to 80 μm of settled water (depending on the latitude, season and time of the day). The comparison of various mechanisms responsible for the gas régime on the planet has revealed the important rôle of the mantle in the formation of the atmosphere. Some contradictions in the isotopic ratios obtained (in particular, the increased $^{15}N/^{14}N$ ratio, while the $^{36}Ar/^{40}Ar$ ratio is considerably lower than on the

Earth) and some other considerations (e.g. the trapping of volatiles in the near-surface layer of permafrost) prevent one from accurately evaluating the outgassing of the Martian interior, although it is obviously much smaller than on the Earth. This becomes clear if one takes into account that no large-scale events typical of global tectonic processes were discovered on Mars (in comparison to the Earth), while the activity of Mars' mantle is obviously insufficient to induce the developed drift of continents or the shift and compression of crustal plates.

Proceeding from the rate of H and Ar^{36} release, Anders and Owen [8], evaluated the full outgassing of water vapour on Mars, which turned out to be equivalent to the partial pressure (about 3.5×10^4 Pa), corresponding to a liquid water layer 9.4 m thick covering the whole surface of the planet. Using data on the isotopic composition of nitrogen, and considering that Mars became outgassed to the same degree as the Earth, they also calculated the maximum pressure of the atmosphere which existed in the past. It came to some 5.25×10^4 Pa of CO_2 and 8×10^2 of N_2. But Mars evidently became outgassed to a much lesser extent than the Earth. Therefore, a more realistic evaluation will be nearly 1.4×10^4 Pa of CO_2 and 2×10^2 Pa of N_2. Such pressure was more than enough for liquid water to exist on the Martian surface in a 9 m layer.

How can we explain the different content of volatiles on the various bodies? Proceeding from his condensation model, Lewis [25, 32, 33] assumes a simple correlation of the volatile content with heliocentric distance. But the observed compositions of planets do not fit into these assumptions. The most obvious mechanism is the great gravitational cross-section of capture of large bodies, which are capable of adding the last accreting material rich in volatiles [8]. Besides, the actual mechanism determining the volatile content turned out to be more complicated, since not all small bodies are depleted in volatiles (for instance, chondrites and sherghotites are not poorer in volatiles than the Earth).

1.4.6 GENERAL PROBLEMS OF THE EXPLORATION OF MARS

As mentioned above, in some planetary properties and the character of its geological processes, Mars takes up an intermediate position between the Earth and the Moon, which is an example of the most ancient stage of the Earth's formation. To know the laws of the evolution of matter on Mars and its differentiation are of utmost importance for specifying conditions determining the character of the general development of planetary bodies by the 'terrestrial' or 'lunar' ways. (It may be expected that the 'Martian' stage in the Earth's evolution follows the 'lunar' stage). Studying the Martian stage is also very important for extending our ideas of the Earth's history. The key problems of its study and, particularly, of elucidating the degree of differentiation of the Martain crust, are evaluation of the total amount of water and other volatiles, the search for the most differentiated rocks (such as granites), the search for sedimentary rocks (as a medium for determining the possible existence of the biosphere in the past), and the search for modern volcanic activity, etc. The apparent contradiction between the present-day dry rarefied atmosphere of Mars and the evidence for flowing water on the Martian surface in the past poses the question of what mechanisms may cause sharp climatic variations on planets. This problem is closely associated with the question of the existence of any life-forms on Mars in the past or at present.

The problem of the existence of life on Mars is of paramount scientific importance. If it turned out to be possible to find traces of living systems on the planet, then we would have proof of the possibility of life on planets other than the Earth, and open up ways for understanding its origin and evolution in the Solar System.

Analysis of the physical conditions on Mars, and their comparison with the conditions on the Earth, shows that life on the Martian surface may be represented by microscopic forms confined only to some localities (in places of the highest humidity and temperature and the lowest radiation levels, etc.).

The first attempts to detect life on Mars made under the Viking programme encountered a number of difficulties and did not provide an unambiguous answer [34]. When evaluating the results of this search on the whole, two factors should be stressed: firstly, in this research use was made only of some potential possibilities for detecting life on Mars; secondly, the results of biological experiments do not rule out the presence of living systems on Mars even in the explored Martian regions with unfavourable conditions.

The problem of the search for life on Mars proved to be more complicated than had been expected earlier. Future missions will require still more complex experiments to confirm the existence of life on Mars in the past or at present.

Recent investigations of Mars by Soviet and American space probes have given answers to many questions, but they also have revealed many new phenomena which have not been adequately explained so far [35]. In the geological field, further development of our views about Mars requires the solution of the following problems:

The character of matter in the Martian crust and its differentiation

What type of differentiation (terrestrial or lunar) prevailed on Mars? Do the relics of the earlier Martian crust have an anorthosite rock composition? Are there granites and other marginal products of the differentiation of matter; a question which is important for resolving the problems of the granitization of the Earth's crust? What is the rôle of meteorite impacts in the Martian crust formation?

The history of activity in the Martian interior

When did the continental crust and volcanoes of the northern plains form? What is the absolute age of Mars' shield volcanism and are there traces of modern volcanism such as is manifested on the Earth, but evidently subsided on the Moon more than 3000 million years ago? What is the palaeomagnetic history of Mars?

The rôle of volatiles, primarily water, in the deep-seated transformations of primordial rocks on Mars

The manifestations of deep-seated processes and ore formation involving water are characteristics of the Earth, but are not observed in lunar rock samples.

What are the specific features of the metamorphic processes on Mars, and are there manifestations of metasomatism and hydrothermal oreformation processes?

The rôle of water in transforming the Martian surface, the specific features of the
outgassing of the planet's interior and the history of its atmosphere
What is the degree of chemical weathering on Mars? Were there warmer and more
humid epochs on Mars, and are they connected with changing acticity of the Sun and
the atmospheric composition of Mars? Are there sedimentary rocks of the terrestrial
type – clays, limestones, soluble salts, etc.? What is the degree of the rock oxidation
on the Martian surface and what process gave rise to its oxidation? Detailed analysis
of the Martian atmosphere.

The search for traces of bygone life
Are there traces of biogenic formations on Mars – the remnants of microorganisms,
life activity – morphological, mineralogical, chemical and isotopic? Are there the
traces of processes akin to the terrestrial soil formation?

REFERENCES

[1] V. I. Moroz, *Physics of the planet Mars*, (In Russian.) Moscow, Nauka, p. 351 (1978).

[2] M. Ya. Marov, *Planets of the Solar System*, (In Russian.) Moscow, Nauka, p. 254, 1981.

[3] T. A. Mutch, R. E. Arvidson, and J. W. Head, *The geology of Mars.* Princeton University Press, p. 262 (1976).

[4] Reports, *Science,* **194**, 57 (1976).

[5] K. P. Florensky, A. T. Basilevsky, and R. O. Kuzmin, *Icarus*, **26**, 219 (1975).

[6] K. P. Florensky, A. T. Bazilevsky, and R. O. Kuzmin, In *Tectonics, structural geology and planetology.* (In Russian.) Moscow, Nauka, p. 281 (1976).

[7] R. O. Kuzmin, *Voprosy Kriologii*, **6**, 7 (In Russian.) (1977).

[8] E. Anders and T. Owen, *Science,* **198**, 453 (1977).

[9] R. W. Shorthill, H. J. Moore, and R. F. Scott, *Science,* **194**, 91 (1976).

[10] Yu. A. Surkov, L. P. Moskalyova and F. F. Kirnozov, Paper presented at the 18th COSPAR session, Varna, Bulgaria, p. 48 (1975).

[11] Yu. A. Surkov, *Gamma-ray spectrometry in space research,* (In Russian.) Moscow, Atomizdat, p. 209 (1977).

[12] Yu. A. Surkov, L. P. Moskalyova and O. S. Manvelyan, In *proc. 11th Lunar and Planet Sci. Conf.* Houston, USA, p. 669 (1980).

[13] G. R. Hunt, L. M. Logan, and J. W. Salisbury, *Icarus,* **18**, 459 (1973).

[14] Yu. A. Surkov, F. F. Kirnozov, and V. N. Glazov, *Kosmich. Issled.,* **14**, 704 (In Russian.) (1976).

[15] A. A. Smyslov, *Uranium and thorium in the Earth's crust.* (In Russian.) Leningrad, Nedra, p. 231 (1974).

[16] A. V. Ronov and A. A. Yaroshevsky, In *The Earth's tectonics.* (In Russian.) Moscow, Nauka, p. 379 (1978).

[17] V. L. Barsukov, L. V. Dmitriyev, and A. V. Garanin, In *Soil from the Moon's highland region,* (In Russian.) Moscow, Nauka, p. 18 (1979).

[18] J. Trombka, In *Cosmochemistry of the Moon and planets.* (In Russian.) Moscow, Nauka, p. 128 (1975).

[19] A. K. Baird, P. Toulmin, and B. C. Clark, *Science,* **194**, 81 (1976).

[20] B. C. Clark, A. K. Baird, and P. Toulmin, *Science, **194***, 1283 (1976).

[21] T. Owen, K. Biemann, and D. Ruchneck, *J. Geophys. Res., **82***, 4635 (1977).

[22] J. W. Morgan and E. Anders, *Geochim. et Cosmochim. Acta*, **43**, 1601 (1979).

[23] T.R. McGetchin and J. K. Smith, *Icarus,* **34**, 512 (1978).

[24] D. H. Green and A. E. Ringwood, *J. Geophys. Res., **68***, 937 (1963).

[25] J. S. Lewis, *Earth and Planet. Sci. Lett.,* **15**, 286 (1972).

[26] A. E. Ringwood and S. P. Clark, *Nature,* **234**, 89 (1971).

[27] A. E. Ringwood, *Icarus,* **28**, 325 (1978).

[28] A. G. W. Cameron, *Moon,* **17**, 377 (1973).

[29] P. Goldreich, *Mon. Not. Roy. Astron. Soc.,* **130**, 159 (1965).

[30] M. N. Toksöz and A. T. Hsui, *Icarus,* **34**, 537 (1978).

[31] M. N. Toksöz and D. H. Johnson, In *Cosmochemistry of the moon and planets.* (In Russian.) Moscow, Nauka, p. 210 (1975).

[32] J. S. Lewis, *Icarus*, **16**, 241 (1972).

[33] J. S. Lewis, *Annu. Rev. Phys. Chem.,* **24**, 339 (1973).

[34] H. P. Klein, M. N. Horowitz and G. V. Vevin, *Science,* **194**, 99 (1976).

[35] K. P. Florensky, A. T. Bazilevsky and G. A. Burba, *An outline of comparative planetology.* (In Russian.) Moscow, Nauka, p. 326 (1981).

1.5 Planetary satellites

Our ideas of planetary satellites have been considerably expanded during the last two decades due to intensive exploration of the Solar System by space probes. A complete history of the Solar System, in particular of our planet, requires data on natural space bodies at different stages of their evolution. The data on the terrestrial planets are not sufficient, while what we know of the outer planets remains rather limited. This explains the growing interest in smaller bodies such as planetary satellites, asteroids and meteorites.

The past history of astronomical observations has only succeeded in discovering the largest satellites and describing their orbits. Modern investigations of small bodies (in particular, planetary satellites) by space probes have shown each to have a face of its own and its own history which seems to be genetically related to that of their parent planet.

Some 54 planetary satellites have been discovered so far. The Earth has a single satellite, Mars two, Jupiter 16, Saturn 17, Uranus 15, Neptune two (possibly three), and Pluto one. Table 1.5.1 lists the physical characteristics and parameters of the satellites' orbits [1–3]. On the basis of their orbits, the satellites are subdivided into regular (moving prograde in nearly circular orbits that have very small inclinations to the equatorial plane of the planet) and irregular (moving either prograde or retrograde in elliptical orbits inclined at a considerable angle to the equatorial plane). The Moon has long been considered an irregular satellite on account of the anomalously large ratio of its mass to that of the Earth (1:81.3), but recent observations of the Pluto/Charon system have shown that Charon is certainly the largest satellite in proportion to the size of its parent planet anywhere in the Solar System.

The sizes of planetary satellites were originally determined visually from ground-based telescopic observations [4], by recording the time of the passage of the satellite in front of a bright star or by measuring the time the satellite takes to pass behind the Moon [5–7], from estimates of the albedo [8–11] and by other methods. Mass and density can in most cases also be determined by ground-based techniques [12–14]. However, more accurate information has been obtained from Mariner 9, Pioneer 10, Voyagers 1 and 2 and other space vehicles. Below we discuss in detail only the larger planetary satellites or those likely to become the subject of

Table 1.5.1 — Physical parameters of the largest planetary satellites and their orbits

Planets	Satellite	Radius (km)	Mass (×10^{20} kg)	Density (×10^3 kg m^{-3})	Orbit radius (×10^3 km)	Revolution period (days)	Eccentricity†	Inclination (degrees)
Earth	Moon	1737.4	735	3.34	384.4	27.3217	0.05490	5.1
Mars	Phobos	13×11×9			9.38	0.3189	0.0150	1.02
	Deimos	8×6×5			23.46	1.262	0.0008	1.82
Jupiter	I Io	1821	892	3.56 ± 0.10	421.6	1.769	0.004	0.04
	II Europa	1565	487	3.04 ± 0.75	670.9	3.551	0.009	0.47
	III Ganymede	2634	1495	1.94 ± 0.08	1070	7.155	0.002	0.21
	IV Callisto	2403	1067	1.82 ± 0.34	1880	16.689	0.007	0.51
	V Amalthea	131×73×67			181.3	0.498	0.003	0.45
	VI Himalia	85			11480	250.6	0.158	27.6
	VII Elara	40			11737	259.7	0.207	24.8
	VIII Pasiphae	18			23500	735	0.38	145
	IX Sinope	14			23700	758	0.28	153
	X Lysithea	12			11720	259.2	0.107	29.0
	XI Carme	15			22600	692	0.21	164
	XII Ananke	10			21200	631	0.17	147
	XIII Leda	5			11 094	238.7	0.148	26.1
	XVI Metis	20			128.0	0.295	0.000	0.0
	XV Adrastea	13×10× 8			129.09	0.298	0.000	0.0
	XIV Thebe	55×50×45			221.9	0.675	0.013	0.9
Saturn	I Mimas	199	0.38	1.2	185.5	0.942	0.020	1.52
	II Enceladus	249	0.81	1.2	238.0	1.370	0.004	0.02
	III Tethys	523	6.25	1.0	294.7	1.888	0.000	1.86
	IV Dione	560	11.6	1.6	377.4	2.737	0.002	0.02
	V Rhea	764	22.7	1.2	527.0	4.518	0.001	0.35
	VI Titan	2575	1370	1.9	1221.9	15.945	0.029	0.33
	VII Hyperion	180×140×113	1.14	—	1481.1	21.277	0.104	0.43
	VIII Iapetus	718	18.9	1.2	3561.3	79.331	0.028	7.52

	Name	Diameter (km)			Distance	Period	Eccentricity	Inclination
IX	Phoebe	110	—	—	12 954.0	550.4	0.163	175
X	Janus	97×95×77			151.5	0.695	0.007	0.1
XI	Epimetheus	69×55×55			151.4	0.694	0.009	0.3
XII	Helene	18×17×14			377.4	2.737	0.005	0.2
XIII	Telesto	15×13×8			294.7	1.888	0.0	2
XIV	Calypso	15×8×8			294.7	1.888	0.0	2
XV	Atlas	19×17×13			137.7	0.602	0.002	0.3
XVI	Prometheus	74×50×34			139.4	0.613	0.004	0.0
XVII	Pandora	55×44×31			141.7	0.629	0.004	0.1
Uranus								
I	Ariel	579	13.0	1.6	191.0	2.520	0.003	0.0
II	Umbriel	585	13.0	1.5	266.3	4.144	0.004	0.0
III	Titania	789	42.5	1.9	435.0	8.706	0.002	0.0
IV	Oberon	761	29.0	1.5	583.5	13.463	0.001	0.0
V	Miranda	240×234×233	0.87	1.5	129.4	1.4135	0.017	0.0
VI	Cordelia	13			49.5	0.330		
VII	Ophelia	15			53.8	0.372		
VIII	Bianca	21			59.2	0.433		
IX	Cressida	31			61.8	0.463		
X	Desdemona	27			62.7	0.475		
XI	Juliet	42			64.4	0.493		
XII	Portia	54			66.1	0.513		
XIII	Rosalind	27			69.9	0.558		
XIV	Belinda	33			75.3	0.622		
XV	Puck	77			86.0	0.762		
Neptune	Triton	1750±250?	1285	—	355.3	5.877	0.000	159.9
	Nereid	345±180?	—	—	5510.0	359.881	0.749	27.2
Pluto	Charon	606			19	6.3867		

†The orbital elements, in particular the eccentricities, of some satellites are all subject to considerable variations.

*The orbital inclinations are referred to the plane of the equator of the primary for inner satellites and to the orbital planes of their primaries for outer areas.

Note: All data on satellite diameters taken from Report of the IAU/IAG/COSPAR Working Group on Cartographic Coordinates and Rotational Elements of Planets and Satellites : 1988.

practical investigations by space probes in the near future. Some of them (the satellites of Mars, Jupiter, Saturn and Uranus) have already been scrutinized by spacecraft. Some, such as Titan, attract ever increasing attention. The interest in the Moon seems to continue, although it is fairly well-known at present.

1.5.1 THE MOON

The Moon has been the subject of special attention for the last two decades. Since it is fairly large, a study of its internal structure and the composition of its crust have provided new insights into the formation of the terrestrial planets, the Earth included. Investigations of the topography, as well as the structure and properties of lunar rocks, have clarified conditions under which the surface of small bodies devoid of atmospheres formed (planetary satellites, asteroids and meteorites). Finally, the study of rock composition and radioactivity has provided important information on cosmic rays, meteoritic flux and solar flares in the remote past. For these reasons the Moon is being intensively studied, especially as it is relatively close to the Earth. The Moon is a natural testing ground for the study of celestial bodies in the Solar System and outer space. About 50 missions, of various kinds, have been launched to the Moon, orbiting around it, landing on its surface and bringing back lunar rock samples from areas of particular interest. The vast amount of essentially new scientific information (especially as regards the lunar soils) will take a long time to process and interpret. At the same time these investigations have updated the main physical characteristics of the Moon (Table 1.5.2).

Table 1.5.2—Main characteristics of the Moon and its orbit

Mass	7.35×10^{22} kg
Mean diameter	3475 km
Mean density	3.34×10^3 kg m^{-3}
Mean distance from the Earth:	384 000 km
perigee	356 410 km
apogee	406 700 km
Period of revolution around the Earth	27.32166 days
Axial rotation period	27.32166 days
Axial inclination of the equator referred to the ecliptic	1° 32′
Orbital inclination	5° 09′
Orbital eccentricity	0.0549
Acceleration due to gravity	1.62 ms^{-2}
Surface temperatures:	
day	407 K
night	120 K
Pressure at the surface (at the morning terminator)	10^{-9} Pa
Intensity of magnetic field (in the wake of the Earth)	4 nT
Geological age	4,400–4,600 million years

Origin and formation of the Moon

Despite much new factual information and considerable progress in understanding the Moon's history, its origin remains a mystery. Paradoxically, each of the long-established hypotheses has received some additional support. There are four principal hypotheses of the lunar origin: the fission hypothesis, according to which the Moon formed from one or more fragments that broke away from the Earth's mantle; a common or joint-origin hypothesis whereby the Moon and the Earth formed as a binary system through accretion of common parent material; capture theories, according to which the Moon had formed elsewhere in the Solar System to be subsequently captured by the Earth; and finally the accretion of the Moon by the fusion of the components in a planetesimal ring which formerly encircled the Earth.

Each of these hypotheses faces a number of serious difficulties, which has resulted in a prolonged period of indecision as to which is most plausible. Data acquired during the past few years allow a more critical examination of these hypotheses, additional constraints being placed on the range of various concepts of the Moon's origin.

The study of lunar rock samples returned to Earth by Soviet and American spacecraft has not given rise to serious objections to the fission hypothesis put forward by G. Darwin as long ago as 1880. Numerous differences in the bulk chemical compositions of the Earth and the Moon, and a significant depletion in lunar siderophile elements , which are satisfactorily accounted for by supposing the Moon to have torn away from the Earth's mantle as a consequence for the Earth's rotation, still induce a number of researchers to support this theory of lunar origin. In particular, the older objections based on difficulties with the energy balance have been overcome by introducing a long (500 million year) phase of geosynchronism — a synchronous rotation of the Earth—Moon system with a distance of about three Earth radii between them. The introduction of such a phase has explained a number of features in the geochemical, morphological, and magnetic history of the Moon. However, the fact that the Moon is itself a differentiated body and has a thermal history of its own, unlike that of the Earth, is not in favour of the Moon having formed by separation from the Earth.

The joint-origin hypothesis developed by Kuiper [15] supposes the Earth–Moon system to be similar to systems of binary stars — two bodies that have formed in close proximity to each other by accretion of similar parent material. Many processes then become understandable, but the low lunar density as compared with that of the Earth remains a problem. The difficulty can be obviated by postulating a physical fractionation during the accretion that would concentrate metallic iron on the Earth, but the mechanism needed to achieve this is not obvious. In the opinion of the proponents of the theory, the close relation between these two simultaneously forming planetary bodies is manifested, for instance, in the coincident isotopic compositions of oxygen in lunar and terrestrial rocks, while that found in meteorites is different.

The capture model put forward by Urey [16] considers the Moon as a relic of the process of generation of primary bodies in the Solar System by which the existing terrestrial planets were formed by the complex mechanisms of accretion and fractionation. The principal argument in favour of the hypothesis rests on differences in the Fe/Si abundance ratio, which until recently had been thought to be much lower in the Sun compared with the Earth and chondrites. The author of the hypothesis explained the low lunar density by the low Fe/Si ratio similar to that postulated for the

Sun and probably of the material in the protoplanetary nebula. However, recent studies have shown that the abundance of iron on the Sun is much larger than estimated previously, so the argument fails. Finally, the very act of capture has an extremely low probability of accurrence.

The hypothesis of the lunar origin by accretion of a planetesimal ring was first proposed by Öpik [17]. He envisaged the ring as somewhat similar to Saturn's rings but much more massive, revolving about the Earth at a distance of 5–8 terrestrial radii from the Earth's surface. In a further development of Öpik's idea, Ringwood [18] assumed the Earth to have possessed a massive primary atmosphere at the later stages of accretion hot enough for a substantial portion of silicates to evaporate selectively. Subsequently the atmosphere dissipated as the Sun passed through a phase of high activity. The decomposition and dissipation of a primary atmosphere with the ensuing expansion and cooling had condensed the silicates as a planetesimal ring around the Earth. The ring was unstable, so its particles coalesced, forming the Moon. A number of facts support the Opik–Ringwood hypothesis. Thus, the low density and some heterogeneity typical of the Moon and evident in its moment of inertia are compatible with its formation out of silicate planetesimals. The extremely low abundance of siderophile elements, together with the absence of a metallic core on the Moon, indicates the removal of some of the iron and practically all the noble metals from the parent material prior to accretion — these elements have obviously remained on the Earth. The Moon is considerably depleted in volatiles as compared with their probable abundance in the Solar System. The loss of these elements is readily understandable if the planetesimal ring had been subjected to high temperatures. On the other hand, the appreciably increased content of refractory elements in lunar rocks provides an additional piece of evidence in favour of fractionation going on during the high-temperature stage in the evolution of planetesimals.

A number of the accretion models of lunar origin developed in recent times involve different mechanisms accounting for volatile depletion on the Moon. Thus, the dynamic model for the formation of the Moon from a circumterrestrial swarm of minor bodies assumes its active accumulation began when the mass of a growing Earth had reached about half of its present value. According to Ruskol's calculations [19], the circumterrestrial swarm was sufficiently transparent at the outer margin for volatile atoms released by evaporation during the collision of solid particles and larger bodies to be partly removed from the swarm by the solar wind. At the same time, the inner, less transparent portion of the swarm would retain most elements owing to subsequent condensation of the evaporated atoms on solid particles. In this way the removal of volatiles from the outer portion of the swarm, a source of lunar material at the later stages of the Moon's formation, must have produced some volatile depletion on the present Moon. There are other explanations of the principal differences in composition (hence in density) between the Earth and the Moon, all of them ultimately in favour of the accretion model.

There is no generally accepted hypothesis as to the Moon's evolution subsequent to its formation. However, most investigators agree on one point; namely, that there have been several periods of activity on the Moon. Evidence for this is found, in particular, in rock age data from samples brought back to the Earth from a number of lunar areas. The earlier periods are related to accretion, when large-scale differentiation of material and formation of a primitive crust took place; the crust can now be found in the highland areas. The later periods are thought to be associated with locally heated material and its local differentiation due to radiogenic heating. All the larger lunar mare basins formed during this period.

Various hypotheses have been put forward to explain the heating and differentiation of material during the early period of the Moon's existence due to rapid heat generation. Heat could be produced directly during accretion by converting the kinetic energy of small particles or planetesimals into thermal energy. However, with the above mechanism of heat generation, the accretion rate becomes an important factor. If the accretion was slow the heat would dissipate into interplanetary space at the rate at which it was generated. Extensive heating of a large mass of material is most unlikely. If accretion is supposed to have occurred rapidly, most of the heat must have remained in the Moon. In that case, according to calculations, conservation of accretion energy may have produced melting in the 300 to 500 km thick outer layer of the Moon.

In recent years the rapid accretion hypothesis has attracted increasing numbers of supporters, so that the heat-generation mechanism due to accretion energy seems to be the most probable for the early history of the Moon.

Isotopic estimates for the age of impact metamorphism have led to the conclusion that meteoritic bombardment, which is a natural sequel to the accretion of material at the preplanetary stage to form planetary bodies, was at a maximum about 4000 million years ago, when large multi-ring basins, like the Mare Orientale and Mare Imbrium, formed during a relatively short period. The same period saw the last stages of the ascent and crystallization of melts that were the strongly fractionated remains of a molten envelope. Rocks from the melts enriched with alkalines, radioactive and rare earth elements and phosphorus occur in the southern part of Mare Imbrium and in the area of ejecta southwest of it, as revealed by gamma-ray surveys from orbit. Soon after the formation of Mare Orientale the flux of impacting bodies rapidly decreased and a second, long stage in the geological history of the Moon began — the mare stage associated with the filling of the lunar basins by high-iron basaltic rocks. Lunar volanism was not vigorous, as is indicated by the relatively small volume of erupted mare basalts; less than 1% of the volume of the crust. As distinct from continental rocks, the mare basalts have largely retained primordial magmatogenic features owing to a considerable reduction in impact metamorphism during that epoch. Thermodynamic investigations into the distribution patterns in olivines of various origins for elements of the iron group provide evidence that the mare basalts formed under more reducing conditions, and at lower temperatures and partial oxygen pressure as compared with the highland rocks. An important feature in lunar geology is the absence of a direct relationship between an impact-explosion phenomenon producing a basin and a volcanic process filling it with mare-type basalts. This conclusion follows from the absolute-age determinations for lunar samples indicating a sizeable time gap between the two processes. For example, it is 300 million years for Mare Serenitatis and 800 to 1000 million years for Mare Imbrium.

Heat generation at the early stage of the Moon's existence could take place due to the solar wind (much stronger at the time) and the decay of relatively short-lived nuclides (for instance, [26]Al).

An analysis of the orbital gamma-ray studies of the lunar surface, as well as of the results of laboratory studies of the rock radioactivity, have enabled an evaluation of the mean contents of Th, U and K both for the 60 km crust 1.08, 0.28 and 700 p.p.m. by weight, respectively) and for the entire Moon (approximately 0.16, 0.045 and 120 p.p.m.) [29]. These data are in good agreement with the estimates for the contents of lunar heat-generating elements obtained from direct measurements of the heat flow in the surface layer by Apollos 15 and 17.

The decrease of magmatic activity at the Moon's surface in the post-mare stage in conjunction with slow rates of subsequent exogenous reworking over 3000–4000 million years have helped preserve geological features and their constituent rocks that had formed at the earlier stages of the Moon's evolution 4000–4500 million years ago. The principal features of the chemical composition of lunar regolith in various areas are largely controlled by the composition of underlying rocks. This is appreciably affected, as has been mentioned above, by the complex of processes associated with meteoritic bombardment.

However, all these heat sources could be of importance only during the first 500 million years. The entire subsequent thermal history of the Moon was obviously associated with radiogenic heating. The generation of heat by the decay of natural radioactive elements — uranium, thorium, and potassium — has been covered by a number of authors [20–25].

To sum up, the lunar thermal history may have looked as follows. According to current theories, the initial stage was characterized by high temperatures due to the Moon being heated during accretion. These temperatures have been sufficient to cause partial melting on the Moon, at least of its outer layers, and subsequent formation of a gabbro-anorthosite crust by flotation of anorthosite crystals that were relatively depleted in radioelements.

The subsequent period of the Moon's thermal history has a stage of rejuvenated activity starting about 10^9 years after the Moon's formation as shown by age determinations for lunar basalts. This stage is associated with radiogenic heating in the deeper regions of the Moon, magmatic redistribution of heat sources, and transfer of radioelements in the course of zonal melting towards the Moon's surface. The crystallization of basaltic magma and deposition of radioelements took place in the upper, cooler layers; the level of radioelement concentration in the crust must significantly exceed the mean level of the radioelement concentration at large depths. In particular, the radioactive basalts (KREEP) from the old Fra Mauro region in the Riphaeus Montes seem to have undergone, during their formation, the most profound differentiation of magma melts, resulting in a high degree of enrichment by radioelements.

There are calculations in some papers showing that even the decay of potassium alone could be sufficient for the heating and melting of lunar material. It cannot be entirely ruled out, however, that the stage of lunar evolution that had terminated by producing basalts and anorthosites proceeded due to a combination of processes. It is possible that a number of factors, such as the kinetic energy of particles or planetesimals, the solar wind, and the decay of radioactive nuclides, have been active in facilitating the intensive melting of at least a third of lunar material.

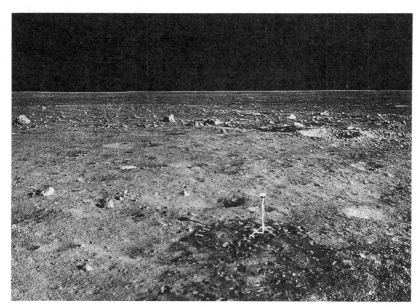

Fig. 1.5.1. — Lunar surface in the region of the south-western part of Mare Tranquillitatis. The picture was taken from the Apollo 11 lunar module.

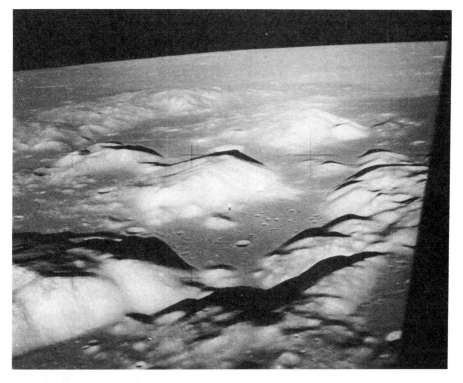

Fig. 1.5.2. — Lunar surface in the Taurus-Littrow region. Picture was taken from the Apollo 17 command module in lunar orbit.

Taking into account the geomorphological study of the Moon's surface, age determinations for rock samples from various areas and, finally, the study of the lunar thermal history, one can divide the Moon's evolution into a number of stages starting from some time during its formation up to the present. Such evolutionary models have been discussed in a number of papers. Thus, the model proposed by Schmitt [26] assumes seven principal stages: (1) formation of the Moon, 4600 million years ago; (2) melting of the outer envelope, 4600–4400 million years ago; (3) formation of the highlands with craters, 4400–4100 million years ago; (4) formation of the huge mare basins, 4100–3900 million years ago; (5) formation of the bright plains, 3900–3800 million years ago; (6) formation of the basaltic mare plains, 3800–3000 million years ago; and (7) formation of the smooth crust, from 3000 million years ago until the present day.

Structure of the surface and the character of rocks
The Moon's surface is fairly well-known at present. The principal morphological types of lunar features had been known from Earth-based observations. Photographs taken by spacecraft have permitted a global mapping with a resolution of about 50 m, as well as large-scale photography of selected areas with as fine a resolution as 10 m. Finally, the landing spacecraft Luna, Surveyor, and Apollo have taken pictures of lunar topography at their landing sites with resolutions down to 1 mm. Figs 1.5.1 and 1.5.2 show photographs of the lunar surface in the mare and highland areas: the southwestern part of Mare Tranquillitatis (this picture was taken by the Appollo II lunar module, and the Taurus-Littrow area (this picture was taken by Appollo 17).

General estimates show that the maria comprise about 16% of the lunar surface. They are situated largely on the visible side (about 30% of the area), only about 3% being on the lunar farside. Lunar mountains usually encircle large mare basins. The maximum height of the lunar mountains is about 4000 m above the mean lunar sphere, the maximum depth being about the same distance below the mean sphere.

The very first satellites of the Moon have shown that the mare areas are covered with basalts. All subsequent investigations of lunar samples have confirmed that most of the maria are covered with basalts with high Fe and Ti contents and a low alkali content compared with terrestrial basalts [27]. Oceanus Procellarum and Mare Imbrium also contain basalts rich in potassium, rare earths, phosphorus, uranium, and thorium. The bulk of lunar highland rocks is represented by gabbro-anorthosites.

The Moon's surface seems to be covered with a layer of fine–grained, loose, fragmentary rock (regolith) whose thickness varies in different places. Fig. 1.5.3 shows the regolith returned to Earth by Luna 16 and operations with it in a receiving chamber.

Lunar rocks typically contain no volatiles, in particular water and oxygen. For this reason iron and other metals occur in the rocks in an unoxidized state. Overall, the lunar rocks are somewhat enriched with lithophiles and depleted in chalcophiles and siderophiles as compared with the principal rocks of the Earth's crust.

Table 1.5.3 shows the chemical composition of highland and mare rocks [28]. We see that the highland rocks are subdivided into two groups in mineral and chemical compositions: the group of anorthositic rocks and that of non-mare basalts.

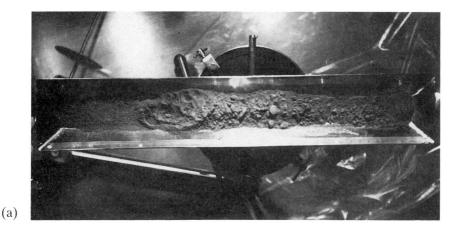

(a)

(b)

Fig. 1.5.3 — Lunar rock (regolith) brought back to the Earth by Luna 16 (a) and operations at
the chamber which receives lunar soil (b).

The anorthosite group is characterized by high concentrations of Al, Ca and Mg
and by a high Mg/Fe ratio. The principal rock-forming minerals in these rocks are
plagioclase, olivine, orthopyroxenes and clinopyroxenes.

Non-mare basalts are characterized by lower concentrations of Al and Ca and are
rich in Fe, Mg and Ti. An important constituent of non-mare basalts is the KREEP
component (basalts with high concentrations of potassium and rare-earth elements).
Compared to anorthosites, the non-mare basalts have less plagioclase and more low-
calcium pyroxenes. As demonstrated by orbital gamma-radiation measurements
[29], the bulk of the highland surface is composed of anorthosites.

Table 1.5.3 — Chemical composition of lunar highland and mare rocks (percentage by weight)

Oxide	Highland rocks[a]						Mare rocks[a]					
	1	2	3	4	5	6	7	8	9	10	11	12
SiO_2	43.97	45.30	46.33	46.60	45.70	47.90	40.20	37.91	47.81	45.50	48.10	45.50
TiO_2	0.02	0.29	0.57	0.64	1.38	1.80	12.28	13.08	1.77	4.04	0.36	0.96
Al_2O_3	35.83	28.70	25.01	19.50	15.84	15.60	7.78	8.86	8.87	13.95	11.20	13.90
FeO	0.36	4.12	4.60	8.60	9.27	10.74	19.77	19.96	19.97	17.77	18.20	18.40
MnO	0.00	0.05	0.08	0.12	0.12	0.15	0.22	0.26	0.28	0.26	0.26	0.24
MgO	0.25	4.35	7.70	10.90	17.89	10.93	8.06	7.99	9.01	5.95	11.0	6.30
CaO	18.95	16.24	14.23	12.60	9.13	9.90	10.27	10.77	10.32	11.96	10.20	13.30
Na_2O	0.34	0.50	0.62	0.42	0.55	0.78	0.52	0.38	0.28	0.63	0.15	0.37
K_2O	0.01	0.09	0.27	0.14	0.22	0.52	0.29	0.04	0.03	0.21	0.1	0.02
P_2O_5	not deter.	0.06	0.21	0.11	0.22	0.60	0.18	0.11	0.08	0.15	not deter.	not deter.
Total	99.73	99.70	99.62	99.63	100.32	98.92	99.57	99.36	98.42	100.42	99.50	99.03

[a] (1) anorthosite, (2) gabbro–anorthosite, (3) anorthosite–gabbro, (4) alumina basalt, (5) non-mare basalt with a low concentration of KREEP components, (6) KREEP basalt, (7) ilmenite basalt, (8) olivine basalt, (9) tridymite gabbro, (10) pigeonite basalt, (11) low-titanium basalt (Apollo 17), (12) low-titanium basalt (Luna 14).

The texture and composition of these rocks indicate that they formed as a result of impact-explosion recycling of crustal material.

Mare rocks are largely represented by low-titanium (less than 6% TiO_2) and high-titanium (more than 8% TiO_2) basalts. The leading rock-forming minerals in mare rocks are clinopyroxene and plagioclase, occasionally olivine and ilmenite. Mare basalts were produced by the partial melting of mafic mantle material. The great diversity of petrological types in mare basalts is due to the differences in the degree and depth of the partial melting.

To sum up, lunar rocks are dominated by pyroxene, olivine, and plagioclase. The bulk mineral composition of lunar rocks is similar to that of terrestrial basalts and anorthosites. However, it is more primitive because of a total absence of water and weathering on the Moon, in contrast to the Earth where the result is a great number of hydrated minerals. For this reason the diversity of rocks and their principal minerals is much less pronounced on the Moon than on the Earth.

The data on the chemical and mineral composition show that lunar rocks from mare regions are similar in their concentration of basic elements to calcium-rich feldspathic achondrites (eucrites) and oceanic tholeiitic basalts, while those from lunar highlands are similar to terrestrial basalts (with a high content of plagioclase) and anorthosites.

A comparison of chemical element abundances and ratios in lunar and terrestrial rocks shows both similar features and significant differences. These data provide evidence in favour of the theory that the lunar rocks formed by the partial melting of material in the inner zone (rich in plagioclase and pyroxene), the segregation of the melt, and its ascent to the Moon's surface.

The study of isotopic ratios in lunar rock samples has determined the mean ages of rock crystallization in individual areas, thus establishing the temporal succession in the origin of present-day topography on the visible side of the Moon's surface. The temporal succession of events deduced from isotopic analyses has borne out the conclusions drawn on the basis of astronomical observations using the superposition principle. The only exception to this chronology is the model age of regolith which is older than that of underlying rocks.

Structure of the Moon's crust and interior

The lunar gravitational field has been studied using tracking data for satellites orbiting the Moon. The evidence obtained indicates that the Moon's gravitational field is irregular and significantly different from a central one. It appears that an anomalies (so-called 'mascons' which stands for mass concentrations) occur above circular maria over 200 km in diameter situated on the visible side (Maria Imbrium, Serenitatis, Humorum, Crisium and Nectaris). The mascons are old features whose age is about 3000–3500 million years. They are supposed to have formed either from large bodies striking the Moon's surface or from some internal mass redistribution. There are certain difficulties in providing convincing proof in favour of either of these two hypotheses. However, the very fact that mascons exist is significant, suggesting, in particular, considerable deviations from the hydrostatic equilibrium in the interior of the Moon (the dynamic compression $\epsilon_d = 0.00063$, about 17 times that of a hydrostatic figure), and the existence of a lunar lithosphere at least several hundred kilometres thick. The presence of mascons also indicates a former differentiation in the Moon's interior. To account for the observed anomalies we need bodies of 50–100 km in size at depths of 25-125 km. If the mascons formed due to an internal redistribution of material, there must be decreased concentrations of mass somewhere around them. No convincing evidence of these is available so far, however.

The Moon's magnetic field has been investigated by numerous spacecraft [30–33, 46]. These investigations have shown that at present the Moon has no magnetic field (magnetic flux density of about 0.05 nT) of its own. At the same time, magnetic anomalies have been discovered on the Moon's surface, mainly in the highlands. The anomalies reach some hundred nanotesla in several areas on the lunar, surface. The principal magnetic carriers are rocks that contain metallic iron.

The study of lunar rock samples brought back to the Earth provides evidence of individual samples that have very high magnetization values. This indicates that the Moon's magnetic field has been stronger in the remote past than the present day value by factors of several thousand. The origin of such a strong magnetic field has not been explained in a satisfactory way. One can just hypothesize that 3000–4000 million years ago the Moon either had a molten core operating as a dynamo or it was cold but was somehow subjected to the effect of a strong magnetic field. In the latter case, the Moon's interior became heated afterwards, and the molten rock retained only a 'memory' of this event.

The study of lunar magnetism will probably yield palaeomagnetic data on the early history of the Solar System, because the Moon has changed little during the several thousand million years of its existence. Such magnetic information formerly recorded in the terrestrial crust has been erased owing to volcanic activity and the ejection of magnetic materials onto the surface.

Little is known about the Moon's internal constitution, which is characterized to some extent by the lunar mean density and moment of inertia. The low mean density of the Moon compared with the Earth ($3.34 \times 10^3 : 5.52 \times 10^3$ km m^{-3}) may indicate that the Moon is much more homogenous. Estimations of the moments of inertia along all the three axes indicate that the radial density distribution is not very much different from a homogeneous one; the density of the Moon's outer envelope must be somewhat higher than that in the deeper interior owing to differences in the composition or temperature. The absence of hydrostatic equilibrium, as well as the existence of mascons under some circular lunar maria, suggests a high degree of rigidity in the outer parts of the Moon. As the mean density of the Moon is much lower than that of the Earth, and the Moon has no general dipole magnetic field, one can suppose that the Moon has no molten iron core.

Some information on the Moon's internal constitution has been obtained by analysing terrestrial seismic data and rocks under various pressures and temperatures. The corresponding models for the internal constitution of the Moon have been constructed by a number of investigators. However, the relevance of such models can only be determined from experimental data obtained on the Moon itself.

Seismometers brought to the Moon by Apollos 12, 14 and 15 have probed the Moon to obtain data on the velocity of lunar seismic waves. The Moon's outer layer shows an interesting feature — the presence of a stratified crust 65 km thick.

Interpretations of seismic data have been attempted. They have been based on experimental information on the penetration velocities of waves in lunar samples brought back to Earth by Luna 16, 20 and 24 and Apollo 11 to 17. Near the surface, down to a depth of 1–2 km, the seismic wave velocity corresponds to a dust layer that has been condensed under its own weight or to crushed rocks – breccia and rock fragments. The lunar crust in the depth interval 2–25 km may consist of basalts similar to those returned to the Earth. The terrestrial equivalent of the lunar crustal layer deeper than 25 km may be, according to seismic data, rocks like gabbro, pyroxenite or anorthosites; they must be enriched with magnesium for depths below 65 km. There is a zone around 1000 km through which seismic waves do not penetrate. The Moon's core consisting of FeS is supposed to lie below this interface. Judging from the high temperature in the Moon's interior and its weak magnetic field, the core must be in a semi-molten state. The Moon's crust is estimated to have a mean density of about 2.9×10^3 km m^{-3}, the mantle 3.35×10^3 kg m^{-3}, and the core over 4×10^3 kg m^{-3}.

The seismometers have recorded moonquakes whose foci lie at depths of 600–1000 km. This indicates that the Moon's interior is in a solid state at least to this depth.

No evidence for present-day volcanic activity on the Moon has been discovered. Moonquakes occur infrequently (700–1000 per year). They are small (Richter magnitude 1–2) and mainly occur during the Moon's passage through perigee or apogee. The Earth's tidal forces probably act as a trigger mechanism in this case. The total seismic energy of the Moon is less than that of the Earth by a factor of 10^6 to 10^8. However, in spite of the absence of volcanic activity and low seismicity, the present-day lunar heat flow is about twice as large as that on the Earth. The lunar flow measured in mare regions (Taurus-Littrow and the Hadley Rille) is 3×10^{-4} W m^{-2} [34] exceeding the theoretical value for a chondritic model of the Moon. This provides evidence of a higher concentration of natural radioactive elements in the lunar crust as compared to the terrestrial crust.

From this value of the heat flow we conclude that the temperature gradient on the Moon must amount to a few degrees per kilometre depth if the thermal conductivity coefficient lies in the range 0.004–0.04 W m^{-2} K^{-1}.

Toksöz and Hsui have shown [23] that a heat flow of about 3×10^{-4} W m^{-2} requires a mean uranium content of about 10^{-4} p.p.m. on the Moon. They assume an initially homogeneous distribution of natural readiactive elements and that condensation falls off exponentially with depth after the differentiation of material on the Moon. Such a concentration and distribution of radioelements must have produced early differentiation of material on the Moon which has cooled sufficiently up to the present time and, having already solidified, continues to cool rapidly. At the same time, the mantle temperature remains fairly high (1100–1300 K).

Radar observations and measurements of temperature and heat radiation have been used to obtain theoretical estimates for the conductivity of the Moon's interior. Calculations show that the outer part of the Moon has a low conductivity of about 10^{-5} $\Omega^{-1 \text{ m}-1}$, while the values for the inner part or the core are as high as 10^{-2} Ω^{-1} m^{-1}. The sharp drop in the conductivity of the outer part (the lunar crust) seems to be due to a loss of oxygen from the surface rocks.

Deep electromagnetic sounding shows [35] that the upper layer, down to depths of 240–300 km, has a low conductivity of about $10^{-6}\ \Omega^{-1}\ m^{-1}$, the conductivity increasing in deeper layers up to 10^{-2}–$10^{-3}\Omega^{-1}m^{-1}$, then dropping to about $10^{-5}\ \Omega^{-1}\ m^{-1}$ at a depth of about 340 km, and increasing again to $10^{3}\ \Omega^{-1}\ m^{-1}$ at a depth of about 940 km. The mean diamagnetic permeability of the Moon as a whole is estimate at 1.03 ± 0.13.

All these geophysical data allow a representation of the Moon's internal constitution. Fig. 1.5.4 is a diagram illustrating the structure, state, and composition of the Moon's interior.

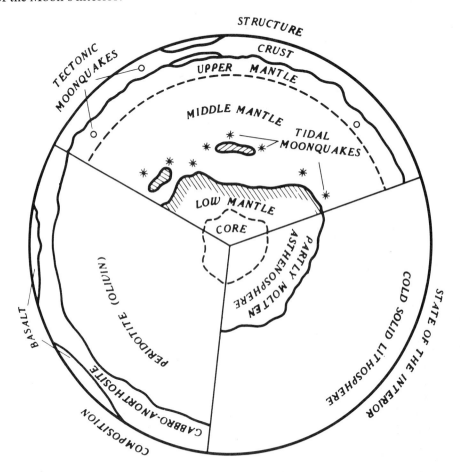

Fig. 1.5.4 — Diagram illustrating the structure, state and composition of the Moon's interior.

A comparison of the Moon and the Earth reveals a certain similarity between the two. The Moon is stratified like the Earth, although its crust and lithosphere make up a greater proportion of the total mass than is the case for the Earth. Both bodies have cores that seem to consist of Fe and FeS. Finally, lunar seismic activity indicates the Moon to be an active body, not only in the past, but also in the present. The Moon has a similar, although more primitive, thermal history.

Future lines of research

Now that we know the Moon well enough, we can point out a number of unique features that distinguish it from all the other bodies of the Solar System: a small mass ratio of the planet to its satellite; great differences in the average compositions of the planet and its satellite; displacement of the centre of mass relative to the centre of the figure (by 2.5 km toward the Earth, because of the thicker lunar farside crust); asymmetry of the surface (virtually all maria on the visible, near-Earth side); an envelope-like internal constitution; anomalous mass concentrations; the old age and primitiveness of the crust; the absence of volatile components; the presence of rock palaeomagnetism, etc. All these features of the Moon's structure determine the spectrum of questions that remain unanswered.

At the same time, in spite of enormous progress in the study of the Moon, the principal aim of lunar investigations remains the development of concepts of the origin and evolution of the Moon, the Earth and the Solar System. This problem also includes the question of where and how the Moon formed. New data seem to favour the formation of the Moon close to the Earth during a single process. However, the hypothesis of a Moon captured by the Earth and the hypothesis of a Moon torn away from the Earth continue to attract the attention of investigators. It is also important to understand whether the formation of the Earth-Moon system is typical of other planet–satellite systems.

The study of the Moon by space vehicles and investigations of lunar soil samples on the Earth have answered a lot of questions posed by classical astronomy. However, these investigations have raised many new problems still awaiting a solution.

Summaries have been attempted by many researchers. Here are some of the questions. What is the Moon's internal structure? What is the evolution of the early lunar crust? What were the intensity and nature of the meteoritic bombardment during earlier times? How did the older lunar crust (in the highlands) form? What is the history of the formation of regolith? What is the rôle of volcanism in the evolution of the Moon and the planets? What are the geochemical and age differences between the areas of thin and thick crust? What are the absolute ages of the basic stratigraphic units? Was there volcanic activity before 3900 million years ago and more recently than 2500 million years ago? What was the source for the Moon's heating and the cause of the differentiation of lunar material? Was the Moon's core fluid in an earlier epoch? What bodies have formed the mare basins? What is the cause of the differences between the Moon's near and far sides? Is there water in the lunar polar regions or has the Moon completely outgassed? Are there any random processes operating on the Moon (for instance, the release of gases)? Are there any traces of cometary or carbonaceous material of impact origin on the Moon? What is the nature of the local magnetic fields? What is the distribution of the Moon's gravitational field? What can be said about terrestrial geological processes on the basis of lunar studies? What has been the influence of the Moon on the Earth's history (through ejections from the Moon, gravitational attraction, and because of the common origin)?

Apart from a purely scientific interest in the Moon, it can, being the closest natural body to the Earth, be used to observe processes going on in space. For example, to investigate the entire spectrum of low-temperature astronomy; to observe the Sun;

for optical astronomy where observations require a dark sky and a long duration; for radio astronomy which requires low radio-noise interference; to measure galactic cosmic rays; to collect meteorites and cosmic dust; and to conduct observations of the Earth.

Finally, out of the same considerations, the Moon has an important practical rôle to play. In particular, the Moon can be used for space communications, for the tracking and launching of spacecraft; for energy generation (solar or potential) for conducting controlled agricultural experiments (farms) aimed at setting up self-sufficient habitable space bases; for conducting medical investigations; for purposeful studies of terrestrial mineral deposits; for development of the technology of low-temperature production processes on the Earth; as a new source for the stimulation of human life processes.

1.5.2 MARS' SATELLITES: PHOBOS AND DEIMOS

The satellites of Mars were discovered in 1877 by the American astronomer Asaph Hall [36]. He called them Phobos (fear) and Deimos (terror) after the two attendants of Ares (Mars), the god of war in the *Iliad*. The motion of both satellites is prograde, the period of Phobos being less, and that of Deimos being greater, than the axial rotation period of Mars. Their orbits are nearly circular. The orbital radius is 9380 km for Phobos and 23460 km for Deimos. Significant advances in man's knowledge of these bodies are due to Mariners 7 and 9 and Vikings 1 and 2. The photographs obtained by these spacecraft have revealed these satellites' surface topography, shapes and sizes [37,38].

Figs 1.5.5 and 1.5.6 show pictures of Phobos and Deimos taken by the Viking 1 spacecraft. Both satellites have non spherical shapes that can be fitted by a triaxial ellipsoid whose major, intermediate, and minor semiaxes are 13.4, 11.2 and 9.2 km for P-hobos and 7.5, 6.1 and 5.2 km for Deimos. The mean square error in approximating the surface of Phobos by a triaxial ellipsoid is (σ) = $\pm$ 1 km for all the three axes. The satellites seem to be spinning suchronously with their rotation about Mars. The synchronous motion must have come about as a result of evolution under the effect of tidal forces.

The surface morphology of the satellites has retained traces of the intensive meteoritic bombardment in the remote past. (The existence of volcanic craters is improbable on such small bodies). This is demonstrated by the presence of numerous overlapping craters covered by a layer of regolith.

The largest craters so far found on Phobos are 10 km (Stickney) and 5 km (Hall) in diameter. As Phobos itself has a mean diameter of only about 22 km, one must conclude that the meteoritic impacts needed to produce those craters seem to have been of such force as to almost destroy the entire satellite. The force of such powerful impacts may be invoked to explain the irregular shape of the limb and the presence of a long linear feature on Phobos. Most of the craters are naturally smaller than this. Their rims have no calderas (as is the case for larger bodies), because the force of gravity is so small there. (The gravitational constant on Phobos is μ = (0.66 $\pm$ 0.12) x 10^3 km^3 s^{-2}). The ejected material has been nearly completely dissipated in circum-Martian space and now revolves around Mars on its own. Some of the younger craters have sharply pronounced rims that can be attributed to either the ejection or

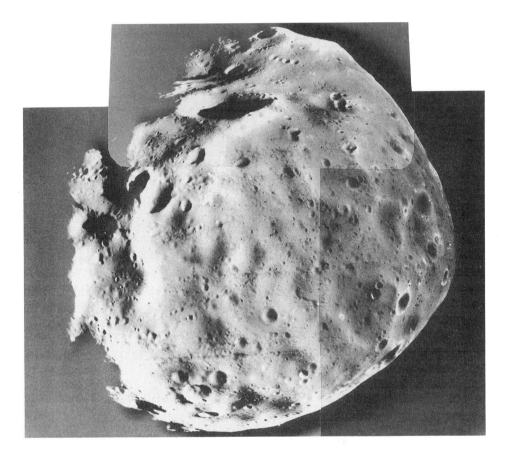

Fig. 1.5.5. (a) Mars' inner satellite Phobos photographed from a distance of 480 km by Viking Orbiter 1. Some features as small as 20 metres across can be seen.

the condensation of material [38, 39].

When one compares the density of craters of differing size on both Phobos and Deimos with that of similar craters on various types of lunar and Martian surfaces, it proves to be very close to that observed in areas of the older lunar crust (such as the lunar highlands). The equilibrium crater density on Phobos and Deimos (i.e. the number of new craters of some size arising in a specified time interval, which is equal to the number of old craters destroyed over the same time) has been used to obtain rough estimates of the age of the satellites, this age value being close to that of the Solar System planets [37].

The study of physical characteristics in the surface layer of small bodies must in the first place address the question: is there or is there not regolith on the surface? On the one hand, the open (unprotected by an atmosphere) surface is continually bombarded by meteorites and cosmic dust, loosening the rock and forming a regolith layer, but, on the other hand, the small size of the bodies and, hence, small gravity allows practically all the material excavated by meteoritic impact to leave the body for outer space (the velocity required to overcome the force of gravity on the satellites discussed is typically 10 m s^{-1}.

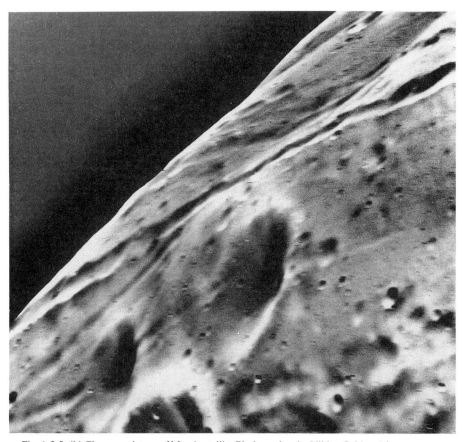

Fig. 1.5.5. (b) Close-up picture of Mars' satellite Phobos taken by Viking Orbiter 1 from a range
of 120 km. The picture covers an area of 3 x 3.5 km. The smallest surface features identifiable
are 10 to 15 metres across.

However, nearly all photometric, polarimetric, and thermal observations of
Phobos and Deimos [40, 41, 38] indicate the presence of some regolith on their
surfaces. In Soter's opinion [42], the velocities at which material is ejected from the
satellites are always too small to overcome the attraction of Mars so that, being
within the attraction field of Mars at orbits close to those of Phobos and Deimos, the
ejected material is ultimately captured again by them after a period of 10^2 to 10^5
years, forming the regolith layer on the surface. Such a mechanism could have
operated when either there were vigorous impacts of large meteorites, or the satellite
surface was composed of hard rock (i.e. was not covered with regolith), as well might
be the case during the initial period of their existence. At present, when these bodies
are covered with regolith, most of the material raised by an impact soon returns to
the surface. From the consideration of crater shapes, Pollack *et al.* [38] estimate the
mean thickness of the regolith layer to be a few hundred metres. Florensky's estimate
[43] for the mean thickness is a few tens of metres. The surface regolith layer has
probably a density of $1–2 \times 10^3$ kg m^{-3}, i.e. a value close to that for the Moon.
However, the regolith thickness seems to be non-uniform. The presence of brighter
areas may indicate not only recent ejecta, but also outcrops of hard rocks not yet
covered with regolith.

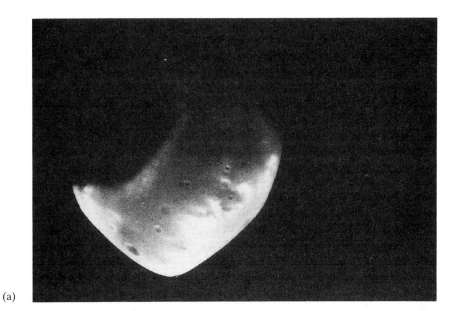

(a)

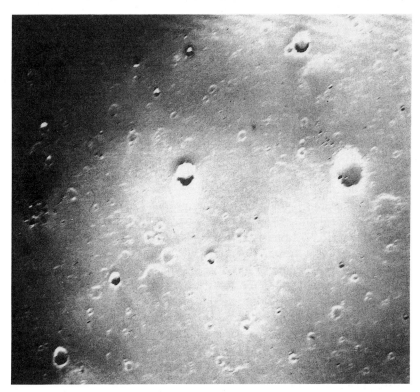

(b)

Fig. 1.5.6. — Mars' outer satellite Deimos, photographed from Viking Orbiter 2: (a) from a distance of 1400 km; only part of the illuminated hemisphere is facing the camera; (b) at a distance of just 50 km, it can be seen that Deimos is saturated with craters, and that large boulders are strewn across the surface. The region shown is 1.2 x 1.5 km in size, and features only 3 m across are discernible.

Infrared measurements [40] conducted from Mariner 9 have yielded the brightness temperature of Phobos: 295 K on the sunlit side and 180 K on the dark side. The surface temperature T_s is related to the brightness temperature T_B by the relation $T_s = T_B \sqrt[4]{ß}$ where $ß = 0.90$, is the surface radiation coefficient. Thus, the surface temperature on Phobos is 305 K on the day side and 190 K on the night side.

Little is known about the thermal structure of the satellites of Mars. The most important characteristic is the mean density, equal to $(1.9 \pm 0.6) \times 10^3 \text{ kg m}^{-3}$ for Phobos and $(1.4 \pm 0.6) \times 10^3 \text{ kg m}^{-3}$ for Deimos. There are two alternative opinions concerning these density values. For example, Soter and Harris [44] suppose that the satellites may consist wholly of small particles so consolidated as to form a hard rock (like carbonaceous chondrites). This consolidation of material may have occurred in an early epoch of the existence of the Solar System as a result of heating due to the solar wind and the decay of short-lived radioactive nuclides. Such a mechanism has repeatedly been proposed to account for the high density of chondrites [33, 45]. In that case the satellites of Mars may have been formed by accretion of Solar-System protomatter in circum-Martian space. Probably as much likelihood can be claimed for another hypothesis; namely, that based on the idea that the interior of the satellites is composed of hard rock like basalts of the terrestrial crust [37]. One is then inclined to think that the satellites are remnants of a former larger body that had undgergone differentiation of its material.

The composition of the satellites is also unknown. Some indirect information on their composition has been obtained only from photometric observations. Repeated albedo measurements [36–38] have yielded a low value: 0.05–0.07; i.e. the satellites are dark in the visible region of the spectrum. The fact that the two satellites have similar albedo values seems to indicate a similar composition. A comparison of the albedo and colour characteristics with those of a number of natural materials shows that the greatest resemblance is to carbonaceous chondrites (or C-type asteroids) and, to a lesser extent, to basaltic rocks. The low albedo for carbonaceous chondrites is due to the high carbon content, and for basaltic rocks due to high iron oxide content (Table 1.5.4).

As the mean density of Phobos and Deimos is below $2 \times 10^3 \text{ kg m}^{-3}$, and the material of carbonaceous chondrites in a nonporous state has a density of 2.4 to $2.5 \times 10^3 \text{ kg m}^{-3}$, the satellites of Mars must be composed of porous material. A typical feature of carbonaceous chondrites is a high content of volatile elements and compounds; in particular, water (up to about 20%), carbon (up to about 5%), sulphur, and rare gases. Some portion of these volatiles may be present as organic matter consisting of complex organic acids, hydrocarbons, and other components. As far as their mineral composition is concerned, carbonaceous chondrites (CI) largely consist of amorphous hydrated silicates, sulphates, and ordinary silicates.

Recently, the Soviet Phobos-2 spacecraft, launched in July 1988, took TV pictures of Phobos at a distance of ~ 320 km that improved our knowledge of the surface relief and the structure of the surface, in addition to refining the accuracy of Phobos' orbit to within just two or three kilometres.

Table 1.5.4 — Mean elemental composition of carbonaceous chondrite CI [47] and terrestrial basaltic rocks [48] (percentage by mass)

Element	Chondrite CI	Basalt
Fe	18.43	8.56
Si	10.53	24.0
Ti	0.04	0.9
Al	0.87	8.76
Ni	0.97	0.016
Co	0.05	0.005
Mn	0.15	0.2
Mg	9.53	4.5
Ca	0.87	6.72
Na	0.55	1.94
K	0.66	0.83
P	0.12	0.14
H	2.21	—
C	3.10	0.01
S	5.49	0.03
O	43.2	43.5

1.5.3 JUPITER'S SATELLITES: AMALTHEA, IO, EUROPA, GANYMEDE, AND CALLISTO

Jupiter has 16 satellites, making the Jovian system rather like a miniature Solar System. All the satellites of Jupiter can be divided into three groups. The group of four outer satellites is composed of relatively small bodies. They revolve in a direction opposite to that in which the planet rotates around the Sun. Their orbits also have high inclinations to Jupiter's equator. In view of these two factors, the outer satellites are considered to be irregular. They are probably captured asteroids. Another group of four satellites is closer to the parent planet and also consists of small bodies. These satellites move prograde, but their orbits have high inclinations, so these satellites are also irregular. They, too, may have been captured by Jupiter. Finally, the group of satellites closest to the planet (Metis, Adrastea, Amalthea, Thebe, Io, Europa, Ganymede, and Callisto) is distinguished by four large bodies (Io, Europa, Ganymede, and Callisto), discovered by Galileo in 1610. For this reason the four largest satellites are called Galilean. All these eight satellites move prograde and have nearly circular orbits close to the plane of Jupiter's equator. The Galilean satellites, Io, Europa, Ganymede, and Callisto are the most interesting. They have sizes similar to that of the Moon (see Table 1.5.1). These satellites have been photographed by the American Voyager 1 and Voyager 2 spacecraft [49, 50]. It has turned out that the satellites are widely dissimilar. It has become obvious that water and other volatiles have played an important part in the history of these bodies. An ice covering has been found on the surface of Europa, Ganymede, and Callisto. Ganymede and Callisto seem to consist of a silicate rock mixed with ice. Io is the most geologically active body [49–51]. Several active volcanoes have been detected and photographed on its surface. It can be seen from Table 1.5.1 that the further a satellite is from the planet, the lower its density, indicating decreasing proportions of the silicate part compared with the volatile fraction (water and ice). The masses of the Galilean satellites are different from the Moon's mass (7.35×10^{22} kg) by factors of less than 2.

Amalthea

This is the third satellite from Jupiter in order of increasing distance. It was discovered less than a century ago, in 1892, by the American astronomer E. E. Barnard. The satellite was photographed by Voyager 1. It has been established that Amalthea is highly irregular in shape, and its surface is heavily cratered. It is possible that the satellite has become irregular because of a collision with a large meteorite. Television observations have revealed its low albedo. It is much darker than the Galilean satellites. The satellite is also reddish in colour. It is, however, unclear whether this colour is typical of the material of the entire satellite or only of its covering (modified surface material). The pictures have been used to determine its size: $262 \times 146 \times 134$ km. (These dimensions are accurate to within about 10%.) The satellite's greatest axis is radial relative to Jupiter; the shortest axis is polar. The satellite revolves around its own axis with a period of just under 12 hours. It rotates around Jupiter with the same period. Thus, the same side of the satellite is constantly towards the planet. It is difficult to say anything definite about the internal constitution and origin of Amalthea. Its small size and low albedo seem to indicate the possible capture of an asteroid of chondritic composition. Although, the red colour would seem to be not in favour of this hypothesis, it is possible that the reddish surface deposits emanated from the Jovian satellite Io, next in order of increasing distance from the planet. If Amalthea formed near Jupiter, then the thermal radiation of Jupiter during the initial epoch of its existence must have heated Amalthea to temperatures around 1500 K [52, 53]. In such a case Amalthea, like Mercury, must consist of refractory material.

Io

Io (Fig. 1.5.7) is the next after Amalthea in the system of Jovian satellites. It is a little larger than the Moon in size. The surface of Io has a high albedo. The polar regions are somewhat darker than the equatorial ones. Io is yellowish or reddish brown in colour. There are extensive light regions and dark craters on this general background. Many craters are surrounded by rings (haloes) of light and dark material. A number of active volcanoes have been discovered on Io, ejecting clouds of material to altitudes of 100–200 km. The explosive character of these observed eruptions indicates a molten interior and the abundance of volatile components [54]. Blue and violet light were scattered by the cloud of ejected material more strongly forwards than backwards. One explanation may be that the erupted material consisted of particles a few micrometres in diameter. Changes in the satellite's volcanic activity were noted during the four-month interval between the Voyager 1 and Voyager 2 encounters. Also, the surface albedo has been observed to diminish in the vicinity of the volcanoes, indicating the ejection of dark material. The albedo change may have resulted from the pyroclastic deposition of ejected material. It should be noted that Io is the only body in the Solar System so far (apart from the Earth) where present-day volcanic activity has been definitely observed. Ground-based spectroscopy has

Fig. 1.5.7 — Jupiter's satellite Io. This view of Io was taken from a range of 862200 km by Voyager 1. Circular features are seen that may be meteorite impact craters or features of internal origin. Irregular depressions are seen that indicate surface modification has taken place. The bright irregular patches appear to be younger deposits masking the surface detail.

discovered [55] an atmosphere on Io that contains a great number of sulphur compounds. Water has not been found. Probably the atmosphere is maintained by present-day volcanic activity resulting in the ejection of vast amounts of H_2S, SO_2 and other compounds. The mean surface temperature is rather low, about 130 K, but some areas of the surface are warmer. The presence of active volcanic craters leads to the rapid rejuvenation of Io's surface (in contrast to the other Galilean satellites), so that craters are rather sparse on average, and the relief is smooth. Long narrow plains with sharp edges have been found, probably indicating tectonic deformation of the crust. The most mountainous areas with rugged relief occur in the polar regions.

The information contained in the relief and surface texture provide some indirect clues to the internal structure. Thus, a mean density close to that of the Moon indicates that Io has an intrinsically silicate composition, while active volcanism testifies to a molten interior. The principal deep-seated source of heat seems to have been Jupiter's tidal effect [56].

Io is close to Jupiter, which has greatly influenced its formation. In particular, Jupiter's intense heat radiation may have removed ice and other highly volatile material from its composition [57]. The accumulation of Io is supposed to have begun soon after the collapse of Jupiter and to have lasted for a short period. The principal chemical components of Io were partially hydrated silicates with a mean density of about 3×10^3 kg m^{-3}. Calculations show [57] that if Io was close to carbonaceous chondrites in composition, then its temperature must have risen above 1000 K for a time less than 1000 million years and the satellite must have been completely differentiated. Salts such as sodium sulphate, epsomite, gypsum and some others must have been carried to the surface.

With its relatively large size, a not very low surface temperature, a smooth relief, and inhomogeneous characteristics, Io is one of the msot attractive potential objects of promising investigations.

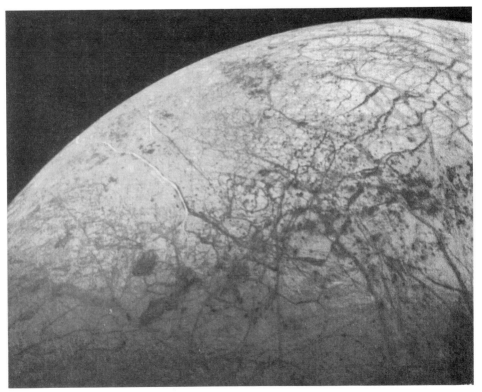

Fig. 1.5.8 — Jupiter's satellite Europa. This image of Europa, the smallest of the Galilean satellites, was acquired by Voyager 2 from a range of 241000 km. The complex patterns on its surface suggest that the icy surface was fractured and that the cracks filled with dark material from below. Very few impact craters are visible on the surface, perhaps indicating that active processes on the surface are still modifying Europa.

Europa

The orbit of Europa (Fig. 1.5.8) is beyond that of Io in order of increasing distance from Jupiter. Europa is somewhat smaller than the Moon. The satellite is creamy white in colour, the polar regions being brighter than the equatorial ones. The surface of Europa is characterized by two types of terrain — darkish spotted areas and uniform, smooth and light-coloured areas. The satellite's surface has a multitude of dark linear features with bright rims. The features cover the entire surface. Some of them are over 1000 km in length, the width reaching 200–300 metres. These features may be faults in the crust [58]. Most of the surface of Europa seems to be covered with ice, especially the polar regions, and with a mixture of rock and ice at lower latitudes [59]. The dark areas are probably covered with small craters. The lighter areas are rather homogeneous, except for the dark linear features and numerous dark spots, most of which are less than 10 km across and are distributed chaotically (these are probably small craters) with spacings of a few tens of kilometres. In addition, the lighter areas have several dark patches of indefinite shapes up to 150 km across.

The extended dark bands (faults) are shallow, probably not more than a few tens, perhaps hundreds, of metres in depth. Very few craters over 20 km across have been discovered. It is supposed that such craters are sparse on the surface of Europa — approximately one per 10^6 km^2. The surface seems to be rejuvenated either by erosional processes or by internal isostatic flattening. Infrared spectral and albedo measurements indicate that most of the surface of Europa is covered with ice or hoar-frost. Consideration of the internal structure of the satellite assumes the existence of a silicate core, with small admixtures of volatile elements (chiefly water), having a radius of 400 km, a water mantle 100 km thick, and an ice crust about 70 km in thickness. This abundance of water (about 10%) in Europa is hypothesized on the basis of the silicate composition and the mean density of 3.04×10^3 kg m^{-3}.

Fig. 1.5.9 — Jupiter's satellite Ganymede. Taken from a range of 313000 km, this picture of Ganymede in the region 30°S 180°W shows features as small as 6 km across. Shown is a bright halo impact crater with fresh material thrown out of the crater. In the background is bright grooved terrain that may be the result of shearing of the surface materials along fault planes. The dark background material is the ancient, heavily cratered terrain — the oldest material preserved on the Ganymede surface.

Ganymede

Ganymede (Fig. 1.5.9) has an orbit immediately beyond that of Europa. It is somewhat larger than Mercury in size and is the largest of the four Galilean satellites, and the largest satellite in the Solar System. Large-scale photographs taken by Voyagers 1 and 2 show that its surface is represented by dark and bright area. High-resolution pictures indicate that the dark areas (of which the largest Galileo Regio has a diameter of 4000 km) on the surface are heavily cratered and are probably older, while the brighter (presumably younger) areas are densely covered with systems of narrow parallel 'sulci', i.e. grooves or furrows overlain by craters. These groove systems vary in extent (from tens to hundreds of kilometres) and in depth (a few hundred metres). The brighter shade of the sulci relative to the environment provides evidence of outcrops of brighter rocks (probably ones containing large amounts of ice). The grooved terrain may have been produced by fractures in the expanding ice crust. Similarly shaded bright rays diverging from the younger craters also seem to indicate the ejection of rock largely mixed with ice. The crater density in the brighter areas is an order of magnitude less than in the dark areas.

The relationship between large and small craters on Ganymede is approximately the same as on the Moon [49]. Large craters 50–150 km across are recorded only in the darker areas of the surface. Craters have more distinct outlines in the brighter areas than in the dark ones. An analysis of craters in the dark and bright areas indicates that the crust of Ganymede became thicker and stronger while cooling during the period between the formation of the dark and bright areas of the surface. The dark areas seem to represent the older crust which had formed several thousand million years ago. They are very similar to the lunar highlands. The principal difference between the large craters on Ganymede and the lunar ones is the greater extent of the ray ejecta of relatively lighter material saturated with ice.

We have no information from which to draw conclusions about the internal structure and composition of Ganymede. However, judging from its low density $(1.94 \times 10^3$ kg m$^{-3})$, one may hypothesize that about half its mass must be water, either liquid or solid. Proceeding from this, and supposing a silicate base, several models for the internal constitution of the satellite have been examined. In particular, the model proposed in [60] allows a differential structure for Ganymede. It supposes that the satellite has a core of radius 1800–2200 km, a fluid mantle consisting of water 400–800 km thick, and a solid ice crust at least 100 km thick.

Callisto

Callisto (Fig. 1.5.10) is the farthest of the four Galilean satellites from Jupiter. Its surface is densely studded with craters tens of kilometres across. This strongly cratered surface dates back to remote times, to the period of intensive bombardment of all bodies formed in the Solar System that terminated about 4000 million years ago. The side facing towards Jupiter is somewhat less densely covered with craters than the outer one, indicating a synchronous rotation of Callisto and Jupiter early on in its existence. Absence of great changes in heights of the relief, and the depths of large craters indicate that Callisto, like Ganymede, had a soft ice crust in the early epoch of its existence. Two huge multi-ringed basins (Valhalla and Asgard) have been discovered on the surface

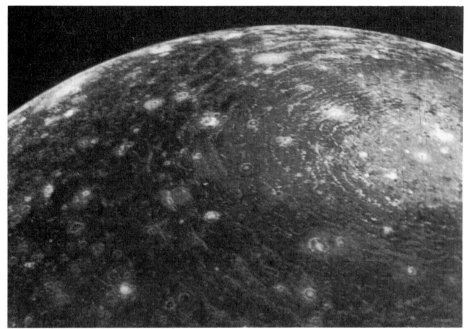

Fig. 1.5.10 — Jupiter's satellite Callisto. Voyager 1 took this picture of Callisto at a range of 350,000 km, and it shows features about 7 km across on the surface. The darker colour of Callisto suggests that its upper surface is "dirty ice" or water rich rock frozen at the cold surface (120 K). Callisto shows far more craters on its surface than Ganymede, leading scientists to believe that its surface is the oldest of the Galilean statellites. The prominent bullseye type feature in this picture is believed to be a large impact basin. The brighter circular spot is about 600 km across.

of the satellite with bright, circular depressions 600 and 200 km (respectively) across in the middle. Concentric rings surround these depressions. The outer diameters of these features are 3000 and 1000 km respectively for the two basins. Even though the entire surface seems to be old, no trace of subsequent volcanic or tectonic processes has been discovered.

An analysis of albedo in the ultraviolet region gives some grounds for belief that Callisto's surface consists of a silicate rock without large amounts of glass-like (as on the Moon) or carbonaceous material [61]. Photometric observations indicate a dark, rough, and porous surface material, i.e. regolith [62]. It has the lowest albedo of the four Galilean satellites. The heat release from the surface of Callisto has been measured [63], providing evidence of a low thermal conductivity in the surface layer, probably accounted for by the high porosity of the rock.

Lewis [64] was the first to suggest that Callisto is a differentiated body in which silicates and other heavy materials have gravitated towards the centre of the satellite, creating a core surrounded by water in a liquid or solid state. Its primary crust may have survived. (Callisto is probably the only Galilean satellite with a primary crust still surviving.) In view of its low density (1.82×10^3 kg m^{-3}), Callisto, like Ganymede, probably consists of silicates and water in a liquid or solid state. The model considered in [60] allows the existence of a silicate core with a radius of 1200 km, a mantle of liquid water about 1000 km in thickness, and a crust about 200 km thick consisting of a mixture of silicates and ice.

Such bodies as Ganymede and Callisto, if they had a cosmic abundance of water and rocky matter, must be differentiated by now, irrespective of whether homogeneous or inhomogeneous accumulation was responsible for their formation. The process of inhomogeneous accumulation first forms a core, then a fluid mantle and a solid crust that consist of water. In such a case the crust must consist of pure ice. In the process of homogeneous accumulation the crust that has emerged as a result of differentiation may consist of a mixture of silicates and ice. It appears that it is this type of crust which exists on Callisto with its low albedo.

A comparison of the crater density in a variety of geomorphological regions can establish a certain sequential order in the formation of these regions. One can also detect some relative sequential order in the formation of the Jovian satellites. To do this one needs to find time shifts in the initial stages on the Galilean satellites relative to events on the Moon or the Earth. There is a comparative estimate [49] (relative to the Earth) for the numbers of asteroids and comets that have arrived in the neighbourhood of Jupiter and may have contributed to the formation of the craters. The authors have come to the following conclusions:

(1) The older parts of the surface (primary crust) on Callisto and Ganymede were cratered during the period of the intensive meteoritic bombardment, i.e. about 4000 million years ago, when the lunar highland crust formed, irrespective of whether the flows were as intensive for these satellites as for the Moon.

(2) The formation of bright spotted surface areas, which began during the period of intensive bombardment and gave the same (relative to the Moon) number of impact craters as that for the dark areas, took some hundred million years.

(3) The surface of Europa must have an age of at least 10^8 years, if the flux of bodies falling on Jupiter was the same as on the Earth and the Moon. If, on the other hand, the flux of bodies falling on the surface of Europa was much smaller than assumed, the surface of Europa could be several thousands of millions of years older. Europa may have frozen immediately after the intensive bombardment. Dating from that time its surface was subjected to prolonged erosion as a result of the transfer of material from the falling bodies.

(4) The great gravitational pull of Jupiter makes the crater formation rate on Io close to or greater than the present-day crater formation rate on the Moon. Hence the absence of craters on Io is compelling evidence that this satellite is the youngest and has the most dynamic surface of all the Solar System bodies.

1.5.4 SATURN'S SATELLITES: TITAN

Titan alone will be considered of all the 17 known satellites of Saturn. This satellite is of special scientific interest and consequently may certainly be regarded as a potential object of future space exploration. Titan is the second largest satellite in the Solar System (after Ganymede) and seems to be the only one having a dense atmosphere. The mass of its atmosphere is about 10 times that of the terrestrial atmosphere. Titan is so far the only body, apart from the Earth, to have an atmosphere mainly composed of nitrogen (although current evidence suggests that nitrogen exists in the atmosphere of Neptune's satellite Triton, and the satellite is cold enough for nitrogen to exist as a liquid on its surface). However, unlike the Earth, the other components of Titan's atmosphere have a strongly reducing character, i.e. consist of molecules enriched with hydrogen. There are many chemical reactions going on in the atmosphere which form various exotic molecules and complex organic polymers. These compounds form a layer of photochemical smog (small particles) which screen the satellite's surface from direct observation. The surface temperature existing on Titan ($-$ 180°C) is near the triple point of methane, and this may lead to the formation of clouds composed of methane droplets in the lower atmosphere, and cliffs of solid methane with fluid methane oceans on its surface. A study of chemical processes occurring in the atmosphere of Titan may make an important contribution to our understanding of the origins of life here on the Earth.

Titan's atmosphere was discovered by Gerard P. Kuiper as far back as the 1940s by ground-based spectroscopy, although at the time the main constituent was thought to be methane. Later ground-based observations discovered other components in the atmosphere of Titan — C_2H_6, C_2H_4, C_2H_2, HCN and others [65–67]. However, more detailed studies were carried out by Voyager 1 [68–71]. This spacecraft flew by Titan at a distance of 5000 km from its surface. The measurements included the temperature profile of the atmosphere and pressure at the surface, the atmospheric composition, the structure of the cloud layer, the magnetic field and the flow of energetic particles in the vicinity of the satellite.

Table 1.5.5 — Characteristics of Titan, Mars, and the Earth

Characteristics	Titan	Mars	Earth
Mass (kg)	1.37×10^{23}	6.42×10^{23}	5.97×10^{24}
Equatorial radius (km)	2575	3397	6378
Gravitation (ms^{-2})	1.44	3.72	9.81
Density ($kg\,m^{-3}$)	1.9×10^3	3.93	5.52
Mean surface temperature (K)	93	215	288
Orbital eccentricity	0.029	0.093	0.017
Orbital inclination (to primary)	0.33°	—	—
Period of rotation (days)	15.945	1.03	1.0
Mass of the atmosphere, ($\times 10^4\,kg\,m^{-2}$)	10.9	0.02	1.0
Surface pressure ($\times 10^2$ Pa)	1600	6	1000
Composition of the atmosphere	N_2, Ar, CH_4	CO_2, N_2	N_2, O_2

Table 1.5.5 presents the main characteristics of Titan, with those of Mars and the Earth being given for comparison purposes. It can be seen from the table that Titan has a nearly circular orbit lying almost in the equatorial plane of Saturn. Titan moves in the direction of Saturn's rotation. This indicates that Titan, in common with most of the other satellites of Saturn, must in all probability have formed within a flattened gas-and-dust disk which surrounded the planet during an early epoch of the existence of the Solar System.

Some understanding of the internal constitution of Titan can only be reached through the use of mathematical models based on its size, mass, and density. The principal components of its interior must be rock (consisting of minerals rich in silicates and iron) and ice (consisting of water and, possibly, ammonia). If the density of the rock component in Titan is supposed to be the same as on Io, Titan must consist roughly of 55% rock and the rest ice.

As Titan is of planetary size (a little smaller than Mercury), its internal temperatures may have been high enough to produce differentiation of its material; as a result, the denser part, i.e. the rock, moved towards the centre, while the ice ascended to the surface. The heat sources might be accretion, radioactive decay, and tidal deformation. However, the most probable heat generation mechanism seems to be accretion. Therefore, the heating of Titan must have taken place during the first 1000 million years of its existence. Even if only about 10% of the kinetic energy of the bodies falling during the accretion is converted into heat, this will be sufficient for all of the rock to move towards the centre of the satellite, and if the value is significantly greater than 10%, then this will enable a complete differentiation of material and the formation of a silicate core, a mantel of fluid water (with some amount of ammonia and methane dissolved in it), and a thin crust of ice. The mantle may remain fluid up to the present time or become frozen (converted into ice). at a much earlier time, depending upon the rate of loss of heat generation in Titan. Fig. 1.5.11 shows the hypothetical internal structure of Titan according to our present state of knowledge [72, 73].

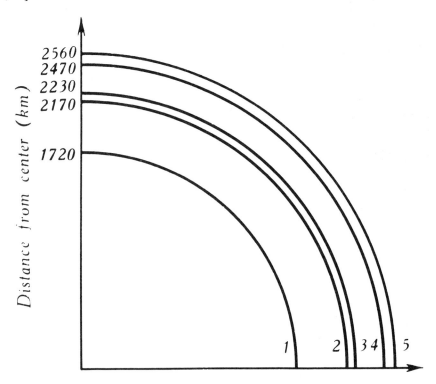

Fig. 1.5.11 — Supposed internal structure of Titan; 1, core composed of hard rock; 2, 3, 4 and 5, ice layers having different crystalline structure and densities of 3.52, 1.43, 1.28, 1.18 and 0.94×10^3 kg m^{-3}, respectively.

Of particular interest is the atmosphere of Titan. Voyager 1 has discovered that 80–95% of it is nitrogen. The rest is probably methane or perhaps argon. The other detected molecules are present in negligible amounts and are derived from the methane and nitrogen that form as a result of chemical reactions due to the solar ultraviolet radiation. The absence of oxygen in these molecules is explained by a lack of its parent material — water, which is in a frozen state in the surface layer of the crust. The ultraviolet and infrared spectra of Titan's atmosphere measured by Voyager 1 are presented in Fig. 1.5.12 [68, 69].

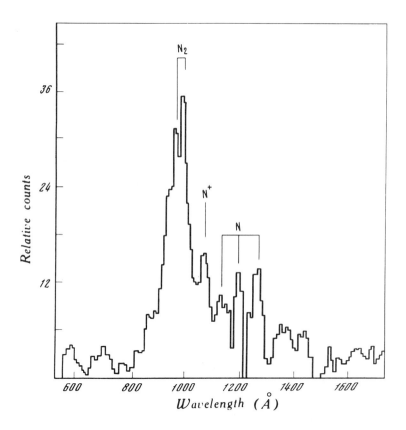

Fig. 1.5.12 (a) — Ultraviolet spectrum of Titan's atmosphere, of which 80 – 95% is composed of nitrogen.

The decomposition of methane molecules in the atmosphere may result in the formation of complex hydrocarbons which are condensed into fine particles. Collision of these particles may give rise to coagulation and the formation of larger particles. These particles, 0.1–0.5 μm in size, seem to be responsible for the formation of the smog layer. The main smog layer is at an altitude of about 200 km. The number of particles per unit volume of the atmosphere is much smaller than on the Earth, but because the layer has a considerable depth, Titan's atmosphere is much less transparent than that of the Earth.

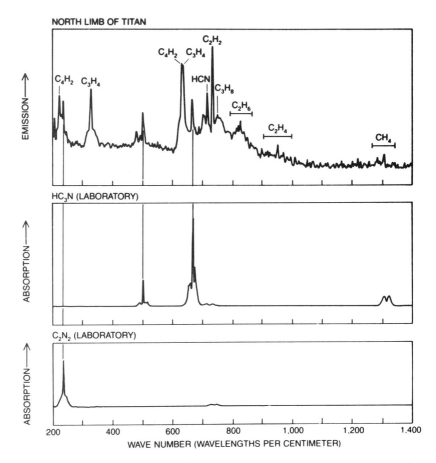

Fig. 1.5.12 (b) — Infrared spectrum of Titan's atmosphere, showing the presence of methane and various other hydrocarbon components.

The pictures taken by Voyagers 1 and 2 have also revealed the presence of a haze (weak mist) layer situated 100 km above the main cloud layer. It has also been noticed that the northern hemisphere of Titan is darker than the southern with a gradual change of brightness through the equator.

One year on Titan is equal to almost 30 terrestrial years. Since its axis of rotation has the same direction as that of Saturn, its inclination relative to the orbit of the Saturnian system around the Sun is also 27°.

Because the winter hemisphere receives less solar heat compared to the summer one, the rate of photolysis of methane and the rate of formation of aerosols must be different for the two hemispheres. Hence the size and composition of aerosol particles (and consequently, the brightness of the corresponding regions) must vary according to the seasons.

The force of gravity and atmospheric turbulence produce the effect that aerosols which have formed at high altitude descend, reach the surface and remain there (because the surface is too cold to cause evaporation). During Titan's lifetime, deposits of complex organic molecules may have covered the surface either in a layer about 1 km thick (if the surface is solid) or be present in the form of a mixture (if the surface is fluid). Thus the surface of Titan may contain more hydrocarbons than any other body of the Solar System.

The amount of methane in the atmosphere of Titan seems to be in a dynamic equilibrium: on the one hand, methane decreases due to the formation of aerosols, and, on the other, it evaporates from the surface of methane ice or liquid. Thus, the quantity of aerosols in the atmosphere depends on the amount of methane on the surface.

The amount of H_2 in the atmosphere according to Hunten's estimates [74] is a few tenths of one per cent. It is constantly formed out of methane, and escapes into outer space. As far as N_2 is concerned, its molecular velocity is too low at the present-day temperatures on Titan to escape into outer space. However, in some cases nitrogen atoms may have higher velocities, provided they form in chemical reactions with the release of heat. Strobel [75] has estimated the amount of nitrogen lost in this manner during Titan's entire lifetime. This amounts to one-tenth of the present-day quantity.

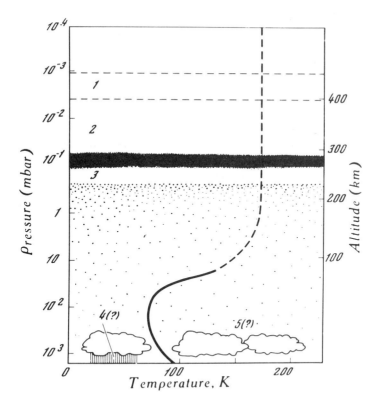

Fig. 1.5.13 — Temperature and pressure profile in Titan's atmosphere: 1, ultraviolet absorption layer; 2, haze from small particles; 3, aerosol layer; 4, methane rain zone (?); 5, methane clouds (?). Note that 1 mbar is equivalent to 100 Pa.

Fig. 1.5.13 shows the change in temperature with altitude and pressure measured by Voyager 1 [76, 77]. The temperature reaches a minimum (about 70 K) at an altitude of about 40 km (tropopause), and gradually increases, both with decreasing altitude (in the troposphere), reaching 93 K at the surface, and increasing altitude (in the stratosphere), reaching about 170 K at altitudes of 120–130 km, and then remaining nearly constant at least as high as 250 km. Radio observations by Voyager 1 have determined the surface pressure as 1.6×10^5 Pa.

As will be evident from Fig. 1.5.13, the tropospheric temperature is slightly higher than the condensation temperature of molecular nitrogen, so that one cannot expect the condensation of nitrogen (cloud formation) near the tropopause, and much less at the surface. The temperature at the surface of Titan is close to the triple point of methane (90.7 K or −182.3°C) at which methane can exist in all three phases. If the actual temperature at the surface is slightly higher than this value (as evidenced by the Voyager 1 measurements), then much of the surface must be covered by fluid methane oceans, while solid methane can exist only in the cold polar regions.

Titan absorbs about 80% of the solar energy incident on it. Aerosol particles and molecules of methane gas absorb nearly all of this energy. However, a small proportion (5–10%) can reach the surface and be absorbed by it. As the absorption of solar energy mainly occurs in clouds, the temperature must decrease towards the surface. Actually, however, it increases due to the 'greenhouse effect' caused by nitrogen, hydrogen, and methane. Since heat is transported at high altitudes by strong winds blowing from the equator towards the poles, it may be conjectured that temperature is nearly independent of latitude in the lower atmosphere and at the surface [76].

The above discussion of the processes going on in Titan's atmosphere are largely hypothetical. These processes are very complex; there are no analogues to this atmosphere; the experimental data are sparse — all these circumstances prevent us from forming definite ideas about the history of the formation of Titan's atmosphere, its present composition and structure. It is quite obvious, however, that this unique satellite and, in particular, its exotic atmosphere are of special interest for understanding the history of our planet, its atmosphere, and possibly the origins of life itself.

1.5.5 GENERAL PROBLEMS OF EXPLORING PLANETARY SATELLITES

Jupiter's Galilean satellites and Saturn's satellite Titan are of special interest for understanding the evolutionary history of Solar System bodies. Their near-planetary sizes have predetermined their evolutionary history, which must to a certain extent be similar to that of the terrestrial planets. For this reason, the study of these satellites is important for the development of ideas about the Earth. The most important questions to be answered in the future include:

– Is there a difference in the mean chemical composition of satellites as a function of their distance from Jupiter?
– Which of the satellites were formed near their planets and which have been captured by planets? What is the nature of the captured satellites?
– Which satellites are active at present? Where do tectonic and volcanic phenomena take place?

- What volatile components have been condensed on the satellite?
- How did the surface of the satellites form? What is the history of crater formation?
- What is the internal structure of the satellites, and are they differentiated bodies?
- Have the satellites their own magnetic fields?

REFERENCES

[1] H. Alfvén and G. Arrhenius, *Evolution of the Solar System*, NASA, SP-345 (1976).

[2] D. Morrison, D. Cruikshank, and J. Burns, In *Planetary satellites*, J. A. Burns (ed.), Tucson, University of Arizona Press (1977).

[3] D. Morrison and D. P. Cruikshank, *Space Sci. Rev.*, **15**, 641 (1974).

[4] A. Dollfus, In *Surfaces and interiors of planets and satellites*, New York, Academic press, p. 46 (1970).

[5] R. W. Carlson, J. C. Bhattachryya, and B. A. Smith, *Science,* **182**, 53 (1973).

[6] B. T. O'Leary, *Science,* **175**, 1108 (1970).

[7] B. T. O'Leary and T. C. van Flandern, *Icarus,* **17**, 209 (1972).

[8] E. Bowell and B. Zellner, In *Planet, stars and nebula*, Tucson, University of Arizona Press, p. 381 (1974).

[9] D. P. Cruikshank, *Icarus,* **30**, 77 (1976).

[10] R. E. Murphy, *Astrophys. J.,* **181**, L87 (1973).

[11] B. Zellner, *Astrophys. J.,* **174**, L 107 (1972).

[12] D. Brower and G. M. Clemence, In *Planets and satellites*, Chicago University Press, p. 31 (1961).

[13] R. L. Duncombe, W. J. Klepszynski, and P. K. Seidelmann, *Fundam. Cosm. Phys.,* **1**, 119 (1973).

[14] G. P. Kuiper, *Commun. Lunar and Planet. Lab.,* **9**, 199 (1972).

[15] G. P. Kuiper, *J. Geophys. Res.,* **64**, 1713 (1959).

[16] H. C. Urey, *Science,* **147**, 1262 (1965).

[17] E. J. Öpik, *Irish. Astron. J.,* **3**, 245 (1955).

[18] A. E. Ringwood and E. Essene, *Science,* **167**, 607 (1970).

[19] E. L. Ruskol, The Earth's physics, *Izv. AN SSSR,* **7**, 99 (In Russian.) (1972).

[20] T. C. Hanks and D. L. Anderson, *Phys. Earth and Planet. Inter.,* **5**, 409 (1972).

[21] J. F. Hays, *Phys. Earth and Planet. Inter.,* **5**, 77 (1972).

[22] M. N. Toksöz, S. C. Solomon, and J. W. Minear, *Moon,* **4**, 190 (1972).

[23] M. N. Toksöz and A. T. Hsui, *Icarus,* **34**, 537 (1978).

[24] H. C. Urey and G. J. F. McDonald, In *Physics and astronomy of the Moon*, Z. Kopal (ed.), New York, Academic Press, p. 213 (1971).

[25] J. A. Wood, *Icarus,* **16**, 229 (1972).

[26] H. H. Schmitt, *Cosmochemistry of the Moon and planets.* (In Russian.) Moscow, Nauka, p. 345 (1975).

[27] A. P. Vinogradov, *Geokhimiya,* **3** 261 (In Russian) (1971); **7**, 763 (In Russian.) (1972).

[28] K. P. Florensky, A. T. Basilevsky, G. A. Burba, In *An outline of comparative planetology.* (In Russian.) Moscow, Nauka, p. 326 (1981).

[29] Yu. A. Surkov, In *Gamma-spectrometry in space research,* (In Russian.) Moscow, Atomizdat, p. 209 (1977).

[30] Sh. Sh. Dolginov, Ye. G. Yeroshenko, and L. N. Zhuzglov, In *Cosmochemistry of the Moon and planets*, (In Russian), Moscow, Nauka, p. 314 (1975).

[31] P. Dyal and C. W. Parkin, In *Proc. 2nd Lunar and Planet. Sci. Conf.*, New York, Pergamon Press, **3**, 2391 (1971).

[32] P. Dyal, C. W. Parkin, and W. D. Daily, In *Proc. 4th Lunar and Planet. Sci. Conf.*, New York, Pergamon Press, **3**, 2925 (1973).

[33] C. T. Russell, P. J. Coleman, and N. Lichtenstein, In *Proc. 4th Lunar and Planet. Sci. Conf.*, New York, Pergamon Press, **3**, 2833 (1973).

[34] M. G. Langseth, J. L. Chute, and S. Keihm. *Lunar Sci.*, **4**, 455 (1973).

[35] N. Ness, In *Physics of the Moon and planets.* (In Russian.) Moscow, Nauka, p. 167 (1972).

[36] A. Hall, *Observations and orbits of the satellites of Mars with data for ephemerides in 1979*, Washington DC, US Government Printing Office (1978).

[37] J. Pollack, In *Planetary satellites*, J. A. Burns (ed.), Tucson, University of Arizona Press, p. 356 (1977).

[38] J. B. Pollack, J. Veverka, and M. Noland, *J. Geophys. Res.*, **78**, 4313 (1973).

[39] H. Jeffreys, *J. Astron. Soc.*, **91**, 169 (1930).

[40] I. Gatley, H. Keiffer, and E. Miner, *Astrophys. J.*, **190**, 497 (1974).

[41] M. Noland, J. Veverka, and J. B. Pollack, *Icarus*, **20**, 490 (1973).

[42] S. Soter, *The dust belts of Mars*, Ithaca (NY), Centre for Radiophysics and Space Research Report N462, p. 37 (1971).

[43] K. P. Florensky, A. T. Bazilevsky, and R. O. Kuzmin, In *Tectonics, structural geology and planetology*, (In Russian.) Moscow, Nauka, p. 281 (1976).

[44] S. Soter and A. Harris, *Icarus*, **30**, 192 (1976).

[45] C. P. Sonnett, D. S. Colburn, and K. Schwartz, *Nature*, **219**, 924 (1968).

[46] Ye. G. Yeroshenko and B. A. Okulsky, In *Geomagnetic studies*, (In Russian.) Moscow, Sovradio, **22**, 75 (1978).

[47] H. B. Wiik, *Geochem. et Cosmochim. Acta*, **9**, 279 (1956).

[48] A. P. Vinogradov, *Geokhimiya*, **7**, 555 (In Russian.) (1962).

[49] B. A. Smith, L. A. Soderblom, and R. Beede, *Science*, **206**, 927 (1979).

[50] B. A. Smith, L. A. Soderblom, and T. V. Johnson, *Science*, **204**, 951 (1979).

[51] L. A. Morabito, S. P. Synnott, and P. N. Kupferman, *Science*, **204**, 972 (1979).

[52] A. G. W. Cameron and J. O. Pollack, In *Jupiter*, T. Gehrels (ed.), Tucson, University of Arizona Press (1976).

[53] J. B. Pollack and R. T. Reynolds, *Icarus*, **21**, 248 (1974).

[54] G. J.. Consolmagno, In *Proc. 12th Lunar and Planet. Sci. Conf.*, New York, Pergamon Press, **2**, 1533 (1981).

[55] R. Hanel, B. Courath, and F. M. Flasar, *Science*, **206**, 951 (1979).

[56] S. Peal, P. Cassen, and R. Reynolds, *Science*, **203**, 892 (1979).

[57] F. P. Fanale, T. V. Johnson, and D. L. Matson, In *Planetary satellites*, J. A. Burns (ed.), Tucson University of Arizona Press, p. 379 (1976).

[58] B. K. Lucchitta, L. A. Soderblom, and H. M. Ferguson, In *Proc. 12th Lunar and Planet. Sci. Conf.*, New York, Pergamon Press, p. 1555 (1981).

[59] C. B. Picher, S. T. Ridgway, and T. B. McCord, *Science*, **170**, 1086 (1972).

[60] G. J. Consolmano and J. S. Lewis, In *Jupiter*, T. Gehrels (ed.), Tucson, University of Arizona Press (1976).

[61] D. Morrison and J. A. Burns, In *Jupiter*, T. Gehrels (ed.), Tucson, University of Arizona Press (1976).

[62] J. Veverka, In *Planetary satellites*, J. A. Burns (ed.), Tucson, University of Arizona Press, p. 210 (1977).

[63] D. Morrison and D. P. Cruikshank, *Icarus,* **18**, 224 (1977).

[64] J. S. Lewis, *Icarus,* **15**, 174 (1971).

[65] F. C. Gillett, W. J. Forrest, and K. M. Merrill, *Astrophys. J.,* **184**, L93 (1973).

[66] F. C. Gillett, *Astrophys. J.,* **201**, L41 (1975).

[67] A. Tokunaga, S. Beck, T. Geballe, and J. Lacy, *Bull. Amer, Astron. Soc.,* **12**, 669 (1980).

[68] B. R. Broadfoot, D. E. Sandel, and D. E. Shemansky, *Science,* **212**, 206 (1981).

[69] R. Hanel, B. Courath, and F. M. Flasar, *Science,* **212**, 192 (1981).

[70] V. G. Kunde, A. C. Aikin, and R. A. Hanel, *Nature,* **292**, 686 (1981).

[71] W. C. Maguire, R. A. Hanel, and D. E. Jennings, *Nature,* **292**, 683 (1981).

[72] J. B. Pollack, In *The new Solar System*, J. Kelly Beatty, B. O'Leary and A. Chaikin (eds.), Sky Publ. Corp. Cambridge, Massachusetts (1981).

[73] T. Owen, 'Titan', *Scientific American*, **246**, No. 2 (February 1982).

[74] D. M. Hunten, *NASA Conf. Publ.,* **2068**, 127 (1978).

[75] D. F. Strobel, *Rev. Geophys. and Space Phys.,* **13**, 372 (1975).

[76] F. M. Flasar, R. E. S. Samuelson, and B. J. Conrath, *Nature,* **292**, 693 (1981).

[77] G. L. Tyler, V. R. Eshleman, and J. D. Anderson, *Science,* **212**, 201 (1981). (1981).

Exploration of planets and satellites by space vehicles

2.1 Gamma-ray spectrometric studies

As mentioned above, gamma-ray spectrometry marked the beginning of the exploration of celestial bodies by space vehicles. As a result it became possible to evolve the first concepts of lunar and planetary material.

The first steps of gamma-ray spectrometry in outer space were very difficult. This was a consequence not only of the many technical problems linked to the construction of onboard instrumentation, but also of the uncertainty in initial data which were to determine the entire philosophy of the experiment ranging from the basic structure of the gamma-ray spectrometer and the details of its operation to the processing and interpretation of information obtained.

For instance, during the preparations for the first experiment to measure gamma radiation of the Moon, we did not know the flux density of gamma radiation caused by cosmic rays in the course of the irradiation of celestial bodies. Therefore, it was hard to choose the optimum parameters of the gamma-ray spectrometer (the size of the crystal, the capacity of channels, the duration of measuring intervals, etc.). During the preparations for the experiment on the space probe which was to make the first landing on Venus, the climatic conditions near the planet's surface were unknown. Therefore, there was uncertainty too as far as the choice of the optimum detector was concerned (a big crystal could fail to withstand high mechanical loads and the high temperature gradient, while a small crystal could fail to gather appropriate statistics during the operating lifetime of the probe on the planetary surface). Finally, the preparations for the experiment to measure the gamma-radiation of Mars involved the uncertainties connected with the absence of knowledge on the composition and density of the Martian atmosphere.

This led to the fact that sometimes the design and operating mode of the instrument proved to be not optimal and the volume of information obtained proved to be lower than was desirable for its reliable interpretation. At the same time, these first experiments were of particular importance for the development of space-based gamma-ray spectrometry and for studying extraterrestrial material.

There is another important factor which should be taken into account. Preparations for experiments in lunar and planetary gamma-ray spectrometry require numerous, sometimes rather complicated, model experiments on accelerators, air balloons and terrestrial rocks in their natural bedding in order to ensure the opportunity of interpreting every bit of information coming from space. This should be borne in mind when getting acquainted with the results of the first experiments in gamma-ray spectrometry of extraterrestrial objects.

With the development of space technology, the gamma-ray spectrometry of extraterrestrial material will be perfected and the scientific problems solved with its assistance will in turn get more complicated. This dynamic development is seen in the few experiments which have already been performed. The first experiment conducted from Luna 10 was relatively simple. But at that time practically nothing was known about lunar material. Therefore, despite the fact that the volume of information obtained was not great, its importance was at the level of a discovery. A more perfect experiment on Apollos 15 and 16 was staged, when already much had been learnt about lunar soil from laboratory studies of samples returned to the Earth. It gave a much larger volume of information and it was the next step in lunar exploration. In the gamma-ray spectrometry of Venus and Mars so far only the first steps have been taken, but they are of very great importance. Apparently in further studies of Solar System material, gamma-ray spectrometry will continue to play a prominent rôle.

2.1.1 GAMMA-RADIATION FROM SOLAR SYSTEM BODIES

The study of gamma-radiation from the Moon and planets is of special significance for further progress in developing concepts of their origin, evolution and present internal structure. Gamma-radiation of Solar System bodies is due to the decay of natural radioactive elements and radioactive nuclides formed by cosmic rays. All our knowledge of the Earth points, in particular, to the fact that natural radioactive elements (uranium, thorium and potassium, and at the early stage of development also the more short-lived nuclides) were determining its thermal history and, consequently, endogenic processes which formed the internal structure and the present-day view of our planet. At the same time, data on the content and rôle of natural radioactive elements on other bodies of the Solar System continue to be rather scarce.

Information of a different character is contained in radioactive nuclides produced during the interaction between cosmic rays and extraterrestrial matter. Even the first data on the radioactivity of meteorites brought to light some radically new possibilities for investigating the history of outer space. Soon the study of radioactivity induced by cosmic rays in different extraterrestrial objects became a highly important tool for solving quite a number of problems in the exploration of the Moon, planets and interplanetary space.

At present, the entire history of celestial bodies investigated by remote-sensing methods or space vehicles, and from them the history of the Solar System as a whole, is reproduced from the radioelements and radionuclides contained in them, some of which were playing an active part in the evolution of the Solar System and others which just bear witnesses to the events of the remote past.

A new aspect in studying the radioactivity of extraterrestrial objects has appeared. Progress in space technology has opened up the possibility of measuring gamma-radiation from the Moon and planets to determine not only the content of natural radioactive elements (U, Th, and K) on them but also of principal rock-forming elements (Si, Al, Mg, Fe, etc.) from the gamma-radiation induced by cosmic rays.

That it was in principle possible to determine the character of surface rocks on the Moon and on the planets from their gamma-radiation was first pointed out by Vinogradov *et al.* [1]. Subsequently this idea was elaborated in some theoretical papers: thus, in the paper by Surkov *et al.* [2] it was shown that the measurement of gamma-radiation at Mars' surface permits us to identify the type of Martian rocks, and papers by Armstrong [3] and Reedy and Arnold [4] discuss certain processes leading to the emission of gamma-quanta at the Moon's surface.

Finally, there appeared an opportunity for experimental verification of these ideas. Gamma-ray spectrometric investigations of the Moon from Luna 10 [5] and Apollos 15 and 16 [6, 7] and of Mars from Mars 5 [8, 9] furnished an opportunity to obtain, for the first time, data on the chemical composition of matter on these celestial bodies and thus to make initial progress in elaborating concepts of their evolution and internal structure.

This method, though rather simple as to its concept and realization in terms of apparatus does nonetheless present certain difficulties as regards the processing and interpretation of the measurements of gamma-radiation caused by the interaction between cosmic rays and extraterrestrial matter. These difficulties are due to a number of circumstances and, above all, to the compositional inhomogeneity of cosmic rays and their energy range, the complexity of the chemical composition of extraterrestrial matter and, lastly, the diversity of processes taking place during the interaction of high-energy particles and nuclei.

2.1.1.1 Galactic and solar cosmic rays

All Solar System bodies are being irradiated by galactic cosmic rays (GCR) and solar cosmic rays (SCR). The nuclear reactions responsible for gamma-radiation are produced almost exclusively by charged particles of GCR and SCR. The bodies possessing a magnetic field (e.g. the Earth) are screened by it from low-energy particles and are irradiated solely by the high-energy component of cosmic rays. Bodies deprived of a magnetic field (e.g. the Moon and meteorites) are irradiated by the lowest-energy particles, i.e. the solar wind.

GCR mainly consist of protons and alpha-particles. Their energy spectrum lies within the range from 0.1 to about 10^{10} GeV. The flux density of GCR is constant over a long period of time. However, at energies of a few GeV and below, the energy spectrum of GCR is significantly influenced by the solar magnetic field. The solar modulation of GCR (the Forbush effect) is responsible for the fact that their flux density decreases by a factor of two to three times during the period of solar maximum. The energy spectrum of GCR can be described by the expression:

$$\psi_1 (E > E_o) = \frac{A}{(M_o c^2 + E_0)^n} , \qquad (2.1.1)$$

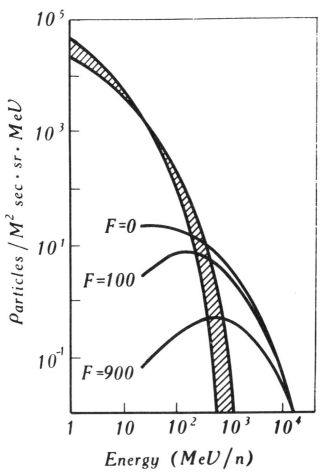

Fig. 2.1.1. — Spectra of galactic cosmic rays (GCR) near the Earth in different periods of solar activity (coefficient $F = 0$ characterizes the spectrum with the absence of modulation, $F = 900$ with maximum modulation) and the solar proton spectrum averaged over a long time (hatched region).

where ψ_1 is the total flux density of particles with energy $E > E_0$ (particles cm^{-2} s^{-1}); E is the kinetic energy of a particle (GeV per nucleon); M_0c^2 is the rest energy of particle (GeV); A and n are constants. Fig. 2.1.1 shows the GCR spectra in the periods of the solar activity maximum and minimum. The intensity of GCR varies not only with time but also in space. This dependence is shown in Fig. 2.1.2 for the orbits of the terrestrial planets. In moving from Mercury's orbit out to Mars' orbit (i.e. a distance of the order of 1AU) the intensity increases nearly by an order of magnitude; in moving further away it will presumably remain almost constant.

SCR appearing in the period of major solar flares likewise consist of protons and heavier nuclei. The flux of SCR may be much higher than that of GCR. However, the energy spectrum of SCR lies within the range of relatively low energies, mainly not above about 300 MeV. Many solar flares are accompanied by emissions in which very few particles with energies above 100 MeV are present. Cyclicity in the

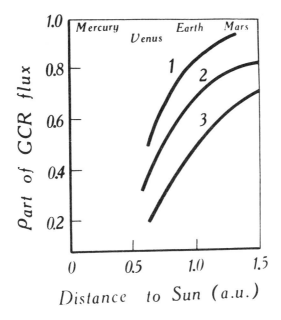

Fig. 2.1.2 — Change in the intensity of GCR with distance from the Sun, for low (1), intermediate (2) and high (3) solar activity.

appearance of SCR is associated with the roughly 11-year cycle of solar activity and with the 27-day period of the Sun's revolution.

The energy spectra of SCR differ for different solar flares and can be described by an exponential function

$$\psi_2 (>P) = \psi_0 \exp (- P/P_0), \tag{2.1.2}$$

where ψ_0 is the total proton flux during a flare (protons cm^{-2}); P is hardness (MeV per nucleon); P_0 is the characteristic hardness of a given flare. Hardness P is related to energy E in the following manner:

$$P = \frac{1}{Z_e} \sqrt{(E^2 + 2M_0c^2E)} \tag{2.1.3}$$

where Z_e is the charge of a particle, M_0 is the rest mass of a particle and c is the velocity of light.

It follows from the foregoing that the energy spectra of GCR and SCR overlap across a broad energy range. However, the range of SCR mainly lies below 100 MeV, while that of GCR mainly above 100 MeV. At the same time, the flux densities and energy spectra of GCR and SCR depend on the level of solar activity. The energy region above approximately 100 MeV is usually considered as a high-energy region. The interaction processes of particles with such energies obey different laws to the interactions in the medium energy region (5–100 MeV). Finally, all charged particles with energies significantly less than the specific binding energy of a nucleon in the nucleus (6–9 MeV), which belongs to the low-energy region, almost invariably fail to produce nuclear reactions.

2.1.1.2 Radionuclides induced by cosmic rays

The interaction of cosmic rays with a thick target (e.g. the surface layer of material on the Moon, planets and meteorites) is accompanied by nuclear reactions due to the effect of primary cosmic particles and secondary particles (nucleons and mesons).

Secondary particles produced in a thick target as a result of bombardment by particles of cosmic origin may be arbitrarily subdivided into two energy groups. All particles with energies above 100 MeV essentially interact in a single way, an ' for numerous nuclear reactions of the cross-sections for the formation of product nuclei are little dependent on the nature of the high-energy particle producing the reaction.

The predominant and strongly interacting particles with energies below 100 MeV in large bodies are neutrons, since many charged particles with energies below 100 MeV lose energy due to ionization losses before being able to interact with the nucleus.

The majority of secondary neutrons are produced with energies of a few MeV by emission from an excited nucleus. The rest are formed in the course of the 'knocking-out' process and have relatively high energies. The total number of secondary neutrons, for instance, born in the surface layer of lunar material is about 1.75×10^5 neutrons m^{-2} s^{-1} [10], or about seven neutrons for every primary nucleon. The spectrum of these neutrons has not yet been measured. However, the spectrum of secondary neutrons was measured at different heights in the Earth's atmosphere. Although the flux densities of neutrons at the surface of the Earth and the Moon are different (due to the Earth's magnetic field and dense atmosphere), the energy and spatial distribution of neutrons must be similar in both cases.

The number of product nuclei appearing in a thick target as the result of some *i*th reaction per unit of time at a depth *d* may in a general form be expressed as:

$$P_i(d) = N \frac{dI}{dE}(E,d)\,\sigma_i(E)\,dE$$

where $\sigma_i(E)$ is an excitation function for this reaction; N is the number of target atoms in a unit mass; and dI/dE (E, d) is the differential flux of interacting particles at the depth d.

To be able to use expression (2.1.4) it is necessary to know the energy distribution of all interacting high-energy particles ($E > 100$ MeV) and medium- and low-energy neutrons ($E < 100$ MeV). Such calculations were performed in [4].

The energy distribution of all strongly interacting particles with energies in excess of 100 MeV at the depth d in a thick target was determined from the relationship:

$$\frac{dI}{dE}(E, d) = K(\alpha + E)^{-2.5} \tag{2.1.5}$$

where α is a parameter determining the distribution form, and K is a normalizing constant. The parameters K and α are functions of depth. The parameter α

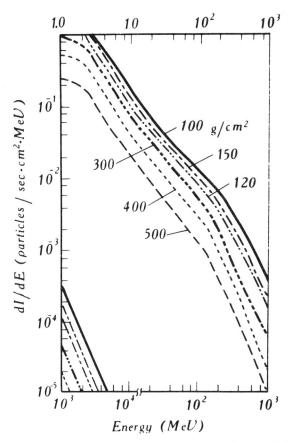

Fig. 2.1.3 — Flux density of all nuclear interacting particles as a function of their energy
and the depth of lunar rock.

decreases with depth because the number of low-energy particles increases with respect to that of high-energy particles. The parameter K is determined for every depth from the total flux of particles with energies in excess of 1 GeV per nucleon.

Calculation of the energy distribution of secondary neutrons with energies between 2.5 and 100 MeV versus depth d was made by using the expression

$$\frac{dI}{dE}(E, d) = K(\alpha + 100)^{-2.5}[M(E) - (\alpha - 50)\,\delta(E)] \qquad (2.1.6)$$

where K and α are the same parameters dependent on depth as those in equation (2.1.5); $M(E)$ and $\delta(E)$ are energy functions in MeV: $M(E) = 94E^{-1} + 603E^{-2} - 300E^{-3}$; $\delta(E) = 0.3E^{-1.26} - 0.00091$.

For $E = 100$ MeV equation (2.1.6) changes into equation (2.1.5) because $\delta(E) = 0$ and $M(E) = 1$ for this energy.

Since many inelastic scattering reactions producing gamma-rays have a maximum cross-section in the case of neutron energies of the order of 1 MeV, it is important in computing the lunar albedo for gamma-rays to know the flux of the latter near the

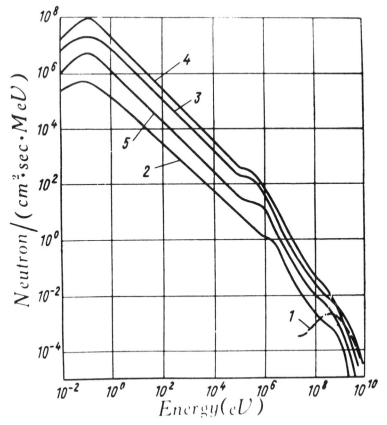

Fig. 2.1.4 — Neutron flux density and energy of neutrons as a function of the depth in lunar rock: 1, galactic particle spectrum; 2, neutron flux density near the surface; 3, at a depth of 300 Kgm^{-2}; 4, at a depth of 10^3 Kgm^{-2}; 5, at a depth of 2×10^3 Kgm^{-2}.

surface of a thick target. The energy distribution of neutrons with energies between 0.5 and 2.5 MeV was computed by using an expression of the form:

$$\frac{dI}{dE}(E,d) = K(\alpha + 100)^{-2.5}[115 - (\alpha - 50)\,0.094][1.3125 + 0.5E - 0.25E^2] \quad (2.1.7)$$

Finally, it was supposed that the flux density of neutrons with energies below 0.5 MeV increases approximately as does $1/E$.

Figs 2.1.3 and 2.1.4 show the flux densities of interacting particles, computed for different depths of rock on the Moon [4, 10]. The total flux of primary protons with energies in excess of 1 GeV per neutron was assumed to be equal to 1.7×10^4 protons m^{-2} s^{-1}, which is the mean value for a solar cycle. The results are given for isotropic irradiation of the lunar surface. The ratio of the total proton flux intensity to the total flux of alpha-particles for energies in excess of 1 GeV per nucleon was assumed to be equal to 10. Particles heavier than helium were omitted. At present the computed data can be compared with the experimental data obtained on lunar specimens, though for an insignificant layer of matter. Fluxes at considerable depths are comparable with measurements made in the Earth's atmosphere.

Table 2.1.1 — Principal long-lived ($T_{1/2} \geqslant 30$ days) cosmogenic radionuclides

Nuclide	Type of decay, radiation	Half-life $T\frac{1}{2}$	Radiation energy (MeV); yield (%)
1	2	3	4
^{3}H	β^-	12.262 years	0.0186 max.
^{10}Be	β^-	1.62×10^6 years	0.555 max.
^{14}C	β^-	5.745 years	0.156 max.
^{22}Na	β^+, EC, γ	2.6 years	0.545 max. — β^+ 1.275 (100) — γ
^{26}Al	β^+, EC, γ	7.16×10^5 years	1.17 max. — β^+ 0.511; 1.12 (4); 1.81 (100) — γ
^{32}Si	β^-	~700 years	0.21 max.
^{36}Cl	β^-, β^+, EC	3.08×10^5 years	0.71 max. — β^- 0.511 (2) — γ
^{37}Ar	EC, γ	35 days	contin. up to 0.81 — γ
^{39}Ar	β^-	263 years	0.565 max.
^{40}K	$\beta^-, \beta^+, EC, \gamma$	1.27×10^9 years	1.36 max. — β^- 0.483 max. — β^+ 1.46 max. (11) — γ
^{44}Ti	EC, γ	48 years	0.068 (90); 0.78 (98) — γ
^{45}Ca	β^-	165 days	0.262 max. β^-
^{46}Sc	β^-, γ	84 days	0.357 max. 0.889 (100); 1.120 (100) — γ
^{48}V	EC, β^+, γ	16 days	0.694 max. — β^+ 0.945 (10); 0.984 (100); 1.312 (97); 2.241 (3) — γ
^{49}V	EC, γ	330 days	contin. up to 0.60 — γ
^{51}Cr	EC, γ	27.5 days	0.320 (10) — γ
^{53}Mn	EC, γ	2×10^6 years	
^{54}Mn	EC, γ	312 days	0.835 (100) — γ
^{55}Fe	EC, γ	2.6 years	contin. up to 0.23 (0.004) — γ
^{56}Co	β^+, EC, γ	79 days	1.49 max. — β^+ 0.847 (100); 1.04 (15) 1.24 (66); 1.76 (15) 2.02 (11); 2.60 (17) 3.26 (13) — γ
^{57}Co	EC, γ	272 days	0.014 (9); 0.122 (87); 0.136 (11); 0.692 (0.14) — γ
^{58}Co	β^+, EC, γ	72 days	0.474 max. — β^+ 0.810 (99); 0.865 (1.4) 1.67 (0.6) — γ
^{59}Ni	EC, γ	~10^5 years	contin. up to 1.06 — γ
^{60}Co	β^-, γ	5.3 years	1.48 max. (0.12); 0.314 max. (99) — β^- 1.173 (100); 1.332 (100) — γ

EC, electron capture.

Table 2.1.1 lists principal cosmogenic radionuclides produced in the course of the interation between cosmic rays and material of the Moon, planets, meteorites and cosmic dust. Cosmogenic radionuclides accumulate in extraterrestrial objects with the time of their presence in outer space. However, in the case of prolonged irradiation the majority of these radionuclides attain an equilibrium content, which is determined by the intensity of cosmic irradiation. The shorter the decay period of a radionuclide, the sooner its content attains an equilibrium, i.e. the amount when the number of produced nuclei (of a given type) becomes equal to that of disintegrating nuclei.

Most of the cosmogenic radionuclides listed in Table 2.1.1 are contained in extraterrestrial objects in such equilibrium quantities that yield about 1–100 decay events $min^{-1}\,kg^{-1}$ of the object.

An analysis of both radioactive and nonradioactive products of nuclear reactions enables us to obtain information on the present-day processes taking place in outer space, as well as to learn about the remote past.

As can be seen from expression (2.1.7), the number of cosmogenic nuclides formed per unit of time depends on the intensity and spectral composition of interacting particles, as well as on the cross-section for the formation of a given nuclide, which itself is a function of particle energy. In principle, knowing these dependences, we may also compute the accumulation rate of any cosmogenic nuclide at any distance from the surface of a celestial body. However, the rigorous computation of the accumulation rate of cosmogenic nuclides in celestial objects is a rather complicated process. Therefore, such computations are made with certain simplifying assumptions [11–15]. In this case, for example, theoretical estimates of the content of cosmogenic nuclides in meteorites [11] were found to agree with experimental ones within a factor of about two.

The formation of cosmogenic nuclides in lunar matter has been discussed in a number of papers. Fig. 2.1.5 shows the distribution of cosmogenic nuclides at different depths in lunar in lunar rock, as calculated in [16]. The calculation was carried out for lunar soil irradiated by GCR. As seen from the figure, the maximum formation rate, for instance, of ^{14}C and ^{22}Na nuclides lies at a depth of about 4×10^2 $kg\,m^{-2}$. Such isotopes as ^{10}Be and ^3H have a maximum computed formation rate lying at a depth betweeen 0 and $1.5 \times 10^2\,kg\,m^{-2}$. Starting at a depth of approximately $1.2 \times 10^4\,kg\,m^{-2}$, the formation rate of radionuclides exponentially decreases with depth.

The contribution of cosmogenic nuclides to gamma-radiation of lunar rocks was estimated for the first time in [1]. Computations were made for 1 g of different types of rock. The number of cosmogenic nuclides was determined on the basis of experimental data from the cross-sections for the formation of nuclides, as obtained in accelerators. The limited experimental data for the cross-sections of formation of nuclides was supplimented through extrapolation for some non-measured cross-sections. It was shown that the main cosmogenic nuclides contributing to the gamma-ray spectrum of lunar rocks are: ^{10}C, ^{16}N, $^{14,19}O$, ^{20}F, $^{22,24}Na$, $^{26,28}Al$ and ^{54}Mn. The formation of cosmogenic nuclides in lunar soil under the effect of secondary nucleons was also discussed in [3,4]. The authors indicate that of all of the radionuclides — the reaction products forming in lunar rock — only four account for a perceptible contribution to the total gamma-ray spectrum of lunar soil, namely, ^{16}N, ^{22}Na, ^{26}Al and ^{54}Mn.

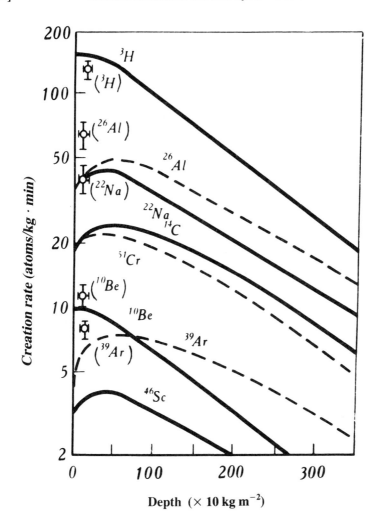

Fig. 2.1.5 — Change in the rate of the formation of cosmogenic nuclides as a function of depth (distance to the surface) in lunar rock. Points are experimental data.

Fig. 2.1.6 shows the gamma-ray spectrum of principal cosmogenic gamma-radiators with energies below 3 MeV contained in lunar soil samples brought back to the Earth. The spectrum was measured using a scintillation spectrometer with NaI (Tl) crystal 76×76 mm in size and with a resolution of about 10% (with respect to E_γ this is about 0.666 MeV). There is the possibility of variation of this spectrum with the solar cycle, which is due to a change in the content of particularly short-lived gamma-radiators, such as ^{22}Na, ^{54}Mn, etc., the formation of which depends on the time elapsed from the moment of the solar flare. The flux of gamma-quanta of ^{26}Al is almost independent of time. The gamma-quanta of ^{40}K, forming principally from Ca, and of ^{50}V, nuclides, forming principally from Fe, Mn, and Ti, make an insignificant contribution to the total flux of gamma-quanta from lunar rock.

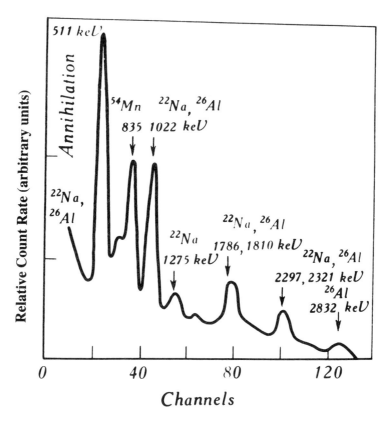

Fig. 2.1.6 — Spectrum of gamma-radiation of cosmogenic nuclides in lunar soil brought back to the Earth by Luna 16. The spectrum is constructed according to experimentally measured radionuclide contents.

The total flux of gamma-quanta due to the decay of cosmogenic nuclides amounts approximately to 8×10^2 and 4×10^2 quanta m^{-2}, respectively, for the minimum and maximum of solar activity, thus make an insignificant contribution to the total gamma-radiation produced by the interaction of cosmic rays with matter. The main contribution is made by gamma-quanta produced during the transition of excited nuclei to the ground state.

2.1.1.3 Gamma-radiation of natural radioactive elements

Natural radioactive elements have played a special rôle in the history of the Solar System. The study of their occurrence on different celestial bodies is a basis for a further elaboration of concepts of the Solar System. However, since the number of adequately investigated extraterrestrial objects is few, this causes certain difficulties in making a quantitative estimate of the abundance of natural radioactive elements in the Solar System.

We can well imagine that, at the earliest stage of the appearance of the solar nebula, radionuclides were homogeneously distributed in the gaseous cloud whose density was decreasing from its central part towards the periphery. The entire subsequent evolution of matter in the Solar System and, in particular, the history of the existence of radionuclides may be subdivided into two main periods — the preplanetary stage when matter was in a gaseous–dusty state, and the planetary stage when matter had concentrated into the large bodies of the Solar System.

At present the radioactivity of planetary matter is chiefly determined by U, Th and K. Their average content on the Earth is estimated either on the basis of the magnitude of the present heat flow from the planet's interior [17] or by assuming it to be equal to their average content in chondritic meteorites [18]. Radioactivity of the planets in the remote past was significantly higher, not only due to a higher content of these elements at that time, but also due to the decay of shorter-lived nuclides with a decay period of about 10^6–10^8 years. The latter had arisen in the epoch of nuclear synthesis and later entered the composition of the Solar System's younger bodies.

Finally, in the preplanetary epoch, and at the early development stage of the planets, there could possibly exist superheavy transuranic elements, the tracks of whose fragments were discovered in certain meteorites and lunar rock specimens [19].

Today we know of about 20 natural radionuclides having decay periods ranging from 10^8 to 10^{21} years. They mostly belong to rare and trace elements, the contents of which in the rocks of the Earth's crust do not exceed small fractions of one per cent. Table 2.1.2 lists some particularly confidently identifiable natural radionuclides found in the Earth's crust. The data were taken from [19–25], the radiation intensity of radionuclides being determined not only by their content in the rock but also by their decay period. As can be seen from Table 2.1.2, a significant contribution to radioactivity can be made only by ^{40}K, ^{232}Th and ^{238}U.

On the Earth, potassium, thorium and uranium are principally contained in the crust, where their concentration is significantly higher than in the mantle. But even within the limits of different types of rocks in the Earth's crust their contents are observed to be varying significantly.

The potassium nuclide ^{40}K disintegrates ($10.95 \pm 0.90\%$) by way of electron capture (accompanied by the emission of gamma-quanta with 1.461 MeV energy), converting into ^{40}Ar, or ($89.05 \pm 0.09\%$) by way of beta-decay, converting into ^{40}Ca. Since we shall further be interested mainly in gamma-radiation, let us note that one gramme of natural potassium emits 3.25 ± 0.07 gamma-quanta per second.

In the course of disintegration ^{232}Th forms a radioactive series (family) consisting of seven radionuclides and terminating in a stable lead nuclide, ^{208}Pb. One gramme of natural thorium (^{232}Th), being in a radioactive equilibrium with daughter products of decay, emits 4.1×10^3 gamma-quanta per second.

As a result of disintegration, ^{238}U gives rise to a radioactive series (family) consisting of eight radionuclides and terminating in a stable lead nuclide, ^{206}Pb. One gramme of ^{238}U, being in a radioactive equilibrium with daughter products of decay, emits 1.23×10^4 gamma-quanta per second.

If we take account of the K, Th and U content in terrestrial rocks and on celestial bodies, as given in [26], and make use of the aforementioned specific activities of these nuclides, we may compute the specific gamma-activity of each rock. The corresponding data are listed in Table 2.1.3. As seen from the table, terrestrial rocks and space bodies differ significantly from one another in gamma-radioactivity.

Table 2.1.2 — Natural radionuclides of the Earth's crust

Radionuclide	Type of decay	Half-life (years)	Abundance of radionuclide (%)	Mean content of radionuclide in the Earth's crust (%)
^{40}K	β^- (89.05%) EC (10.95%)	1.27×10^9	0.0119	2.35
^{50}V	EC	4×10^{14}	0.24	0.02
^{87}Rb	β^-	4.7×10^{10}	27.85	8×10^{-3}
^{115}Zn	β^-	6×10^{14}	95.77	10^{-5}
^{130}Te	β^-	10^{21}	34.49	10^{-6}
^{138}Ba	β^-	10^{15}	71.66	0.05
^{138}La	β^-, EC	7×10^{10}	0.089	6.5×10^{-4}
^{144}Na	α	3×10^{15}	23.87	1.7×10^{-3}
^{147}Sm	α	6.7×10^{11}	15.07	7×10^{-4}
^{150}Nd	β^-	10^{16}	5.60	
^{176}Lu	β^- (33%) EC (67%)	2.4×10^{10}	2.60	1.7×10^{-4}
$^{178(?)}$W	α	6×10^8	2.5×10^{-7}	7×10^{-3}
^{187}Re	β^-	4×10^{12}	62.93	10^{-7}
$^{190(?)}$Pt	α	?	?	2×10^{-5}
^{209}Bi	α	2.7×10^{-7}	100	10^{-5}
^{232}Th	α	1.39×10^{10}	100	10^{-3}
^{235}U	α	7.13×10^8	0.72	2×10^{-6}
^{238}U	α	4.51×10^9	99.28	3×10^{-4}
^{247}Cm	α	$>4 \times 10^7$	?	?

However, the total flux of gamma-quanta does not constitute an unambiguous characteristic of the content of each of these radionuclides separately. At the same time, it is the separate content of each of these radionuclides that is the most important characteristic of many geochemical processes. In laboratory and field conditions the separate determination of K, Th and U is usually made not from the total flux but from the spectral composition of the gamma-radiation.

2.1.1.4 Natural radioactive elements on the Earth

It is common knowledge that U, Th and K are distributed very irregularly within the Earth's crust. They are contained in maximum quantities in acid rocks, in lesser quantities in intermediate rocks, less still in basic rocks and, finally, very insignificantly in ultrabasic rocks. Table 2.1.4 lists the average contents of natural radioactive elements in the Earth's most widespread rocks [26–28]. Being generally aware of the processes leading to the formation of these rocks on the Earth, we may consider the behaviour of natural radioactive elements and their rôle in the evolution of matter on other planets

Table 2.1.3 — Gamma-radioactivity of terrestrial rocks and extraterrestrial objects

Radionuclides	Specific activity ($\times 10^{-2}$ quanta g^{-1} s^{-1})				
	Granites	Basalts	Dunites	Chondrites	Moon's crust
^{40}K	11.05	2.60	0.103	0.29	3.70
^{232}Th	7.38	1.23	2.05×10^{-3}	1.64×10^{-2}	1.16
^{238}U	4.31	0.62	3.69×10^{-3}	1.85×10^{-2}	0.64
Total	22.74	4.45	0.109	0.328	5.50

Table 2.1.4 – Content of natural radioelements in different types of earth rock formations

Type of formation	Rocks	Content of radionuclides p.p.m.		
		$K \times 10^4$	U	Th
Acidic	Granites, granadiorites (quartzporphyrites, reolites, dactites)	3.4 (1–6)	3.5 (1–20)	18 (6–40)
Neutral	Diorites (andesites)	2.3 (1–4)	1.8 (1–3)	7 (6–30)
Basic	Gabbro (basalts) anorthosites	0.8 (0.05–3.0)	0.5 (0.03–4)	3.0 (0.05–10)
Ultrabasic	Dunites, peridotites, harzburgites (picrites)	0.03 (0.001–0.1)	0.003 (0.001–0.8)	0.005 (0.001–1.0)

The average proportion by weight of the natural radioelements is given followed by the range in parentheses.

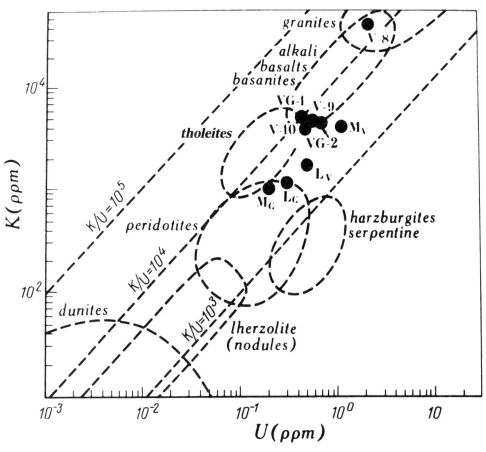

Fig. 2.1.7 — K–U systematics of data according to the content of natural radioactive elements in widespread terrestrial rocks.

Fig. 2.1.7 presents in K–U coordinates the data on particularly representative terrestrial rocks. Such systems based on double-logarithmic graphs are often employed in geochemical and cosmochemical examinations.

Petrographic and petrochemical investigations of oceanic rock samples have enabled us to turn our attention to the character of the genetic interrelationship of basalts and ultrabasites which subdivide into two basic groups of rock: lherzolites and harzburgites [29]. In this case, lherzolites are classified as matter of the upper mantle and harzburgites as a remnant after melting out of primitive basalts. These considerations also appear to be supported by the K-U systematics.

As seen from Fig. 2.1.7, the region of the mean values of the K/U ratios for lherzolite modules of oceanic areas occupies a narrow band within $(2–3) \times 10^3$, i.e. lies significantly below that of the K/U ratios for the succession of theoleiitic basalts (K/U $\approx 7 \times 10^3$) and the ground mass of alkaline basalts (K/u = $(1–2 \times 10^4)$. It would be natural to suppose that an increase of the K/U ratio in these rocks, must be accompanied by its decrease in other formations interrelated to the former ones by a single genetic process. The rocks in question are apparently harzburgites. Thus, in examining the data on K/U ratios a noteworthy fact is the branching-out of the lherzolite band of K/U ratios into two series significantly different from each other. The upper series beginning with oceanic tholeiitic basalts is characterized by a higher K/U ratio, while the lower series, represented by harzburgites, by a lower K/U ratio.

A decrease of K/U ratios in harzburgite rocks of the rift zones is due to a very high uranium content for ultrabasic rocks. Proceeding from a number of factors we may suppose that their high uranium content results from secondary enrichment, in the course of reworking of these rocks by mantle outgassing, by products containing uranium. What is important here is that uranium had enriched rock directly associated with the mantle. The rift areas are free from any influence of the continental crust and, therefore, all variations of K/U ratios stem exclusively from the differentiation in mantle matter and its products.

Thus, proceeding from the assumption put forth for the first time by Vakita [30] to the effect that the lherzolite modules represent the upper mantle material, and taking into account the distribution scheme of K/U contents presented in Fig. 2.1.7, we may suppose that the potassium content in primary mantle matter is not above 3×10^{-4} and that of uranium 0.1 p.p.m.

In estimating the mean contents of U, Th and K for the Earth as a whole we usually proceed from the following considerations:

(1) the magnitude of the mean heat flow at the Earth's surface is assumed to be equal to about 6×10^{-2} W m^{-2}.
(2) the relationship of radioelements in the upper mantle's rocks is extended to material of the entire Earth;
(3) the limits of the potassium content on the Earth are assessed from ^{40}K on the basis of the data on the content of daughter ^{40}Ar in the planet's atmosphere, allowance being made for the possible magnitude of its fractional release [31, 32].

Supposing that the heat flow is in equilibrium with heat formation and that the bulk of the heat is generated in the course of the disintegration of uranium and thorium, MacDonald [17] obtained for the Earth the mean content of U ≈ 0.031 p.p.m. Similar estimates based on thermodynamic calculations were given by other researchers too; particularly in [168] the average values were obtained (by supposing that radioelements are absent in the Earth's core) for U of 0.035 p.p.m. and for Th of 0.14 p.p.m. in the case of Th/U = 4.

As regards the estimates of the average potassium content on the Earth, the value of about 100 p.p.m. obtainable from the K/U ratio of about 3×10^3 is, in our opinion, to be preferred to the value of about 350 p.p.m. which was computed from the commonly used ratio K/U $= 10^4$; the more so since about 100 p.p.m. agrees better with the range of possible potassium contents 90–170 p.p.m., as estimated from the data on the daughter^{40}Ar.

2.1.1.5 Natural radioactive elements in the Solar System bodies

Although the fractionation of volatile elements and compounds between the terrestrial planets and the giant planets is accepted as being caused by temperature differences at different distances from the Sun, the problem of fractionation dependent on heliocentric distance within the confines of the terrestrial planets remains unsolved. However, certain notions about fractionation can be obtained both from an examination of the various condensation models of the formation of planets from the protoplanetary cloud and from the analysis of indirect data on the structure of the planets.

Supposing that the U and Th ratios change little or do not change at all within at least 4 AU, let us consider, as in the foregoing discussion, the contents and relationships of U and K alone.

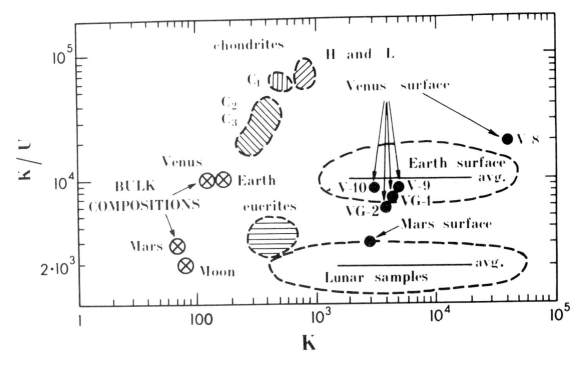

Fig. 2.1.8 — K–U systematics of data according to the content of natural radioactive elements in rocks of the Earth, Venus, Mars, the Moon and some meteorites.

Fig. 2.1.8 gives the K/U ratio as a function of the K abundance on Venus, the Earth, Mars, the Moon and in some meteorites. It is seen that the abundances of U and K, as measured by the gamma-ray spectrometric method, are more like the terrestrial values than the lunar or meteoritic ones.

Taking account of the difficulties in obtaining these data, it is nevertheless possible to make a certain extrapolation to the composition of rocks on Venus on the basis of a correlation between K content and the Si and Al contents, as is observable among rocks on the Earth, the Moon and in meteorites. The potassium content in the Venera 8 area favours the presence of sialic rock, while the Venera 9 and 10 and VeGa 1 and 2 areas, depleted in K, favour the presence of simatic rock.

The rock compositions, as measured by Veneras 13 and 14 and VeGa 2 show that Venus is differentiated, since these compositions are different from primitive meteoritic rocks (see Fig. 2.1.8) and are close to differentiated terrestrial rocks. As seen from the figure, the abundances of natural radioactive elements on the Moon, planets and in meteorites conform to the general concepts of the evolution of matter in the Solar System. According to these concepts, the protoplanetary matter, from which all of the Solar System bodies subsequently formed, had acquired in the course of its chemical evolution a compositional inhomogeneity reflected in the composition of the Moon, planets and meteorites. This compositional inhomogeneity of protoplanetary matter was principally determined by the relationship of volatile and refractory elements and their compounds.

In the course of the evolution of protoplanetary matter, the volatile elements and compounds moved to the periphery of the cloud (in the low-temperature region), while refractory elements moved closer to the Sun (in the high-temperature region). This process of differentiation of matter in the preplanetary period was naturally reflected also in the occurrence of radioactive elements (and particularly in their relationships) in the Solar System. Thus, for instance, over the range of distance from Mercury (about 0.4 AU) to the asteroid belt (about 2–4 AU) the K/U ratio varies by nearly five orders of magnitude.

Thus, the subsequently formed different bodies of the Solar System inherited those quantitative relationships of radioactive elements that had been presented in the formation areas of the bodies concerned.

The formation pattern of the Earth–Moon planetary system appears to be somewhat more complicated. In spite of the identity of preplanetary matter in the supply zone of these two bodies, the differences in the condensation conditions (pressure, temperature) led to a difference in their chemical composition. According to the condensation models, the Earth's metallic core could form prior to the beginning of condensation of low-temperature magnesium silicates. Correspondingly, a relative shortage of iron on the Moon can be associated with the fact that in the latter's accretion a significant proportion was accounted for by high-temperature condensates enriched with refractory elements (among them U and Th).

On the other hand, an important rôle in the deficiency of volatiles on the Earth and on the Moon is to be attributed to the mechanism of the interaction between the solar wind and the particles of the swarm being formed. According to the model elaborated by Ruskol [33], the effect of the solar wind would have been particularly important on the Moon at the terminal stage of the accretion of its surface layers. In that period the transparency at the circumterrestrial swarm periphery was great enough to enable the atoms of volatile elements, which had been released during the evaporation of matter in collisions of solid particles and bodies, to be partly removed from the swarm by the effect of the solar wind.

Following the formation of planets, matter was subject to further evolution. As is known, in the course of differentiation of planetary matter the crust was being enriched with natural radioactive elements, particularly potassium.

While in the case of the Moon the differentiation of matter was relatively insignificant, the Earth and Venus underwent far-reaching differentiation in the course of their thermal history; appropriate evidence for this is found, in particular, in high K/U ratios of the surface magmatic rocks as compared to the assumed ratios of the mean contents of radioelements throughout the planets.

This is how we may interpret the abundance of natural radioactive elements in the Solar System, as observed today, and their rôle in the evolution of matter in celestial bodies.

2.1.2 GAMMA-RAY SPECTROMETRIC INSTRUMENTATION FOR SPACE RESEARCH

Progress in gamma-ray spectrometric techniques over the past two decades has been marked by important achievements. Elaboration of gamma-ray spectrometric instrumentaion and methods has been dealt with by numerous researchers, applying gamma-ray spectrometry to the solution of diverse problems. The use of gamma-ray spectrometry and, particularly the description of the instruments and methodologies employed in laboratory, field and logging investigations have become the subject of quite a number of monographs [34–39]. A number of papers deal with the gamma-ray spectrometric instrumentation finding application in space research [40–43], as well as that used in the investigation of meteorites, cosmic dust and lunar soil samples brought back to the Earth by space vehicles [44–53].

On account of the extremely low content of natural and cosmogenic radionuclides in extraterrestrial objects, investigation of their radioactivity mostly involves the use of low-background scintillation gamma-ray spectrometry endowed with high-efficiency detectors of gamma-radiation. At the same time, development of large-volume semiconductor detectors likewise opens up the possibility of using them for the aforementioned purposes.

The gamma-ray spectrometric instrumentation used for the study of extraterrestrial matter with the aid of space vehicles comprises in the simplest case a multi-channel scintillation gamma-ray spectrometer possessing a number of specific features to meet the requirements expected of onboard equipment. The detector used in such a spectrometer can be either a solid scintillator, e.g. NaI(Tl) or CsI(Tl), or a gas scintillator, e.g. Xe. A more sophisticated version of such apparatus is a gamma-ray spectrometer with a semiconductor detector. To maintain continuously a low temperature for the semiconductor detector, there is a need to develop special on-board cryogenic facilities, as well as to make use of amplitude analysers with a great number of channels, and this significantly complicates the spectrometer design. Finally, in the apparatus intended for obtaining more extensive information on the composition and properties of extraterrestrial matter, various excitation sources of gamma-radiation are employed together with the gamma-ray spectrometer. Possible sources for this use are: neutron generators based on the nuclear reaction $T(d,n)^4He$, either Po–Be or Ra–Be isotopic sources based on the reactions $(\propto, n)$, or heavy elements (e.g. ^{252}Cf) which emit neutrons as a result of spontaneous fission.

Although the design principles of gamma-ray spectrometric instrumentation for use in the laboratory and in space research are generally similar, the onboard equipment is notable for some important differences. These are, first and foremost, small overall dimensions, low weight and lower power-consumption. The onboard equipment must, moreover, be capable of performance within a wide temperature range and under the impact of great linear and shock accelerations and vibrations. Finally, it must be able to carry out all measurements automatically, including the execution of the preset operational program, automatic correction of operating modes, as well as sending out the accumulated information to the space vehicle's telemetry. All these requirements of the onboard equipment, as could be expected, call for the working out of different solutions to design and methodological problems associated with the development of gamma-ray spectrometric instruments to be used in space research.

Later in the text we shall be concerned with the specific design of gamma-ray spectrometric instrumentation intended for exploring extraterrestrial matter, maximum attention being given to the facilities developed and used for studying gamma-radiation on the Moon, Venus and Mars by space vehicles.

2.1.2.1 Scintillation detectors and detection units

To clarify adopted terminology we shall agree that the name of the radiation detector will be applied to a direct receiver and converter of gamma-radiation (i.,e. a scintillation crystal), and the name of the detection unit to a crystal combined with a photomultiplier (possibly together with a voltage divider), and all the devices securing the reception, amplification and transmission of the electric signal to the analysing device will be called a sensor. The last term is not universally accepted, but it is widely used in space research, because the sensor itself (a unit of this designation) is often brought outside the framework of a space vehicle, the rest of the electronic devices being arranged inside it.

The choice of the gamma-ray detector is made by considering the following parameters:

— the resolution of the detector which determines the complexity of the spectrum that can be analysed;
— the efficiency of the detector which determines the lower limit in measuring gamma-ray activity;
— linearity, stability and other parameters determining the quality of information obtained;
— simplicity of processing the information obtained.

Today's gamma-ray spectrometry is practically entirely based on three classes of detectors — scintillation, gaseous, and semiconductor. The principal functional elements of scintillation detection units are scintillators and photomultipliers.

Table 2.1.5 — Basic properties of some scintillators used in gamma-ray spectrometry

Scintillators	Emission spectrum maximum (nm)	Time of flash (µs)	Density ($\times 10^3$ kg m^{-3})	Efficiency with respect to anthracene
NaI(Tl)	420	0.25	3.67	2.1
CsI(Tl)	565	1.1	4.51	1.0
CsI(Na)	565	0.65	4.51	1.75
Anthracene	440	0.032	1.25	1.0
Plastic scintillator	350–450	0.0025–0.005	1.06	0.28–0.48
Liquid scintillator	355–450	0.0015–0.008	0.86	0.27–0.49

Table 2.1.5 lists some characteristics of scintillators used in gamma-ray spectrometry. At present, among the scintillators listed in Table 2.1.5, NaI(Tl), CsI (Tl) and plastics are mainly used both in the onboard and laboratory gamma-ray spectrometers intended for the study of extraterrestrial matter. Let us note that inorganic scintillators, as compared with organic, have a time of flash two orders of magnitude longer and a registration efficiency of gamma-quanta one order of magnitude higher, thus enabling the two classes of scintillators, between them, to be used for solving a wide range of problems.

Table 2.1.6 lists the main characteristics of spectrometric photomultipliers used in scintillation gamma-ray spectrometry in the USSR. It is easy to see that the maximum spectral sensitivity region of the majority of photomultipliers mostly corresponds to the emission spectrum maximum of an NaI(Tl) crystal and organic scintillators. The strength characteristics of photomultipliers improve as their size decreases. The smaller the photomultiplier the less its intrinsic noise.

One of the main units of gamma-ray spectrometric instrumentation is the detection unit. Scintillation spectrometers consist, as a rule, of a scintillator and a photomultiplier which, being structurally integrated in a single unit and confined within a single pressurized body, have received the name of a 'scintiblock'. The scintiblock determines the main parameters of a gamma-ray spectrometer and the quality of information obtained with its aid. Development of scintiblock designs intended for operation under conditions of space experiments calls for careful examination of the properties of scintiblocks and photomultipliers, optical glues and sealing agents.

There have been developed by now quite a number of scintiblocks of different types and sizes [54–60] endowed with superior strength characteristics.

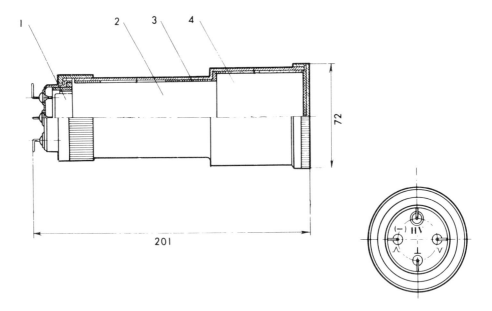

Fig. 2.1.9 — Structure of the single-crystal scintillation detection unit: 1, voltage divider; 2, photomultiplier; 3, antimagnetic screen; 4, scintillation crystal. Dimensions in millimetres.

Table 2.1.6 — Design dimensions and specifications of photomultipliers (FEU)

Parameter	FEU-129	FEU-125	FEU-54	FEU-55	FEU-58	FEU-83	FEU-92	FEU-93	FEU-97	FEU-110	FEU-118	FEU-119	FEU-139	FEU-141	FEU-148
1. Maximum size ($h \times h$)	52×122	170×190	22×75	22×75	22×75	36×100	40×113	52×110	52×110	80×125	52×110	40×115	80×125	38×70	40×110
2. Working diam. of photocathode (mm)	40	150	12	12	12	25	25	40	40	63	40	25	63	25	25
3. Mass (g)	130	1000	25–40	25–40	40	80	150	140	140	200	140	180	200	120	140
4. Type of photocathode	BiAgCs	SbNaKCs	SbCs	BiAgCs	SbCs	AgOCs	SbCs	SbCs	SbCs	SbKNaCs	SbKNaCs	SbKNaCs	SbKCs	SbKNaCs	SbKCs
5. Spectral sensitivity region (nm)	310–740	300–850	300–650	310–770	300–650	100–1200	300–650	300–650	250–650	300–900	300–850	300–850	300–650	300–850	300–650
6. Light sensitivity ($A lm^{-1}$)	4.5×10^{-5}	8×10^{-5}	2×10^{-5}	2×10^{-5}	1.5×10^{-5}	2.5×10^{-5}	2.5×10^{-5}	3×10^{-5}	3.5×10^{-5}	8×10^{-5}	10×10^{-5}	8×10^{-5}	9×10^{-5}	—	5.5×10^{-5}
7. Supply voltage (V)	1500	1650–2200	1550	1550	2000	1700–2200	1700–2000	1600	1700–2400	1500–2000	1400	1500–2000	1850	1700	2100
8. Light anode sensitivity ($A lm^{-1}$)	10	10–100	10	10	30	10–100	30–100	10	30–10000	10–100	10	10–100	100	30	100
9. Energy resolution with a gamma-radiation source ^{137}Cs (%)	—	10	15	—	—	—	11	11	11	11	10.5	12	9.0	11	9.5
10. Maximum pulse amplitude (A)	—	—	—	—	9×10^{-2}	—	—	—	—	—	—	0.1	8	—	—
11. Working temperature range (°C)	-60 +70	-60 +70	-60 +70	-60 +70	-60 +70	-60 +55	-60 +60	-60 +70	-60 +70	-60 +70	-60 +70	-60 +85	-60 +70	-60 +85	-60 +85
12. Vibration strength (ms^{-2})	98.1	98.1	98.1	98.1	147	—	147	98.1	98.1	98.1	98.1	196	98.1	196–294	194
13. Minimum service life (hour)	2.000	2.000	1.000	1.000	1.000	1.000	2.000	3.000	2.500	2.000	2.000	3000–5000	3000	2000	5000

Fig. 2.1.9 illustrates the design principle of one of the simplest scintiblocks. Arranged inside it is a scintillator, a photomultiplier and a voltage divider with terminals supported on high-voltage insulators. The voltage divider resistors are soldered directly onto the photomultiplier legs. Exclusion of a photomultiplier socket significantly adds to the dependability of the device. Fig. 2.1.10 shows the electrical circuit of this scintillation detection unit.

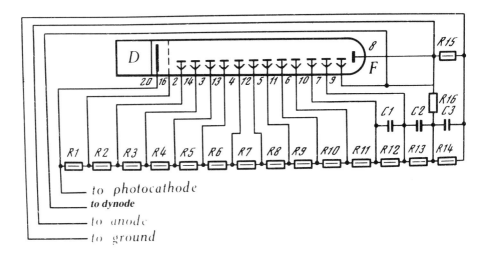

Fig. 2.1.10 — Circuit diagram of the single-crystal scintillation detection unit shown in Fig. 2.1.9.

In recording gamma-radiation in outer space there arises the need to eliminate the background of charged particles. If we assume, according to the data available, the flux of charged particles to be equal to $5 \times 10^4 \, \mathrm{m}^{-2} \, \mathrm{s}^{-1}$ and the cross-sectional area of 63×63 mm crystals to be about 40 cm^2, then the count rate of charged particles in outer space will amount to about 200 pulses per second. This value is close to the count rate of gamma-quanta within the 0.3–3.0 MeV energy range observed when measuring the natural radioactivity of rocks of the basalt type.

To reduce or eliminate the background of these charged particles, scintiblocks with combined detectors have been developed. The arrangement of the detectors is illustrated in Fig. 2.1.11 (a, b). The operating principle of the detector shown in Fig. 2.1.11 (a) involves the different response of the scintillators comprising it to excitation by gamma-quanta and charged particles. For this reason, pulses of different shape (amplitude and length) arise at the multiplier output. The next electronic circuit — the shape discriminator — solves the problem of subtracting the charged particle background. The pulse length from a NaI(Tl) crystal, which is determined by the time of flash, is about 250 ns, while the length of pulses from a plastic scintillator (flash time 5 ns), which is mainly determined by the photomultiplier inertia, is about 20 ns. This difference is quite sufficient for confident separation of the signals.

To make the optimal choice for the design of such a scintiblock that is capable of securing an adequate resolution and effective light collection from a plastic scintillator, investigations were carried out into different combinations of a NaI(Tl) crystal, an

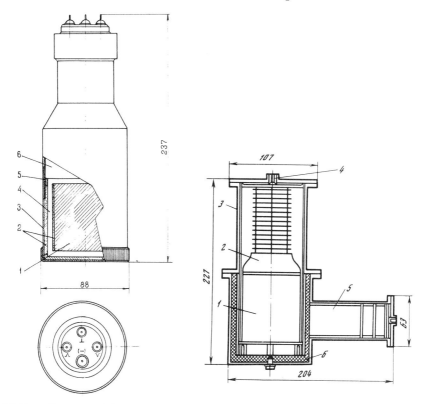

Fig. 2.1.11 — Structure of the combined scintillation detection units (a) with a combined scintillator and one photomultiplier: 1, scintillation crystal; 2, light reflector; 3, buffer gasket; 4, plastic scintillator; 5, antimagnetic screen; 6, photomultiplier; 7, hermetically sealed body. (b) with a combined scintillator and two photomultipliers; 1, scintillation crystal; 2, photomultiplier; 3, hermetically sealed body; 4, expansion valve; 5, photomultiplier; 6, plastic scintillator. Dimensions in millimetres.

MgO reflector and a plastic scintillator. Fig. 2.1.12 shows the diagrams of different models of combined scintillators and gamma-spectra of a ^{137}Cs course obtained with them. A spectrum obtained with a NaI(Tl) crystal alone is shown for comparison. The scintillation unit shown in Fig. 2.1.11(a) was used in the gamma-ray spectrometer installed aboard the Mars 5 probe [8, 61].

The use of a detector, illustrated in Fig. 2.1.11(b), produces a similar effect, i.e. the elimination of the charged-particle background in recording gamma-quanta. In this design the NaI(Tl) crystal is registering gamma-quanta and charged particles, while the plastic-scintillator registers charged particles alone. Each scintillator is scanned by its photomultiplier. Pulses from the photomultipliers arrive at the discriminator circuit which admits to the analyser only those pulses that are due to gamma-quanta. This detector was used in the gamma-ray spectrometers installed in the command modules of Apollos 15 and 16 [60].

The main parameters of scintillation units, determining their quality and suitability for use in instrumentation, are: the energy resolution, the efficiency, the pulse amplitude for an optimal magnitude of high voltage, the settling-in time of the working mode, stability, etc.

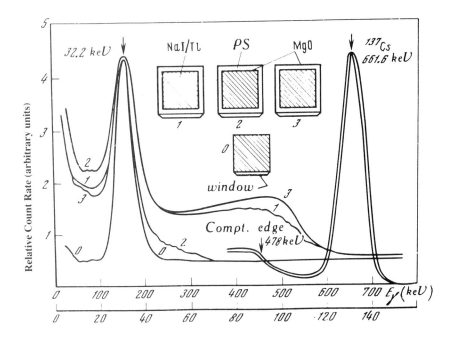

Fig. 2.1.12 — Spectra of the gamma-radiation of the ^{137}Cs nuclide obtained with scintillation detection units, the structure of which is given in Fig. 2.1.11(a) having different configurations of the light reflector.

The energy resolution of detection units can to a first approximation be expressed in the form: $R = (R_s^2 + R_p^2)^{1/2}\%$; where R_s and R_p are the proper resolution of the scintillator and photomultiplier, respectively. R_s is mainly determined by the conversional efficiency of the scintillator, the degree of its optical and spectral homogeneity, and the quality of optical contact. The R_p is dependent on the intensity of light pulses, the quantum yield of the photocathode, the photoelectron collection coefficient onto the first emitter, and the secondary-electron emission coefficient of the first emitter. To obtain maximum energy resolution of the scintiblock, there is also a need to choose a photomultiplier having a maximum quantum sensitivity in the light-emission wavelength region of the scintillator in use.

Investigations of scintillator parameters (resolution, light yield, spectral sensitivity) and photomultiplier parameters (relative amplification, resolution, working régime settling-in time, stability, behaviour in magnetic fields), carried out in [61–67], made it possible to estimate the effect of the above factors and to work out adequate criteria for the selection of photomultipliers and crystals and for the choice of crystal–photomultiplier pairs.

In developing an electronic–optical system, such as the scintiblock, an important factor proves also to be the choice of the immersion compound for ensuring an intimate contact between the scintillator and the photomultiplier. The compound must secure a high light transmission within the wavelength range of recorded radiation, and maintain this property within the scintiblock operating under the conditions of mechanical loading, as well as within a wide temperature range.

NaI(Tl) crystals are spectrometric scintillators finding a particularly large-scale application. However, a number of disadvantages, such as fragility and hygroscopicity, restrict the possibility of using them in apparatus intended for operation under the conditions of high temperatures and mechanical loads. The CsI(Tl) crystals are non-hygroscopic and, being endowed with plasticity, are capable of withstanding shocks, vibrations-and and abrupt temperature differences across a wide range. The presence of Cs ($Z = 55$) instead of Na ($Z = 11$) results in a higher registration efficiency for gamma-radiation. But the CsI (Tl) crystals suffer from certain disadvantages: long time of flash (see Table 2.1.5), a certain amount of phosphorescence, poorer resolution due to a lower conversional efficiency compared to NaI(Tl), and a less favourable position of the peak of the luminescence spectrum (in the 560 nm region).

In a gamma-ray spectrometer more than 99% of the amplification achieved by the entire system is accounted for by the photomultiplier. Dependent on its parameters are the main characteristics of both the detection unit and the gamma-ray spectrometer as a whole. The main requirements of photomultipliers are the following: parametric stability during long-term operation, low settling-in time within the working régime, good amplitude resolution, high anode sensitivity (amplification), low intrinsic radioactivity, low noise level, and high strength characteristics. The last requirement is most adequately met by photomultipliers having a shutter-type dynode system.

Particularly important for onboard gamma-ray spectrometers is the performance capacity of scintillation detectors and their components (scintillators and photomultipliers) within a wide temperature range, because if detectors are mounted on an outside boom, it is difficult to secure a sufficiently stable temperature régime. The maximum permissible temperature limits appear to be mainly determined by photomultipliers (volatility of the caesium coating on the photocathode at $+60°C$ and collapse of the kovar-glass solder joint at -60 to $-70°C$).

With a change in temperature the energy resolution of the detector changes too. For instance, in the case of detectors with high-quality crystals in the region of positive temperatures the energy resolution deteriorates at about 0.04% per centigrade degree temperature rise.

2.1.2.2 Highly effective xenon detectors

General characteristics
Over the past few years gamma-radiation detectors based on solid [68–70], liquid [71–73] and gaseous compressed [74–76] xenon have been put to use. Their main advantage is high efficiency which is due to the large atomic number of xenon, and the fact that xenon detectors can be large in size.

The use of detectors filled with solid and liquid zenon involves some difficulties, because they call for rather sophisticated cryogenic technology ensuring the maintenance and stabilization of the temperature throughout the entire working volume of the detector. That is why compressed xenon detectors will generally be employed more extensively than liquid or solid xenon detectors.

Compressed xenon detectors have some advantages over detectors of other types:

— greater efficiency as compared with ionization chambers;

— **better** energy resolution as compared with gas-discharge and scintillation detectors;
— a larger working volume and hence a higher efficiency as compared with semiconductor detectors.

The main characteristics of these detectors are their high efficiency in recording gamma-radiation, good energy resolution, and high speed determined by the velocities of electron and ion drift.

The efficiency of recording, or the probability of the interaction of an ionizing particle with the detector working gas, is determined mainly by two factors — the charge of the atomic nucleus Z and the density of the absorbing medium ρ. That is why such a heavy gas as xenon is an effective absorber of gamma-ray quanta. The dependence of the probability of the interaction on Z is complicated because it is determined by several processes: the photoelectric effect ($\propto Z^5$), the Compton-effect ($\propto Z$) and pair formation ($\propto Z^2$).

The recording efficiency (Q) can be evaluated from the relationship:

$$Q = P(E)\,(1\text{-}e^{-\mu l \rho}) \qquad\qquad (2.18)$$

where $P(E)$ is the ratio of the number of events in the full absorption peak to the total number of interactions in the detector.

$P(E) = 0.108468\ C^{\,0.346163}\ E^{\,-2.0495\,C\,-0.33182}$
   where $C = 0.372$;
          E, energy of the gamma-ray quantum (MeV);
          μ, mass attenuation coefficient for xenon;
          ρ, density of xenon (g cm^{-3}); and
          l and d, length and diameter of the detector (cm).

For instance, for the detector with $l = d = 30$ cm and $\rho = 1$ g cm^{-3} and $E = 1$ MeV the recording efficiency (Q) is about 33%.

The limiting energy resolution is another important characteristic of the detector. This value can be assessed from the report [78]:

$$R = 2.36\ \sqrt{}\ (\text{FW/E}) \times 100\%, \qquad\qquad (2.1.9)$$

where E is the energy of the gamma-ray quantum;
      W, energy necessary to form an electron-ion pair; and
      F, Fano factor for xenon,
      $W_{Xe} = 21.9$ eV [81]
      $F_{Xe} = 0.13$ [78].

For example, for $E = 1$ MeV, $R \approx 0.4\%$. However, this value characterizes the spread of energies resulting only from the statistics of the interaction of the ionizing particle with the working gas. The attainable energy resolution is actually worse by almost an order of magnitude. The lower energy resolution achieved in the experiments is due to the fact that it depends not only on statistical processes but also on the noise of the amplifier channel.

Finally, another important characteristic of the detector is the operation speed, which depends on the collection time of electrons formed in the detector while, in its turn, electron collection time depends on the purity of the working gas. If there are electrically negative admixtures in the working gas, the capture of electrons takes place, as a result of which the magnitude of the charge collected by the signal electrode depends on the place of ionization in the detector. That is why the working gas must be of high purity. The mobility of electrons depends also on the intensity of the applied field and on the density of gas. Electron mobility in pure xenon with a density of about 8×10^2 kg m^{-3} in an electric field of about 10^3 kVm^{-1} is approximately 10^3 m s^{-1}. It was established that the addition of several per cent of hydrogen or nitrogen to xenon increases the drift velocity 5–8 times [79,80]. The drift velocity can be evaluated from the following expression [81].

$$V_d = \frac{eE(3-h)}{3mNa} \frac{G(3-h/2h+2)}{G(3/2h+2)} \left[\frac{2(h+1)M}{3m} \left(\frac{eE}{mNa} \right)^2 \right]^{-\frac{h}{2h+2}}$$

(2.1.10)

where e is the electron charge;
m, the electron mass;
M, the molecular mass;
D, diffusion coefficient;
$\mu = V_d/E$, mobility;
$G(x)$, gamma function;
N, gas density (atoms m^{-3});
a, h constants.

With respect to the method of recording secondary electrons, detectors based on compressed xenon can be subdivided into three groups: (1) ionization chambers, (2) gas-discharge proportional counters, and (3) scintillation proportional counters.

Ionization chambers are widespread particle detectors with a large energy release (alpha-particles, protons and fission fragments). They offer limited opportunities for recording gamma-radiation due to their low efficiency. However, the use of such an effective filler as compressed xenon brings them into the class of detectors preferable for recording gamma-radiation [75].

Due to gas amplification, the compressed xenon gas-discharge proportional counter provides, in principle, the opportunity to attain higher energy resolution compared with the ionization chamber, because of the lack of noise in the amplifier channel. However, other factors, such as the strong dependence of the gas amplification coefficient on the stability of the high voltage and on the design parameters of the counter (the inconstancy of the thread diameter, fringe effects, etc.), bring about the situation when the resolving power of real proportional counters does not reach the limiting value ($\leqslant 1\%$). These factors are considered in detail in [79,80]. The best resolution reached in this work is about 5% for the energy $E_\gamma = 59.8$ keV. In multithread counters or in counters with a large working volume the resolution is about 20%.

The scintillation proportional counter records not electrons but the flashes caused by them. Being accelerated in strong electric fields, electrons excite working gas molecules which split into atoms, emitting energy quanta according to the $A_2 \rightarrow 2A + h\nu$ reaction. The radiation spectrum is a narrow continuum in the ultraviolet region with a maximum at about 173 nm for Xe. These counters have particular advantages in recording gamma-radiation due to their high efficiency and resolution. However, their use for recording gamma-radiation involves great difficulties. To record gamma-radiation it is necessary to have a large density of working gas, which requires the use of very high voltages. For instance, already at a pressure of about 6×10^5 Pa it is necessary to have a field of about 1.5×10^3 kVm^{-1} in order to cause flashes in the working gas.

Thus, when we need to record gamma-radiation by compressed xenon detectors, ionization chambers seem to have advantages over gas-discharge and scintillation proportional counters.

Ionization chambers based on compressed xenon

The simplest version of the compressed xenon ionization chamber is described in [78]. The chamber is a steel pipe 50 cm long and 6 cm in diameter. Xenon with a slight hydrogen admixture is the working gas of the detector. The pressure of gas is about 3.7×10^6 Pa ($\rho x_e = 2.7 \times 10^2$ kg m^{-3}). The purity of gas corresponds to a lifetime of electrons before their capture by admixtures of over 10^3 μs. The full time of electron drift from the cathode to the anode is 8.4 to 8.9 μs. The energy resolution of the ionization chamber is 6% for $E_\gamma = 662$ keV and 4.3% for $E_\gamma = 1332$ keV.

Such a chamber can be used for the purposes of gamma-ray spectrometry. Spectra will have sufficiently good resolution. However, in such chambers energy resolution can be improved still further when the signal electrode is shielded from positive ions of small mobility, and when its electrical capacity is reduced (since in this case noise decreases). Chambers having the signal electrode shielded are called drift chambers. One such drift chamber based on compressed xenon is shown in Fig. 2.1.13. It is described in [75,76]. The drift field in the chamber is created by two distributive electrodes manufactured from foil-covered glass plates. On the foil-covered side, strips 1 mm wide with a pitch of 2.56 mm are cut. The signal is taken from the central electrode (thread) which is the anode. These three electrodes mounted on the fluoroplastic frame represent a drift cell. The drift cell together with the voltage

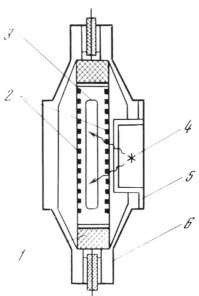

Fig. 2.1.13 — Diagram of the compressed xenon drift ionization chamber: 1, fluoroplastic holder; 2 distributive plates; 3, signal electrode (anode); 4, source of gamma-ray quanta; 5, flange; 6, body (cathode).

divider is housed in the steel body. The voltage divider is used for focusing the field on the anode thread. To eliminate the induced charged, the divider resistances are shunted by capacitors.

Such a drift cell can be efficiently used for recording gamma-ray quanta with energies of 0.05–1.5 MeV. Restrictions on the use at low energies are determined by noise in the cell and on the use of high energies to improve efficiency. To record gamma-ray quanta with higher energies or to enhance the efficiency of the detector, use can be made not of one, but of a set of drift cells; alternatively, the volume version of the drift ionization chamber can be employed [75, 76].

The diagram of such a chamber is given in Fig. 2.1.14. The chamber has the shape of a cylinder with the inner part (of the working part) 74 mm in height and 93 mm in diameter. The signal electrode (anode) is made in the form of a grid composed of nine threads 0.1 mm in diameter with a pitch of 8 mm. The signal electrode is surrounded with screen grids. Distribution rings are housed in space between the screen grids and the wall of the chamber which forms the cathode. The rings ensure a homogeneous drift field in the working region of the chamber. Voltage between the rings falls due to their semiconductor glass support. In fact, this support is a high-resistance (about 1.5×10^8 Ω voltage divider.

The signal electrode has the form of a grid, so as to have a minimum capacity with the large area of the detector. Besides, such an electrode can be shielded more efficiently than a planar electrode.

This chamber possesses a high energy resolution. In the mixture of Xe and 0.5% H_2 at a pressure of 18×10^5Pa, an energy resolution of about 1.5% has been obtained when $E_\gamma = 1.115$ MeV [78]. A chamber of this type can be used to measure the

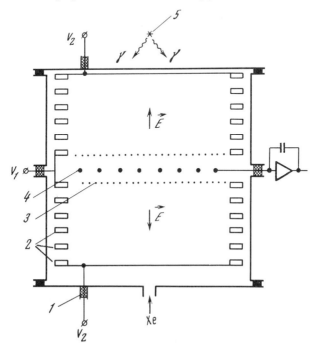

Fig. 2.1.14 — Diagram of the compressed-xenon volume drift ionization chamber; 1, high-voltage input; 2, distributive rings; 3, screen grid; 4, signal electrode; 5, source of gamma-ray quanta.

energies of gamma-ray quanta within the range 0.1–10 MeV. By way of an example, Fig. 2.1.15(a) gives some spectra measured by the volume drift chamber.

(a)

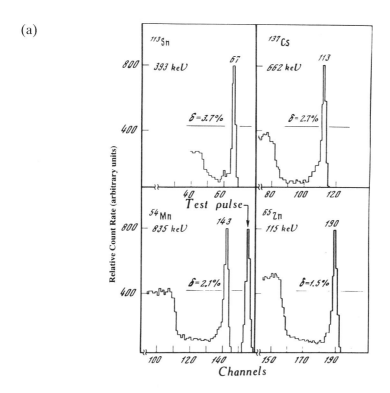

(b)

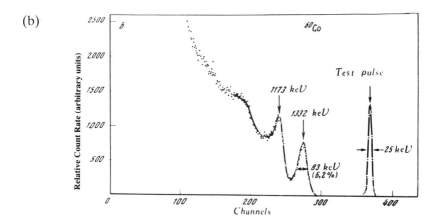

Fig. 2.1.15 — Spectra of typical gamma-radiation sources measured by ionization chambers; (a), filled with compressed xenon (the chamber is shown in Fig. 2.1.14; and (b), filled with liquid xenon (the chamber is shown in Fig. 2.1.16).

Ionization chamber based on liquid xenon.
Due to its high density ($\rho = 3.1 \times 10^3$ kg m^{-3}) liquid xenon is an excellent detecting medium. The Fano factor for liquid xenon is very low ($F = 0.05$), being comparable with that of germanium. Both these parameters enable one to make a liquid xenon detector with an energy resolution close to the resolution of the semiconductor Ge (Li) detector, and with an efficiency higher than that of the scintillation NaI (Tl) detector. In creating a liquid xenon detector with such high characteristics it is necessary to obtain xenon of very high purity.

Fig. 2.1.16 presents a diagram of a liquid xenon ionization chamber [72]. The diagram also shows a part of the cryostat adjacent to the chamber. The ionization chamber consists of two grid ionization sections each of which has a collector, a grid and a common cathode. Such a two-section structure makes the space for the electron drift smaller. Inside the chamber is 50 mm in diameter and 35 mm in height. Each grid is placed at a distance of 13 mm from the cathode and 4 mm from the collector. The sensitive volume (the region between the grid and the cathode) of the chamber is about 50 cm^3.

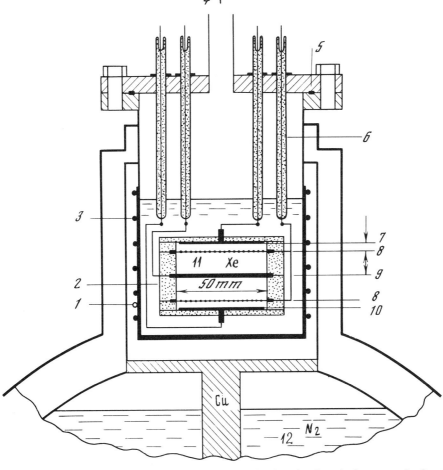

Fig. 2.1.16 — Diagram of the liquid xenon drift ionization chamber: 1, thermocouple; 2, ceramic holder; 3, heater; 4, aperture for pumping out and filling with gas; 5, metal gasket; 6, glass feedthrough; 7, collector; 8, grid; 9, cathode; 10, collector; 11, liquid xenon.

The cathode and collectors are stainless steel disks 50 mm in diamter and 1 mm thick. The grids consist of tungsten threads 10 μm thick covered by gold and platinum. The critical ratio of the electric fields between the grid and the collector to the field between the cathode and the grid is 1.53 and, therefore, the inefficiency of the grid is just 0.9%. Electrodes are mounted on ceramic holders. The chamber is housed in the stainless steel body mounted on the upper part of the cryostat. As usual, the cold conduit of the cryostat is made of copper. Liquid nitrogen is used as a cooling agent. It is worth noting that the structures of solid xenon chambers have no fundamental differences from the design of liquid xenon chambers. Their difference lies only in the fact that xenon is cooled to lower temperatures (about 150 K) so that it is in the crystalline state. The energy resolution of solid xenon chambers is approximately the same or slightly higher than that of liquid xenon chambers.

By way of example Fig. 2.1.15(b) gives the spectrum of gamma-radiation of ^{60}Co measured in the above-described chamber. For a collimated source an energy resolution of 6.9% for the 1322 KeV line has been obtained. These data show that the energy resolution of the liquid xenon detector is better than for the NaI (Tl) scintillator 76 $\times$ 76 mm in size.

The compressed- and liquid-xenon ionization chambers considered in this section can be used as highly effective detectors for gamma-ray spectrometers employed in space research. Like all devices, xenon detectors have their draw-backs (high pressure and voltage in the case of compressed xenon, and the necessity to have a cryostat in the case of liquid xenon). However, such merits as high efficiency, the large effective area, the adequate energy resolution, etc. explain their use in cosmic gamma-radiation spectrometry.

2.1.2.3 Semiconductor detectors and detection units

A large-scale application of semiconductor detectors (SCDs) during laboratory investigations of different kinds of radiation has enabled their characteristics to be examined in much detail and permitted the range of problems where their use is particularly feasible to be determined. The main advantages of SCDs for use in gamma-ray spectrometry reside in their higher energy resolution as compared with scintillation detectors and proportional counters. This fact is particularly important in the measurement of gamma-radiation spectra resulting from the interaction between cosmic rays and objects of a complex chemical composition. The gamma-radiation spectra in this case turn out to have multiple components to such a degree that their discrete components practically defy recognition.

At the same time, SCDs finding application today in gamma-ray spectrometry have a relatively low efficiency, the reason for this lying in the extreme difficulty of developing large detectors (in excess of 100–150 cm^3). This restricts the possibility of using them for measuring gamma-radiation spectra of weakly radioactive samples of terrestrial rocks, lunar soil, meteorites, tectites, etc. Certain difficulties in using SCDs in spectrometers are also associated with the need to employ sophisticated cryogenic techniques to ensure the low-temperature régime that is necessary for the storage and functioning of SCDs.

There are available quite a number of original review papers dealing with the characteristics [83–94], designs [95–107] and applications of SCDs [108–119] for measuring the intensity and spectral composition of gamma-radiation under terrestrial conditions. On the other hand, the first steps have been taken in using gamma-ray spectrometers with SCDs for space research [43, 113, 120–123]. We shall be concerned solely with this limited experience in the development and application of onboard gamma-ray spectrometers with SCDs.

Table 2.1.7 — Main characteristics of semiconductor materials used in SCDs

Material	Forbidden zone width (eV)	Temperature (K)	Energy of formation of electron–hole pair (eV)
Si	1.12	300	3.61
Si	1.16	77	3.76
SiC	2.2–3.3	300	—
Ge	0.74	77	2.98
GaAs	1.4	295	4.2
CdTe	1.47	300	4.43
HgI_2	2.13	300	6.5
GaSb	—	77	0.77
ZnSb	—	0	0.265
ZnAs	—	77	0.43

Table 2.1.7 lists the basic characteristics of semiconductor materials used in the manufacture of gamma-ray spectrometric detectors. Numerous semiconductor materials available in adequate purity and quality can be used in gamma-ray spectrometric detectors. However, growing a unified crystalline structure of sufficiently large volume is a matter of great difficulty. What is more, an important factor for gamma-ray spectrometry is a high atomic number Z for at least one of the constituents of the crystal.

Because the cross-section of photoelectric absorption increases in proportion to Z^5, of Compton scattering in proportion to Z, and of the formation of pairs in proportion to Z^2, detectors with $Z > 32$ appear to have particularly favourable prospects. However, among them germanium and silicone alone (as seen from Table 2.1.7) are obtainable in sufficiently high purity. Furthermore, it has become possible today to grow a germanium crystal of great size. Detectors available today have a sensitivity volume up to about 150 cm^3, and an energy resolution of 2–3 keV (for ^{60}Co, $E_\gamma = 1.33$ MeV).

SCDs have a significantly lower efficiency in gamma-quanta registration compared to the scintillation detectors. Thus, for instance, the efficiency of Ge (Li) detectors for gamma-quanta with 1 MeV energy is about a fifth of that of an NaI(Tl) detector of the same size [124]. Si(Li) detectors have a lower efficiency than Ge(Li) detectors, though under optimal operating conditions their resolutions are approximately the same.

The region of optimal working temperatures for Ge(Li) detectors lies within 150 – 200 K, and for Si(Li) detectors within 100 – 150 K. This régime is not easy to maintain in long term economical self-contained systems. Accordingly, attempts are being made to develop SCDs which do not need such considerable cooling. In particular, attempts have been made to develop use detectors from cadmium telluride or mercury iodide, but these have a wide forbidden zone. For this reason, their conductivity even at normal temperature is extremely low. Therefore, it has so far been possible to develop such detectors only if they are of small size.

Development of gamma-ray spectrometers with SCDs for space research involves numerous difficulties stemming from the special requirements made of onboard instruments.

The general requirements made of onboard equipment are minimal possible overall dimensions, weight, and power consumption; high strength characteristics; a broad temperature range; and noise resistance (to network interference, electromagnetic induction and microphone noise). However, in gamma-ray spectrometric research, according to the aim of the experiment, there arise certain specific requirements concerning the energy resolution, efficiency, detector orientation, etc. Many of these characteristics being interrelated, we are compelled to make compromise solutions to achieve the optimal design of the entire detector model. Given such a great number of different restrictions, developing even the simplest model of a detector proves to be a fairly difficult task. Until today only Ge (Li) detectors have been used in gamma-ray spectrometers carried by balloons, rockets and man-made satellites. What involves particularly great difficulties today is not the development of SCDs meeting the requirements made of space instruments, but the development of a cryostat capable of securing the functioning of the spectrometer for a sufficiently long period of time.

The cooling of SCDs results in a reduction in noise and an increase in its resolution. Optimal temperature régimes in the operation of SCDs have been principally achieved by using liquid nitrogen as a cryogen, which at a given pressure has a definite temperature (the boiling point of liquid nitrogen at atmospheric pressure is 78 K). Designs of cryostats with liquid nitrogen intended for space research were discussed in detail in [120,122,123]. The great weight of the cryogen and its large consumption for maintaining the low temperature of the detector do not yet permit a gamma-ray spectrometer with SCDs to be used in the study of planets on a flight which would take many months. Presumably, more useful in this respect will be cooling devices based on the Peltier effect [126–128]. However, it has not yet been possible to use these to achieve cooling below 180–200 K (which is sufficient for a Si(Li) detector); furthermore, they consume a great deal of energy.

It appears that in the near future we shall not be able to develop lightweight cryogen systems capable of functioning for a sufficiently long time. But another way of solving this problem is emerging. The development of new technology for germanium purification and crystal growing has made it possible to manufacture germanium of such high purity that its compensation with lithium proves unnecessary. Detectors based on ultra-pure germanium can be stored at an ordinary temperature and cooled only when at work. As to their characteristics, the detectors based on ultra-pure germanium are practically identical with Ge(Li) detectors. The characteristics of detectors based on pure germanium are discussed in [53,107,129,130].

Conventional Ge(Li) detectors are made of the n–p type of germanium in a coaxial or planar shape. The concentration of acceptor impurity is, as a rule, 10^{20} m^{-3}. To obtain a larger sensitivity region, lithium ions are introduced into crystals by drifting in the electric field. The last stage of this operation is carried out at a low temperature. After that, the crystal is placed in a vacuum cryostat where a pressure of 1.3×10^{-3} Pa and a temperature of 80–90 K are maintained all the time. A higher temperature or pressure brings about irreversible processes in the crystal and the deterioration of its characteristics.

Papers [131, 132] contain the description of capsulated detectors with a solid dielectric. In these detectors the Ge(Li) crystals are kept not in vacuum, but in a certain organic compound. At a normal temperature the compound is liquid and at the temperature of liquid nitrogen it is a solid substance with a very low conductivity (e.g. hexane). The use of a solid filler led to an improved sealing of the crystal and to a significant improvement in the strength characteristics of the detector. Fig. 2.1.17.

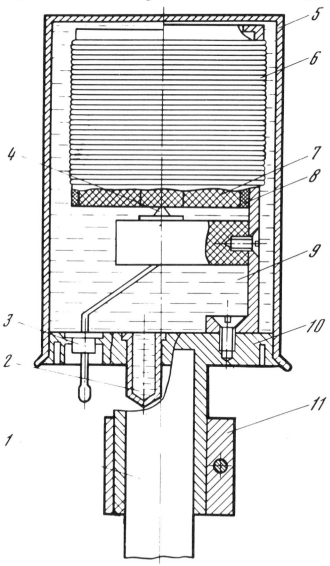

Fig. 2.1.17 — The structure of the capsulated gamma-radiation detector: 1, cold conduit; 2, exhaust tube; 3, signal output; 4, dish-shaped spring; 5, body; 6, kapron cord; 7, crystal; 8, indium gasket; 9, filter; 10, leg; 11, mounting clamp.

shows the schematic layout of such a capsulated detector intended for operation under conditions of a high mechanical load and, particularly, in space vehicles. The detector is a cylindrical capsule. Its housing consists of two main components — a flask and a leg made of an aluminium alloy and tightly interconnected with one another. Arranged inside the housing is a Ge(Li) crystal 80 cm³ in volume. The crystal is likewise cylindrical in shape and at its lateral surface (n-region) is pressed against the post of the leg by means of a kapron thread through an indium washer. The pressure of a disk spring ensures a fixed position of the crystal and contact of its base (p-region) with an insulated terminal. This terminal is vacuum-tight and a high-voltage of 3000 V is applied to it, the leakage current being not above 5×10^{-11} A. An exhaust tube in the leg of the capsule is used to bring in the organic filler. Once the organic filler is in place, the tube is pressurized. On the outside of the capsule leg there is a socket for bringing in and fixing the cold conduit.

The necessity of working with gamma-radiation sources of low specific activity stimulated the development of large-size detectors [133]. In particular, at the Oak Ridge National Laboratory a composite detector for space research representing a kind of assembly of separate Ge(Li) crystals has been developed. (see Fig. 2.1.18).

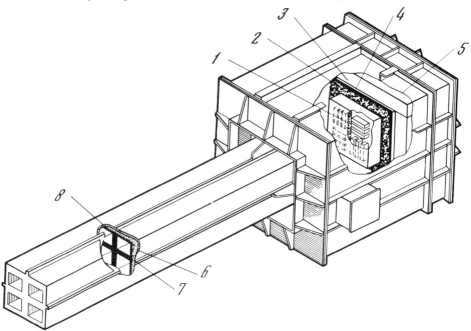

Fig. 2.1.18 — The structure of compound gamma-radiation Ge (Li) detector: 1, Ge (Li) crystal; 2, lead screen; 3, plastic scintillator; 4, epoxy resin; 5, aluminium body; 6, polyurethane foam heat shield; 7, aluminium ribs; 8, epoxy resin.

The working area of the detector in this case totals 200 cm² The detector is in the shape of a cube. Arranged at its centre is an assembly of Ge(Li) crystals, which is surrounded by a lead shield securing a solid angle of view. Outside of the lead shield there is a plastic scintillator which gives protection against charged particles of cosmic origin. The detector housing is made of aluminium. Thermo-insulation of Ge(Li) crystals and of the coolant conduit is achieved by using polyurethane foam and epoxy resins. This detector was developed for space research under the Apollo programme, but has not yet been used.

Measurements of gamma-radiation by using a gamma-ray spectrometer with SCDs, sent up in a balloon, were first reported in [122]. The Sun's gamma-radiation spectrum within the $0.03 - 6.3$ MeV range was measured by a Ge(Li) detector of 15.3 cm^3 cross-section (27.6 cm^3 volume). The detector was surrounded with the shield NaI(Tl) crystals serving as a collimator for the SCD. The SCD was cooled by liquid nitrogen through a coolant conduit. The detector's resolution was less than 6 keV for energies beyond the measurement range. The work took place at a height of about 40km, where the residual atmospheric layer was 47 kg m^{-2}. Gamma-radiation spectra were recorded by a 4096-channel pulse-amplitude analyser. The cryogenic system provided for the cooling of the Ge(Li) detector during the five-day flight of the spectrometer aboard the balloon.

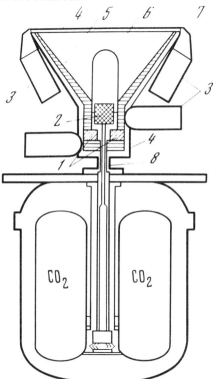

Fig. 2.1.19 — Structure of the single crystal semiconductor detector with a cryostat for space research; 1, steel shield; 2, Ge (Li) detector; 3, photomultiplier; 4, plastic scintillator; 5, high-density shield; 6, vacuum cover; 7, light pipe; 8, housing for thermal link.

Fig. 2.1.19. shows the design of the first gamma-ray spectrometer with SCDs used in space research [43]. The instrument was developed at the Lockheed Company's space research laboratory. It was carried by the US polar Earth satellite 1972-076B in 1972 and was intended to be used for the study of terrestrial and extraterrestrial gamma-radiation within the 40 keV to 2.8 MeV energy range. The instrument's energy resolution was $3.5 - 4.0$ keV (with respect to $E\gamma = 1.33$ MeV, ^{60}Co). Gamma-radiation was recorded by a Ge(Li) crystal 50 cm^3 in volume. The crystal was mounted on a special cryostat which was resistant to vibrations arising during the launching of the satellite. The Ge(Li) crystal was surrounded with a tungsten protective collimator restricting the angle of view (this shield chiefly removed the gamma-radiation appearing in the satellite materials being irradiated by cosmic rays) and with a plastic scintillator eliminating the recording of cosmic rays and charged particles created by them. The gamma-radiation spectra were recorded by a 4096-channel pulse-amplitude analyser. The low temperature of the SCD was maintained by a special cryostat with a solid CO_2 cryogen. Thermal contact between the crystal and the cryogen was effected by a copper coolant conduit. The cryostat contained 14 kg of solid CO_2, thus providing for the spectrometer operation in outer space for one year. The cryogen was placed in a circular container surrounded with fibreglass. The working temperature of the detector was maintained around 130 K, and was determined by the sublimation temperature of CO_2 (126 K). The spectrometer in question was used to obtain important information on the intensity and spectral composition of gamma-radiation in the Earth's environment. This kind of spectrometer can be employed for the study of fairly intensive gamma-radiation sources or whenever long-term measurements are necessary. However, for the measurement of short-term processes (solar flares) such a detector is a little effective. Accordingly, a gamma-ray spectrometer with a more efficient detector has been developed at the California Institute of Technology's Jet Propulsion Laboratory [134]. Its design principle is schematically shown in Fig. 2.1.20. The spectrometer consists of a combined detector, a cooling system and the registration electronics. Gamma-radiation is recorded by four Ge(Li) crystals.

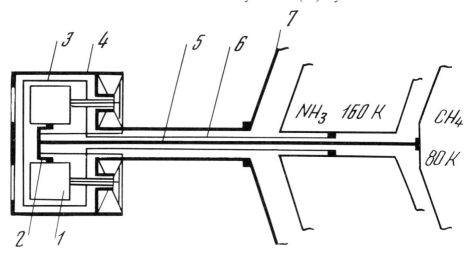

Fig. 2.1.20 — Structure of the four-crystal semiconductor detector with cryostat for space research developed at NASA/JPL; 1, Ge(Li) crystal in the primary container; 2, crystal aluminium holder; 3, secondary container; 4, aluminium cryostat; 5, primary silver cold conduit; 6, secondary silver cold conduit; 7, external envelope of the refrigerator.

All crystals are packed in pressurized containers maintaining contact with the cryogen through a coolant conduit. To secure a specific angle of view, the Ge(Li) crystals are surrounded with a scintillation shield of CsI(Na) setting up a cone with a 27° angle, at the vertex of which there is a hole for the coolant conduit. Signals from CsI (Na) are taken by 12 photomultipliers. The Ge(Li) crystals are of a cylindrical shape, each 60 cm^3 in volume. The efficiency of each of the crystals is about 15% with respect to that of the NaI(Tl) crystal 76 × 76 mm in size for the 1.33 MeV line of the ^{60}Co nuclide. The Ge(Li) crystals operate at a temperature of about 80 K, which is achieved by double-step cooling. The Ge(Li) crystals alone are maintained at such a low temperature. Along with all the primary packing containers they are placed into a secondary common container kept at a temperature of about 165 K. The secondary container is, in its turn, confined within the external cryostat housing at normal temperature. The primary and secondary detector containers maintain thermal contacts with the cryogens via a coaxial device made of high-purity silver.

The high thermal characteristics of the cryostat called for the use of specially selected structural materials and coatings for the vacuum containers. Activated charcoal (a highly porous form of carbon) is used as a getter in the cryostat. The cryostat has a separate evacuation system which is not connected with that of the cooling devices. The magnitude of thermal loads from the primary and secondary containers of the Ge(Li) detector along with their heat-transfer devices is 98 W and 162 W, respectively.

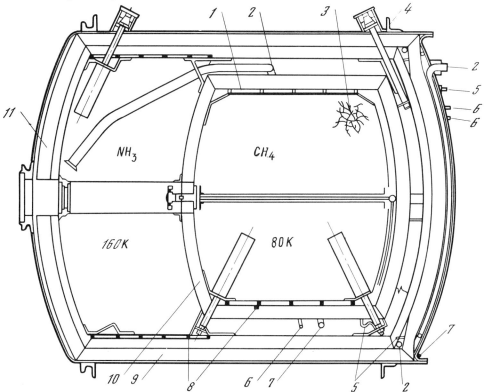

Fig. 2.1.21 — Two-stage cooler of the Ge (Li) detector for space research: 1, activated charcoal getter; 2, hole for ammonia; 3, aluminium wool; 4, places for mounting the cooler; 5, hole for methane; 6, hole for liquid nitrogen; 7, glass fibre shield; 8, cooling coil for liquid nitrogen; 9, vapour-cooled shield; 10, primary tank supports; 11, multilayer insulation.

Fig. 2.1.21. shows a double-stage cooling device used in the spectrometer concerned. Its operating principle is based on the fact that the cryogens are maintaining the required temperatures through direct sublimation into space vacuum at a controlled rate. The cooling device operates quite passively once the cryogens have been frozen, by forming liquid nitrogen through the coils arranged inside the cryogenic reservoirs. In the case of a double-stage cooler the active existence time is longer than in the case of a single-stage one. In a double system, a primary cryogen (methane) is surrounded with a secondary one (ammonia), the latter being endowed with a higher thermal efficiency and operating at a higher temperature than is necessary for a Ge(Li) dectector. For a two-year time of active existence of the system, the primary reservoir contains 16 kg of solid methane at 8×10^2 Pa pressure and a temperature of 80 K, and the secondary reservoir 30 kg of solid ammonia at a pressure of 2×10^3 Pa and a temperature of 160 K. To secure adequate thermal insulation, both the primary and secondary reservoirs with cryogens are suspended inside the cryostat housing on fibreglass braces.

The preamplifiers in the spectrometer are installed directly on the cryostat. All conductors from the crystals to the preamplifiers are confined within metallized mylar screens so as to secure electromagnetic protection and reduce to a minimum both the magnification of sounds and the effect of thermal flow. Signals from each of the crystals are directed to their respective preamplifier, amplifier and pulse analyser, which has 8192 channels.

The above spectrometer for space research has adequate physical characteristics (energy resolution, registration efficiency, length of active existence, etc.), but it is fairly sophisticated as regards design and maintenance.

2.1.2.4 Functional diagrams of onboard spectrometers

Multichannel amplitude analysis in the direct transmission regime
The volume of information to be relayed from aboard the space vehicle depends, on the one hand, on the complexity of the measured spectrum and, on the other, on the length and accuracy to be achieved in obtaining the relayed data. These two requirements being interdependent, the usual practice is to select an optimal version providing the minimum permissible volume of relayed information to achieve a specific task. For instance, in determining the content of natural radioactive elements under the conditions on the Earth or Venus, we may confine ourselves to counting the number of pulses from a single spectrometric detector in three broad energy channels, information (2^{15}–2^{16} pulses in volume) being memorized in each. Relaying of this information by recording the amplitude code of each of the pulses involves the transmission or storage of about 0.5 million bits of information. Transmission by the same method of a more complex gamma-ray spectrum (for example, that of the Moon or Mars) with the use of a 256-channel analyser calls already for the transmission or storage of more than 100 million bits of data.

In numerous cases, a limited speed of data transmission from space vehicles and rigorous requirements made of the economical aspects of onboard systems account for the necessity of processing spectrometric signals from radiometric detectors directly aboard the space vehicle. Such systems are employed, as a rule, aboard space vehicles sent towards remote objects — Venus, Mars and other planets.

Processing and storage of measurement results aboard a space vehicle makes it possible to reduce the volume of relayed information (which is highly important from the point of view of power consumption) or to carry out a repeated transmission (should there have been faults or interference during the transmission of the data) and, finally, to carry out information transmission in those periods of time when communication with the space vehicle is possible. At present we can identify several stages in the development of onboard multichannel spectrometric instrumentation.

Among the first ones to be used in space research were multichannel spectrometers with ultrasonic delay-line recorders, which were employed with much success aboard the Soviet space vehicles Cosmos 60, Luna 10 and 12, Venera 8, as well as in experiments with balloons. Progress in developing more advanced memory devices based on other principles gradually ousted analysers with delay-line memory devices on account of certain shortcomings inherent in them, which will be discussed later. In place of these, analysers with magnetic-core memory started to be successfully used in space research. Thus, the American space vehicle Ranger made use of a 32-channel analyser [135] and the Soviet space probes Mars 5, Venera 13 and 14 of a 256-channel analyser [136,140] with a magnetic-core memory. Finally, use is being made today of spectrometers with parallel-type analysers consisting of single-channel analysers tuned to be different signal levels. Such analysers are noted for their high operating speed and are simple in adjustment and maintenance. However, the number of channels in them does not, as a rule, exceed 10, since the large volume of the equipment and its power consumption restrict the use of multi-channel systems of this type.

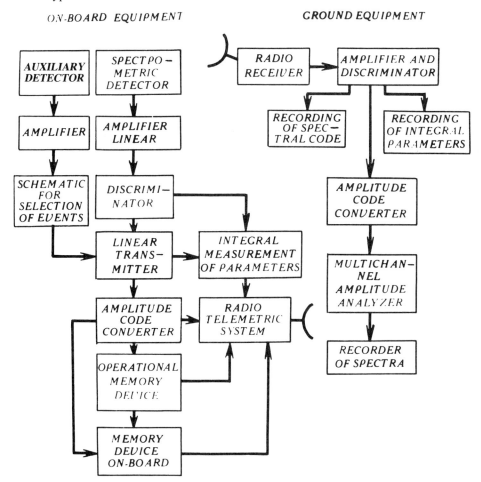

Fig. 2.1.22 — Typical functional diagram of onboard and ground-based equipment used in securing spectrometric measurements.

To record information from all the systems aboard, including spectrometric data, use is made of devices of the tape-recorder type installed in the space vehicle. Thus, for instance, tape-recorders aboard Apollos 15 and 16 recorded information from the gamma-ray and alpha-particle spectrometers in real time in the form of an eight-digit amplitude code for each incoming pulse [60,6].

At the same time, quite often transmission of the amplitude code of each pulse with a subsequent sorting-out among the spectrometer channels involves the use of ground-based devices. Under such a measurement scheme, which we shall call amplitude analysis in the direct transmission régime, we have aboard the space vehicle only part of the spectrometer, including the detector and the input device converting the investigated parameter into a digital code. Such was the scheme of the experiment used for studying the chemical composition of the Moon's surface by the roving space vehicles Lunokhod 1 and 2 [137–139].

A typical functional diagram of both the onboard and ground-based equipment employed in securing spectrometric measurements with direct transmission is shown in Fig. 2.1.22.

The diagram can be even simpler if ancillary devices and certain other units are absent from the space vehicle. However, at present the majority of spectrometric measurements are made in outer space according to the full scheme. In particular, auxiliary pickups are used to eliminate the background of charged particles of cosmic origin in measuring the gamma-radiation from the planets; the onboard memory is used to accummulate data during long-term measurements of micrometeorite fluxes, solar and galactic cosmic rays, etc.

In the absence of memory devices, information on the amplitude of each incoming pulse is relayed and an analysis of the radiation is possible solely with an operating communication line. This significantly restricts the possible applications of such apparatus. However, in the case of direct transmission, the system is simple enough and the volume of onboard equipment is not great. A typical functional diagram of such an analyser is presented in Fig. 2.1.23. The specific versions of these devices generally contain several detectors, preliminary analysis circuits and logical circuits that have been omitted from the block diagram. As will be clear from the block diagram, analysis of a signal from a detector cannot be made except in the transmission régime, the input being blocked in this case both during processing time and during transmission of the preceding pulse code. In the case of low transmission speeds as, for instance, with objects in remote outer space, the time resolution of such apparatus turns out to be rather low.

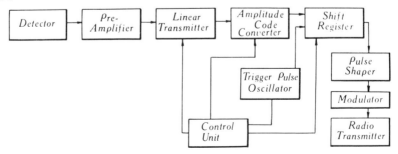

Fig. 2.1.23 — Typical functional diagram of the equipment used for direct transmission of spectrometric information.

With respect to quality, the main characteristics of analysing equipment relaying the code of each signal in the direct transmission régime are as follows:

— small volume of onboard equipment and, consequently, a higher dependability;
— the possibility of obtaining information about intensity variations with time;
— low information transmission speed;
— work not to be undertaken in periods other than those coinciding with communication sessions.

The recording of the amplitude code of each pulse in onboard memory may, of course, reduce the dead-time of the system. This however, will be so only if the rate of onboard-to-ground transmission does not impose restrictions on the total volume of relayed information.

Thus, in the case of remote space objects, the amplitude analysis in a direct transmission régime may have a limited application. Realization of the advantages inherent in the real-time transmission of each pulse code is possible in experiments aboard Earth satellites and long-term lunar vehicles. The case in point is the aforementioned experiments aboard Lunokhods 1 and 2.

Multichannel amplitude analysers with ultrasonic delay line memory.
The gamma-ray spectrometers discussed in this section comprise multichannel pulse analysers. They are considered here as a single family because all of them have ultrasonic delay-line memory. Analysers of this type, because of their compactness and sufficient realiability, satisfied the requirements of the first space experiments despite significant dead time (of the order of 1 ms for up to 100 channels) [40,41].

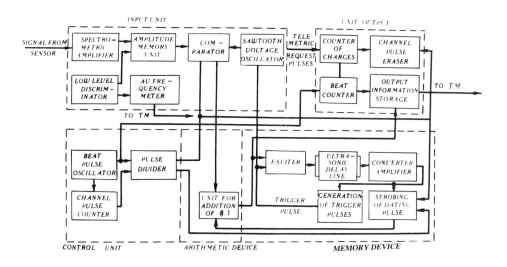

Fig. 2.1.24 — Functional diagram of an onboard pulse analyser with ultrasonic delay-line memory.

A functional diagram common for this type of analyser is given in Fig. 2.1.24. The analyser consists of an input unit where the pulse amplitude is compared with a standard analogue signal, an arithmetic device responsible for addition to the analyser channels, a memory unit, a control unit presetting the succession of analyser operations in time, and the unit which outputs the spectrum to telemetry.

Once converted and shaped in the input unit, the analysed pulse arrives, via a low-level discriminator, in the memory unit. If a pulse arriving from the sensor exceeds the discriminator threshold, the pulse charge will be stored in a capacitor. The analysed signal is then compared with a signal from a sawtooth voltage oscillator, which is set into operation in a periodic régime by a start trigger pulse. Once the sawtooth voltage has reached the memorized pulse amplitude, a comparison signal is shaped, to be gated by the next channel pulse from the control unit, and sent to the arithmetic device as a unit addition pulse (+1) into the correct channel. Should the pulse amplitude have failed by the moment of comparison to reach the value of the sawtooth voltage, comparison will take place in the next memory cycle. Thereupon the memory capacitor is quickly discharged, and the input unit is ready for reception of the next signal from the sensor.

The memory device is built on the principle of the ultrasonic delay-line. Conversion of shaped information pulses (videopulses) into signals with radio-frequency filling is performed by an exciter. The exciter output is connected to an input piezoconverter on the delay-line, which sets up acoustic signals that propagate along the line. Once the acoustic signal has reached the end of the line, an output piezoconverter transforms it once again into radio pulses. Attenuation of the signal in the line (about 50–60 db) is compensated for by a converter-amplifier which detects the signals and converts them once again into videopulses. The output signal from the converter-amplifier is fed via a gating unit and the unit-addition block in the arithmetic device to the exciter input. Thus, the dynamic storage of information is achieved.

The arrival of a unit-addition pulse at a given channel enables its contents to be increased by one unit and thus permits us to carry out the statistical analysis of pulses with respect to their amplitudes, i.e. to accumulate the spectrum.

The beginning of counting time in the delay line is determined by the start trigger pulse, the length of which (about $5\mu s$) is significantly greater than that of the information pulses (about $0.3\mu s$), thus permitting it to be identified in a special unit during the recording of information. The start pulse also arrives at the control unit input and puts the waiting clock-pulse generator into operation. A four-digit counter of channel pulses feeds out every 16th clock pulse. The channel pulses thus obtained are used to control the recording of information in memory and for gating channels of unit-addition pulses from the input device. The control signals are shaped by a pulse distributor having two outputs — one for the channel pulses and one for the clock pulses. Signals from the distributor are used to achieve an independent gating (prior to being sent to the exciter) of signals corresponding to channel pulses and to information pulses.

The output device enables us to achieve a digit-by-digit multiple output of accumulated information. The telemetry interrogation pulses, initially phased by start trigger pulses, are sent to a digital counter which memorizes the number of the digital being brought out into the channel. The code is transmitted from the digital counter into the clock counter, the latter determining the place in memory of the digit being brought out. Information being brought out from the given memory unit to telemetry is memorized in the storage unit for output information. Once all the digits of a particular channel have been brought out, the corresponding channel pulse is eliminated in the memory device, and the procedure is repeated for the next channel. As a result of the output of the entire volume of information, the channel pulses in the memory unit are obliterated. During the reregistering of information they will be automatically recorded once again from control unit signals, and a new output cycle can be commenced.

Different models of analysers, within the framework of the design structure outlined above, possess individual specific features associated with the tasks pursued

Table 2.1.8 – Main characteristics of analyzers with an ultrasonic delay-line memory

Space vehicle	Type and length of delay (t_d) of an ultrasonic line (μs)	Number of channels	Mean dead tim (μs)	Differential non linearity (%)	Integral non linearity (%)	Form of output information	Number of output digits	Power supply (W)	Mass of analyser (kg)
Luna 10	metallic $t_d = 500$	32	250	≤2	≤1	Analogue	12	2.5	3.9
Venera 8	monocrystalline $t_d = 1500$	64	800	≤2	≤1	Analogue	15	2.5	6
Luna 22	monocrystalline $t_d = 1500$	100	800	≤2	≤1	Digital	16	2.7	5

by particular specific experiments.

Table 2.1.8 summarizes the main characteristics of some analysers in the family described.

In conclusion it should be noted that progress in developing memory devices based on other principles, and the successful application of analysers based on them in space research has led to a gradual replacement of spectrometers of the family described above. At the same time, the development and successful application of spectrometers with the ultrasonic delay-line memory in space probes marks a certain stage in the continued development of multichannel instrumentation for gamma-ray spectrometry in space research, which enabled us to obtain some important scientific results.

Onboard multichannel analysers with the ferrite-core memory
Although possessing some positive characteristics, onboard amplitude analysers using ultrasonic delay-lines have, at the same time, turned out to be less promising than ferrite-core analysers. The latter are somewhat superior with respect to measurement and operational characteristics, as well as improved power consumption. Such analysers were used in gamma-ray spectrometers installed aboard Mars 5, Veneras 8, 13 and 14, and Apollos 15 and 16. We shall dissuss here the arrangement of one of them — the onboard pulse analyser used in the gamma-ray spectrometer carried by the interplanetary space probe Mars 5 [8,136,140]. Its functional diagram is given in Fig. 2.1.25. It consists of the following units: a pulse-height-to-digital converter, a counter unit with a decoder, magnetic high-speed

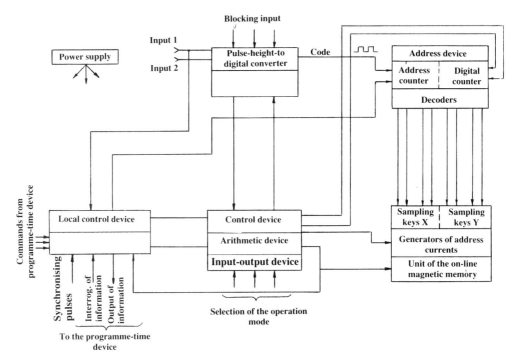

Fig. 2.1.25 — Functional diagram of the onboard pulse analyser with magnetic-ferrite core memory
carried aboard the space probe Mars 5.

storage, a control unit (containing, besides the control unit, an arithmetic device and
an output device), a local control device and a power-supply unit.

The pulse-height-to-digital converter performs the conversion of the pulse height
into a serial unit code, the number of pulses being proportional to the pulse
amplitude.

The binary counter and decoder convert the serial unit code into the address-key
control voltages for the magnetic high-speed memory, as well as handling the
reception of signals from the peripheral devices and their conversion into the parallel
code control voltages. The binary counter is functionally divided into an address and
a digital counter. It has 12 digits, its resolving time is 2μs and its maximum operating
frequency 4 MHz. Information readout is effected by the serial unit code and the
parallel binary code applied to the digital counter input and to the setting inputs of
the counter triggers, respectively.

The magnetic high-speed storage is accumulating and storing discrete information
during the processes of measurement and output. The storage capacity is 4096 binary
units, the number of addresses 256, and the number of digits 16.

The control device is responsible for synchronisation of the operation of the
analyser units. It provides for information readout with and without destruction,
information output on the receipt of interrogation signals from peripheral devices,
the addition of a unit during information recording, the recording of an arbitrary
code, the registration of additional information in the zero channel, the
commutation of the magnetic storage's readout – entry currents, and control over
starting and stopping the programme.

Finally, the local control device is responsible for converting commands from external devices into analyser operation control signals, for forming interrogation signals about information stored in the analyser, and handling synchronisation signals and information output from the analyser to an external device.

The analyser operates in the following manner. Signals from an external detection unit are sent to the pulse-height-to-digital converter which converts the detection-unit signal amplitude into a series of standard pulses, the number of which is proportional to the amplitude (serial unit code).

The series of pulses from the pulse-height-to-digital converter arrives at the input of the address device to be converted by an eight-digit address counter into the binary address code of the channel in which the arrival of the pulse is to be recorded.

Upon termination of the series of pulses from the pulse-height-to-digital converter, a pulse initiating the signal registration cycle (at the selected address) arrives at the control device.

As the magnetic high-speed storage in the analyser is of the series type, successive access to the digits of the selected address is made with the aid of the digital counter in the address device, the state of which changes in response to the clock pulses coming from the control device. The arithmetic device and the control device in the analyser perform the operation of adding a unit to the contents of a storage channel at the selected address. The succession of the above operations and time relationships between them are preset by the analyser control device. At the end of the registration cycle, the control device will send a signal to the input device to prepare it for reception of the next pulse for measurement from the detection unit, because throughout the time needed for amplitude codification and registration the pulse-height-to-digital converter is 'locked'.

Commands from external devices, interrogation about information stored in the analyser, and synchronisation of information interrogation and output to external devices are performed with the aid of the local control device linked up the central control device. In feeding control signals and pulses to the analyser control-device mode selection and testing inputs the following analyser programmes are realised: information readout in response to interrogation signals from external devices either with or without destruction of information, recording of information, and testing ('linear set').

The analyser was employed as part of the gamma-ray spectrometer installed in the Mars 5 probe which was put into a satellite orbit around the planet in February 1974. Its principal characteristics are as follows: the gamma-ray spectrometer has 256 channels, the channel capacity is $(2^{15} - 1) = 32,767$; gamma-radiation is recorded by a NaI(T1) detector 63 x 63 mm in size enveloped by a protective plastic scintillator; the energy range of measurements is 0.5–10 MeV; the integral nonlinearity of the analyser is not in excess of $\pm1\%$, a differential one not in excess of $\pm2\%$; the spectrometer resolution at the 0.622 MeV line of the radionuclide ^{137}Cs is not more than 10%; and the spectrometer dead-time is given by:

$$\tau = \tau_0 + mT + \tau_n, \qquad (2.1.11)$$

where $\tau_0 = 5 \mu s$ is the constant part of the dead-time; m is the number of code pulses (channel number); $T = 0.3$–$0.4 \mu s$ is the succession period of the generator's pulses of a code series; $\tau_n = \tau_p n$ is the access time to the memory device; $\tau_p = 5 \mu s$ is the time of a single access to the memory device; m is the number of accesses in the operation involving addition of a unit to the channel contents.

Promising multichannel analysers.

Recent progress in microelectronics offers the possibility of constructing multichannel analysers which have their working memory on semiconductor integrated circuits. The use of semiconductor structures enables us to increase the operating reliability of the memory and its speed, to reduce the weight, overall dimensions and power consumption, as well as to simplify the communication circuits with the other units of the instrument. A significant increase in the operating speed of memory devices on integrated circuits with a sampling time within 100 ns will open up the possibility of reducing the recording cycle down to some fractions of a microsecond in the case of a parallel version of the analyser memory device, whilst in the case of a parallel-series memory device the recording time will not exceed a few microseconds.

The number of analyser channels is determined in each case by the experimental requirements at the celestial object, but lies within the range 1024–4096 channels, the channel capacity word length being 16–18 binary bits.

The change-over to a new elemental base offers the possibility of increasing the frequency of the code pulse series up to 100–200 MHz in the analogue-to-digital converters operating on the Wilkinson principle, thus reducing the maximum dead time during the conversion to 5–20 μs. In constructing analogue-to-digital converters using the method of digit-by-digit 'weighting', the dead time of the conversion amounts to several microseconds.

The use of specialized microprocessors in multichannel analysers permits us not merely to simplify their architecture, but also to reduce the volume of information relayed via telemetry channels, due to the primary processing power aboard.

Thus, future multichannel analysers will be distinguished by a great number of channels, high operating speed, enhanced operational reliability and lower power consumption while possessing the same overall size and mass.

2.1.3   STUDY OF THE MOON'S GAMMA-RADIATION

2.1.3.1   Background gamma-radiation

Measurements of the cosmic gamma-ray background is of special significance in studying the gamma-radiation of the Moon and planets. What we mean by the cosmic gamma-ray background is the flux of gamma-ray quanta in interplanetary space falling on the detector. However, it is practically impossible to measure this background in a pure form, since any kind of detector will record simultaneously the gamma-radiation produced as a result of the interaction of cosmic rays with material of the space vehicle and detector. However, the less the mass of material in the proximity of the detector, the less this contribution. In a limiting case the gamma-ray background must be of cosmic origin alone.

A number of experiments [5, 141–146] have dealt with measuring the flux density of gamma-ray quanta in the Earth's upper atmosphere using balloons; above the atmosphere from meteorological rockets and satellites; and in outer space at a considerable distance from the Earth with the aid of interplanetary probes. As a result, it was found that in outer space there exists a flux density of gamma-ray quanta with an energy in excess of 1 MeV, with an intensity of about 1-10 quanta^{-2} s^{-1}.

Simultaneously it became clear that a significant flux of background gamma-radiation arises due to the interaction of charged cosmic particles with the material of the space probe aboard which the gamma-radiation detector is installed. The processes responsible for the appearance of this gamma-radiation are similar to those arising as a result of the interaction with material of the Moon, planets and meteorites.

The longest measurements of background gamma-radiation in outer space were made from Ranger 3. Although this space probe failed to fulfil its principal mission, i.e. measuring the Moon's gamma-radiation, it enabled the purest spectra to be obtained, to which the contribution from the gamma-radiation of the space probe itself was infinitesimal. During the flight of the space probe towards the Moon for nearly 30 hours, the gamma-radiation background was measured by a detector mounted on a telescopic boom (1.8 m long). In this case the solid angle concealed by the space probe was less than 1/20th part of the total space. The contribution from charged particles of cosmic and solar origin was eliminated by the Foswich circuit. Measurements were made within the 0.1–2.6 MeV range.

The number of gamma-ray quanta recorded with a 'pulled-in' boom was found to be nearly twice as great as with an 'extended' boom. In the latter case, the counting rate within the 0.5–2.1 MeV range was $(2.7\pm0.1) \times 10^3$ quanta m^{-2} s^{-1}, while in the case of gamma-ray quanta with energies in excess of 2.1 MeV it was $(6.7\pm0.2) \times 10^3$ quanta m^{-2} s^{-1}. During the flights of Lunas 10 and 12 towards the Moon the gamma-radiation background necessary for interpreting the gamma-radiation spectra of the lunar surface was also measured. Integral values of the background measured in different experiments are listed in Table 2.1.9.

Simultaneously with measuring the density of the gamma-radiation flux from certain space probes, the gamma-radiation background spectra were also measured. Fig. 2.1.26 shows gamma-ray spectra obtained when Lunas 10 and 12 were at a distance of about 230000 km from the Earth. The detector aboard Luna 10 was housed inside the space probe and that of Luna 12 was outside. This figure also shows the gamma-ray spectra obtained by Cosmos 60 (detector inside the space vehicle) and by Ranger 3 (detector at a 1.8-m distance from the probe's frame).

A characteristic feature of the gamma-ray spectra measured from Lunas 10 and 12 is an exponential decrease in the number of gamma-ray quanta with energies up to about 1.5 MeV and an insignificant decrease in the case of greater energies. The spectrum is observed to contain a significant number of gamma-ray quanta with energies over 1.5 MeV. A relatively high count-rate in the terminal spectrometer channels ($E\gamma > 3$ MeV) is an indication of the presence of gamma-radiation with even larger energies, this being in agreement with the data obtained by Ranger 3 for $E\gamma > 2.1$ MeV.

The spectra obtained by Cosmos 60 are observed to contain peaks associated with the inelastic interaction of cosmic protons with the material of the spacecraft's body (principally aluminium). Obviously, the same peaks, though less distinctly, manifest themselves in other spectra. The insignificant difference in the gamma-ray spectra (for energies beyond 1 MeV) obtained from Ranger 3, Cosmos 60, and Lunas 10 and 12 is apparently due to the differences in the dimensions of the crystals used.

The above spectra enable us to establish the intensity limits of certain lines which must be particularly distinct in the background spectrum of gamma-radiation. This is the annihilation line at 0.51 MeV and the hydrogen neutron capture line at 2.23 MeV. These lines are bound to arise at stellar surfaces or in interstellar space under

Table 2.1.9 – Data on the gamma-radiation background, as measured by different space probes

Year	Space probe	Instrument	Gamma-quanta energy range (MeV)	Flux density, ($\times 10^4$ quanta m^{-2} s^{-1})	References
1959	Second Soviet space rocket	Scintillation counter, NaI(T1) 40 x 40 mm	0.045–0.45	3.2±0.1	[141]
1960	Weather rockets, balloons	Scintillation counters	0.35–0.65 0.65–1.00 1.00–1.45 1.45–1.85	~0.8 ~0.2 ~0.1 ~0.005	[143,145]
1962	Ranger 3	32-channel scintillation gamma-ray spectrometer, CsI(T1), 75 x 75 mm with subtraction of the charged-particle background	0.5–2.1 >2.1	0.27±0.01 0.67±0.02 (1.8 m from the space probe frame)	[144]
1965	Cosmos 60	16-channel scintillation gamma-ray spectrometer, NaI(T1), 40 x 40 mm with subtraction of the charged-particle background	0.3–0.2	1.7±0.1	[142]
1966	Luna 10	32-channel scintillation gamma-ray spectrometer, NaI(T1), 40 x 40 mm with subtraction of the charged-particle background	0.3–0.7	1.20±0.08 2.44±0.09	[5]
1966	Luna 12	32-channel scintillation gamma-ray spectrometer, NaI(T1), 40 x 40 mm with subtraction of the charged-particle background	>0.3	2.85±0.09	[140]

1971	Apollo 15 Apollo 16	512-channel scintillation gamma-ray spectrometer, NaI(T1), 76 x 76 mm with subtraction of the charged-particle background	0.55–8.6	~1	[7,147]
1975	Mars 5	256-channel scintillation gamma-ray spectrometer, NaI(T1), 63 x 63 mm with subtraction of the charged-particle background	1.0–9.0	1.85	[8,9]

Table 2.1.10 – Background gamma-radiation within the 0.5–2.0 MeV range according to data from different space probes

Parameter	Luna 10 (detector inside space probe)	Luna 12 (detector near space probe)	Cosmos 60 (detector inside space probe)	Ranger 3 detector near space probe)	Ranger 3 (detector at 1.8-m distance)
Flux density ($\times 10^4$ quanta m^{-2}s^{-1})	1.40	1.6	0.98	0.54	0.27
Mass of the space probe (kg)	860	860	1600	350	350

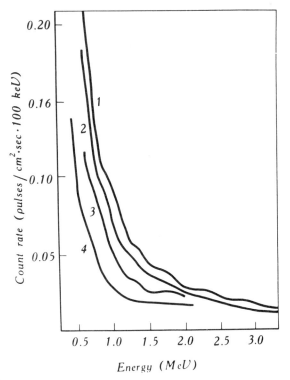

Fig. 2.1.26 — Spectra of the background gamma-radiation measured by lunar probes: 1, Luna
12; 2, Luna 10; 3, Cosmos 60; 4, Ranger 3.

the effect of any form of nuclear activity. The upper limits established in the aforementioned experiment aboard Ranger 3 are 1.5×10^2 quanta $m^{-2} s^{-1}$ for the 0.51MeV line and 3×10^2 quanta $m^{-2} s^{-1}$ for the 2.23MeV line.

The absence of any distinct peaks in the given spectra is an indication that the contribution of the monoenergy lines from a quiet Sun and the total galactic medium is small compared with the continuous spectrum (continuum). The continuous spectrum is observed to fall off sharply according to the $E^{-2.4}$ law down to the 1.0–1.5 MeV energy range and less steeply in the case of greater energies. A characteristic feature of all spectra is a great number of gamma-ray quanta with high energies ($E\gamma$ >3.0 MeV).

In measurements from Luna 10, the gamma-ray background within the 0.3–3.0 MeV energy range accounted for 60–70% of the entire flux of gamma-ray quanta, as measured in lunar orbit. The consequences of such a high background are the great statistical errors in determining the contribution of the natural and induced gamma-ray activity of lunar rocks.

Table 2.1.10 lists data on the gamma-radiation background within the 0.5–2.0 MeV energy range, as obtained from space probes of different mass.

As seen from Table 2.1.10, the background value is determined by the mass of the space probe and the position of the detector. The lowest background is observed for the detector mounted on the boom of the small space probe Ranger 3. The position of the same detector near the frame of Ranger 3 nearly doubled the background. The Luna 10 and 12 space probes are heavier than Ranger 3 and, correspondingly, have a greater background. The background on Cosmos 60, despite its larger mass, was found to be lower than on Luna 10 and 12, because Cosmos 60 was making measurements in the proximity of the Earth, where the flux of cosmic radiation is inferior to that in remote outer space on account of the screening effect of the Earth's magnetic field.

It has to be borne in mind that the difference in the gamma-ray background could also be due to a variation in the flux density of cosmic rays (mainly associated with the 11-year cycle of solar activity), since measurements were made at different times. The count-rate of gamma-ray quanta during the flights of Lunas 10 and 12 (within the statistical errors) continued to be constant, thus testifying to the absence of significant solar flares in those periods.

2.1.3.2 Investigation of the Moon's gamma-radiation by Lunas 10 and 12

On April 3, 1966 the Luna 10 probe was put into a selenocentric orbit, thus becoming the Moon's first man-made satellite. Nearly nine months later another lunar satellite — Luna 12 — was launched. Table 2.1.11 lists their orbital parameters.

Scientific instrumentation aboard the space probes was intended for studying the Moon and circumlunar space. The instruments comprised a multichannel scintillation gamma-ray spectrometer intended for measuring the spectral composition of the Moon's gamma-radiation [5].

Information from the gamma-ray spectrometers was relayed via telemetry communication channels in an eight-digit code. Gamma-radiation spectra recorded from a lunar orbit were selected within 10–12 min. Termination of the spectrum selection was made automatically upon overfilling one of the analyser channels. Spectrum selection time was recorded by the spectrometer timer, its reading being also relayed via telemetry.

Table 2.1.11 – Orbital parameters of Lunas 10 and 12

Parameters	Luna 10	Luna 12
Apogee	1015 km	1740 km
Perigee	350 km	100 km
Revolution time	2 hour 58 min	3 hour 25 min
Orbital inclination to equatorial plane	72°	20°

Commands for the gamma-ray spectrometer switch-on and information read-out were relayed from the Earth via a command-relay line. It was possible to receive information from the instrument either simultaneously with the spectrum selection or following it (due to overfilling of the channel).

The space probes were put into elliptical orbits and, therefore, the distance to the Moon was continuously varying. In accordance with the variation of the solid angle subtended by the Moon's surface at the moment of measurement, the relationship between the lunar gamma-radiation and gamma-ray background fluxes was continually changing. The count rate of gamma-ray quanta in orbit can be written down in the form:

$$I_O = I_m \left(\Omega / 2\pi\right) + I_\psi (1 - \Omega/2\pi) \qquad (2.1.12)$$

where I_m, I_ψ are the count rates of gamma-ray quanta at the Moon's surface and in the Earth-Moon flight trajectory, respectively; Ω is the solid angle subtended by the Moon at the moment of measurement from a lunar orbit:

$$\Omega = 4\pi \left[(R + h - \sqrt{(h\,(2R + h))} \,/ 2(R + h) \right] \qquad (2.1.13)$$

where R is the Moon's radius (1738 km), and h is the height of the spacecraft above the Moon's surface.

The solid angle Ω, for example, in measurements from Luna 10, was varying from 0.9π (h=350 km) to 0.46π (h=1 015 km).

During the active lifetime of the space probe, measurements of gamma-radiation spectra within the 0.3 - 3.0 MeV energy range were made in 14 areas of the lunar surface. Simultaneously in 56 areas, the integral count rate of gamma-ray quanta within the 0.3 - 0.7 MeV energy range was measured. Fig. 2.1.27 (curve 1) shows one of the primary gamma-ray spectra obtained when the probe was in lunar orbit. Also shown for the same orbital point is the background spectrum (curve 2) due to the interaction of cosmic rays with the probe's material (screening by the Moon being taken into account).

Compared to the count-rate of gamma-ray quanta, as measured in the flight trajectory, the count-rate in a lunar orbit was increased. Owing to the Moon's screening effect, the background due to the irradiation of the space probe by cosmic particles in lunar orbit amounted to 78-88% of the background in the flight trajectory. The count rate of lunar gamma-ray quanta, as recorded by the spectrometer, was also varying with the changing distance to the surface.

In Fig. 2.1.27, curves 3 and 4 refer to measurements reduced to the Moon's surface. Curve 3 depicts a gamma-ray spectrum at the Moon's surface together with

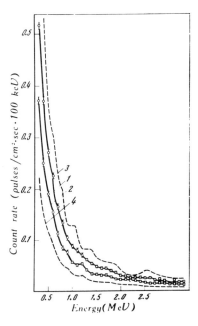

Fig. 2.1.27 — Spectra of gamma-radiation of the Moon; 1, spectrum measured from lunar orbit; 2, spectrum of background in orbit; 3, spectrum (1) reduced to the surface; 4, spectrum (2) reduced to the surface.

the background due to the irradiation of the probe, while curve 4 refers to the background alone. The increase in the ratio between the spectra of the Moon's surface together with the background and that of the background alone to a value of 3.2 is due to the increase of the solid angle in which the Moon's surface is visible and to a decrease of the background on account of greater screening from cosmic radiation.

Lunar gamma-ray spectra differ significantly in shape from the spectra of terrestrial rocks. As noted above, the shape of the gamma-ray spectra of terrestrial rocks is mainly determined by the uranium, thorium and potassium content. The spectrum of lunar gamma-radiation is closer in shape to the spectrum measured in outer space, the shape of the latter being determined by the interaction processes between cosmic particles and the material of the satellite.

In these measurements the upper registration boundary of the spectrum was 3.2 MeV. At the same time, the character of the spectrum indicates that it also contains gamma-ray quanta with energies in excess of 3.2 MeV.

All gamma-ray spectra measured above different areas of the lunar surface are similar in shape. Weakly manifested in the spectra are practically the same peaks from gamma-ray quanta arising chiefly in the course of the inelastic interaction, including inelastic scattering of the proton component of cosmic rays by rock-forming elements: oxygen, aluminium, magnesium and iron.

The measurement of the natural radioactivity level and determination of the concentration of natural radioelements involved subtraction of the gamma-radiation spectrum due to the interaction between cosmic rays and dunite rocks from the Moon's gamma-radiation spectrum obtained. To a first approximation we accepted the shape of the spectrum either by calculation on the basis of an average chemical composition of lunar rock or plotted on the basis of model experiments using accelerators.

Gamma-ray spectrometers carried by Lunas 10 and 12 had been preliminarily calibrated under terrestrial conditions on standard specimens with a known content of natural radioactive elements – potassium, thorium and uranium.

Apart from gamma-ray spectra, Lunas 10 and 12 measured the integral count rate of gamma-ray quanta within the 0.3–0.7 MeV energy range during brief communication sessions. Measurements were made in 56 surface areas and covered extensive territories of both the visible (nearside) and far sides of the Moon. On the basis of the trajectory data all the areas were subdivided into two groups – the maria and the highlands — and the average count rate of gamma-ray quanta was determined for these two types of morphological province. This subdivision into two groups is of an approximate nature, as seen from Fig. 2.1.28.

Fig. 2.1.28 shows for different altitudes the ratio of the gamma-ray quanta flux, I arriving at the detector from an area described by the radius, R, to the total flux from the lunar surface I_{max} as a function of the R value. As seen from these curves, owing to the great distance of the spacecraft from the Moon, the gamma-radiation was recorded by the probes from a large area of the lunar surface, which in most cases comprised simultaneously (but to a different degree) both the mare and highland parts.

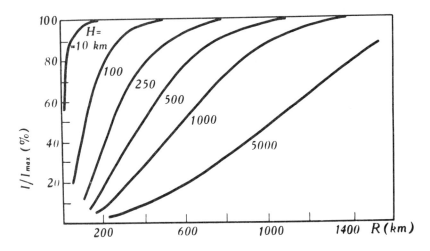

Fig. 2.1.28 — Flux of gamma-ray quanta as a function of the area of the emitting surface of the Moon.

Table 2.1.12 – Count rate of gamma-quanta above lunar and terrestrial rocks

Measurement object	Count rate, ($\times 10^4$ pulses m^{-2}s^{-1})	Instrument calibration object	Count rate, ($\times 10^4$ pulses m^{-2}s^{-1})
Lunar maria	1.78	Acid rocks (calculated)	0.90
Lunar highlands	1.51	Basic rocks (calculated	0.21
Increase of intensity	0.27	Acid rocks (measured)	1.28
in mare areas		Basic rocks (measured)	0.21
over highland areas		Ultrabasic rocks (calculated)	0.002

Table 2.1.12 lists the mean count-rates of gamma-ray quanta for the mare and highland areas, as measured by Luna 10.

The count-rate of 1.78 $\times 10^4$ pulses m^{-2}s^{-1} principally relates to the Mare Humorum and Mare Nubium area lying on the Moon's visible side whilst the count-rate of 1.51 $\times 10^4$ pulses m^{-2}s^{-1} was recorded for a highland massif on the far side of the Moon. As shown, the count rate of gamma-ray quanta above lunar maria is about 1.15–1.2 times as high as above lunar highlands. The same table presents both calculated and measured count rates of gamma-ray quanta above different terrestrial rocks — acidic, basic and ultra-basic. Model experiments were carried out above granitic and basaltic rock massifs (in Armenia and Karelia). If an excess of the count rate of gamma-ray quanta above the maria (as compared to the highlands) is to be entirely attributed to natural radioactivity, then from a comparison with the data obtained on the standards it follows that the composition of the maria corresponds to terrestrial basaltic rocks. The highland areas having a lower activity level possess, in this case, a composition similar to primary or weakly differentiated rocks. A contribution to gamma-radiation above lunar maria from the disintegration of potassium, thorium and uranium in with 0.3–0.7 MeV energy range approximately amounts to 10–15%. It is even less above lunar highlands.

2.1.3.3. Main results of studying the Moon's gamma-radition from Lunas 10 and 12

Prior to the flights of Lunas 10 and 12 our concepts of the character of lunar rocks were quite conflicting. They embraced the entire range of known terrestrial rocks from ultrabasic to acid. At the same time, if we disregard details, many researchers presumed that lunar maria were, in effect, areas covered by erupted lava similar in composition to the Earth's basaltic rocks.

In this respect, the data on the Moon's gamma-radiation, for the first time, furnished experimental confirmation of the validity of such concepts. In all mare areas where measurements were made, the gamma-radiation level of natural radioactive elements corresponded to terrestrial basaltic rocks with a low content of uranium, thorium and potassium (i.e. primitive or oceanic basalts). However, mare areas in different parts of the lunar surface also differed in radioactivity level. And although measurements were made from high-altitude orbits (and, therefore, in all cases we obtained information averaged over a large area), our attention was drawn by certain tendencies in the variations of radioactivity in lunar maria. Thus, for instance, an area with a particularly high radioactivity was observed, lying in the vicinity of Mare Humorum and Mare Nubium. No high radioactivity level is observable in eastern maria – Mare Australe, Mare Marginis, Mare Crisium and Mare Smythii. Presumably, these maria differ slightly in the composition of their rocks.

As regards the Moon's highlands, prior to the staging of these experiments the majority of researchers were inclined to think that, similarly to the Earth's continents, lunar highland were made up of acid rocks similar in composition to terrestrial granites. At the same time some of the papers put forward an idea about the Moon's surface being mainly composed of primary nondifferentiated matter compositionally similar to stony meteorites, i.e. chondrites. Suppositions were also made to the effect that stony meteorites falling on the Earth were of lunar origin [148]. This supposition was confirmed later in [172].

As can be seen from the aforementioned results of measurements, a high content of natural radioactive elements, as exists in terrestrial granites, was not observed anywhere on the lunar highlands. Furthermore, the flux of gamma-ray quanta of natural radioactive elements above the highlands was found to be lower. This enabled the authors [5] to suppose that the Moon's highland rocks may be compositionally similar to the Earth's ultrabasic rocks. In their opinion, the rocks of the Moon's highland massifs are not similar to those of terrestrial continents, as was often assumed earlier. The low radioactivity level of the lunar highlands is evidence to the effect that they must be composed of either weakly differentiated or non differentiated primary matter.

If we take into account the mean ratio $K/U \approx 2800$, as is known today for the Moon [140], and the ratio $Th/U \approx 4$, similar to the Earth, we may estimate the mean content of uranium, thorium and potassium in certain areas of the Moon's surface. Thus, for the basins of western maria they amount to 1–2, 4–8, and 2000–4000 ppm, respectively.

Nowadays, after lunar soil samples from different areas of the Moon have been returned to the Earth and carefully analysed, we may also estimate the character of rocks from other lunar areas (from which no soil has yet been returned to the Earth) by proceeding from the above-discussed results of gamma-radiation measurements.

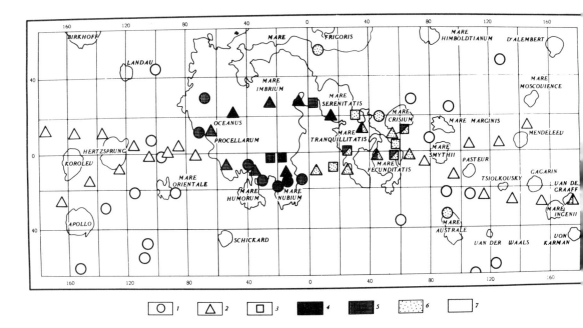

Fig. 2.1.29 — Contour map of the Moon. It shows the regions where the radioactivity of rocks was measured: 1, Lunar 10 and 12; 2, Apollos 15 and 16: 3, Lunar samples. Radioactivity: 4, high; 5, medium; 6, low; 7, very low.

Fig. 2.1.29 presents a contour map of the lunar surface. The map indicates areas in which the radioactivity of rocks was measured by Lunas 10 and 12, and Apollos 15 and 16, as well as areas in which rock specimens were collected, to be afterwards investigated on the Earth. The flux of gamma-ray quanta from the lunar surface, which with a certain assumption can be considered to be proportional to the concentration of natural radioelements, is subdivided on the basis of density into four groups. Let us note that despite a significant difference (by at least one order of magnitude) in the concentration of natural radioelements in separate lunar soil specimens brought back to the Earth, the flux density of the gamma-ray quanta varies by not more than about 1.5 times. This is accounted for by two factors: firstly, an insignificant variation of the mean content of natural radioelements; and, secondly, the fact that the main contribution to the Moon's gamma-radiation is made by cosmogenic radionuclides, rather than by natural radioelements.

As evident from the map, a particularly high radioactivity level is observed in the basins of western lunar maria, a lower one in eastern maria and the lowest of all on continental and high-mountain massifs of the Moon's visible and far sides. Such a distribution of radioactivity could be understood, particularly after lunar soil samples had been analysed on the Earth. It is accounted for by the presence of two radically different types of crustal matter on the Moon: the highland (gabbro–anorthositic composition) and the mare (basaltic composition).

The ground mass of the Moon's highland crust is composed of gabbro–anorthosites, i.e. rocks in which feldspar is predominant. These rocks are known to be outcropping at the old, strongly cratered surface. Their absolute age is 4000–4500 million years. They compose the old primary crust formed in the early period of the Moon's existence. This crust arose as a result of the fusion process during the impact heating of the upper (fairly extensive) mass of the Moon in the process of its formation.

The area of the lunar maria accounts for about 15% of the lunar surface. The maria are mainly covered by basaltic rocks 3200–3800 million years old. These rocks were formed in a later period than the highland rocks due to heating of the Moon's interior as a result of the accumulation of radiogenic heat and the impacts of large meteorites breaking through the thin feldspar crust and opening the way for exit onto the surface of more differentiated (basalt) rocks.

The presence of two types of crust, highland and mare, having a different nature is fairly distinctly reflected on the map of the Moon's radioactivity, where there are seen both the mare areas noted for their high level of radioactivity and the highland areas with a relatively low radioactivity level and content of radioelements. The rest of the areas with an intermediate radioactivity (such as Van de Graaff, etc.) apparently consist of a mixture of anorthositic and basaltic rocks.

Comparing the content of radioelements on the Moon and on the Earth, we may point out the following. The mean content of radioelements on the Moon is higher than on the Earth, while their mean content in the lunar crust is lower than in the Earth's crust. This indicates that differentiation processes of matter on the Moon were not as intensive as on the Earth and, as a result, the enrichment of the crust with radioelements on the Moon turned out to be at least by one order of magnitude lower than on the Earth.

2.1.3.4 Investigation of the Moon's gamma-radiation from Apollos 15 and 16

In 1971–1972 the manned space vehicles Apollos 15 and 16 were launched towards the Moon. In contrast to the previous Apollo launchings, these space vehicles carried scientific instruments intended for the study of the Moon and circumlunar space during the presence of the orbital command module in a satellite orbit around the Moon. These instruments also included gamma-ray spectrometers to be used for a continued investigation of the Moon's radioactivity. The gamma-ray spectrometers installed aboard Apollos 15 and 16 were used to determine the content of natural radioactive elements (uranium, thorium, potassium) in lunar rocks, and to estimate the content of principal rock-forming elements (oxygen, magnesium, aluminium, silicon and iron) [7,147].

The spectrometer consisted of a sensor mounted on a boom 7.6 m long and an electronic analysis unit mounted inside the instrumentation compartment of the space vehicle. The sensor incorporated a NaI(TI) crystal of a cylindrical shape, 76 x 76 mm in size, for registering gamma-radiation and a protective plastic scintillator for eliminating the recording of charged particles of cosmic origin. Both scintillation detectors were combined with the corresponding photomultipliers and were operated according to the anticoincidence scheme. The spectrum was recorded in a direct-transmission régime. The resolution of the spectrometer was about 8%.

Measurements were made from lunar orbit at distances of 100–120km above the lunar surface. The orbital inclination angle to the equator was 29° for Apollo 15 and 10° for Apollo 16. Therefore, only the Moon's equatorial regions were investigated, i.e. about 20% of the lunar surface. The spectra were measured within the 0.55 – 8.6 MeV energy range.

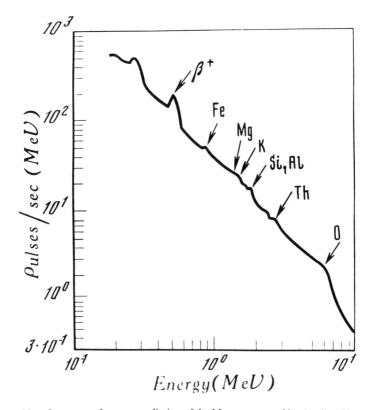

Fig. 2.1.30 — Spectrum of gamma-radiation of the Moon measured by Apollo 15 in the energy range of 0.1–10 MeV.

Fig. 2.1.30 shows one of the measured spectra. The spectrum exhibits some indistinctly expressed energy peaks which are mainly due to the interaction of cosmic rays with the principal rock-forming elements. The main peaks lie within the energy range below 3 MeV. At higher energies, the oxygen peak alone can be identified, the content of this element in lunar rocks accounting for about 50% of the total mass.

It is easy to see that this spectrum is similar to the spectra obtained earlier by Lunas 10 and 12, although they were measured in different lunar areas and at different times. The reason for this lies in the fact that their shape is mainly determined by the gamma-radiation induced in lunar rock by cosmic rays. As regard the determination of the content of natural radioactive elements, the optimal conditions occur for thorium in which the 2.61-MeV energy band almost fails to be overlapped by other elements; the uranium and potassium contents can be determined with lesser accuracy.

In measurements from an altitude of about 100 km the angular resolution with respect to the areas considerably differing in their content of radioactive elements was about 2.5° (about 70 km). This permitted a comparison of the radioactivity of different areas of the lunar surface, over which the space vehicles were flying, to be carried out.

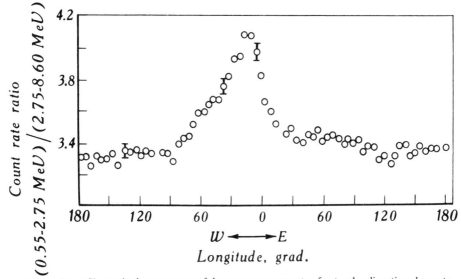

Fig. 2.1.31 — Change in the count rate of the gamma-ray quanta of natural radioactive elements measured during one orbit of Apollo 15 around the Moon.

Fig. 2.1.31 shows a variation in the count rate of gamma-ray quanta, as measured from lunar orbit during one revolution about the Moon. The variation in the ratio of the count-rate within the 0.55–2.75 and 2.75–8.60 MeV ranges principally reflects the variation in the uranium, thorium and potassium contents in the rocks. For the given trajectory this ratio was changing from about 3.3 for a highland massif to 4.0 for a particularly radioactive area in the western mare basins.

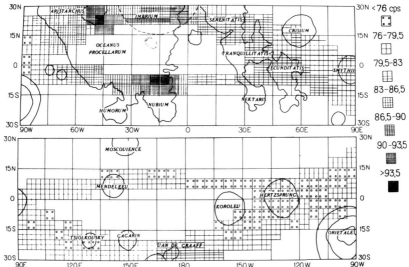

Fig. 2.1.32 — Distribution of natural radioactive elements in the equatorial part of the lunar surface

Fig. 2.1.32 shows the equatorial part of the lunar surface for the visible and far sides on which the measured count-rates (the number of gamma-ray quanta per cm^2 of the detector area in 1 sec within the 0.55–2.75 MeV energy range) over different surface areas are indicated. The count rates are given for lunar surface areas 5° x 5° in size. The average count-rate within this energy range in the case of Apollo 16 was 4.6% higher than that of Apollo 15, which is in good agreement with the ratio of the fluxes of cosmic particles observed at respective times. For those areas which were covered by both space vehicles, weighted mean values are given. The count-rate was varying from 73 to 94 pulses s^{-1}, i.e within about 25%. In this case good reproducibility of values was observed for repeatedly scanned areas, as well as for areas overlapped by both vehicles.

2.1.3.5 Main results of studying the Moon's gamma-radiation from Apollos 15 and 16

As seen from the data given in Fig. 2.1.32, a particularly radioactive area proves to be that of the basins of western maria on the Moon's visible side, which is in good agreement with the data obtained by Lunas 10 and 12. The level of radioactivity in this area is much higher than in the eastern maria on the Moon's visible side and more so than anywhere in the highland areas of the Moon's surface. Radioactivity was found to be high in the northern part of the basins of western maria (the maximum level being at the Aristarchus crater) and in the southern part of western maria (the maximum level being south of Fra Mauro), thus enabling us to assume the presence of high radioactivity also in the central part of the western mare basin where no measurements have been made.

All the eastern maria on the Moon's visible side revealed low radioactivity levels. However, in this part, areas with high radioactivity were identified too. The highest radioactivity with respect to the surrounding highland massif was observed in Mare Tranquillitatis, Mare Foecunditatis, Mare Crisium and Mare Smythii. At the same time, no increase in radioactivity was observed in Mare Serenitatis. The highest radioactivity level in the eastern maria was recorded in Mare Crisium.

Highland areas on both sides of the Moon revealed a low radioactivity level, except for the areas bordering on the western maria where an intermixing of rocks is highly probable. This points to the fact that the highlands had been formed prior to the formation of the Oceanus Procellarum with adjoining maria. At the same time, on the Moon's far side, the highland part (180°–90°E) was found to be slightly more radioactive than the western part (90°W–180°). For instance, there is an insignificant radioactivity maximum in the vicininty of the Van de Graaff crater, where a large magnetic anomaly has also been recorded. As noted by the authors of papers [7,147], a certain difference in the flux of gamma-ray quanta above eastern maria and highland massifs is possibly explained not by the content of natural elements, but rather by a difference in the chemical composition of the rocks.

From the analysis of the shape of the peaks belonging to uranium, thorium and potassium an assessment of the K/Th and K/U ratios was made. They were found to be low for all areas of the lunar surface as compared to those for terrestrial rocks (about 2500 and 10000, respectively). These ratios are slightly higher for western maria than for eastern ones (as was noted in lunar specimens investigated on the Earth).

The radioactivity data obtained as a result of these measurements correlate with numerous other properties of lunar matter that are known for different areas of the lunar surface.

In the first place, gamma-radiation is observed to be correlated with data on the chemical composition. Extensive information available today on the chemical and mineral composition of rocks returned to the Earth from different lunar areas enables one to identify them with terrestrial analogues on the basis of the natural radioactive elements contained in them.

In papers [16,149] attention is given to a correlation between the content of natural radioactive elements and the lunar surface relief. Wherever the relief is higher, the radioactivity is lower, and vice versa. Generally this would be expected, since all the maria having basaltic rocks (i.e. a high uranium, thorium and potassium content) lie below the highlands predominantly composed of anorthositic rocks (noted for a low content of uranium, thorium and potassium). However, no differences between separate maria or between different areas of the highland massif had been observed earlier.

Attention was also drawn to a correlation between the radioactivity level and the magnitude of the magnetic field. In particular, in the area of the Van de Graaff crater a coincidence between maximum gamma-ray activity and the maximum magnetic field was noted.

The results of gamma-radiation studies from Apollos 15 and 16 in combination with other correlating data obtained in the study of lunar surface characteristics have enabled the experimenters to put forward some general considerations on the nature of the western mare basins which are covered by a highly radioactive rock [16,149].

It is presumed that in the particularly radioactive areas discovered by the Apollos, a considerable mass of the rock is represented by KREEP basalts. In other places of the western mare basins its content is apparently lower on account of intermixing with a less radioactive rock. In this case, an exceptionally high content of KREEP basalts in the western mare basins is explained by one of the following assumptions: (a) high radioactivity was once the property of a large alien body, the falling of which onto the Moon contributed to the formation of the entire region; (b) the size and velocity of a falling alien body (which could also be non-radioactive) were so great that it was capable of throwing out (or pouring out in the form of magma) the material from a depth larger than could do any other impact on the Moon's surface; (c) the primary (primitive) surface lunar rock was inhomogeneous both in depth and over the surface; (d) perhaps both factors (b) and (c) are responsible.

2.1.4 STUDY OF MARS' GAMMA-RADIATION

2.1.4.1 Calculation and construction of the spectra of Mars' gamma-radiation

Mars' gamma-radiation spectra were calculated by Surkov *et al* [2], Metzger and Arnold [150]. Calculation and plotting of the spectra in [2] was carried out using the data obtained by measurement of the Moon's gamma-radiation [5], as well as the results of model experiments on balloons and using accelerators [13,151,152]. Plotting was made for some particularly widespread rocks of the Earth, the Moon and meteorites. In the first stage of the work the model spectra were obtained from balloons. After that, containers of rock, the layer of which was about 500 kg m^{-2}

containers with rock, the layer of which was about 500 kg m^{-2} thick, were raised to an altitude of 33–34 km. The atmospheric layer above the rock was about 200 kgm^{-2}, i.e. quite close to the conditions at the Martian surface.

Emission cross-sections of gamma-ray quanta, as measured from balloons, can be used as a first approximation for the plotting of gamma-ray spectra expected to be present at the Martian surface. However, in this case the data obtained from balloons needed to be reduced to the measurement conditions on Mars.

The first stage of such a correction involved the normalization of gamma-ray spectra measured from balloons with respect to the gamma-ray spectra of lunar rocks, as measured by Luna-10 [5]. In this case, the normalising coefficient was determined as a result of the alignment of the spectra in the energy range in excess of 2.7 MeV where gamma-radiation is determined solely by the interaction of cosmic rays with the rock and is little dependent on the latter's composition. Such a method of normalisation permits us to take account of the factors which are specific to an experiment in outer space (the infinite, as compared to model experiments, size of the rock, the continuous spectrum of cosmic radiation, the effect of solar cosmic radiation, etc.).

The second stage involved a recalculation of the gamma-ray spectra thus normalised to the measurement conditions in a satellite orbit around Mars. In this case, the following considerations formed the basis of the calculations. The flux of gamma-ray quanta, I, recorded by the detector, is determined by the parameters:

$$I = Bn_o SG\sigma \tag{2.1.14}$$

where $B = Nd/A$ is the number of nuclei per m^2; n_o is the density of the proton flux, (particles m^{-2}s^{-1}); S is the surface area from which gamma-radiation is recorded (m^2); A is the weighted mean atomic number of the rock; G is a geometric factor; N is the Avogadro number; d is the thickness of the rock layer, from which gamma-radiation is recorded (Kg m^{-2}); σ is the emission cross-section of gamma-ray quanta (m^2).

Since the proton flux falling onto unit area of the lunar and Martian surfaces may be considered similar, because the Martian atmosphere will cause only some insignificant distortion of the primary spectrum of cosmic rays (this having no significant effect either on the cross-section or on the thickness, d), then for $\sigma_1 = \sigma_2$ and $d_1 = d_2$ the fluxes of gamma-ray quanta, as recorded by the detector in satellite orbits around the Moon and Mars, can be written down as follows:

$$I_1 = qS_1G_1; \quad I_2 = qS_2G_2; \tag{2.1.15}$$

where $q = Bn_o\sigma$ is the flux of gamma-ray quanta from unit area of the surface, similar for the Moon and Mars above (henceforth index 1 refers to the Moon, index 2 to Mars).

The quantity SG is determined in the following manner. If the distance from the detector to the planet is comparable to the radius of the planet, the latter surface can be regarded as a sphere, while the thickness of the rock layer, from which gamma-radiation is recorded, can be neglected in calculating G. Thus, the problem boils down to determining the flux of gamma-ray quanta from an impervious sphere covered by a thin layer of radiating matter. The solution of a similar problem for a hollow sphere is given in [153]. However, while in the case of a hollow sphere, the integral is taken over the entire surface of the sphere, in the given case the integration is made solely over the surface from which gamma-radiation is recorded. Consequently, in solving the given problem we may write down the value of the flux of gamma-ray quanta recorded by the detector in the following form:

$$I=\int_0^{s} \max \ qG_sdS$$

$$(2.1.16)$$

where G_s is a geometric factor allowing for the fraction of gamma-radiation recorded by the detector from each unit area; S_{max} is the maximum area from which gamma-radiation is recorded.

As a result of the integration we obtain an expression:

$$I=q\ [R/2(R+H)] \times \ln(1+2R/H),$$ $$(2.1.17)$$

where R is the planetary radius; H is the distance from the detector to the planetary surface. Then from expressions (2.1.15)–(2.1.17) we obtain a relationship enabling us to make a recalculation of the flux of gamma-ray quanta in a satellite orbit around the Moon in relation to that in a satellite orbit around Mars:

$$I_2=I_1\ [R_2\ (R_1+H_1)/R_1\ (R_2+H_2)] \times [\ln(1+2R_2/H_2)/\ln(1+2R_1/H_1)],$$ $$(2.1.18)$$

Calculations made in [173] enabled gamma-radiation spectra to be constructed for different rocks for measuring conditions at different distances from the Martian surface. The gamma-ray spectra were calculated for a scintillation gamma-ray spectrometer with an NaI(Tl) crystal 70x70 mm in size and with a 9% resolution (with respect to ^{137}Cs). Given as an illustration in Fig. 2.1.33 is an expected gamma-radiation spectrum at a distance of 2000 km from Mars, which is formed both by the interaction of cosmic rays with the planetary surface, assuming that the latter is made up of silicate rock (basalt), and by the decay of natural radioelements contained in the rock.

As seen from Fig. 2.1.33, the spectrum proves to be rather complex, the reason for this lying in the abundance of discrete lines and the great contribution of the background count. The spectrum is observed to comprise peaks belonging to annihilation radiation (0.51 MeV), potassium (1.46 MeV) and thorium (2.61 MeV).

As pointed out above, we may expect the existence on Mars of silicate rocks, different iron compounds, specifically haematite (Fe_2O_3) and limonite ($2Fe_2O_3 \cdot 4H_2O$). The presence of ice-covered spaces is not excluded. Therefore, investigations were undertaken into the cross-section for the formation of gamma-ray quanta within the 0.6 – 5.2 MeV energy range as a function of the effective mass number of the rocks and compounds that are assumed to be present on Mars during their irradiation by cosmic rays. These have revealed a prominent dependence of the cross-section (and, consequently, of the flux density of the gamma-ray quanta) on the mass number of

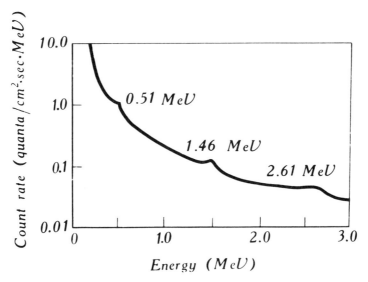

Fig. 2.1.33 — Martian gamma-radiation spectrum calculated for the altitude of a satellite orbit around Mars of 2000 km.

the target. Thus, from the magnitude of the integral flux of gamma-ray quanta we may in principle also determine the character of Martian rocks. However, gamma-radiation spectra contain a great deal of information. In particular, the fluxes of gamma-ray quanta from granite and haematite are similar, the ratio $I\gamma$ (1–2 MeV)/$I\gamma$ (2–3 MeV) for them, however, being about 1 and 10 respectively.

For a distance of 40000–50000 km from the Martian surface, the factor G is three orders of magnitude smaller than for a distance of 10000 km. Consequently, measurements at more than 40000–50000 km distances can be employed for estimating the background due to the gamma-radiation from the space vehicle.

If the distance from the detector to the surface is significantly less than the planetary radius, then in calculating the flux of gamma-ray quanta in a satellite orbit we must take account of the thickness of the rock layer from which the quanta emerge. In this case the flux of gamma-ray quanta will be determined by the numerical integration of the expression.

$$I = 4\pi q \int_{R-\Delta R}^{R} \int_{\theta}^{\theta_{max}} r^2 \sin\theta \, /a^2 \exp(\mu_1 x + Z) \, dr \, d\theta \qquad (2.1.19)$$

where θ is the angle between the line connecting the detector to the centre of the planet and the line connecting the centre of the planet to the point of emission of a gamma-ray quantum; r is the distance from the centre of the planet to the emission point of a gamma-ray quantum to the detector; R is the planet's radius; μ_1 is the absorption coefficient for a gamma-ray quantum of a spherical layer; x is the length of path travelled by a gamma-ray quantum in the spherical layer; θ_{max} is the maximum angle of view; $\theta_{max} = R/(R+H)$; ΔR is the thickness of the layer from which gamma-ray quanta fly out; H is the distance from the detector to the planetary surface. The thickness of the spherical layer over which integration is carried out is determined from the emergence of about 90% of gamma-radiation coming out of it:

$$I/I_0 = \exp(-\mu_1 x) \qquad (2.1.20)$$

where $\mu_1=\rho_1/16\ \sqrt{E\gamma}$ is the rock density. Absorptioon of gamma-ray quanta by the atmosphere is allowed for by the expression.

$$Z= \int\limits_{0}^{1} \mu_2(l)dl, \qquad\qquad (2.1.21)$$

where μ_2 is the absorption coefficient of gamma-ray quanta by the atmosphere; $l=(a-x)$ is the length of path travelled by a gamma-ray quantum in the atmosphere.

The absorption coefficient of gamma-ray quanta in the atmosphere is dependent of height, H, since the density of the atmosphere varies with height according to an exponential law:

$$\rho_\alpha = \rho_0 \exp(-\alpha H), \qquad\qquad (2.1.22)$$

where ρ_0 is assumed equal to 2×10^{-2} kg m^{-3}; and $\alpha = 0.114$ km^{-1}.

Fig. 2.1.34 shows the radius of an effective area as a function of height H for several values of $E\gamma$. It is seen from the figure that, for instance, for $E\gamma = 3$ MeV and a height of 2000 km the radius of an effective area amounts to 1600 km (an effective area is that part of the planet's surface from which the flux of gamma-ray quanta amounts to 90%), the radius of an area from which 50% of the gamma-ray quanta flux is recorded being about 900 km. The contribution of gamma-radiation from the atmosphere to the gamma-spectrum recorded in orbit can be estimated in the following way. As pointed out above, the formation cross-section of gamma-ray quanta with energies from 1 to 3 MeV is almost invariable within a wide range of proton energies (for $E_p > 100$ MeV). Therefore, to estimate the relative contribution

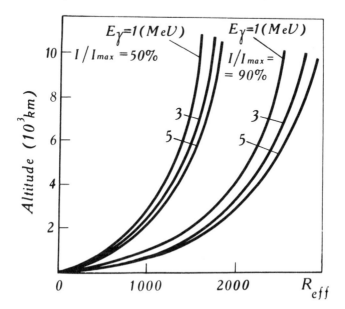

Fig. 2.1.34 — Radius of the effective area as a function of the height of a satellite orbit and gamma-radiation energy.

of gamma-radiation from the planet's atmosphere and rock we may use the integral cross-sections for the formation of gamma-ray quanta from rock-forming and atmosphere-forming elements, as measured using an accelerator. The composition of the Martian rock can be arbitrarily assumed to be basaltic and the atmosphere as consisting of CO_2. Then the integral cross-sections for the formation of gamma-ray quanta can be expressed as follows:

for the rock $\quad\quad \sigma_2 = I_2 A_2/(d_2 n_2 N G_2);$ (2.1.23)
for the atmosphere $\sigma_3 = I_3 A_3/(d_3 n_3 N G_3).$ (2.1.24)

From the experiments using an accelerator in the case of proton energies of about 660 MeV it follows that $\sigma_2 \approx 3\sigma_3$. The values of n_2 and n_3 can be assumed equal, because the flux of cosmic particles is practically equal for the rock and the atmosphere. Finally, the calculation of the geometrical factor, G, for the rock and for the atmosphere reveals that with a thickness of atmosphere up to about 200 kg m^{-2} for measurements at an altitude of not less than 1000 km $G_2 \approx G_3$. Then, the flux density of gamma-ray quanta from the atmosphere takes the form:

$$I_3 = (I_2 A_2 d_2)/(3 A_3 d_3),$$ (2.1.25)

where A_2 and A_3 are the mean mass numbers of the rock and the atmosphere; d_2 and d_3 are the thicknesses of the layers of the rock and the atmosphere from which gamma-radiation is registered; I_2 is the flux density of gamma-ray quanta from the rock, as determined from formula (2.1.23) and equal to 7.5 gamma-quanta s^{-1}.

The bulk of gamma-radiation arrives from a layer with a thickness of the order of the free path of gamma-ray quanta $L=1/\mu$. For the gamma-ray quanta with energies from 1 to 3 MeV the mean value of $L = d_2$ in rocks amounts to about 200 kg m^{-2} [154]. Then from relationship (2.1.25) for an atmosphere consisting entirely of CO_2 we shall obtain the values of $I_3 = 2.8$ gamma-quanta s^{-1} for $d_3 = 200$ kg m^{-2}.

Thus, information on the character of the rocks can be obtained not only from spectral measurements, but also from the flux density of gamma-ray quanta.

2.1.4.2 Sensitivity and resolution limits of the gamma-ray spectrometric method in the exploration of Mars

As is known, the particularly intense lines in the gamma-radiation of natural radioactive elements are the following: for ^{40}K, 1.46 MeV; for U, 1.76 MeV; and for Th, 2.62 MeV. The maximum sensitivity of the laboratory setups with an NaI (Tl) detector 70 x 70 mm in size is, correspondingly, about 1 pulse s^{-1} for 10^4 ppm K, about 0.3 pulse s^{-1} for 1ppm U; and about 1 pulse s^{-1} for 1ppm Th in the case of the 2π geometry.

The above values were used in [150] and the minimum potassium concentration that can be measured from different satellite orbits was calculated. The calculation was carried out by making use of the following expression for the flux of gamma-ray quanta recorded by the detector, which characterises the gamma-radiation intensity line:

$$B = PGKt$$ (2.1.26)

where P is the detector sensitivity in the photopeak region, referred to a unit of time and a unit content of the element; G is the planet's geometrical factor at orbital height; K is the transmission coefficient for gamma-radiation through Mars' atmosphere for a true optical thickness; t is the time of measurement.

In this case the total background in the photopeak energy interval is determined as follows

$$B_t = A_o \Delta E t \left[B_m GK + (1 - \Omega_m) B_s \right] \qquad (2.1.27)$$

where A_o is the detector's isotropic area; ΔE is the photopeak energy width, B_m is the background of cosmogenic radioactivity per unit area and unit energy; B_s is the background caused by the interplanetary flux; Ω_m is the solid angle which Mars subtends from orbit.

The minimum identifiable concentration of any element, as represented by the gamma-ray line, has the form

$$C_{min} = (B/N) \, B_t^{\,1/2} / B, \qquad (2.1.28)$$

where B/N is the desirable significance of the data. Therefore, by substituting (2.1.26) and (2.1.27) in (2.1.28) we obtain

$$C_{min} = (B/N) \left\{ A_o \Delta E [B_m GK + (1 - \Omega_m) B_s] \right\}^{1/2} / [PGKt^{1/12}) \qquad (2.1.29)$$

Substituting the corresponding values of all the quantities in this equation, we can calculate the minimum concentration or uranium, thorium and potassium, as determined from a satellite orbit around Mars.

Table 2.1.13 The minimal identifiable potassium content in Martian rock

Mean orbit height (km)	Measurement time (hour)	Minimal content K_{min} (x10⁴ppm)	Mean orbit height	measurement time (hour)	Minimal content K_{min} (x10⁴ppm)
500	1	0.27	2000	10	0.13
1000	1	0.30	2600	10	0.14
2000	1	0.46	2000	100	0.40
1000	10	0.096	2600	100	0.045
1600	10	0.11			

Table 2.1.13 lists as an illustration the respective calculated data obtained in [150] for potassium ($P \approx 0.9$ pulse s⁻¹ for 10⁴ppm K). The calculations were made for different distances of the detector from the Martian surface. As seen from Table 2.1.13, the lower the satellite orbit (i.e. the closer the position of the detector to the planet's surface) and the greater the measurement time, the lower the potassium concentrations that can be identified in the Martian rock.

However, the optimal orbital height in case of a non-collimated detector is determined by the required areal resolving power (the lower the orbital height, the higher the resolution in area), as well as by the relevant statistics (the latter calling for a higher orbit to secure a longer time of collecting information over the flown surface area). An optimal combination of the areal resolving power and the sensitivity in determining elements in the Martian rock is achieved when the orbital height secures a relevant statistical error.

At the same time, the areal resolving power is affected by other factors, such as the intensity of the gamma-ray line, and the contrast between adjacent areas (the difference in the content of elements). In the case of low concentration and insignificant contrast the limiting factor happens to be the statistical representativeness of the data. In this case, what we need is a large survey area, i.e. a higher orbit.

The measurement time, t, which is necessary to identify the given concentration of an element, can be determined from equation (2.1.29). The maximum number of separate areas that can be mapped will be determined by dividing the total counting time for the entire radiating surface by the time needed to achieve registration with a given statistical error. For a given orbital height the size of the separate area decreases with the increasing flux density of the gamma-radiation. In the case of a low content of radioactive elements the size of the separate area is restricted by the counting statistics, rather than by the spatial resolving power. In this case, mapping from relatively high altitudes is more feasible.

Understandably, a particularly convenient orbit for studying Mars' gamma-radiation proves to be one perpendicular to the equator. In this case, a maximum area of the Martian surface will be scanned. A circular satellite orbit around Mars enables us to have many measurement points (continuous measurements in a limiting case), while an elliptical orbit permits measurements to be practically made only in proximity to the periapsis. However, in the latter case there is a possibility of making alternative measurements of the cosmic background (in apoapsis) and of Mars' gamma-radiation (in *periapsis*). In the case of a circular orbit, measurements of the cosmic background are possible solely in a flight trajectory towards Mars. It is to be borne in mind, however, that during long-term measurements the background may change due to variations in solar activity.

2.1.4.3. Study of Mars' gamma-radiation from Mars 5

In February 1974 the Mars 5 probe was put into a satellite orbit around Mars. The probe was revolving around the planet in an elliptical orbit, its apoapsis and periapsis being 32560 km, and 1760 km, respectively. The inclination of the spacecraft orbit to the equator of the planet was about 35°, and one revolution period was 24 hours 53 min.

The space probe carried scientific instrumentation intended for the investigation of the composition, structure and properties of the Martian atmosphere and surface. The scientific instruments comprised a 256-channel gamma-ray spectrometer for measuring the spectral composition of Mars' gamma-radiation [87]. The scintillation spectrometer consisted of a detection unit with an NaI(TI) crystal 63 x 63 mm in size, mounted on a boom outside the probe, and electronic equipment, providing for analysis, storage and transmission of information, which was situated inside the probe.

In accordance with the working programme of the space probe, a series of measurements were carried out on the Earth–Mars flight route and in the planet's environs.

Flight-route measurements made it possible to determine the background gamma-ray radiation due to the interaction of cosmic rays with the structural materials of the space probe. Six measurement sessions were held for gamma-ray spectra at distances of 61.2, 85.4 and 93.8 million kilometres from the Earth and six sessions of

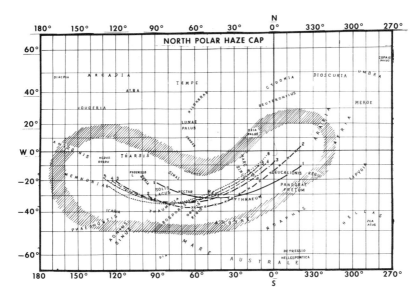

Fig. 2.1.35 — Schematic map of Mars on which sections of the flight trajectories of Mars 5, where gamma-ray spectra were measured, are plotted.

measurements near Mars at a distance of about 2000 km from the planet's surface. The measurement duration of gamma-radiation spectra in each session was 60 minutes.

Fig. 2.1.35 shows a map of Mars on which projections of the flight trajectories in which gamma-radiation spectra were measured are given. The outer boundary of the hatched strip delineates a region corresponding to an effective area from which 90% of gamma-radiation is collected, the inner boundary 50% of gamma-radiation.

As seen from the figure, in all the measurement sessions from Mars 5 the detector was scanning an area confined between 25°N and 50°S in latitude and 130°W and 320°E in longitude, i.e. chiefly the areas: Thaumasia, Argyre, Coprates, Lacus Phoenicis, Sinus Sheba and the Bay of Pearl.

Firstly, the mean content of natural radioactive elements for the region as a whole was determined. This region comprises mountainous massifs Tharsis, Coprates, etc. Therefore, the effect of the planetary topography was measured by a method similar to the aforementioned one used in determining the dependence $I=f(H,S)$. The calculation results have revealed that in measurements at altitudes of 500 km and higher, the gamma-ray flux increases by 0.6% from an isolated mountain 20 km in height and 100 km in base diameter. Should the entire surface scanned by the detector be covered by mountains with a height of 20 km, we may expect up to a 10% increase in the gamma-ray flux. In the investigated area of Mars, according to present-day concepts, there exist small numbers of mountains of significant height and therefore the effect of the relief can be regarded as unimportant.

As indicated above, of special significance in such measurements is the background (its magnitude, spectral composition and variability with time). In the period concerned there were no intensive solar flares. Therefore, the background was fairly constant and the problem boiled down solely to the collection of sufficient statistics. The count-rate of background gamma-ray quanta within the 1–9 MeV

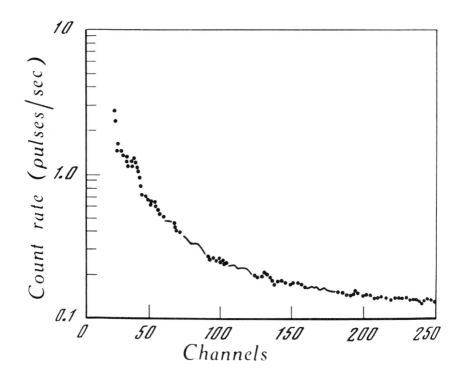

Fig. 2.1.36 — Martian gamma-radiation spectrum measured by the spacecraft Mars 5 from a
distance of about 2300 km.

energy range, as measured in all the measurement sessions, coincides within
statistical errors, and amounts to 59.9 pulses s^{-1}.

Fig. 2.1.36 shows one of the spectra measured from a satellite orbit around Mars.
To obtain the general characteristics of an extensive area lying within the
aforementioned coordinates, the gamma-radiation spectra measured in the vicinity
of Mars were subject to summation and averaging to bring down the statistical errors.
An averaged count-rate of gamma-ray quanta within the 1–9 MeV energy range
amounts to 95 ± 0.2 pulses s^{-1}. In this case the effect, i.e. Mars' gamma-radiation,
amounts to 37.6 ± 0.3 pulses s^{-1}, the effect/background ratio being equal to 0.65.

Components due to the decay of natural radioactive nuclides and to the nuclear
interaction of cosmic rays with the atmosphere and rock were identified in Mars'
gamma-ray spectrum. The solution of this problem involved the use of data obtained
in the course of experimental modelling using accelerators and with balloons of
various processes leading to the emission of gamma-ray quanta [151,152], as well as
by measurements of gamma-radiation from granite and basalt in their natural
bedding on the Earth.

Assuming that the Martian atmosphere consists of CO_2, the gamma-radiation
spectra of carbon and oxygen were measured in an accelerator. The modelled
gamma-ray spectra were used to construct the gamma-ray spectrum of the Martian
atmosphere.

In accelerator experiments, targets of finite dimensions with thicknesses of the
order of a proton free path length were irradiated. Coefficients for recalculating the

gamma-ray spectrum modelled on an accelerator to the 2π-geometry were determined from the data obtained in the course of the measurements of gamma-radiation of natural radioelements in rock in the geometry used in the accelerator, as well as in the 2π-geometry when measuring the rock in its natural bedding on the Earth. The transformation of the gamma-ray spectrum to the measurement conditions at a height of 2000 km above Mars' surface was achieved by calculation on a computer in accordance with expression (2.1.19); by assuming the atmosphere to extend for 50 km .

Furthermore, the gamma-radiation spectrum of the Martian atmosphere was calculated from the results obtained by high-altitude balloons and rockets for the Earth's atmosphere [155-158]. The calculation was made in two stages. At first, gamma-radiation spectra within the energy interval ΔE_γ =0.5–2.5 MeV, measured for the values of the residual thickness of the atmosphere, d, equal to 70, 260, 570, 1250 and 2700 Kg m^{-2}, were extrapolated to the thickness $d=0$ Kg m^{-2}. The extrapolation was carried out with the use of a second-order polynomial. The intensity and shape of the gamma-ray spectrum in the region $E_\gamma>2.5$ MeV were reproduced on the basis of the data given in [150]. Thereupon, the differences in the thickness (Kg m^{-2}) of planetary atmospheres was taken into account, since the atmospheric mass per unit area of the surface is much larger for the Earth than for Mars, the figure for the latter being about 180 Kg m^{-2}. Therefore, part of the gamma-radiation of the Earth's atmosphere arrives from a depth greater than 180 Kg m^{-2}. To obtain the gamma-ray spectrum of Mars' atmosphere, the fraction of radiation from the upper layer of the Earth's atmosphere 180 Kg m^{-2} thick was calculated. Since the composition of the Earth's atmosphere differs significantly from the Martian one, the values of the mean mass numbers are equal to 15 and 22, respectively. Therefore, the effects associated with a higher escape of gamma-ray quanta from the Earth's atmosphere compared to that of Mars was also evaluated. In this case use was made of the data on the escape of gamma-ray quanta in the inelastic interaction of protons with different nuclei, obtained in [152,159].

From the gamma-radiation spectra of the atmosphere, calculated by the two above described methods, an averaged spectrum was obtained. The subtraction of this spectrum from the measured gamma-radiation spectrum of Mars (after subtraction of the background) yielded the spectrum of the Martian rock. (Within the 1–9 MeV energy range the count-rate of gamma-ray quanta from the atmosphere and from the rock was 11 ± 3 and 26 ± 3 pulses s^{-1}, respectively.)

The spectrum of the Martian rock thus obtained is due to the decay of natural radionuclides and to the interaction of cosmic rays with the elements constituting the rock. This spectrum was processed on a high-speed computer by using the data from experimental modelling on accelerators. .

Table 2.1.14 lists the results obtained in the processing of gamma-ray spectra of the Martian rock.

Since the area where gamma-ray spectrometric measurements were made is characterized by a diversity of forms and types of rocks, the thorium and uranium content was estimated by taking into account the geological structure of the area concerned [9]. In the investigated area the entire observed diversity of relief forms and rock types can be reduced, with a certain amount of generalization, to two principal types: old highland formations and the younger volcanic formations. Other formations observed in this territory, for instance valleys of a fluvial pattern and field

Table 2.1.14 – Content of elements in the Martian rock measured from Mars 5

Element	Content (%)
0	44
Si	17
Al+Fe	19
K	0.3
U	0.6*
Th	2.1*

* parts per million

of aeolian dunes, occupy here a relatively small part of the area, and their contribution to the recorded gamma-radiation can be neglected.

Highland formations on Mars are characterized by the presence of a great number of large craters and this renders Mars' highlands similar to lunar highlands. Volcanic formations in the investigated territory are represented by the Tharsis plateau (including the shield volcano Arsia Mons) and the plains confined to the floors of depressions, e.g. the Argyre basin. The former are morphologically similar to areas of development of shield basalt volcanism on the Earth. The latter resemble the basaltic plains of the lunar maria.

The first and the last flight trajectories being displaced with respect to one another during these space flights, the space probe was measuring the gamma-radiation from areas which consisted, to a varying degree, of highland and volcanic areas of the surface. If one proceeds from the geomorphological analysis data for the territory shown in Fig. 2.1.37 (the map was compiled from the photos obtained by Mars 4, Mars 5 and Mariner 9) and from the mean contents of U, Th and K for the entire investigated area listed in Table 2.1.14, it is possible to determine the contents of these elements for the two geomorphological provinces separately. For that, we have to solve the system of two linear equations which have the form:

$$q_x \iiint\limits_{S_1 \; l \; t} I(S,l,t)\,ds\,dl\,dt + q_y \iiint\limits_{S_2 \; l \; t} I(S,l,t)\,ds\,dl\,dt = q \iiint\limits_{S_1+S_2 \; l \; t} I(S,l,t)\,dS\,dl\,dt$$

$$q_x \iiint\limits_{S'_1 \; l \; t} I(S,l,t)\,ds\,dl\,dt + q_y \iiint\limits_{S'_2 \; l \; t} I(S,l,t)\,ds\,dl\,dt = q' \iiint\limits_{S'_1+S'_2 \; l \; t} I(S,l,t)\,dS\,dl\,dt$$

$$(2.1.30)$$

where $I(S,l,t)$ is the flux of gamma-ray quanta at a given moment of time (t), i.e. at a given point in the orbit, produced by a unit volume of the surface rock layer with a unit concentration of radioactive elements; q_x and q_y are the concentrations of radioactive elements in the surface subdivisions considered; $\overline{q}$ and $\overline{q}'$ are the averaged concentrations of radioactive elements over the entire surfaces scanned by the detector; S_1, S_2, S'_1 and S'_2 are the surface areas relating to the investigated types of Mars' surface subdivisions, in different measurement sessions; l is the thickness of the surface rock layer, which is chosen on the assumption that 10% of incident

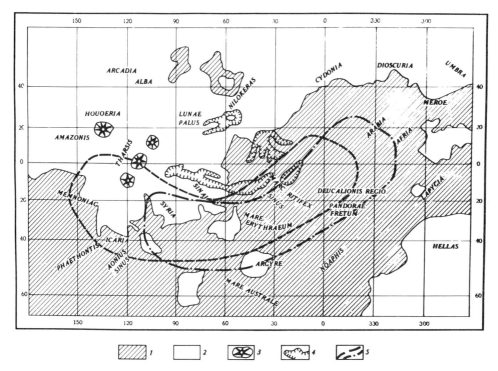

Fig. 2.1.37 — Geological scheme of the region of the Martian surface over which gamma-ray spectrometric measurements were performed: 1, ancient crust; 2, depression; 3, young volcanoes; 4, valleys; 5, boundaries of gamma-radiation measurements.

radiation passes through the rock layer, and takes values from 12 cm for gamma-ray quanta with 0.5 MeV energy to 38 cm for gamma-ray quanta with 5 MeV energy.

Computation of the integrals in the above system of equations is based on the results of calculating gamma-ray quanta fluxes as a function of the height of space probe above the Martian surface and the area scanned by the detector [140]. What we mean here by the planetary surface is the surface layer of a definite thickness l.

From the altitude of passage of the space probe and the results of these calculations, there was obtained for each measurement session a function expressing the flux of gamma-ray quanta coming from the entire surface of the planet scanned by the detector as a function of time. Integration of this function over each of the times of measurement represents respectively the integrals standing in the right-hand parts of each of the equations of the compiled system. The calculated fraction of the flux of gamma-ray quanta, coming from 1 km^2 of the planet's surface, as a function of the distance to the intersection point between the surface and the space probe to planet-centre line enables us to determine the contribution of gamma-radiation from different geological subdivisions of the surface to the total recorded gamma-ray flux, i.e. gives the values of the integrals in the right-hand parts of the equations.

Calculation results and certain data on the thorium and uranium content in typical rocks of the Earth and the Moon are listed in Table 1.2.15 [9].

It follows from these data that with respect to the thorium and uranium content, the volcanic rocks in the investigated territories on Mars are similar to the basalts typical of numerous geological formations on the Earth and the Moon, such as

Table 2.1.15 – The thorium and uranium content in different types of rocks on Mars, the Earth and the Moon

Planetary body	Type of rock	Th (ppm)	U (ppm)	Th/U
Mars	Volcanic rock	5.0±2.5	1.1±0.8	4.5
	Highland rock	0.7±0.35	0.2±0.14	3.5
Earth	Ultrabasic rocks	0.08	0.03	2.7
	Tholeiitic oceanic basalts	0.18	0.1	1.8
	Alkaline olivine basalts	3.9	1.0	3.9
	Platform plateau basalts	2.5	0.8	3.1
	Geosynclinal basalts	2.4	0.7	3.9
	Granites, granodiorites, granitogneisses	15.6	3.9	4.0
Moon	Analysis of the rock samples returned to the Earth:			
	ANT group rocks	0.73	0.22	1.55
	KREEP material	9.3	2.8	3.4
	Mare basalts with a high Ti and K content	3.98	0.68	5.8
	Mare basalts with a moderate Ti and K content	1.18	0.64	1.9
	Mare basalts with a high Ti and a moderate K content	0.61	0.16	3.9
	Orbital gamma-ray spectrometry in the equatorial zone:			
	Highland formations (ANT)	0.80	0.21[a]	—
	Mare formations (basalts)	1.2–8.4	Not determ.	—

Calculated by assuming Th/U=3.8, as is typical of lunar rocks

alkaline olivine basalts, platform plateau basalts of the Earth, and lunar mare basalts with a high potassium content. Terrestrial tholeiitic basalts of the oceans and lunar mare basalts with a high titanium content and a moderate potassium content are characterised by perceptibly lower thorium and uranium concentrations and do not have any analogues among Martian volcanites investigated in the given experiment.

Highland formations on Mars, as revealed by these calculations, have lower thorium and uranium contents compared to the studied Martian volcanites and differ very much from the matter of the Earth's granitic continents and from lunar KREEP material, which are characterized by significantly higher contents of these elements. In comparison with the rocks of the anorthosite-norite-troctolitic (ANT) group which are widespread on lunar highlands, the investigated highland formations on Mars do not exhibit any perceptible differences either in thorium content or in uranium content.

2.1.4.4. Main results of studying Mars' gamma-radiation from Mars 5

Comparing the uranium, thorium and potassium, contents measured by Mars 5 with the contents of these elements in terrestrial rocks, it is not difficult to see that they are particularly close to terrestrial rocks of the basic composition. Such a high content of natural radioactive elements on Mars is an indication that they are principally confined within the planet's upper envelope. According to Toksöz's calculations [160] even the average uranium content 0.037 ppm should already have led to the fusion and differentiation of Martian matter, if one offers any plausible model of its thermal history.

The measured level of the content of natural radioactive elements refers to an extensive surface in Mars' southern hemisphere, its area being 4.2×10^5 km^2. If we assume that in the rest of the areas of the Martian surface a similar quantity of natural radioactive elements is present, and accept the average uranium content on Mars to be about 0.02 ppm [161], we may estimate the thickness of the Martian crust.

Let us take two extreme cases. In the first case we shall assume a homogeneous distribution of natural radioactive elements in the crust; in the second case we shall assume decrease of their quantity with depth according to the law:

$$H(r) = A_o \exp[-(R-r)/h], \qquad (2.1.31)$$

where $H(r)$ is the content of radioactive elements at the depth r; A_o is the content at the surface; and h is the crust thickness. Then in the first case the thickness of the Martian crust must be $20-30$ km, and in the second case nearly twice as much. If we suppose that natural radioactive elements have failed completely to diffuse out into the Martian crust (part of them remaining in the mantle), the thickness of the crust in either case must be correspondingly less. The ratio K/U $\approx 3 \times 10^3$, as measured by Mars 5, may, apparently, be taken as the upper limit for Mars as a whole, since in the process of differentiation of Martian matter this ratio for the surface rock could be only increasing. In the given case the enrichment of the Martian crust with uranium, thorium and potassium is two orders of magnitude higher than for the planet's mantle. However, a lower K/U ratio for the Martian crust as compared to the Earth's crust appears to be evidence in favour of lesser differentiation on Mars.

The measured potassium content on Mars enables us to estimate the argon content in the Martian atmosphere by taking account of the aforementioned estimates of the thickness of the Martian crust, or vice versa: we can make an independent determination of the Martian crust's thickness by taking into account an estimate of the argon content in Mars' atmosphere, as given in [162]. Hence, in accordance with a modelled distribution of radioactive elements we may obtain the argon content in the Martian atmosphere as being equal to 20–40%. This content is significantly superior to that measured by Viking 1 (1–2%). The Martian atmosphere was unexpectedly found to contain much less argon than could be expected as a result of the outgassing of matter in the course of the melting of the crust. Such a small quantity of argon must testify either to the fact that Mars is a weakly differentiated planet, or to the existence in its history of a period when the temperature of the exosphere was significantly higher than at present, or to the termination of the outgassing process in the early period of Mars' existence when an intensive dissipation of argon into outer space was taking place.

The formation of Mars in a low-temperature region gives grounds for supposing that Mars has retained sulphur and, consequently, its core consists of Fe–FeS. In this case, we may assume that potassium is partly present in Mars' core in the sulphide phase. This fact must have caused the differentiation of Mars' matter at an early stage. If Mars was developing similarly to the Earth, its thermal activity must have reached its peak during the first $3000-3500$ million years [160]. However, even now Mars must have a hot interior. Having passed its peak of activity, it is cooling down at a relatively slow rate.

The presence of an appreciable amount of potassium on Mars enables us to form an idea of the past of the planet's atmosphere as well. Obviously, in the period of Mars' maximum activity, during melting out of the planetary crust, there was taking place an isolation of volatiles that could compose a denser atmosphere. The absence of such an atmosphere on Mars at present can be explained either by the loss of volatiles at an early stage of Mars' existence or by their presence (chiefly as carbon) dioxide) in a bound state in the Martian rocks. These arguments are based so far on the unique data obtained by the authors of the experiment [8] in processing the results obtained in studying Mars' gamma-radiation by Mars 5. At the same time, the data obtained refer to one of the areas at the Martian surface and, therefore, may not be representative of the planet as a whole. Elaboration of more comprehensive concepts of Mars' internal structure, as well as of the origin and formation of its surface rocks, calls for further studies of Mars' gamma-radiation in other surface areas of the planet.

The content of natural radioelements is known to be a good indicator of the geochemical type of the substance and can be employed in identifying the type of rocks. Therefore, considerable differences between volcanogenic and continental formations of Mars in the thorium and uranium contents should, apparently, be interpreted as differences in the general geochemical type of their constituent material. A similarity of the investigated volcanites on Mars in respect of their thorium and uranium content with basalts of certain formations on the Earth and the Moon should, obviously, be considered within a broader framework: as a similarity between the types of rock, is in good agreement with the typically 'basaltic' morphology of these formations. A similarity of the investigated highland formations on Mars in respect of their thorium and uranium content with the ANT-group rocks typical of lunar highlands is found to be in good agreement with the fact that in both morphology and structure, Mars' cratered highlands closely resemble the lunar highlands.

Summing up what has been said above, the authors of [9] consider the data obtained to be an indication of the fact that on Mars, as on the Earth and the Moon, two radically different types of crustal material are available. Mars' volcanic formations with a basaltic surface morphology are similar to basalts also with respect to their level of the thorium and uranium content. Data on the mafic character of Martian soil at the Viking 1 and Viking 2 landing sites being taken into account, we may, apparently, speak of a fundamental geochemical similarity between basalts of the Earth, the Moon, and Mars, which does not of course preclude the existence of certain features specific to each. The old formations of the Martian highlands are definitely different with respect to their thorium and uranium content from granitoidal rocks of the Earth's continents and are more like the ANT association of the lunar highlands, but, possibly, they do represent some yet unknown chemical type of planetary crustal matter.

2.1.5. STUDY OF VENUS' GAMMA-RADIATION

2.1.5.1. Study of gamma-radiation of the Venusian rock by Venera 8

In July 1972 the Venera 8 probe approached the planet and, having entered its atmosphere, performed a smooth parachute descent onto the illuminated side of its surface near the morning terminator. The space probe carried scientific instrumentation intended for further investigations of the atmospheric parameters and climatic conditions existing at the surface of the planet. Furthermore, the probe was to study for the first time the character of the bedded rocks on the planet's surface at the landing site of the space vehicle. Therefore, Venera 8 was carrying a gamma-ray spectrometer to determine the content of natural radioactive elements in the Venusian rock from their gamma-radiation [41,163].

A gamma-ray spectrometer was used for the study of the Venusian rock because under the rigorous climatic conditions at Venus' surface it is rather difficult to make use of any other methods, all of which involve taking detectors or rock sampling devices outside a pressurized, thermostatically-controlled compartment. In contrast, the gamma-spectrometer was housed entirely inside the pressurized compartment of the lander and recorded gamma-radiation emitted by radioelements in the rock that was penetrating through the space probe's outer envelope.

A favourable condition for the determination of natural radioactive elements was the absence of radiation induced by cosmic rays in the Venusian rock; such radiation is an interference in taking such measurements on those celestial bodies which either have an insignificant atmosphere or are devoid of one altogether.

The gamma-ray spectrometer was installed in the descent module of Venera 8. Structurally the spectrometer was made up of three blocks — a detection unit and two electronic units performing the analysis, memorization and codification of information. All the blocks were mounted inside a pressurized, thermostatically-controlled compartment. Functionally the instrument consisted of a scintillation detector, a 60-channel amplitude analyser and an intensitometer for the counting of gamma-ray quanta. The energy interval of gamma-ray quanta recorded by the spectrometer lies within the range 0.3 – 3.0 MeV. The energy resolution of the gamma-ray spectrometer, as measured with respect to ^{137}Cs ($E = 0.662$ MeV), was about 11%. The intensitometer provided for measuring the total count rate of gamma-ray quanta with energies in excess of 0.3 MeV.

The gamma-ray spectrometer detector (NaI(Tl) crystal) was housed in the lower part of the descent module. The layer of material screening the detector (thermal protection, the descent module body and component units) amounted to not more than 200 Kg m^{-2} and consisted mainly of light elements.

In accordance with the operating programme of the Venera 8 descent module, the total count rate was measured during its descent to the planetary surface. The spectral composition of gamma-radiation was measured solely at the planetary surface.

Three measurements were made of the total count-rate during the descent, and one measurement upon landing at the surface. The count-rate measured during the descent showed no perceptible variations. After the descent module had landed on the planetary surface, an increase in the total count rate was recorded, the reason being an additional effect from the planetary surface. Measurements of the total count-rate of gamma-ray quanta enabled us to evaluate the effect due to the gamma-radiation induced by cosmic rays in the material of the space probe, to simultaneously determine the total level of gamma-radiation of the Venusian rock, and thus to judge qualitatively the content of natural radioactive elements in it. Measurements of the gamma-ray spectrum of the Venusian rock were started immediately after the space probe had landed and were completed within 42 min. Information stored by the spectrometer was transmitted channel by channel simultaneously with the spectrum accumulation and was relayed twice. The first gamma-ray spectrum was relayed approximately in the middle of the data collection process, and the second one at the end.

To be able to determine the content of natural radioactive elements in the Venusian rock from their gamma-ray spectrum, one should know the following: the gamma-ray spectrum of the background of the spectrometer installed in the descent module; the contribution of the radiation induced by cosmic rays in the material of the descent module; gamma-ray spectra of the standards (reference rocks); the scattering and absorption of gamma-radiation from the rock by the Venusian atmosphere.

To be able to measure the gamma-radiation background due to the contamination of the object by natural radioactive elements, the descent module, along with the spectrometer installed in it, had been placed into a tunnel made into a mass of dunite rock, which is known for its extremely low uranium, thorium and potassium content. (On account of the great thickness of the rock mass, a contribution from gamma-radiation due to cosmic rays may be ignored in this case.) It was determined that the total value of the background within the 0.3 – 3.0 MeV energy range amounts approximately to 10% of the value measured for the same period of time at Venus' surface.

The fact that the count rate recorded during descent did not vary significantly, testifies to the absence of any prominent contribution from the decay of short-lived (minute- and hour-long) radionuclides that could be produced in the structural materials of the probe under the impact of cosmic radiation. As for the decay of long-lived radionuclides (with a decay period of several days and longer), their contribution to the radioactivity of the descent module is at least one order of magnitude less than the background due to natural radioactive elements. Thus, the recorded background of the lander received a certain contribution due to the space probe being irradiated by cosmic rays, which could practically consist solely of sodium, iodine, and thallium radionuclides (with a decay period ranging from several hours to several days) produced in the material of the detector irradiated by cosmic rays.

Amongst the possible gamma-radiators appearing in the course of the irradiation of these elements, only ^{24}Na($T^{1/2} \approx 15$ hours, $E_{\gamma 1} = 1.37$ MeV and $E_{\gamma 2} = 2.75$ MeV) could make a sizeable contribution. The rest of the radiators have a low energy ($E <$ 1 MeV) or a low yield ($\eta < 1\%$) and thus could make no significant contribution to the background spectrum. It was determined from model and theoretical calculations that the possible effect of ^{24}Na does not exceed 5% of the measured values of U, Th and K contents.

The calibration of the instrument under terrestrial conditions was achieved by the experimenters [41,163] by making a series of measurements on outcropping rocks having a known uranium, thorium and potassium content. In this case, to bring the conditions of measurement closer to the experimental conditions on the planet, the instrument was placed inside an analogue of Venera 8 (measurements being made in approximately 2π-geometry above granite, granodiorite and andesite–basalt masses). To reduce these calibration spectra to a specfic uranium, throrium and potassium content, representative specimens of the rocks concerned were taken at the sites of the measurements. The determination of natural radioactive elements in them involved the application of radiochemistry and low-background radiometry methods with the use of international standards.

Lastly, in processing the Venusian gamma-ray spectra it was necessary to take account of the scattering and absorption of the radiation emanating from the planet by the surrounding atmosphere. This fact is of great importance because the calibration spectra of terrestrial rocks were taken under different conditions.

The calculation by the beam method leads to the following relationship of the content in the planetary rock of monoradiators of energy $E\gamma$ as a function of the number of gamma-ray quanta, I, crossing the surface of the detector (which to a good approximation can be assumed to be spherical) within a unit of time:

$$I = [(\pi r^2 N)/2\mu_o\, E_2(\mu,h), \qquad (2.1.32)$$

where N is the number of gamma-ray quanta emitted by a unit volume of rock per unit of time: μ_o and μ are the linear attenuation coefficients of gamma-ray quanta in the radiating rock and in the planetary atmosphere respectively; h is the height of the detector above the rock; r is the detector's radius; and E_2 is King's function:

$$E_2(x) = \exp(-x) \int_x^\infty \exp(-t)\, t^{-1}dt \qquad (2.1.33)$$

Making use of expression (2.1.33) for determining the flux of gamma-quanta recorded by the detector at the Earth's and Venus' surface and assuming μ_o to be in both cases approximately similar, we obtain the following expression for the coefficient allowing for the effect of the Venusian atmosphere:

$$K = I_v/I_e = E_2(\mu_v, h)\, /E_2(\mu_e, h), \qquad (2.1.34)$$

where I_e and I_v are the fluxes of gamma-ray quanta fluxes recorded by the detector above the Earth's and Venus' surfaces respectively: and μ_e and μ_v are linear attenuation coefficents of monochromatic radiation in the Earth's and Venus' atmospheres respectively.

In computing King's function $E_2(\mu_e, h)$ and $E_2(\mu_v, h)$ in expression (2.1.34), a corresponding linear attenuation coefficient is taken for each energy.

If we take account of the fact that the gamma-radiation of the rock was scattered and absorbed not only by the atmosphere but also by the material of the descent module, then in the given case we should use the mean-weighted coefficients $\overline{\mu}_e$ and $\overline{\mu}_v$. Then,

$$\overline{K} = [E_2(\overline{\mu}_e.h)]\, /[E_1,(\overline{\mu}_v, h)] \qquad (2.1.35)$$

The above remarks being taken into account, the content of natural radioactive elements in the Venusian rock was determined. To this end, two well-known methods were employed: the method involving a comparison of the areas of peaks in the Venusian and in the calibration gamma-ray spectra and the least-squares method.

In the first case, following the subtraction of the space probe's background, as measured on dunite, the areas of particularly characteristic peaks, expressed as the number of pulses were computed for each calibration spectrum. Thus, the known potassium, uranium and thorium contents in calibration rocks were correlated with the areas of peaks corresponding to the aforementioned energies. Therefore, the determination of the potassium, uranium and thorium content in the investigated Venusian rocks simply became a mere recalculation of the respective peak areas by allowing for the K coefficients in the content of the elements.

In the second case, following subtraction of the same background, a pure Venusian spectrum was resolved by the least-squares method into three components (disregarding the contribution from gamma-radiation induced by cosmic rays).

As a result of processing the spectra, the following contents of natural radioactive elements in the Venusian rock were obtained: potassium 4.0±0.2%, uranium $(2.2±0.5) \times 10^{-4}\%$ and thorium $(6.5±0.8) \times 10^{-4}\%$ (the content being given in percentage by mass, the errors being statistical).

If one takes account of any error in determining the contents of the elements in the calibration rocks, and error due to the drift of the spectrometer scale and to the contribution of the gamma-radiation induced by cosmic rays, then the total errors should be increased for the potassium determination by up to 10%, and for the uranium and thorium determination by up to 30%.

The data obtained indicate that Venera 8 was taking measurements in an area with a relatively high content of natural radioactive elements in the investigated rocks, as compared to the Earth's crust and, especially, the Earth's mantle. With respect to the uranium, thorium and potassium content, the rock in question is particularly close to the Earth's magmatic rocks of the alkaline basalt type with a high potassium content.

2.1.5.2. Study of gamma-radiation of the Venusian rock by Veneras 9 and 10
The Venera 9 and 10 space probes which landed on Venus' surface in October 1975 were expected to pursue the task of further exploration of the planet. The unique photographs of Venus' surface obtained with their aid enabled us to form an idea of the processes that have led to the formation of the present-day appearance of the planet. However, no matter how informative they are, the pictures relayed to the Earth contain no data on the character of the Venusian rocks or their composition. To obtain these data, the space probes carried gamma-ray spectrometers which enabled the content of natural radioactive elements in the rock to be determined from their gamma-radiation [164].

Gamma-radiation of the Venusian rock being solely due to the decay of natural radionuclides and the contribution to the background of the lander from cosmogenic radionuclides being insignificant (as was established in the preceding experiment from Venera 8), Veneras 9 and 10 carried gamma-ray spectrometers of a simplified model. The spectrometers recorded gamma-radiation solely in three energy intervals: 1.15–1.55 MeV, 1.55–2.3 MeV and 2.3–3.0 MeV. Each of these intervals is characterized by a particularly intensive line of potassium, uranium, and thorium, respectively.

The instrument was switched on during the descent of the lander through the planet's atmosphere at a pressure of about 7×10^5 Pa and until its landing on the surface it was recording the background gamma-radiation. Prior to starting measurements at the planetary surface, the earlier collected information was erased from the storage of the instrument to enable new data to be accumulated into it throughout the operating time of the space probe. Stored information was brought out of the instrument to a telemetry system every 2.7s throughout the descent period of the lander through the atmosphere. Once it had landed on the surface, the instrument was cyclically interrogated every 4 min.

A continuous output of information made it possible to exercise control over the correct operation of the instrument under conditions of increasing temperature inside the lander, as well as to make observations of the decay of relatively short-lived radionuclides that could be produced in the structural elements of the space probe.

As a result of the experiment, it was possible to measure the count-rate of gamma-ray quanta within the stated energy intervals during the descent of the space probe through the planet's atmosphere and following its landing on the planetary surface. Measurements made during the descent were conducted within a time interval of about 50 min. Futhermore, the count-rate within this period did not change (within the statistical error).

Following the landing on Venus' surface, an increase in the count-rate within every energy range of the instrument was recorded, the reason being the presence of natural radioactive elements — uranium, thorium and potassium — in the surface rock layer. The higher count-rate barely changed throughout the measurement period at the planetary surface.

The differences between the count-rates during the descent and after the landing, which were exclusively due to the effect of the planetary surface rocks, were compared with the results of a preliminary calibration of the gamma-ray spectrometer, which had been performed on natural outcrops of various terrestrial magmatic rocks having a known chemical composition. To bring the measurement conditions for the terrestrial rocks closer to the experimental conditions at the planet's surface, the instrument being calibrated was placed inside an analogue of Veneras 9 and 10. The count rates obtained within the selected energy ranges permitted the content of natural radioactive elements to be determined in Venus' surface rock layer at the Venera 9 and 10 landing sites. The results, computed by the inverse matrix technique, are given in Table 2.1.16. These data were subject to

Table 2.1.16 – The K, U and Th content in the rocks of Venus and the Earth (percentage by mass)

Planet	Rock	Potassium	Uranium ($\times 10^{-4}$)	Thorium ($\times 10^{-4}$)
Venus	Explored by:			
	Venera 8	4.0 ±0.2	2.2 ±0.5	6.5 ±0.8
	Venera 9	0.47±0.08	0.60±0.16	3.65±0.42
	Venera 10	0.30±0.16	0.46±0.26	0.70±0.34
Earth	Intermediate oceanic tholeiite	0.14	0.1	0.18
	Intermediate basalt	0.85	0.6	2.7
	Intermediate granite	3.47	4.8	17

corrections to allow for a difference in the density of the Earth's and Venus' atmospheres. For comparison, the same table lists the mean contents of uranium, thorium and potassium at the Venera 8 landing site and in terrestrial rocks.

The data obtained indicate that in both surface areas of the planet, rocks were encountered which are close in their content of natural radioactive elements to terrestrial rocks of the type of oceanic tholeiitic basalts. Furthermore, the potassium, uranium and thorium concentration in the bedded rocks at the Venera 10 landing site was found to be slightly lower and, possibly, these rocks have a more basic composition (a lower content of silicon dioxide and other features) as compared to those at the Venera 9 landing site.

2.1.5.3. Study of gamma-radiation of the Venusian rock by VeGas 1 and 2

In contrast to the landing areas of Veneras 8, 9 and 10, which were in upland rolling plains or in smooth lowlands, those of VeGas 1 and 2 were in the region of the gradual transition from an upland rolling plain to a high-mountain area. In this area we may expect the intermixing of rocks with a significant contribution from the rock of the high-mountainous massif on Aphrodite Terra. Difficulties of guaranteeing a soft-landing of space vehicles directly in a high-mountainous area were reasons for the choice of this piedmont area.

The content of natural radioactive elements in the Venusian rock was determined by a scintillation gamma-ray spectrometer. The instruments, as in the earlier landers, were fully housed inside a pressurized, thermostatically-controlled compartment.

The gamma-ray spectrometer consisted of two units: a detection unit and a pulse amplitude analyser. The detection unit comprised a gamma-radiation detector (CsI(Tl) crystal 63 x 100 mm in size), a photo-multiplier and auxiliary electronic circuits providing the low-voltage supply and signal amplification. The pulse amplitude analyser comprised 128 energy channels each having a capacity of (2^{16} − 1) pulses.

The spectrometer registered gamma-radiation within the 0.3 − 3.0 MeV energy range. The energy resolution of the spectrometer is about 10% with respect to ^{137}Cs radiation (0.662 MeV).

Apart from the spectral information being stored in the analyser, the instrument registers the mean count rate within three energy intervals. This information is directly sent to telemetry in the form of slowly changing voltage levels. (Such measurements allow an increase in the reliability of the experiment.) To achieve stability control for the spectrometer energy scale, a gamma-ray reference is introduced into the detector.

The execution of the experiment involved initial measurements during the parachute descent trajectory of the space probe for the purpose of recording background radiation caused by the presence of radioactive elements in the structural materials of the lander and in the instrument itself. Once the probe had landed, both background radiation and radiation from the investigated rock were registered. To record background variations, the information stored in the spectrometer appeared at the output every 3 min.

The uranium, thorium and potassium contents from the Venusian rock spectra were determined on the basis of a preliminary calibration of the spectrometer as part of the lander on naturally bedded terrestrial rocks.

During the calibration measurements the instrument was housed inside the mock-up of the lander so that the calibrations on the Earth and the measurements on Venus would be made under similar conditions. The detector of the gamma-ray spectrometer was placed at an altitude of about 50 cm over the rock to be analysed and was partly shielded from it by elements of the lander structure. The calibrations have shown that under conditions of a dense atmosphere, 90% of the radiation entering the detector comes from the Venusian surface, from the rocks occurring within a circle 4–4.5 m in diameter. During the processing of the experimental data, account was taken of the absorption of recorded gamma-radiation by the atmosphere of Venus and by the material of the lander.

Fig. 2.1.38. shows the gamma-spectra of Venus rocks measured at the VeGa 1 and 2 landing sites over a 190-second period.

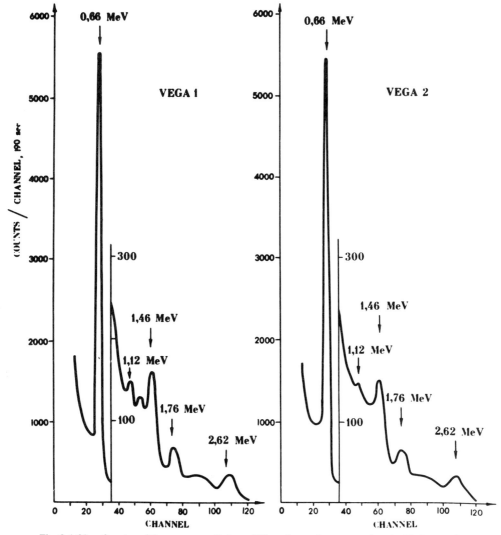

Fig. 2.1.38 — Spectra of the gamma-radiation of Venusian rocks measured at the VeGa 1 and 2 landing sites.

The spectra measured on Venus contain variable components which have appeared due to radioactivity induced by the spacecraft. This hinders the use of a conventional statistical method for the decomposition of spectra into the components appearing due to the radiation of uranium, thorium and potassium. Therefore, the authors [170,171] have used the method of calculating the contents from intercepted peaks and the method of calculating count-rates in the optimum chosen energy intervals of spectra. In both cases it was taken into account that the experimental spectra contained a component changing in time.

The data obtained as a result of the experiment are shown in the Table 1.3.4. The same table lists data obtained for Venusian rocks at other locations on the planet.

As is evident from the Table 1.3.4, at the landing sites of VeGa 1 and VeGa 2 the rocks with fairly similar and relatively low contents of natural radioactive elements have been detected. Using the petrochemical classification of magmatic rocks based on the alkali–silica diagram and the established relationship between the class of rocks and the content of natural radioactive elements in them, it can be assumed that the chemical composition of the investigated rocks is close to basic rocks — tholeiitic basalts and gabbros.

The all-round consideration of these data together with earlier data on the composition of Venusian rocks in different regions of the planet's surface made it possible to take further steps in the development of concepts of the geological structure of Venus.

2.1.5.4. Measurements of the density of the Venusian rock by Venera 10

The density of the rock is, in effect, a parameter with which its principal physical and mechanical characteristics are closely associated. It also characterizes the formation conditions of the rock and its subsequent evolution. Therefore, density may serve as an important diagnostic feature of the type of rocks when investigating them with the aid of space probes.

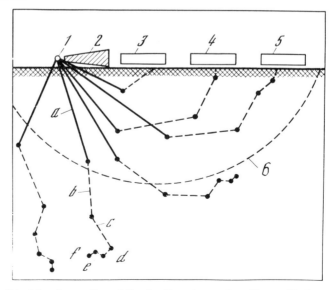

Fig. 2.1.39 — Principle of operation of the densitometer used on Venera 10; 1, gamma-radiation source; 2, screen; 3, 4 and 5, gamma-radiation detectors; 6, boundary of the effective layer; a, primary gamma-ray quantum; b, f-sequence of scattering of gamma-ray quanta.

Information available at present on the density of Venus' surface rocks has been obtained from determinations of their dielectric permeability by radar measurements form the Earth [165,166]. On this evidence the density of the surface layer is 1.5×10^3 Kgm^{-3} to 2.8×10^3 gm/cm^{-3}.

The first direct determination of the surface layer density ws made in 195 [161,167] by Venera 10. The density determination technique used for this purpose involved an application of the effect of the Compton interaction of gamma-ray quanta with electrons in the atoms of the rocks concerned.

Fig. 2.1.39 illustrates the operating principle of the densitometer used at the lander. Gamma-ray quanta emitted by an isotopic source are scattered by the rock and are recorded by three detectors mounted at different distances from the source. From the count rate of gamma-ray quanta in the detectors the rock density is determined. The presence of three detectors makes it possible to allow to a certain degree for the irregularity of the surface upon which the densitometer is placed.

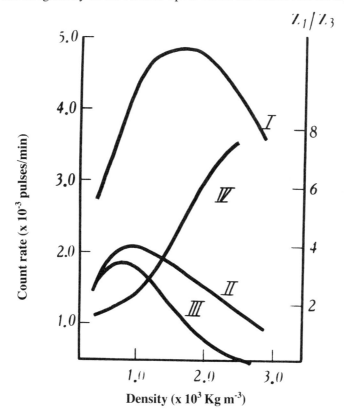

Fig. 2.1.40—Count-rate of gamma-ray quanta as a function of rock density: I, count-rate of the detector with a base of 100 mm; II, 180 mm; III, 250 mm; IV, count rate-ratios I/III.

Fig. 2.1.40 gives the count rates as a function of rock density for detectors with different bases. The curves have an inversion for a specific (critical) density value. The critical density value and the gradient of the branches are determined by the distances between detectors and the source, as well as by the energy spectrum of the recorded radiation.

Structurally the radiation densitometer employed on Venera 10 consisted of two units: a detection unit brought out on the rock surface and an electronic unit arranged inside the thermostatically-controlled pressurized compartment of the lander. The position of the densitometer on the Venusian rock is seen in panoramic photos (see Fig. 1.3.4.).

The main difficulty in developing a radiation densitometer was due to the necessity of securing the stable performance of the outside detection unit for the period of time needed to obtain a representative result under the high temperature and pressure conditions existing at the Venusian surface. The use of effective thermal protection for the detection unit was not easy on account of the pronounced deterioration of the unit's measuring capabilities as a result of the additional scattering mass, as well as because of restrictions placed on the mass and overall size of the instrument. The difficulties stem from the fact that at a temperature of 500°C many electrotechnical materials either break down or change their physical parameters to such an extent that their use is out of the question.

A dividing sheild — a complex-profile collimator made of tungsten alloy of density 1.9×10^4 kg m^{-3} – was placed in the non-pressurized part of the densitometer. This shield, apart from its direct purposse, i.e. protecting the detectors from the direct impact upon them of gamma-radiation from the source, brought down the radiation load on the instrumentation compartment of the lander. At the same time, by collimating the gamma-radiation, the screen preventing a distorting effect of the atmosphere on rock-density measurements. The ^{137}Cs isotope with a gamma-ray quanta energy of 0.66 MeV and with an activity of about 1 mg equivalent of radium was used as a gamma-radiation source. Three groups of detectors forming three independent densitometers with base length 100, 180 and 250 mm were housed inside the detection unit.

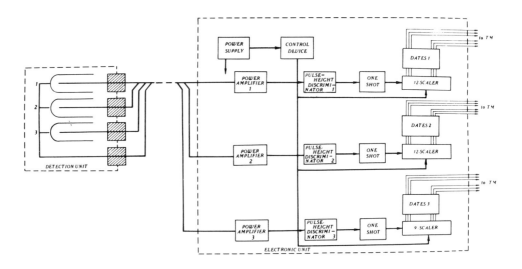

Fig. 2.1.41 — Functional diagram of the radiation densitometer: 1, 2 and 3, gamma-radiation detectors.

The functional layout of the densitometer is illustrated in Fig. 12.1.41. Electric signals produced in gas-discharge counters were sent via a screened cable into the electronic unit to the respective preamplifiers (PA1–PA3) and thereafter to the lower-level discriminators (LLD1–LLD3). The discriminators were based on Schmitt triggers with the use of differential amplifiers in the circuit arrangement.

The recording part of the instrument consisted of integrated circuits. It comprised various signal formers — monostables (F), counting registers (CR1–CR3), and buffer cascades (electronic keys BEC1–BEC3), the latter exercising uncoupling between the register outputs and the telemetry system (TM) inputs. The monostables F formed signals that were suitable for a subsequent recalculation, with a pulse length of about 10 μs and an amplitude of about 5V.

Counting registers were, in effect, the principal elements of the instrument memory. They stored information arriving from the detectors. The registers were synchronous counters with trigger inputs and had memory capacities of 12, 10 and 9 bits, respectively.

The control device (CD) served for setting the counting register triggers into the initial state when the instrument was switched on and a corresponding command was sent from the programme-timing device of the lander.

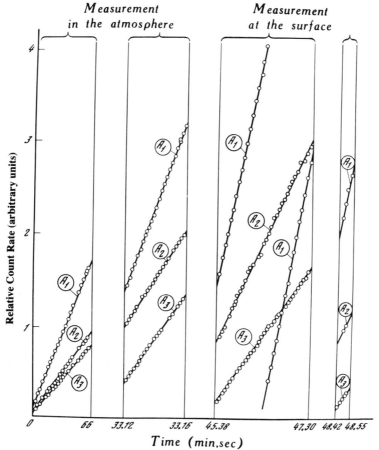

Fig. 2.1.42 — Primary telemetry information for operation of the radiation densitometer.

A precision power supply source (SS) in the instrument supplied stabilized voltage to the electronic units of the instrument. The power consumption of the instrument was not more than 2 W. The operating programme of the lander provided for functioning of the instrument in the planet's atmosphere to compare its parameters with those obtained earlier on the Earth, and to assess its operational stability under conditions of rapidly increasing temperature and pressure. Densitometer readings were continuously relayed to the Earth throughout the descent period. After landing, information was brought out in cycles at 2–4 min intervals. Fig. 2.1.42 illustrates part of the primary telemetry information relayed at the landing stage of the descent, as well as during the operation of the instrument at the planetary surface.

An increase in the count-rate at the end of the descent period took place in conformity with the increasing density of the atmosphere. The count-rates with the detection unit in its transport position, during the calibration on the Earth, and at the initial stage in the atmosphere differed only within the limits of statistical error.

The count-rates of the three detectors, as obtained at the Venusian surface lead to different density values both in the pre-inversion and the post-inversion region, thus serving as an indication of the fact that the detection unit was lying on an irregular surface. Supporting evidence was furnished by the panoramic photograph relayed by Venera 10.

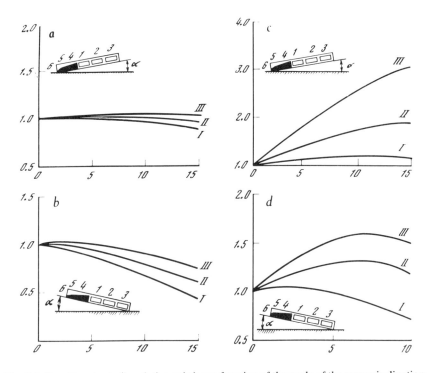

Fig. 2.1.43 — Count rate (in relative units) as a function of the angle of the sensor inclination to the surface of the rock under study (in degrees). (a) and (b), in the pre-inversion region; (c) and (d), in the trans-inversion region. The location of the sensor is shown in the diagram where 1, 2 and 3, detectors; 4, screen; 5, body; 6, source; α, angle of inclination; I, II and III, curves corresponding to detectors 1, 2 and 3.

As seen in the panorama (see Fig. 1.3.4), the detection unit contacts the rock at its left-hand side where the gamma-radiation source is set up. The relevant dependence of the densitometer readings in this case is illustrated in Fig. 2.1.43. In accordance with this dependence the searched-for density can lie solely in the post-inversion region of the curves. The count rate of the first (short base) densitometer, on account of a gap underneath the detector, may be overestimated by not more than 17% (for a 10° surface gradient underneath it), which corresponds to an upper density limit of 3.16×10^3 kg m^{-3}. The lower limit of 2.17×10^3 kg m^{-3} was determined with respect to the first densitometer under the condition that there was no gap underneath the pickup.

Using the measurement results of the other two densitometers (with intermediate and long bases) it was possible to estimate the surface gradient beneath the first of the densitometers as being equal to 5–6°, which is confirmed by the panoramic image.

The dependence illustrated in Fig. 2.1.43 being taken into account, this gradient corresponds to a density of 2.8×10^3 kg m^{-3}.

Using the relationships between the readings of all three densimeters enabled the construction, moreover, of a surface model from a material with density 2.88×10^3 kg m^{-3}, in which count-rates similar to those obtained at Venus' surface are reproduced. Thus, after allowing for the errors in the count-rate determinations, the gradient of graduation curves and the errors associated with the graduation, the surface density of Venusian rocks amounts to 2.8 ± 0.1 kg m^{-3}.

The data obtained indicate that the outcropping rocks visible in the panorama of the Venusian surface are represented by a sufficiently compact rock which has been little altered by surface processes. The layer thickness to which the above density is attributed amounts to 10–15 cm.

Presumably, the bedrock at the Venera 10 landing site, the outcrops of which are seen on the panoramic photograph, is relatively young and has not been subject to significant erosion. However, rock as compact as that does not occur everywhere. For instance, at the landing site of Venera 13 (and, possibly, of Venera 9) the rock was found to be much weathered (at least, on the surface) and, correspondingly, less strong and compact.

2.1.5.5 Main results of studying the gamma-radiation and density of rocks from the Venera and VeGa spacecraft

The composition and properties of matter of the Solar System bodies are known to be the result of both fundamental processes taking place in the primary protoplanetary nebula and of large-scale planetary processes, such as, for instance, the differentiation of planetary matter into envelopes. As regards specific areas of the surface of the Earth and other planets of the Solar System, the formation of the chemical composition and properties of their constituent rocks were also greatly influenced by the physical and climatic conditions which existed at the surface of the planet in question. In particular, as far as Venus is concerned, which has a dense and sufficiently active atmosphere, a high temperature and pressure at the surface and, finally, a relatively smoothed relief, it would be reasonable to assume a significant effect of erosion on the formation of its surface. Evidence in favour of possible intensive erosion at the planet's surface can be seen in the outward appearance of disintegrated rock (see the panoramic photograph obtained by Veneras 9 and 13), in the high wind velocity at the cloud-layer level and in the weak strength of the rocks, as measured by Veneras 13 and 14. However, the degree of erosion of the rock in different surface areas is variable, the explanation lying, apparently, not in the difference of physical conditions, but rather in the age of the rock.

The thorium, uranium and potassium content data point to the existence of igneous rocks in all investigated areas of the planet's surface. The rock at the Venera 8 landing site was found to be particularly rich in natural radioactive elements. Among terrestrial rocks, such a high uranium, thorium and potassium content is found in alkaline basalts or granite, which are particularly rich in radioelements (see the K–U systematics in Fig. 2.1.17). At present we may with greater confidence label this rock potassium alkaline basalt, rather than granite. Appropriate evidence is found in the fact that the rock at the Venera 13 landing site (which lies in the same geomorphological province and has about the same potassium content as the Venera 8 rock) has turned out to be alkaline basalt. Data obtained by Veneras 9 and 10 enable us on the basis of the K–U systematics to attribute the investigated rocks to the transitional zone between tholeiitic and alkaline basalts, i.e. to rocks which are products of the relatively shallow differentiation of the planet's primary matter.

The fact that the investigated rock is of a basaltic composition is confirmed, moreover, by measurements of its density. The density of $2.7–2.9 \times 10^3$ kg m^{-3}, according to terrestrial analogues, corresponds to the denser basalts of low porosity. Such a kind of rock is typical of lava effusions of viscous magmas on the Earth. However, a less compact rock also appears to be widespread on Venus. It resembles terrestrial volcanic tuffs which are formed following the deposition of ash thrown out by volcanic eruptions. Such kind of tuff-like layered rock is observable in the other investigated areas (see, for instance, the panoramic photographs from Veneras 13 and 14 in Fig. 1.3.5).

The K/U ratio for investigated Venusian rocks was found to be pretty close to that typical of the majority of magmatic rocks on the Earth (about 10^4). This fact can be taken as evidence that if processes leading to the alteration of the chemical composition of primary matter (whatever their nature could be) did take place on Venus, they were on the whole similar to terrestrial ones.

Thus, the data on the character of the Venusian rock, which were obtained with the aid of the Venera and VeGa probes, agree with the concepts evolved from the results of investigations of the planet's atmosphere. Today we may well think that the evolutionary path of Venus has been similar to that of the Earth. Apparently, it, like the Earth, passed, long ago, through a stage of heating of its interior and differentiation of its matter into envelopes. At present it is hardly possible to determine how far this process has proceeded, but the identification on Venus' surface of rocks strongly enriched with uranium, thorium and potassium is an indication of their melting out from primary matter occurring in the planet's interior. The great quantity of carbon dioxide in Venus' atmosphere is an indication that the process of effusion or eruption of magmatic rocks on the surface has either terminated relatively recently or is even continuing at the present time.

Comparison of the data available on the Moon, the Earth, Venus and Mars indicates that a single geochemical process appears to be taking place on all these bodies, dividing them into envelopes, the uppermost of which, i.e. the crust, turns out to consist predominantly of basalts. Presumably, all terrestrial planets have a similar internal structure, although each of them has some essential differences due to its origin, primary composition, mass, etc., as a result of which each of the planets is at present at a particular stage along the single evolutionary pathway of the development of the Solar System bodies.

REFERENCES

[1] A. P. Vinogradov, Yu. A. Surkov, and L. P. Moskalyova, In *Moon and planets* (ed.) A. Dollfus, Amsterdam, Pergamon Press. p. 71 (1967).

[2] Yu. A. Surkov, L. P. Moskalyova, and A. N. Khalemsky, *Space Res.,* **11**, 181 (1971).

[3] T. W. Armstrong, *J. Geophys. Res.,* **77**, 524 (1972).

[4] R. C. Reedy and J. R. Arnold, *J. Geophys. Res.,* **77**, 537 (1972).

[5] A. P. Vinogradov, Yu. A. Surkov, and G. M. Chernov, *Kosmich. Issled.,* **5**, 874 (In Russian) (1967).

[6] J. R. Arnold, J. I. Trombka and L. E. Peterson, Report at 16th COSPAR, Constanz, DDR (1973).

[7] A. E. Metzger, J. I. Trombka, and I. E. Peterson, *Science,* **179**, 800 (1973).

[8] Yu. A. Surkov, L. P. Moskalyova, and F. F. Kirnozov, Report at the 18th COSPAR, Varna, Bulgaria (1975).

[9] Yu. A. Surkov, L. P. Moskalyova, and A. T. Bazilevsky, In *Proc. 11th Lunar and Planet. Sci. Conf.* New York, Pergamon Press, 669 (1980).

[10] T.W. Armstrong and R. G. Alsmiller, In *Proc. 2nd Lunar and Planet Sci. Conf.,* New York, Pergamon Press, **2**, 1729 (1971).

[11] A. P. Vinogradov, A. K. Lavrukhina, and L. D. Revina, *Geokhimiya,* **11**, 955 (In Russian) (1961).

[12] K. L. Lyubarsky, Dissertation for a Cand. Sc. degree, the Joint Institute for Nuclear Research, Dubna, (typescript), 125, (In Russian) (1966).

[13] K. H. Ebert, and H. Wänke, *Ztschr, Naturforsch. A.,* **Bd12**, 766 (1957).

[14] T. P. Kohman, and M. L. Bender, *Nuclide production by cosmic-rays in meteorites and on the Moon,* Report, N. NYO-844-72 36 (1967).

[15] J. P. Schedlovcky and G. V. S. Rayudu, *J. Geophys. Res.,* 69, 2231 (1964).

[16] R. C. Reedy, J. R. Arnold and J. I. Trombka, *J. Geophys. Res.,* 78, 5847 (1973).

[17] G. J. F. MacDonald, *J. Geophys. Res.,* **69**, 2933 (1964).

[18] H. C. Urey, *Proc. Nat. Acad. Sci. US,* **41**, 127 (1955).

[19] N. Bhandari, S. G. Ehat, and D. L. Lal, *Nature,* **230**, 219 (1971).

[20] Yu. A. Surkov, A. A. Vorobyov, and V. A. Korolyov, *Atomanaya energiya,* **9**, 477 (In Russian) (1960).

[21] V. V. Cherdyntsev, Ye. A. Isabayev, and Yu. A. Surkov, *Geokhimiya,* 4, 373 (In Russian) (1960).

[22] D. C. Dunlavey, and G. T. Seaborg, *Phys. Rev.,* **92**, 206 (1953).

[23] C. M. Lederer, J. H. Hollander, and I. Perlman, *In Table of isotopes,* NewYork, Wiley, p.594 (1967).

[24] T. Schlomka, *Ztschr. Naturforsch. A.*, **7**, 637 (1952).

[25] E. C. Waldron, V. A. Schultz, and T. P. Kohman, *Phys. Rev.*, **93**, 254 (1954).

[26] A. P. Vinogradov, *Geokhimiya*, **7**, 555 (In Russian) (1962).

[27] N. P. Yermolayev, and O. P. Sobornov, *Geokhimiya*, **6**, 803 (In Russian) (1973).

[28] A. A. Smyslov, In *The basic principles and the technique of radiogeochemical mapping of rocks*. (In Russian) Leningrad, Nedra, p.23 (1968).

[29] L. V. Dmitriyev and G. B. Udintsev, *In Studies on the problem of the rift zones of the World Ocean*. (In Russian) Moscow, Nauka, Vol 1. p.176 (1972).

[30] H. Vakita, H. Hagasawa, and S. Uyeda, *Earth and Planet. Sci. Lett.*, **2**, 377 (1967).

[31] P. M. Hurley, *Geochim. et Cosmochim. Acta*, **32**, 273 (1968).

[32] J. W. Larimer, *Geochim. et Cosmochim. Acta*, **35**, 769 (1971).

[33] Ye. L. Ruskol, *Izv. AN SSSR*, The Earth's physics, **7**, 99 (In Russian) (1972).

[34] N. A. Vartanov and P. S. Samoilov, In *Applied scintillation gamma-ray spectrometry*. (In Russian) Moscow, Atomizdat, p.406 (1975).

[35] S. V. Iokhelson, Yu. Ye. Kazakov and Ye. D. Stukin, In *Proceedings of the 3rd radiochemical conference in the city of Obninsk*. (In Russian) Moscow, Hydrometeoizdat, p.176 (1972).

[36] R. M. Kogan, I. M. Nazarov, and Sh. D. Fridman, In *The fundamentals of the gamma-spectrometry of natural media*. (In Russian) Moscow, Atomizdat, p.468 (1969).

[37] A. N. Silantyev, In *Spectrometric analysis of radioactive samples of the environment*. (In Russian) Leningrad, Hydrometeoizdat, p.183 (1969).

[38] J. Arnold, J. Trombka, and P. Gorenstein, *J. Anal. Chem.*, **44**, 26A (1972).

[39] A. L. Yakubovich, Ye. I. Zaitsev, and S. M. Przhiyalgovsky, In *Nuclear-physical methods of analysis of mineral raw materials*. (In Russian) Moscow, Atomizdat, p.415 (1969).

[40] B. G. Yegiazarov, B. N. Kononov, and S. S. Kurochkin, *Kosmich. Issled.*, **4**, 265 (In Russian) (1968).

[41] Yu. A. Surkov, F. F. Kirnozov, and O. P. Sobornov, *Kosmich. Issled.*, **11**, 781 (In Russian) (1973).

[42] D. J. Forrest, E. L. Chupp, and J. M. Ryan, *Solar Phys.*, **65**, 15 (1980).

[43] G. H. Nakano, W. L. Imhof, and R. G. Johnson, *IEEE Trans. Nucl. Sci.*, **NS-21**, 159 (1974).

[44] O. P. Sobornov, In a Dissertation for a Cand. Sc. degree, Moscow, Vernadsky Institute of Geochem. and Analyt. Chem. of the USSR Academy of Sciences, (In Russian) p.169 (1974).

[45] Yu. S. Surkov, A. S. Shtan, and I. N. Ivanov, *Space Res.*, **12**, 33 (1972)

[46] Yu. A. Surkov, F. F. Kirnozov, and I. N. Ivanov, *J. Radional. Chem.*, **18**, 169 (1973).

[47] Yu. A. Surkov, and G. A. Fedoseyev, *Kosmich. Issled.*, **11**, 926 (In Russian) (1973).

[48] Yu. A. Surkov, G. A. Fedoseyev, and O. P. Sobornov, In *Lunar Soil from Mare Foecunditatis*, (In Russian) Moscow, Nauka, p.417 (1974).

[49] Yu. A. Surkov and G. M. Kolesov, *Isotopenpraxis*, **12**, 392 (1976).

[50] Yu. A. Surkov and Yu. I. Belyayev, *Trends in analytical chemistry*, **4**, 18 (1985).

[51] M. Chaika, E. Sabo, and A. K. Lavrukhina, *Geokhimiya*, **9**, 1106 (In Russian) (1967).

[52] D. Y. Jerome and J. C. Philippot, In *Regolith from the highland region of the Moon*. (In Russian) Moscow, Nauka, p.402 (1979).

[53] J. C. Laul and R. A. Shmitt, In *Regolith from the highland region of the Moon*, (In Russian) Moscow, Nauka, p.389 (1979).

[54] A. M. Radyvanyuk, V. F. Yevtushenko, and S. A. Baldin, In *The development of nuclear and isotopic instrument making*. (In Russian) Moscow, Atomizdat, Vol 1, p.111 (1970).

[55] V. F. Evtushenko, G. A. Kibalchich, and V. A. Suliga, *Monocrystals, scintillators and organic luminophors*, **5**, 307 (1970).

[56] Yu. A. Surkov, O. P. Sobornov, and I. A. Lebedev, *Pribori i technika experimenta*, **2** (In Russian) (1977).

[57] Ju. A. Tsirlin, A. R. Daich, and A. M. Radyvanyuk, In *Scintillation blocks*, (In Russian) Moscow, Atomizdat (1978).

[58] A. E. Metzger, In *Gamma-ray astrophyics*, NASA SP-339, Washington (1973).

[59] T. M. Harrington, J. H. Marshall, and J. R. Arnold, *Nucl. Instr. and Meth.*, **118**, 401 (1974).

[60] Catalogues of Cuartz and Silice (Paris), Harzshaw (The Netherlands), Canberra (USA) and others.

[61] A. H. Werkeiser, and T. G. Miller, *Nucl. Instrum. and Meth.*, **75**, 167 (1969).

[62] G. I. Yakhnis, R. A. Govorova, and M. Ye. Dovgan, *Monocrystals, scintillators and organic luminophors*, **5**, 302 (In Russian) (1970).

[63] J. Toshinobu, *Bull. Jap. Petrol. Inst.*, **13**, 97 (1971).

[64] L. A. Matalin, In *Electronic methods in nuclear physics*. (In Russian) Moscow, Atomizdat (1973).

[65] J. Arens and B. G. Taylor, *Nucl. Instrum. and Meth.*, **108**, 147 (1973).

[66] Yu. A. Tsirlin, In *Light-collection in scintillation counters*. (In Russian) Moscow, Atomizdat (1975).

[67] C. E. Fichtel and J. I. Trombka, In *Gamma-ray astrophysics*, NASA SP-453, Washington (1981).

[68] A. P. Vinogradov, K. P. Florensky, and A. T. Basilevsky, *Dokl. AN SSSR*, **228**, 570 (In Russian) (976).

[69] V. G. Grebennik, V. Kh. Dodokhov, and V. A. Zhukov, The study of the properties of the counter filled with solid xenon, *Dubna*, (Preprint P13-11 165, Joint Institute for Nuclear Research) **12** (In Russian) (1977).

[70] I. M. Obodovsky, and S. G. Pokachalov, *Fiz. nizkikh temperature*, **8**, 829 (In Russian) (1979).

[71] M. C. Gadenne, A. Lansiart, and A. Seigneur, *Nucl. Instrum. and Meth.*, **124**, 521 (1975).

[72] J. Prunier, R. Aelemand, and M. Laval, *Nucl. Instrum. And Meth.*, **109**, 257 (1973).

[73] H. Zaklad, S. E. Dezenzo, and R. A. Muller, *IEEE Trans. Nucl. Sci.*, **NS-19**, 206 (1972).

[74] N. B. Vagraftik, In *Handbook on thermophysical properties of liquids.* (In Russian) Moscow, Nauka (1972).

[75] A. M. Galper, V. V. Dmitriyenko, and A. S. Romanyuk, *Izv. AN SSSR, Phys.*, **45**, 649 (In Russian) (1981).

[76] A. S. Romanyuk, Paper for a Cand. Sc. degree, (In Russian) Moscow, The Moscow Engineering and Physics Institute, p.127 (1981).

[77] A. Porelli, and R. P. Gardner, *Nucl. Instrum. and Meth.*, **159**, 177 (1979).

[78] D. F. Anderson, T. T. Hamilton, W. H. M. Ku, and R. Novick, *Nucl. Instrum. and Meth.*, **163**, 125 (1979).

[79] V. B. Dmitriyenko, A. S. Romanyuk, and Z. M. Uteshev, *Elementary Particles and Cosmic Rays*, **5**, 72 (In Russian) (1980).

[80] S. S. Huang and G. R. Freeman, *J. Chem. Phys.*, **68**, 1355 (1978).

[81] G. D. Alkhazov, A. P. Komar, and A. A. Vorob'ev, *Nucl. Instrum. and Meth.*, **48**, 1 (1967).

[82] V. G. Grebennik, V. Kh. Dodokjov, and V. A. Zhukov, *Priobory i Tekhnika Experimenta*, **5**, 62 (In Russian) (1978).

[83] Yu. K. Akimov, In *Semiconductor nuclear particle detectors and their use.* (In Russian) Moscow, Atomizdat, p.255 (1967).

[84] V. S. Vavilov, L. A. Goncharov, and T. N. Pavlov, *Atomnaya Energiya,* **32**, 335 (In Russian) (1972).

[85] G. A. Armantrout, *IEEE Trans. Nucl. Sci.*, **NS-14**, 503 (1967).

[86] R. D. Baertsch, and R. N. Hall, *IEEE Trans. Nucl. Sci.*, **NS-17**, 3, 235 (1970).

[87] Dan Okuba, *IEEE Trans. Nucl. Sci.*, **NS-17**, 61 (1970).

[88] W. E. Drummond, *IEEE Trans. Nucl. Sci.*, **NS-18**, 91 (1971).

[89] P. Glazow, *Nucl. Instrum. and Meth.*, **80**, 141 (1970)

[90] J. L. Irigaray and G. Y. Petit, *Nucl. Instrum. and Meth.*, **80**, 264 (1970).

[91] J. M. Mayer, *Nucl. Instrum. and Meth.*, **63**, 141 (1968).

[92] S. Santhanam, P. P. Webb, and S. Monaro, *IEEE Trans. Nucl. Sci.,* **NS-16**, 75 (1969).

[93] P. Suominen, *Nucl. Instrum. and Meth.*, **101**, 25 (1972).

[94] A. J. Tavendale, *Nucl. Instrum. and Meth.*, **84**, 314 (1970).

[95] N. I. Adamovich, V. I. Zuyev, and T. F. Pavlovskaya, *Proceedings of the conference on nuclear instrument-making.* (In Russian) Leipzig, p.131 (1970).

[96] A. V. Arefyev, *Priobory i Tekhnika Experimenta*, **4**, 138 (In Russian) (1966).

[97] H. E. Bosch, L. R. Gatto, and M. Behar. *Nucl. Instrum. and Meth.*, **68**, 88 (1969).

[98] S. Buhler and L. Marcus, *Nucl. Instrum. and Meth.*, **50**, 170 (1967).

[99] J. F. Detko, *Nucl. Instrum. and Meth.*, **94**, 395 (1971).

[100] M. M. El-Shishini and W. Zobel, *IEEE Trans. Nucl. Sci.*, **NS-13**, 359 (1966).

[101] C. M. Fleck, and W. Neidstätter, *Nucl. Instrum. and Meth.*, **66**, 304 (1968).

[102]J. Fouarge and R. Delporte, *Nucl. Instrum. and Meth.*, **99**, 81 (1972).

[103]H. F. Franke, *Nucl. Instrum. and Meth.*, **72**, 107 (1969).

[104]J. Lippert, *Nucl. Instrum. and Meth.*, **32**, 360 (1965).

[105]H. Masursky, *J. Geophys. Res.*, **78**, 4009 (1973).

[106]C. E. Minner, *Nucl. Instrum. and Meth.*, **55**, 125 (1967).

[107]P. O. Schlosser, D. W. Miller, and M. S. Gerber, *IEEE Trans. Nucl. Sci.*, **NS-21**, 658 (1974).

[108]A. S. Aloyev, N. A. Vartanov, and Yu. Ye. Kazakov, *Pribory i Tekhnika Experimenta*, **1**, 228 (In Russian) (1972).

[109]V. I. Melentyev, V. V. Ovechkin, and V. S. Rudenko, *Pribory i Tekhnika Experimenta*, **1**, 45 (In Russian) (1967).

[110]E. P. Sheretov, *Measurement, Control, Automatization,* **11–12**, 29 (In Russian) (1980).

[111]A. Mc. G. Beech, J. K. Parry, and D. F. Urquhard, *Nucl. Instrum. and Meth.*, **27**, 169 (1964).

[112]J. A. Cooper, N. A. Wogman, and R. W. Perkins, *IEEE Trans. Nucl. Sci.*, **NS-15**, 407 (1968).

[113]J. A. Cooper and R. W. Perkins, *Nucl. Instrum. and Meth.*, **99**, 125 (1972).

[114]G. E. Goldon, K. Randle, and G. G. Goles, *Geochim. et Cosmochim. Acta.*, **32**, 269 (1968).

[115]C. R. Gruchn, J. V. Kane, and W. H. Kelly, *Nucl. Instrum. and Meth.*, **54**, 268 (1967).

[116]M. W. Hill, *Nucl. Instrum. and Meth.*, **36**, 350 (1965).

[117]S. R. Lewis and N. H. Shafrir, *Nucl. Instrum. and Meth.*, **93**, 317 (1971).

[118]D. Morrison and D. P. Cruikshank, *Icarus*, **18**, 224 (1977).

[119]C. D. Schrader, and R. J. Stinner, *J. Geophys. Res.*, **66**, 1951 (1965).

[120]R. P. Caren, *Cryog. Technol.*, **15**, 115 (1968).

[121]W. L. Kraushaar, *Astronaut. and Aeronaut.*, **7**, 28 (1969).

[122]G. A. MacGregor, I. Turiel, and R. Bettenhausen, *Rev. Sci. Instrum.*, **35** (1971).

[123]O. A. Testard, J. Leny, and J. Leszyszyn, *Cryogenics*, **9**, 137 (1970).

[124]R. Henck, P. Siffert, and A. Coche, *Nucl. Instrum. and Meth.*, **60**, 343 (1968).

[125]V. G. Kunde, A. C. Aikin, and R. A. Hanel. *Nature*, **292**, 686 (1981).

[126]I. N. Arsenyev, I. S. Dneprovsky, and L. A. Popeko, *Atomnaya Energiya*, **28**, 165, (In Russian) (1970).

[127]I. S. Dneprovsky, A. M. Vakhonina, and L. A. Popeko, In *Proceedings of the All-Union Research Institute of Instrument Making*, **13**, 22 (1970).

[128] T. G. Korzyuk, In *Applied nuclear spectroscopy*, (Ed.) V. G. Nedovesov (In Russian) Moscow, Atomizdat, Vol 1, 233 (1970).

[129]R. H. Pehl, R. C. Cordi, and F. S. Goulding. *IEEE Trans. Nucl. Sci.*, **NS-19**, 265 (1972).

[130]R. Stuck, J. P. Ponpon, and P. Siffert, *IEEE Trans. Nucl. Sci.*, **NS-19**, 270 (1972).

[131]B. K. Akinshin, Ye. M. Margolin, and E. Ye. Pakhomov, *Pribory i Tekhnika Experimenta*, **4**, 71 (In Russian) (1973).

[132]B. K. Akinshin, and Yu. Ye. Stolypin, *Pribory i Tekhnika Experimenta*, **3**, 29 (In Russian) (1977).

[133]G. H. Nakano and W. L. Imhof, *IEEE Trans. Nucl. Sci.*, **NS-18**, 258 (1971).

[134]D. B. Hick, and A. S. Jacobson, *IEEE Trans. Nucl. Sci.*, **NS-21**, 169 (1974).

[135]A. E. Metzger, M. A. Van Dilla, and E. C. Anderson, *Nucleonics*, **20**, 64 (1962).

[136]Yu. A. Surkov, L. P. Moskalyova, and F. F. Kirnozov, *Space Res.*, **16**, 993 (1976).

[137]G. Ye. Kocharov, S. V. Viktorov, and N. F. Borodulin. In *The Lunokhod 1 mobile laboratory on the Moon*. (In Russian) Moscow, Nauka, Vol 1, 89 (1971).

[138]G. Ye. Kocharov, S. V. Viktorov, *Dokl. AN SSSR*, **214**, 71 (In Russian) (1974).

[139]G. Ye. Kocharov, S. V. Viktorov, In *Space Research, B.*, **12**, 13 (1972).

[140]Yu. A. Surkov. *In Gamma-spectrometry in space research* (In Russian) Moscow, Atomizdat, p.209 (1977).

[141]S. N. Vernov, A. Ye. Chudakov, and P. V. Vakulov, *Dokl. AN SSSR*, **125**, 304 (In Russian) (1959).

[142] A. P. Vinogradov, Yu. A. Surkov, and L. P. Moskalyova, In *Report to the 7th COSPAR Meeting*, Vienna, p.71 (1965).

[143]W. L. Kraushaar, G. W. Clark, and G. P. Garmine, *Ap. J.*, **177**, 341 (1972).

[144] J. R. Arnold, A. E. Metzger, and E. C. Anderson, *J. Geophys. Res.*, **67**, 4878 (1962).

[145]J. A. Northrop, and R. L. Hostetler, *Bull. Amer. Phys. Soc. Ser.2*, 6, 52 (1961).

[146]G. J. Perlow, and C. W. Kissinger, *Phys. Rev*, 84, 572 (1951).

[147] A. E. Metzger, J. I. Trombka, and R. C. Reedy, In *Proc. 5th Lunar Sci. Conf.* New York, Pergamon Press, Vol 1, 1067 (1975).

[148]H. Urey, In *Experimental space exploration* (In Russian) Moscow, Foreign Literature Publishing House, p.83 (1961).

[149]J. I. Trombka, J. R. Arnold, and I. Adler, In *Proc. Soviet.-Amer. Conf. on Cosmochem. of the Moon and Planets*. Moscow, p.128 (1974).

[150] A. E. Metzger and J. R. Arnold, *Appl. Opt, 9*, 1289 (1970).

[151]Yu. A. Surkov, and L. P. Moskalyova, In *The All-Union Conference on the Physics of Cosmic Rays. Summaries of reports*. (In Russian). Tashkent, The Publishing House of the USSR Academy of Sciences (1968).

[152]Yu. A. Surkov, L. P. Moskalyova, and R. Ya. Zulkarneyev, In *Applied nuclear spectroscopy*. (Ed.) V. G. Nedovesov (In Russian), Moscow, Atomizdat, Vol 3, p.246 (1972).

[153] T. V. Gorshkov, In *Gamma-radiation of radioactive bodies*. (In Russian) Leningrad, Leningrad University Press, p.139 (1956).

[154] V. S. Barashenkov, In *The interaction cross-section of elementary particles* (In Russian) Moscow, Nauka, p.531 (1966).

[155] A. S. Lenin, In *The study of atmospheric gamma-radiation with energies of 0.3 to 3.0 MeV and higher than 100 MeV*. Paper for a Cand. Sc. degree, (In Russian) Moscow. The Moscow Engineering and Physics Institute (typescript) (1973).

(In Russian) Moscow. The Moscow Engineering and Physics Institute (typescript) (1973).

[156] L. Peterson, R. Jerd, and A. Jacobson, The study of X-radiation on balloons, *Uspekhi fiz. nauk*, **95**, 689 (In Russian) (1968).

[157] A. M. Romanov, In *Proceeding of the 6th All Union annual space physics* (In Russian). Apatity, The Kola branch of the USSR Academy of Sciences, Preprint, **1**, 111 (1969).

[158] K. P. Beuermann , *J. Geophys. Res.*, **16**, 4291 (1971).

[159] W. Zobel, F. C. Mainshein, and R. J. Seroggs, *Prepr. ORNL*, **3506**, US, 34 (1965).

[160] M. N. Toksöz, and D. H. Johnston, In *Soviet-Amer. conf. on cosmochem. of the Moon and planets*. Moscow, p.210 (1974).

[161] Yu. A. Surkov, and G. A. Fedoseyev, In *Cosmochemistry of the Moon and planets*. (In Russian). Moscow, Nauka, p.358 (1975).

[162] *Viking-1: Early results*. NASA SP-408, 67 (1976).

[163] A. P. Vinogradov, Yu. A. Surkov, and F. F. Kirnozov, *Dokl. AN SSSR*, **208**, 576 (In Russian) (1973).

[164] Yu. A. Surkov, F. F. Kirnozov, and V. N. Glazov, *Kosmich. Issled.*, **14**, 704 (In Russian) (1976).

[165] N. N. Krupenio, In *The estimate of the density of the material in the surface layers of the Moon, Mars and Venus*. (In Russian). Preprint of the Institute of Space Research of the USSR Academy of Sciences, **Pr-212** (1975).

[166] A. D. Kuzmin, and M. Ya. Marov, In *The physics of the planet Venus*. (In Russian) Moscow, Nauka, p. 408 (1974).

[167] Yu. A. Surkov, F. F. Kirnozov, and V. K. Khristianov, *Space Res.*, **17**, 651 (1977).

[168] S. R. Taylor, In *Planetary Science: A Lunar perspective*. Houston (1982).

[169] J. W. Head, J. B. Garvin, D. B. Campbell, G. H. Pettengill, H. Masursky *et al.*, In *Abstracts of XVII Lunar and Planetary Science Conference* (Houston) p.327 (1986).

[170] Yu. A. Surkov, F. F. Kirnozov, and V. N. Glazov, In *Abstracts of XVII Lunar and Planetary Science Conference* (Houston) p.847 (1986).

[171] Yu. A. Surkov, F. F. Kirnozov, and O. P. Sobornov, *Pisma Astron. Zh.*, **12**, 114 (In Russian) (1986).

[172] L. E. Nyquist, *J. Geophys. Res., Supplement*, **89**, B631 (1983).

2.2 X-ray spectrometric studies

The X-ray spectrometric analysis of extraterrestrial matter as a remote-sensing technique used in space research appears to be second in potential only to gamma-ray spectrometry. It enables us, from a satellite orbit around a planet (if the latter has no atmosphere), or from a landing vehicle, to determine the content of main rock-forming elements and rare elements in the surface rocks of planets and satellites. This method is finding large-scale application in laboratory investigations and there are available at present some monographs [1–4] dealing with the principal techniques, apparatus design and applications. We shall be concerned solely with onboard equipment and details of its application in space research.

The first simple experiment in the study of X-ray radiation from the Moon was installed on the orbiting Luna -10 automatic lunar station in 1966 by Mandelshtam *et al.* [5]. In that experiment and somewhat later in the Lunokhod 1 (1970) and Lunokhod 2 (1973) rovers, use was made by Kocharov *et al.* [6–8] of more-sophisticated onboard equipment for the X-ray radiometric analysis of lunar soils. In the experiments concerned, the excitation of fluorescent radiation was achieved by the use of tritium sources. The content of rock-forming elements was determined in the Mare Imbrium and in the vicinity of the crater Le Monnier. In 1972 Surkov *et al.* [9] discussed the possible use for the same purposes, i.e. analysis of extraterrestrial matter, of a nondispersive X-ray fluorescent analyser using plutonium-238, as a source of alpha-particles. In 1972 Adler *et al.* [10–12] described an experiment carried out with the aid of an X-ray spectrometer set up on the orbiting command modules of the Apollo-15 and Apollo-16 space vehicles. Data were obtained on the relative content of three elements (Mg, Al, Si) in surface rocks of the Moon's equatorial region. In 1973 Clark *et al.* [13–14] described a measurement technique and apparatus for the analysis of Martian soil, in which the excitation sources of fluorescent radiation were ^{55}Fe and ^{109}Cd. Later this equipment was set up in the Viking 1 and Viking 2 space vehicles. It was used to determine the composition of Martian rocks in the landing areas of the vehicles. In 1981 Surkov *et al.* [15] described X-ray radiometric analysis in a quite different field — the investigation of the elemental composition of Venusian clouds. The sources of excitation of fluorescent radiation in the sample of collected aerosol were ^{55}Fe and ^{109}Cd. The elemental composition of the aerosol was determined. Finally, in 1982 in the Venera 13 and Venera 14 space probes the elemental composition of Venusian rocks in the landing areas was determined for the first time. Rock specimens were taken by a sampling device, brought inside the lander and irradiated by the ^{55}Fe and ^{238}Pu sources. Induced fluorescent radiation was analysed by a multichannel X-ray spectrometer. The contents of elements from Mg to Fe were determined [16–20].

In all of the aforementioned experiments, proportional counters with different gas fillings were used as detectors of fluorescent radiation.

In recent years semiconductor detectors using Si(Li) or Ge have found their way into laboratory X-ray spectrometry. In space research no X-ray spectrometers with semiconductor detectors have yet been used, though it is quite obvious that their application has good prospects.

2.2.1. PRINCIPLES OF X-RAY RADIOMETRIC METHOD

Interaction of charged particles or photons with some matter is accompanied by either a partial or a complete transmission of their energy to atoms, as a result of which the electrons in the inner orbits, become excited and leave the atoms. The resultant vacancies in the inner shells are filled by electrons from the outer shells. This transition is accompanied by the liberation of energy which is emitted in the form of photons of fluorescent radiation. The energy of the photons corresponds to the difference between the energies of the two shells and is a characteristic one for specific shells and elements. The spectrum of fluorescent radiation of each of the elements consists only of several lines called K, L, M, etc. depending upon the shells from which the electron transition takes place. However, these lines are also endowed with a finer structure – K α_1, K α_2 K α_3, etc. depending upon the subshells from which the electron transition takes place. The energy of transition of each of the series increases with the increasing atomic number of the element. Thus, by measuring this energy we are able to identify the corresponding element, whilst by measuring the photon flux we can determine the concentration of the given element.

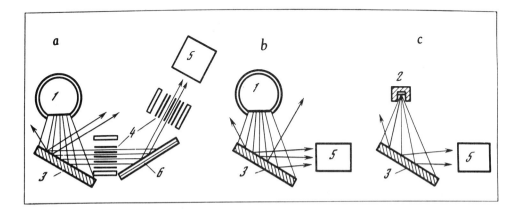

Fig. 2.2.1 — Diagram of X-ray fluorescence analysis: a, dispersive method; b, non-dispersive (crystal-free) method; c, X-ray radiometric method; 1, X-ray tube; 2, radioisotope source; 3, sample under study; 4, collimator; 5, detector; 6, crystal.

In the classical method of analysis the excitation of fluorescent radiation is achieved with the aid of an X-ray tube, whilst separation of X-rays with respect to wavelengths (and, consequently, with respect to energies) is performed by using their diffraction by crystals in accordance with Bragg's law $n \lambda = 2d \sin \theta$ (where d is the crystal grating parameter, θ is the angle of diffraction, λ is the quantum wavelength, and n is the order of diffraction). Schematically this method is shown in Fig. 2.2.1(a). X-ray radiation from the X-ray tube falls on the analysed specimen. The excited fluorescent radiation is collimated and sent onto the crystal. In this case, the X-ray quanta are scattered at different angles with respect to the direction of the X-ray beam, the angle being dependent on the wavelength. Thus, the intensity of the quanta at a certain angle is proportional to the concentration of the element in the irradiated specimen. This method of analysis is known as the dispersive method.

Another method of X-ray fluorescent analysis involves the use not of the wave properties (i.e. dispersion at crystals), but rather of the capacity of the quanta to produce ionization of atoms, which is proportional to the quantum energy absorbed by the ionized medium. Schematically this method is shown in Fig. 2.2.1(b). The analysed specimen is, as before, irradiated from an X-ray tube, whilst secondary fluorescent radiation falls directly into a detector, causing ionization in the latter. The magnitude of ionization caused by a quantum is proportional to the energy of the quantum (should the latter be completely absorbed in the detector). Therefore, by measuring the number of quanta of a specific energy we may determine the concentration of the corresponding element in the specimen. This method of analysis is known as the non-dispersive (or crystal-free) method.

The use of an X-ray tube as a source of excitation of fluorescent radiation involves a number of difficulties, the most serious of which is the need for a high-voltage source of about 100 kV. This accounts for the fact that radioisotopic sources emitting either X- or alpha-radiation have won large-scale application in the excitation of fluorescent radiation (particularly in apparatus of small size). The method of X-ray fluorescent analysis employing radioisotopic sources is commonly known as X-ray radiometry (see Fig. 2.2.1(c)).

The X-ray radiometric method is the one that has so far been mainly used in space research. It is the potentialities of this method that we shall be discussing here in greater detail. Usually when making use of radioisotopes as the sources of excitation of fluorescent radiation and of proportional gas counters as detectors it is found to be possible, in principle, to determine all the elements of the periodic table, starting with magnesium (its characteristic radiation $K_\alpha = 1.25$ keV) to the heaviest elements, if their content in the analysed specimen is not less than 10^3 to 10 ppm. To achieve the excitation of fluorescent radiation of different elements there is a need for radioisotopic sources of particles or quanta with different energies. The line of an element is found to be more prominently excited, if this exciting energy is slightly higher than the energy of characteristic radiation of the element being determined. The energies of fluorescent radiation of rock-forming elements and rare trace elements, their content being within the sensitivity limits of the method lie principally within the range of about 1–10 keV. To achieve the excitation of fluorescent radiation within the above energy ranges, use is made of radioisotopic sources listed in Table 2.2.1.

Table 2.2.1 – Principle radioisotopic sources employed in X-ray radiometry

Radio-isotopic source	Type of decay; half-life	Energy of gamma-rays and X-rays, (keV)	Energy of alpha-particles (MeV)	Type of X-rays
T/Ti	β; 12.3 years	4.5 extending up to 18		K_α (Ti)
T/Zr	β; 12.3 years	2.05 extending up to 18		L_{ser}(Zr)
^{55}Fe	EC; 2.6 years	5.9		$K_{\alpha (Mn)}$
^{57}Co	EC; 270 days	6.4		$K_{\alpha (Fe)}$
^{109}Cd	EC; 470 days	22.6		$K_{\alpha (Ag)}$
^{47}Pm/Al	β; 2.7 years	1.49		$K_{\alpha (Al)}$
^{170}Tm	β; 129 days	52		$K_{\alpha (Y)}$
^{210}Po	α; 0.38 years		about 5.3	
^{238}Pu	α; 86 years	13–17	about 5.5	L_{ser} (U)
^{239}Pu	α; 24000 years	13–17	about 5.15	L_{ser} (U)
^{241}Am	α; 458 years	14–18	about 5.5	L_{ser} (Np)
^{242}Cm	α; 0.44 years		about 6.1	

In the excitation of the characteristic radiation of principal rock-forming elements the T/Zr source is mostly used. A differential spectrum of its radiation is shown in Fig. 2.2.2(a). As seen in the figure, the spectrum of the source has a peak due to K-lines of Zr with a mean energy of 2.03 keV and a broad maximum in the region of 5–6 keV. This source can be conveniently employed to achieve the excitation of fluorescent radiation in either the lightest elements (N, O, Na) or the heaviest rock-forming elements (Cr, Mn, Fe, Ni, Co). Unfortunately, a peak with 2.03 keV energy happens to be a certain interference in determining the elements with $Z = 12$–15, in the case of which the particularly intensive K-lines lie in the same region. To achieve the excitation of elements in this region, such as K, Ca, and Cr, use is commonly made of a T/Ti source which has a radiation spectrum with a broad maximum in the 4.51 keV region (Fig. 2.2.2(b)). Finally, to achieve the excitation of fluorescent radiation from heavier elements (Ti, V, Cr) use is made of either a ^{55}Fe source, the spectrum of which is likewise given in Fig. 2.2.2(c) or of alpha-sources. A source of ^{55}Fe$^{Kcapt.}$ Mn+$K_{5.9\,keV}$ excludes the possibility of determining either Mn either, but it is suitable in the case of lighter elements. The alpha-sources listed in the Table above do not have narrow intense peaks and are therefore suitable for a wide range of rock-forming and rare elements. While slowing down in the matter, alpha-particles expend their energy mainly in the ionization of valence electrons.

The probability of deeper electron shells being ionized sharply declines. This is associated with the fact that alpha-particles, being endowed with a relatively low velocity, are unable to transmit to the electron a significant portion of their energy. Therefore, the ionization efficiency for deeper-lying shells is dependent on the binding energy of the electron at the given level (i.e. on the atomic number of the element) and on the energy of alpha-particles in the source. The excitation efficiency of fluorescent radiation by a T/Zr source is proportional to E^5, whilst the efficiency of excitation by alpha-particles per decay event is about 10^4 times as high as with the use of a T/Zr source.

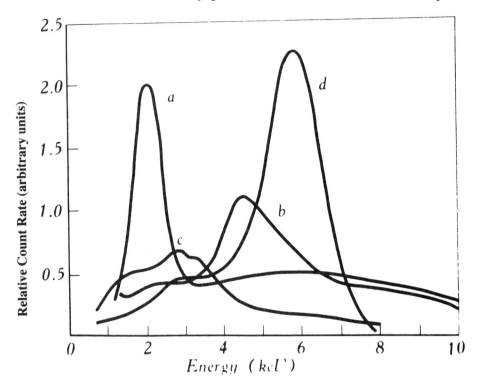

Fig. 2.2.2 — Fluorescent radiation spectra of some radioisotope sources: a, T/Zr; b, T/Ti; c, ^{55}Fe; d, ^{238}Pu.

Shown in Fig. 2.2.2(c) is a soft spectrum of a ^{238}Pu alpha-source. Apart from alpha-particles with about 5.5 MeV energy, there arises in the decay of ^{238}Pu an intensive line of X-radiation with 43 keV energy (not shown in the figure) and a secondary radiation due to transitions of the K, L, M etc. series of the product of plutonium decay ^{234}U, thus permitting an effective excitation of the K-series of a group of elements with $Z \simeq 12+30$.

Fig. 2.2.3. shows the fluorescence yield versus the atomic number of the element in the irradiated specimen. It is seen that alpha-particles more efficiently excited the light elements, approximately down to Fe-Ni (particularly efficient for Na, Mg, Al, Si).

As with excitation sources, radiation detectors are selected in accordance with the energy range containing the characteristic radiation of the elements to be determined. In principle, the higher the energy of fluorescent radiation, the thicker can be the counter window and the higher the atomic number of the main working filler gas. Futhermore, care is also taken lest the filler gas should have in the working energy range its proper radiation (escape peak) that may arise during its irradiation by a given radioisotopic source. Table 2.2.2. lists the main characteristics of those detectors (proportional counters) that have been employed in space research.

As seen from Table 2.2.2, all of the counters were filled with a mixture of inert gases (in different proportions) with an insignificant addition of CO_2 to reduce the working voltage supplied to the counter. The material of the counter window in all cases was beryllium, which is notable for its low photon absorption coefficient. The

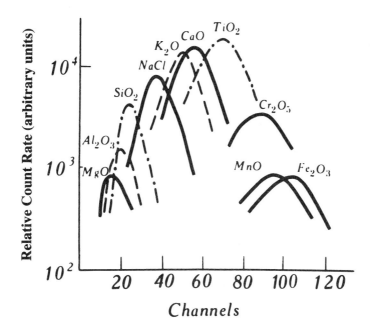

Fig. 2.2.3—Intensity of fluorescent radiation as a function of the order number of the element.

Table 2.2.2 — The Composition of filler gas and window material in proportional counters

No.	Filler gas	Counter window	Elements measure	Space vehicles
1	Ar(90%), CH$_4$(10%)	Al+synthetic film, 10μm	From Mg to Fe	Lunokhod 1 Lunokhod 2
2	Ar(90%), CO$_2$(9.5%) He(0.5%)	Be, 25 μm	Mg,Al,Si	Apollo 15 and Apollo 16
3	Mixtures He, Ne, CO$_2$, Xe	Al, 5 μm Be, 25 and 50 μm	From Mg to Fe	Viking 1 and Viking 2
4	Kr(90%), CO$_2$(10%)	Be, 50 μm	S,Cl,Hg	Venera 12
5	Kr(90%), CO$_2$(10%)	Be, 40 μm	From Mg to Fe	Venera 13 and Venera 14
6	Kr(90%), CH$_4$(10%) Xe(90%), CH$_4$(10%)	Be,~35 μm Be,~35 μm	From Mg to Fe From Co to Zr	VeGa 2

minimal window thickness under which the necessary strength and vacuum tightness are still preserved appears to be 25 μm. In certain cases the beryllium window is additionally covered with filters (a thin magnesium or aluminium layer) to secure discrimination of lines belonging to the neighbouring elements. In [14] the window of one of the counters was made of 5-μm thick aluminium which simultaneously served as a filter.

Fig. 2.2.4. a and b shows by way of example the fluorescent radiation spectra of the main types of rocks in the Earth's crust. The spectra were obtained by irradiating the

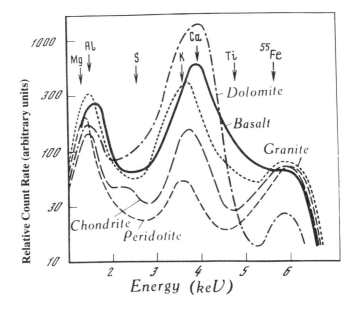

(a)

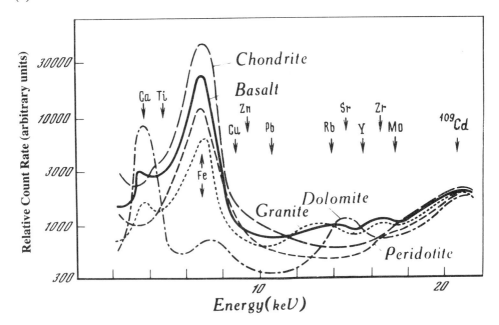

(b)

Fig. 2.2.4 — Fluorescent radiation spectra of the main types of the rocks of the Earth's crust
excited by sources [55]Fe, a, and [109]Cd, b, [20].

rocks with soft (5.9 keV) and hard (22 keV) radiation from ^{55}Fe and ^{109}Cd sources, respectively. As seen from the given spectra, in the region of the main rock-forming elements there are mainly observable three integral (unresolved by proportional counters) peaks: (Mg, Al, Si), (K, Ca) and (Fe, Ni). However, despite the limited resolution of the given detectors, the spectra are seen to have quite clear-cut differences, thus enabling us even visually to determine the nature of the rock (in approximate classification) and in the case of mathematical processing confidently to determine their elemental composition. Despite the nonresolution of the left-hand peak, for instance, it is seen that Al predominates in basalt and granite and Mg in peridotite. As seen from the middle peak, K predominates in granite and Ca in the rest of the rocks. Clearly observable in chondrite is S. In the harder part of the spectrum (obtained by irradiating rocks with a ^{109}Cd source) there are clearly discernible differences in the region of the rare elements Pb, Sr and Zn.

Table 2.2.3 — Minimal concentrations of elements in different rocks,
as determined with the instrument employed in the Viking spacecraft

No.	Element	Min. concentration (%)	Type of rock (matrix)
1.	Mg	2.0	Ultrabasic rocks
2.	Al	2.0	Basalt
3.	Si	0.4	Dolomite
4.	P	1.5	Basalt
5.	S	0.8	Basalt
6.	Cr	0.3	Igneous rocks (all kinds)
7.	K	0.02	Silicate
8.	K	0.15	Basalt
9.	Ca	0.02	Silicate, dunite
10.	Cr	0.5	Estimate
11.	Ti	0.04	Silicate
12.	Ti	0.15	Basalt
13.	Fe	0.03	Silicate
14.	Ni	0.8	Iron silicate
15.	Cu	0.5	Granite
16.	Zr	0.1	Granite
17.	Rb	0.003	Granite
18.	Sr	0.003	Basalt
19.	Y	0.01	Estimate
20.	Zr	0.004	Andesite
21.	Rb	0.005	Syenite
22.	Th	0.008	Syenite
23.	U	0.008	Syenite

Table 2.2.3. indicates the minimal concentration of rock-forming elements, as determined with an instrument employed in the Viking spacecraft [21]. Data are given only for 20 elements since the remainder of the elements are present in rocks in lower concentrations. As seen from the Table, the elements lighter than Mg cannot be measured at all (their radiation being absorbed by the material of the counter window). Mg and Al can be measured only if their content is not below several per cent. The rest of the rock-forming elements from Si to Fe are measurable in quantities ranging from some tenth to some hundredths of one per cent. Finally, rare

elements from Rb to heavy elements can be measured in quantities up to some thousandths of one per cent.

2.2.2   X-RAY RADIOMETRIC ANALYSIS OF VENUS' ROCKS FROM VENERAS 13 AND 14

The flights of Soviet and American space vehicles to Venus have greatly added to our knowledge of its atmosphere and surface. However, the absence of data on the chemical composition of surface rocks proved an insurmountable barrier for the elaboration of valid concepts on the origin and formation of Venus. Accordingly, the Venera 13 and Venera 14 space probes for the first time pursued the task of determining the composition of Venusian rocks in the landing areas. The space probes reached Venus in March 1982. They carried out television photography of the landing areas, investigated the characteristics of Venus' atmosphere and for the first time determined the elemental composition of the rocks at the landing sites.

The landing areas had been so chosen as to be able to obtain data on the relief and the composition of the rocks in particularly typical geomorphological provinces of the Venusian surface. Venera 13 was investigating rocks on a hilly upland while Venera 14 did so in a more low-lying area having a relatively smooth relief. These two types of provinces characterize the major part (more than 80%) of the planet's surface. Therefore, the obtained data on the chemical composition of rocks are sufficiently representative for the Venusian surface. They enable us to interpret from a new viewpoint the formation mechanism of Venus' surface and crust.

The method of analysis and the equipment used aboard the Venera 13 and Venera 14 space probes are described in [17, 91], the experimental results and geochemical interpretations of the data obtained are discussed in [16, 20].

2.2.2.1   Design and operating principle of the equipment

Development of automatic equipment for determining the composition of rocks under the real climatic conditions prevailing at Venus' surface is, in effect, a highly complicated problem. Accordingly, the elaborate experimental technique enabled some of the operations to be carried out under real Venusian conditions (sampling by drilling, reducing the atmospheric pressure around the rock, transportation of the sample inside the lander), and other operations to be executed under relatively normal conditions inside the lander (irradiation of the sample, spectral measurements, information coding and memory storage). Analysis of the elemental composition of the rock was carried out by the X-ray radiometric method.

The rock specimen was taken for analysis with the aid of a rock sampling device (RSD) which is a small-size drilling set capable of taking samples by drilling in rock of practically any hardness, corresponding to terrestrial types. The depth of drilling and the volume and mass of the taken rock sample depend on the specific operating conditions of the drill set and, as revealed by model experiments under conditions simulating the real ones, are sufficient for carrying out an analysis of a representative sample for the content of principal rock-forming elements.

Fig. 2.2.5 shows the scheme of the experiment for the analysis of the composition of rock at the lander site used with the Venera 13 and Venera 14 space probes. As seen from the figure, the analytical equipment was inside the landing vehicle; arranged outside was only the drilling device and the device for transporting the sample inside the lander.

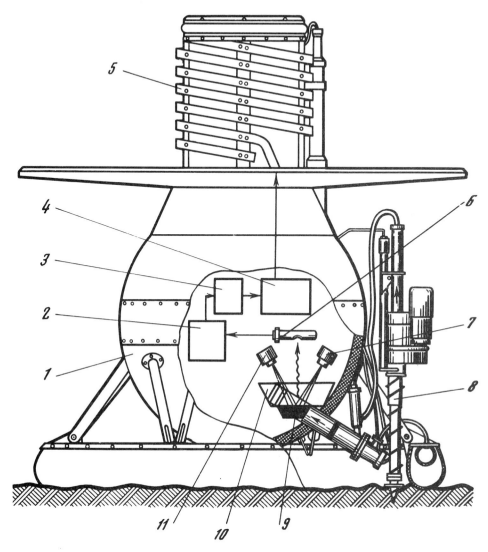

Fig. 2.2.5 — Diagram of X-ray fluorescence analysis at the landers of VEneras 13 and 14.1, probe body; 2, amplification and commutation unit; 3, pulse amplitude analyser; 4, telemetry system; 5, antenna; 6, detector; 7, ^{55}Fe source; 8, soil sampler; 9, soil sample; 10, soil receiver; 11, ^{238}Pu source.

Once the lander had soft-landed, the engine of the drill set was switched on and the drill column was lowered to bring it into contact with the ground surface. Thereafter, drilling and sampling of the rock specimen were carried out, the sample being fed via a pipeline into the sample container. Once the container had been filled, it was hermetically sealed and the atmospheric gas was pumped out into a ballast reservoir. (Residual pressure in the sample container amounted in this case to about 5.3 x10^3 Pa. Thereupon, a transport channel was used to bring the sample container into the sample receiver arranged in the measuring cell of the X-ray fluorescent spectrometer.

The investigated specimen was irradiated in the sample receiver by radioisotopic sources. The arising fluorescent radiation was recorded by detectors, the signals from which were fed, via preamplifiers and amplifiers, into a multichannel pulse analyser. The information stored in the analyser was periodically sent to a telemetry system and relayed to the Earth. Structurally the X-ray fluorescent spectrometer is in the form of two units: the detection unit and the multichannel pulse analyser. Both units were arranged inside a sealed, thermostatically controlled compartment of the lander. For controlling and monitoring the operation of the X-ray fluorescent spectrometer there had been developed a special laboratory control desk, imitating commands received from the onboard programme-timing device of the lander and receiving, in place of the telemetry system, the coded information from the spectrometer.

Detection unit

The design of the detection unit and its arrangement in the lander are shown in Fig. 2.2.6. The detection unit is enclosed within an outer double titanium frame designed

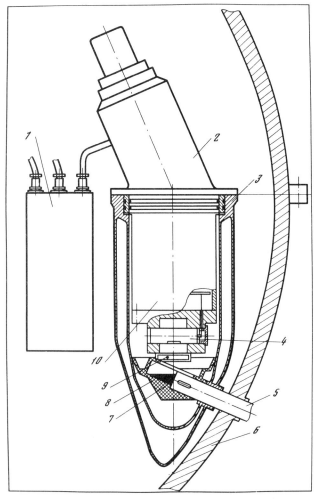

Fig. 2.2.6 — Structure and location of the detection unit at the lander: 1, pulse amplitude analyser; 2, detection unit lid; 4, counter; 5, lock; 6, lander body; 7, sample under study; 8, soil receiver; 9, radioisotope source; 10, electronic unit.

to withstand a 10^7 Pa pressure. The space between the walls of the frame is filled with a cooling agent. The high strength of the frame guarantees a safe performance of the rest of the equipment in the lander even if, in the case of an emergency, the hot dense Venusian atmosphere should break through the data channel. Inside the detection unit there are three divided compartments: the lower compartment houses the measuring cell, the middle one the electronic devices (preamplifiers, amplifiers, supply sources), and the upper one pressure and temperature pickups.

The housing of the middle compartment is in the form of a hermetically sealed cylinder to which the analytical cell is fixed from below. Arranged inside the cell are four counters set up in pairs in mutually perpendicular directions. Fixing of the counters is achieved with the aid of sealed lids provided with rubber packings. Electrical connection of counters with signal converters is effected through hermetic lead-ins in the cylinder bottom. Mounted at the outer butt-end surface of the housing bottom are the radiation sources, care being taken to ensure that their radiation flux is directed towards the investigated sample. The housing of the electronic compartment with electronic elements arranged inside it is hermetically joined to the pressurized container lid. Pressurization of this joint is achieved with the aid of ring packings. To achieve electrical insulation of the housing from the hermetic container lid, the fixing of the housing to the lid is made through insulation bushings and washers. Electrical connection of the detection unit with the object is achieved with the aid of a joint hermetically fixed at the lid of the hermetic container.

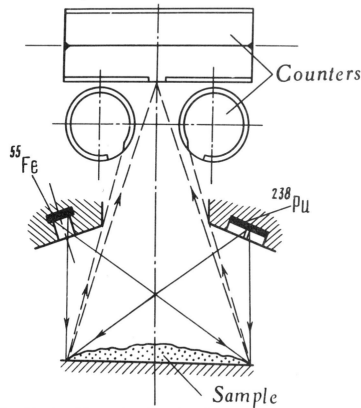

Fig. 2.2.7 — Mutual location of the sample under study, radioisotope sources and detectors in the X-ray fluorescence spectrometer.

Fig. 2.2.7 shows the mutual arrangement of the investigated specimen, gas-discharge counters and radioisotopic sources inside the measuring cell of the detection unit. The instrument makes use of three radioisotopic sources and four gas-discharge counters. In the given measurement geometry the specimen is simultaneously irradiated by all of the sources, whilst the excited fluorescent radiation falls simultaneously on all of the counters.

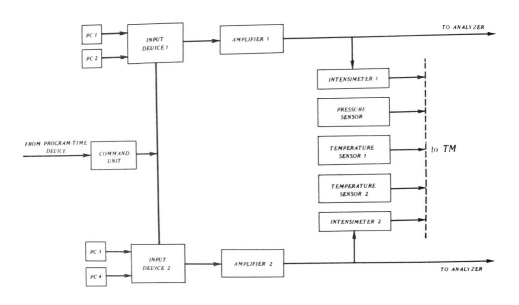

Fig. 2.2.8 — Functional diagram of the detection unit. PC1 and PC2 close counters; PC3 and PC4, far counters; RM1 and RM2, count-rate meters; TM, telemetry.

Fig. 2.2.8 shows the functional scheme of the detection unit. Fluorescent radiation is recorded by four sealed-off proportional counters. Pulses from the counters arrive at the input devices 1 and 2. Arriving simultaneously at the input device ID1 are pulses from the two counters (PC1 and PC2) lying closer to the investigated sample. According to the commands sent from the programme-timing device, the input device lets through for analysis the pulses from one of the counters. The input device ID2 for the counters (PC3 and PC4) lying farther from the sample operates in a similar manner. Signals from the spectrometric amplifier outputs arrive at the two inputs of the channel analyser of the amplitudes of the statistically distributed pulses. The same signals are sent to the inputs of two differential discriminators (intensimeters) the signals from which in an analogue form are sent out to the telemetry system (TM). Also sent out to the telemetry system are readings of the pressure sensor, measuring the pressure inside the detection unit, and of two temperature pickups.

Radioisotopic sources of alpha- and X-radiation
Radioisotopic sources and radiation detectors are the principal elements of the instrument, their choice and arrangement being essentially determined by the

Table 2.2.4 – Characteristics of radioisotopic sources used in the instrument

Source	Half-life	Type of decay	Particle energy (MeV)	Yield	Energy of gamma- and X-rays (keV)	Atomic numbers of excited elements	Activity of sources (mCi)
^{55}Fe	2.6 years	EC	—	100	5.9 (K-radiation of Mn)	12-24 (K-series)	2 x 125
^{238}Pu	86 years	α	5.46	28	13-17 (L-radiation of U)	(K-series)	50
			5.49	72	43.5 (gamma-radiation of Pu)	50-82 (L-series)	

requirements of the experiment. The atomic numbers of the main rock-forming elements lying within the 12–27 range, the choice of radiation sources was made so as to achieve an effective excitation of these elements, while at the same time avoid setting up an interfering background in the measured energy range of fluorescent radiation. The instrument incorporates one ^{238}Pu source and two ^{55}Fe sources; their characteristics are given in Table 2.2.4. The choice of these sources was made on the following considerations: alpha-radiation of ^{238}Pu excites X-ray fluorescence of the lightest elements, Mg, Al, Si; that of ^{55}Fe excites the characteristic radiation of the heavier elements, K, Ca, Ti; and finally, the X-ray radiation of ^{238}Pu excites the elements with even greater atomic numbers, from 24 to 35.

As revealed by methodological studies, in the given instrument, for the chosen source–sample–counter geometry the yield of characteristic radiation by the group (Mg, Al, Si) in the case of excitation by the ^{238}Pu sources is 2–3 times as high as in the case of excitation produced by an ^{55}Fe source (for the sources indicated in Table 2.2.4). On the other hand, the use of ^{238}Pu alone does not permit us to determine elements in the group (K, Ca, Ti) under concentrations equal to fractions of one per cent.

The source of alpha-radiation used in the instrument is in the form of a rectangular ceramic plate 42 x 16 mm in size, upon which is deposited and fixed a preparation of ^{238}Pu of 50 millicurie (mCi) activity. The path of the particles with about 5.5 MeV energy in the nitrogen filling the measuring cell of the instrument, under a working pressure in the cell equal to about 5.3×10^3 Pa, amounts to about 70 cm, whilst the maximum distance of the investigated specimen from the sources is 6 cm. Therefore, practically the entire flux of alpha-particles emitted by the source towards the specimen falls on the latter's surface without a significant change of energy.

The ^{55}Fe source is in the form of a disc pressed into a frame. The window for the exit of the radiation is made of beryllium foil. To improve the measurement geometry, collimators are mounted onto the sources. The collimator for the ^{238}Pu source is made of molybdenum in the form of a grating with 10 x 6 mm mesh size and 4 mm height. The collimator for the ^{55}Fe source is made of copper plate with a cylindrical hole of 5 x 5 mm size. Such collimation brings down the background level of scattered radiation, while at the same time preserving a sufficiently large sample-irradiation area.

Dectectors of X-radiation

The gas-discharge proportional counters used in the instrument have a working volume of 18x57 mm and an input window diameter of 6 mm. The counter filling is

90% Kr and 10% CO_2, the pressure being 2.9×10^4 Pa. The counter housing is made
of stainless steel 0.3 mm thick. The anode of the source is a tungsten filament of 0.1
mm diameter. The input counter window is made of vacuum-tight beryllium foil
about 40 μm thick. The detection unit, which accommodates the soil receiver and the
sample, is filled with dry nitrogen under about 5.3×10^3 Pa pressure to avoid effusive
effects while bringing in the soil sample. Tests made under conditions simulating the
real ones have shown that the pressure in the measuring cell after the soil sample has
been brought in will increase by not more than 3.3×10^2 Pa.

Attenuation of X-radiation in the nitrogen medium is characterized by the
transmission coefficient:

$$K_{N_2} = I_1/I_0 = exp\,[-\mu_1\rho_1x_1],\qquad(2.2.1)$$

where I_0 and I_1 are the fluorescent radiation fluxes prior to and after the passage
through the nitrogen medium; $\mu_1=\mu(E)$ is the mass attenuation coefficient in
nitrogen; ρ_1 is the density of nitrogen under the pressure P; x_1 is the distance from the
surface of the analysed specimen to the input-counter window.

In the instrument, the input counter windows are at distances $x_1=50$ mm and
$x_2=70$ mm from the sample receiver bottom. Fig. 2.2.9 (a) gives the values of the
transmission coefficient of X-radiation through the nitrogen absorber for these
distances and two pressure values.

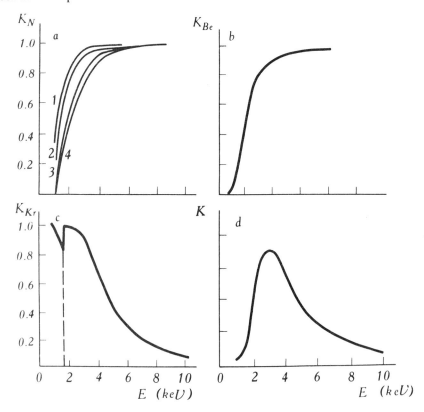

Fig. 2.2.9 — Absorption of fluorescent radiation in different media: a, in nitrogen; b, in
beryllium; c, in krypton; d, efficiency of recording radiation.

Fig. 2.2.9(b) gives the transmission coefficient of X-radiation through beryllium foil versus the energy of fluorescent radiation:

$$K_{Be} = \exp[-\mu_2 \rho_2 x_2) \qquad (2.2.2)$$

where: μ_2, ρ_2, x_2 are the mass attenuation coefficient, density and thickness of beryllium, respectively.

The absorption of fluorescent radiation by krypton inside the counter is shown in Fig. 2.2.9(c). The absorption coefficient in krypton is characterized by the expression:

$$K'_{Kr} = 1 - \exp[\mu_3 \rho_3 x_3] \qquad (2.2.3)$$

The curve was plotted for a krypton absorber of 15mm thickness for the gaseous mixture composition (90% Kr and 10% CO_2) and a pressure in the counter equal to 2.9×10^4 Pa.

Within the range of recorded energies there is observed an absorption jump for $E \sim 1.6$ keV (L series of Kr).

The total absorption of radiation emitted from the specimen, which is due to the absorption of radiation in nitrogen, beryllium and krypton (disregarding geometry), is determined by the relationship:

$$K = K_{N_2} K_{Be} K'_{Kr} \qquad (2.2.4)$$

As follows from the K versus energy curve (see Fig. 2.2.9(d)), the maximum recording efficiency of X-radiation by the given instrument corresponds to energies of about 3 keV.

The energy resolution of the instrument with respect to the line $Mn_{K\alpha}$ (5.9 keV) corresponds to 20-25%, depending on the detector resolution. Under working loads not greater than 10^3 pulses sec^{-1} the energy resolution and the gas amplification coefficient are almost invariable. During the preparation and conduct of the experiment the total number of pulses recorded by each of the counters did not exceed 10^7, i.e. much below the performance capacity of such types of counters, which is equal to 10^9 pulses. The performance capacity was assessed practically with respect to the batch of counters that were employed for compiling a library of spectra of different types of rocks.

Multichannel analyser.
Electrical signals from proportional counters arrive via spectrometric amplifiers at the amplitude-to-digital converter of the pulse analyser. The pulse analyser's functional diagram is shown in Fig. 2.2.10. Signals from the detection unit come to the inputs 1 and 2 of the amplitude-to-digital converter, which converts the amplitude of the incoming signal into a series of standard pulses, the number of which is proportional to the amplitude (serial unitary code). A series of pulses from the amplitude-to-digital converter arrives at the input of the address counter to be converted by the latter into the binary code-address of the channel into which the arrival of the pulses is to be recorded.

To achieve the separation of the analyser's channels into two groups there is available in the linear gate unit of the amplitude-to-digital converter a logical circuit interconnected with the last trigger of the address counter. This trigger is set in the position 1, if a signal appears at the input 2 of the amplitude-to-digital converter. Thus, recording of signals with respect to the input 2 is made in the second group of channels, whilst that with respect to the input 1 is done in the first group of channels.

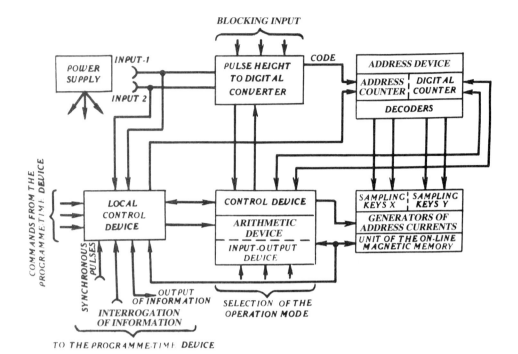

Fig. 2.2.10 — Functional diagram of the pulse-amplitude analyser of the X-ray fluorescence
spectrometer.

(Interconnected with the address counters are decoders for the sampling keys of the
coordinate buses of the on-line magnetic memory. Upon termination of a series of
pulses, a pulse from the amplitude-to-digital converter is sent to the control unit, this
pulse initiating a cycle of signal recording for the selected address in the first or
second group of analyser channels. The magnetic memory in the analyser is of the
sequential type. A consecutive request to selected address locations is achieved with
the aid of a counter, the condition of which is changed by clock pulses sent from the
control unit. An arithmetic device is used to perform the operation of adding a unit
to the contents of the magnetic memory channel for the selected address. The
sequence of the above operations and the time relationships between them are set by
the control unit. At the end of the recording cycle the control unit gives a signal to the
input device that it is ready to receive the next pulse from the detection unit for
measurement, since for the time period necessary for the codification of the
amplitude and its recording the amplitude-to-digital converter is blocked.

Commands from external devices, interrogation of the information stored in the
analyser and information output to the telemetry system are achieved with the aid of
a local control device interconnected to the control unit. In sending control voltages
and pulses the following operational programs of the spectrometer are carried out by
analyser control unit: selection of information, and output of information on request
from external devices with either destruction or preservation of the information. The
local control unit performs, moreover, the switching of the groups of counters in the
detection unit.

The mass of the analyser is 3.5 kg and power consumption 5 W. This analyser was
described in [17,21]. Table 2.2.5 lists the main characteristics of the X-ray
fluorescence spectrometer as a whole.

Table 2.2.5 – Main characteristics and parameters of X-ray fluorescent spectrometer

Mass	8 kg
Power Supply	9 W
Number of analyser channels	256 (2 x 1 28)
Channel capacity	$(2^{16}-1)$ pulses
Measured energy range	1.1–8 keV
Energy resolution	20–25% with respect to 5.9-keV line
Range of principal determined elements	From Mg to Fe
^{238}Pu source activity	50 mCi
^{55}Fe source activity	125 mCi

2.2.2.2. Testing and preflight preparation of the equipment

Design, manufacture, and preparation of the equipment for space flight necessitated a large volume of tests both on separate elements and on the apparatus as a whole. One of the principal elements of the instrument, which determines its measurement and operational characteristics, is the proportional gas-discharge counter. As seen from Fig. 2.2.9(b) and formula (2.2.2) absorption of radiation within the 1-3 keV energy range is greatly dependent on the thickness of the counter window. To enhance the determination sensitivity in the case of elements with low radiation energies it would be desirable to reduce the counter-window thickness. On the other hand, operational reliability and lifetime of the counter and, consequently, of the instrument as a whole require that the input counter window should be sufficiently strong. The presence of microholes, or a lack of stability of the material of the input counter window to pressure variations, are the main causes behind a breakdown of the instrument. Accordingly, much attention was given to the choice of material for the input window. Tests on the counters had revealed that to preserve their working capacity for a long period of time it was necessary that the input counter window be absolutely impermeable to gas (better than $10^{-8}1\mu$ ms^{-1} and should retain its mechanical strength under multiple pressure variations from 5 x 10^2 to 10^5Pa. Accordingly the counter window was made of beryllium about 40μm thick, although a higher efficiency could be achieved with a thinner foil.

Another element determining the instrument characteristics and influenced by external factors is the alpha-source ^{238}Pu. The safety film around the source, whilst being sufficiently thin to be able to let through the radiation of ^{238}Pu must at the same time be radiation-resistant and able to protect the source against the effects of the surrounding medium. As a check ·on the safety of the sources under testing conditions corresponding to the conditions of a long-term space flight and Venus' surface, the sources were tested for the effect of external factors: mechanical loads and the physico-chemical impact of the medium in the hermetic container of the detection unit were simulated. The tests had thrown light on the necessary technological specification when preparing the safety film and the design measures contributing to preservation of the source. Similar tests were made on the X-ray source, ^{55}Fe, though requirements for the radiation strength of its covering are not as essential as in the case of ^{238}Pu.

When preparing instruments for being set up aboard the spacecraft, both separate units and entire instruments were subjected to complex tests. Prior to and after the tests the spectral characteristics of the instruments must be the same. Climatic tests were conducted within the temperature range from $-50°C$ to $+50°C$. In this case, within the working temperature range, the spectral characteristics of the instrument did not essentially change, whilst the variation of the amplification coefficient was not above 4%.

Special attention was given to testing the spectrometer together with the rock-sample-delivery mechanism. These tests were undertaken both under normal climatic conditions and in a special chamber simulating conditions at Venus' surface (temperature up to 500°C and pressure up to 10^7Pa).

Under normal climatic conditions the main purpose of the tests on the instrument jointly with the sample delivery mechanism was to throw light on the distribution pattern of the rock sample in the sample receiver. This was necessary above all for undertaking model experiments and for acquisition of the library of standard rock spectra.

Tests in the chamber simulating conditions at Venus' surface made it possible to achieve complete modelling of the sampling process, introduction of the sample into the sample receiver, recording of the spectra and determination of element concentrations under real conditions.

All the tests on the instrument as a whole, both autonomous and complex ones, were conducted with the aid of the specially developed ground-control-measuring apparatus securing the possibility of assigning a working cyclogram for the spectrometer, bringing out information onto the computer.

Methodological studies

Successful performance of the analytical equipment at Venus' surface was the result of a large volume of methodological work, in the process of which numerous problems related to the instrument design, measurement and processing of fluorescent X-radiation spectra have been studied and solved.

Rigorous restrictions with respect to mass, overall dimensions and power supply, and specific requirements to meet mechanical and climatic conditions had greatly influenced the choice of the type of detector, measurement geometry, working régime, and, in a final analysis, the design of the instrument as a whole. Special attention was given to selecting an optimal measurement geometry, i.e. the mutual arrangement of radioisotopic sources, radiation detectors and analysed rock sample. In the course of long-term tests on the instrument, jointly with the sample-delivery mechanism, investigations were made into possible dusting of the radioisotopic sources and radiation detectors by the rock, as a result of which an optimal atmospheric pressure of about 4×10^3 Pa in the instrument's measuring cell was found. Since the magnitude of the pressure may affect the intensity of the analytical lines of the elements in the soft region of the spectrum, methodological studies were undertaken into the intensities of peaks and forms of spectra of different rocks and certain oxides while varying the pressure in the zone of analysis from 2×10^3 to 3.1×10^4 Pa.

The results of these investigations were used to introduce the necessary corrections into the spectra measured at Venus' surface.

An important factor in X-ray fluorescent spectral analysis is preparation of the sample. To secure reliable operation of the equipment no devices for sample formation had been incorporated into the sample-delivery mechanism. The rock sample was brought into the measuring cell in the same structural form as it had been taken in by the drill set.

Therefore, a cycle of model experiments was undertaken to investigate the dependency of form of the spectrum on particle size in the rock sample, the weight of the sample, and the position of the sample in the sample receiver. Measurements were made for one and the same rock by varying one of the parameters, the rest being held constant. Particle size varied from 0.25 to 5 mm and, weight from 0.3 to 7 g. Numerous versions of the sample arrangement were also investigated. The results of these investigations were taken into account in processing the spectra measured at Venus' surface and in calculating systematic errors of the determinated concentrations of principal rock-forming elements. The most probable distribution of the rock sample in the sample receiver was used in the course of preflight calibration of the equipment and in acquiring the library of standard rock spectra.

Preparations for the experiment involved measurements of the resolution and efficiency of detectors, determinations of the dependence of amplification coefficients of the spectrometer channels and of the drifting of the 'zero' of energy scales with temperature, as well as determinations of the performance capacities of gas-discharge counters.

A special cycle of methodological work was devoted to studying the spectrum of an empty sample receiver. The sample receiver and all the walls of the measuring chamber are coated with fluoroplast and, therefore, in the absence of a sample in the sample receiver the detectors will be recording only scattered X-radiation from the radioisotopic sources. The spectrum of scattered radiation of the radioisotopic sources in the case of an empty sample receiver represents a curve with two well-expressed peaks. The peak lying in the middle part of the spectrum is due to the scattering of X-radiation from the ^{238} Pu source. The second peak is due to the scattering of X-radiation from the ^{55}Fe source having the energy of 5.9 keV. These peaks can be well approximated by a sum of Gaussian distributions

$$f(x) = a_1 + a_2 x + a_3 \exp\left[- \frac{(x-a_4)^2}{2a_5{}^2} \right] + a_6 \exp\left[- \frac{(x-a_7{}^2)}{(2a_8{}^2} \right] \qquad (2.2.5)$$

where the coefficients a_i are to be determined by the least-squares method. The gravity centres of these peaks were used as checks on the instrument energy scale. Fig. 2.2.11 gives the spectra of an empty sample receiver, as measured on the spectrometer, and an approximation of these spectra by a sum of Gaussian distributions.

Fig. 2.2.12. gives for certain elements the intensity of fluorescent radiation versus concentration. Used as a matrix was Li_2CO_3. As seen from the figure, in the case of the lightest elements (Al, Si) the dependence of the count rate upon concentration is relatively weak, close to a linear one. With a greater atomic number for the element there is observed a more prominent dependence under low concentrations and, vice versa, a weaker dependence under high concentrations (see K, Ti).

Figs. 2.2.13. and 2.2.14. show by way of example the spectra of fluorescent radiation of certain rocks, as measured by the spectrometer described. Fig. 2.2.13.

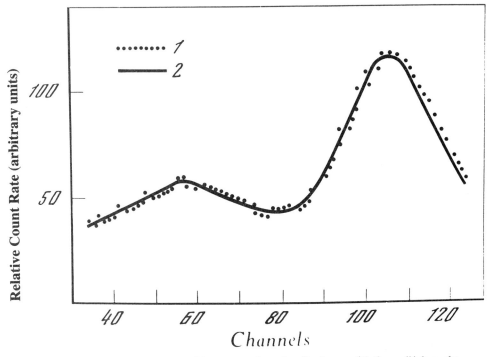

Fig. 2.2.11 — Fluorescent spectra of the empty soil receiver (background) before soil is brought into it: 1, measured spectrum; 2, theoretical spectrum.

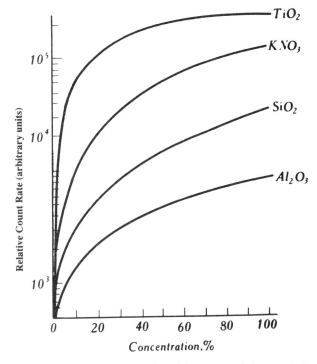

Fig. 2.2.12 — Radiation intensity as a function of the content of elements in the sample.

shows the spectra of granite, excited separately by the ^{238}Pu and ^{55}Fe sources. It can be seen that radiation of light elements (Mg, Al, Si) is weakly excited by the ^{55}Fe source and strongly by the ^{238}Pu source. In the region of heavier elements (K, Ca, Ti) the reverse is true. A simultaneous use of both sources yields a possibility of effectively exciting the fluorescent radiation over the entire range of rock-forming elements from Mg to Fe, as is illustrated in Fig. 2.2.14. This figure shows the spectra of rocks widely occurring in the Earth's crust — granite, basalt, dunite.

2.2.2.3. Processing of X-ray fluorescent spectra

The complex physical conditions of the Venusian experiment necessitated the use of unsophisticated and reliable detectors, i.e. proportional gas-discharge counters. The limited energy resolution of the instrument, which is the result of this, accounts for certain features found in measuring the intensity of spectral lines and in determining the contents of separate elements. In X-ray fluorescent radiation spectra of rocks the analytical lines of principal elements are observed to be distributed into three groups: (1) magnesium, aluminium, and silicon; (2) potassium, calcium, and titanium; (3) manganese and iron. Therefore, identification in such spectra of analytical lines of separate elements leads to great errors and this, in its turn, does not permit traditional methods of relationship and multiple regression equations to be used for spectrum processing [2]. Accordingly, as the first stage in spectra processing use was made of a statistical method for the comparison of the analysed spectra with the library spectra of standard rocks with a known chemical composition. This method is based on the use of correlation analysis and Pearson's correlation criterion (criterion χ^2. A sign of the adequacy of the two distributions — for the analysed and library spectra — is the maximum value of the correlation coefficient r and the minimum χ^2.

The values of χ^2 are determined from the formula:

$$\chi^2 = \frac{1}{n-1} \; \Sigma_i \; \frac{(x_i \text{-} y_i)^2}{y_i} \; , \tag{2.2.6.}$$

where x_i is the number of counts in the channel for the analysed rock spectrum, y_i is the number of counts in the channel for the standard rock spectrum, and n is the number of channels.

Calculation of the values of paired correlation coefficients is made from the expression

$$r = \frac{\sum_{i=1}^{} (x_i \text{-} \overline{x})\,(Y_i \text{-} Y)}{(n\text{-}1)\,S_x S_y} \tag{2.2.7.}$$

where x, y, n have the same values as in formula (2.2.6.), and x, y are the number of counts for the analysed and standard rock averaged for all of the spectrum channels.

$$S_x = \sqrt{\frac{\Sigma_i (x_i \text{-} x)^2}{(n\text{-}1)}} \quad S_y = \sqrt{\frac{\Sigma_i (Y_i \text{-} \overline{Y})^2}{(n\text{-}1)}} \tag{2.2.8.}$$

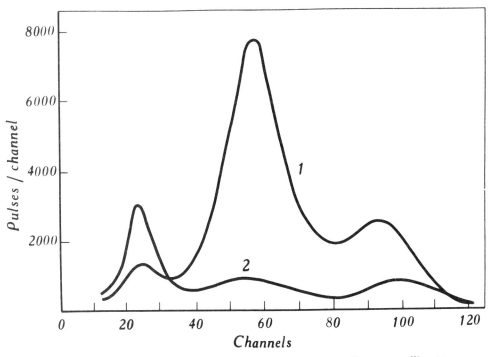

Fig. 2.2.13 — Spectra of fluorescent radiation excited in granite by the ^{55}Fe (1), and ^{238}Pu (2), sources.

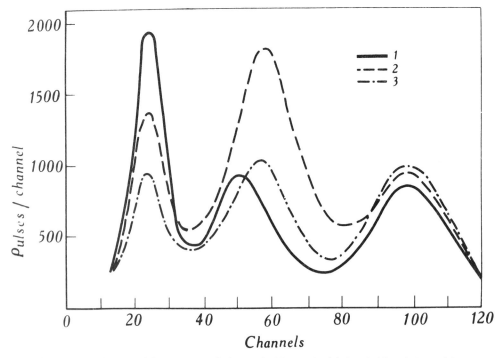

Fig. 2.2.14 — Spectra of fluorescent radiation excited in granite (1), basalt (2) and dunite (3) by ^{238}Pu and ^{55}Fc sourccs uscd simultancously.

Realization of the given method of analysis called for the compilation of a library of standard rock spectra. Accordingly, with an instrument analogous to onboard instruments, a library of 200 rocks with a known elemental composition were measured. In further discussions this library will be called 'basic'. The instruments to be installed in the Venera-13 and Venera-14 spacecraft were used in the period of their preflight calibration to measure 15–20 standard spectra of different types of rocks in each. This library will be referred to as 'instrumental'. It was measured, together with the spectra of the oxides of the elements from Mg to Fe, using all of the instruments. The basic library is represented by different types of terrestrial rocks significantly different in their composition. The choice of rock standards was made in such a way that within the confines of a single type there should be maximum differences in the concentrations of rock-forming elements.

Table 2.2.6 presents the functional diagram of the first stage of spectral analysis in a computer (HICOR program) [20]. Realization of this program resulted in the determination of a preliminary composition of the analysed rock. Should a discrepancy be observed in any region of the analysed spectrum with the standard spectrum selected after the HICOR program, an iterative method based on a variation of the concentrations of analysed elements (ITERA program) would be additionally employed. A functional diagram of this program is given in Table 2.2.7. [20]. Simultaneously, the analogue instrument was used to carry out experimental modelling of the rock spectra measured on Venus, involving variation of the concentrations of separate elements. Until convergence of the standard and analysed spectra within the composition determination error was obtained, about 10 iterations were necessary, as a rule.

The program of preparation for the experiment involved an analysis of control rock samples. Once the analysis was completed, the processing results were compared with library data for the given rocks. The analysis results were found to be coincident with library data within the experimental errors.

2.2.2.4. Measurements on the surface of Venus

Once the descent vehicle had landed on Venus' surface the work of the X-ray fluorescent spectrometer was carried out in accordance with a preset cyclogram (Fig. 2.2.15). During the first 32 s after landing the first group of counters (a nearby and distant one) measured the spectra of an empty sample receiver. Afterwards these spectra were output. Simultaneously, information was being sent from the temperature pickups, a pressure pickup and intensimeters. The next stage involved the measurement over 192 s of the spectra of an empty sample receiver by a second group of counters (likewise a nearby and a distant one) and output of the corresponding information. About 4 min after landing a rock sample was brought into the sample receiver with the aid of the sample-delivery mechanism. The next stage of work involved successive measurements of the rock spectra alternately by the first and second group of counters with the output of information following acquisition of each set of spectra. Measurements were being made during the entire time of active operation of the landers on Venus' surface. The Venera -13 lander was operating on Venus' surface for 127 min, in the case of the Venera -14 lander, 53 min.

During the period of active operation on the surface, the Venera -13 lander measured 38 spectra, and Venera -14 measured 20 spectra. The length of measurement of each of the spectra by the first-group counters was 384 s, and by the second-group of counters 192 s.

Table 2.2.6. – Block Scheme of 'HICOR' Program

Introduction of the spectra of reference rocks form the basic $A_i = f(E)$ or from the instrumental $\beta_i = f(E)$ libraries

↓

Introduction of the spectrum of the rock analysed $S_i = f(E)$

↓

Introduction of the limits for the section of spectrum of the rock analysed, M_1 — first, M — last channels

↓

Obtaining the X^2 values for the rock analysed and reference rock

$$\chi^2 = \frac{1}{n-1} \, \Sigma_m \frac{(x_m - y_m)^2}{y_m}$$

χ_m — number of impulses in the channel for the rock analysed,

Y_m — number of impulses in the channel for the reference rock,

$$m_1 < m = m_2 - m_1 + 1$$

↓

Obtaining the r values for the rock analysed and reference rocks

$$r = \frac{\Sigma_m (\chi_m - \chi)(y_m - y)}{(n-1) S_x S_y} \; ; \qquad y = \frac{\Sigma_m y_m}{} \; ; \qquad x = \frac{\Sigma_m x_m}{n}$$

$$S_x = \sqrt{\frac{\Sigma_m (x_m - x)}{n-1}} : \qquad S_y = \sqrt{\frac{\Sigma_m (y_m - y)_2}{\Sigma_m (y_m n - 1)}}$$

↓

Selection of these reference rocks having maximum r and minimum X^2 with respect to the rock analysed.

↓

Is it necessary to analyse another part of the spectrum of the rock analysed?

YES

NO ↓

Output of the results

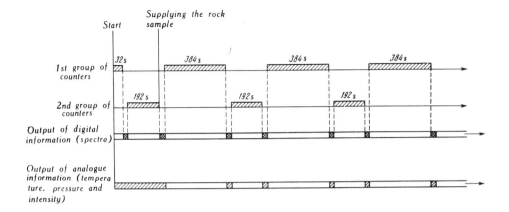

Fig. 2.2.15 — Cyclogram of the operation of the X-ray fluorescence spectrometer at the Venusian surface.

Throughout the working cycle of the instrument, analogue information was also periodically transmitted from the pickups installed in the instrument: a pressure pickup, two temperature pickups and two intensimeters. The entire analogue information testified to normal performance of the instrument. Fig. 2.2.16. shows by way of example the fluorescent radiation spectra of the Venusian rock samples taken in the landing areas of the Venera -13 and Venera -14 space probes. Both the spectra were measured over 192 s by one of the close-lying detectors.

2.2.2.5   Analysis of spectra and the results of experiments
The first stage of processing involved an analysis of the spectra of an empty sample receiver: the gravity centres of scattered radiation peaks were determined. Since the energies corresponding to the maxima of these peaks are known, calibration channel versus energy curves could be plotted for the moment of sample measurement. This enabled reliable determination of the position of the peaks of principal rock-forming elements in the spectra of the Venusian rock.

The values of the amplification coefficients and 'zero drifting' necessary for spectral transformation were determined in two ways. The first involved determination of the gravity centres of the energy lines of oxides (for library spectra) and of scattering peaks of an empty sample receiver (for Venusian spectra), and obtaining by the least squares method of the line $E = a + bn$, where n is the number of the channel, a and b are parameters of the channel-energy line.

Then the values of the variations of the amplification coefficient G and of the drifting of the spectrometer scale zero D were determined as follows:

$$G = b_i/bk; D = \frac{1}{b_k} (a_k - a_i)$$

where a_i, b_i and a_k, b_k are parameters of channel–energy lines, correspondingly, for the analysed Venusian spectra and library spectra.

The second method consisted of an alignment of the spectra of an empty sample receiver, as measured on Venus, with those of an empty sample receiver in a

Table 2.2.7. – Block Scheme of 'ITERA' Program

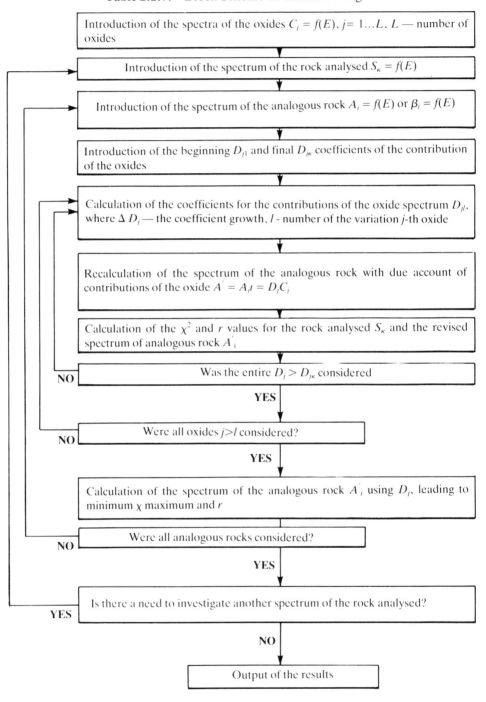

Introduction of the spectra of the oxides $C_j = f(E)$, $j= 1...L$, L — number of oxides

Introduction of the spectrum of the rock analysed $S_\kappa = f(E)$

Introduction of the spectrum of the analogous rock $A_i = f(E)$ or $\beta_i = f(E)$

Introduction of the beginning D_{j1} and final $D_{j\kappa}$ coefficients of the contribution of the oxides

Calculation of the coefficients for the contributions of the oxide spectrum D_{jl}, where ΔD_l — the coefficient growth, l - number of the variation j-th oxide

Recalculation of the spectrum of the analogous rock with due account of contributions of the oxide $A' = A_l l = D_l C_l$

Calculation of the χ^2 and r values for the rock analysed S_κ and the revised spectrum of analogous rock A'_i

Was the entire $D_j > D_{j\kappa}$ considered

NO

YES

Were all oxides $j>l$ considered?

NO

YES

Calculation of the spectrum of the analogous rock A'_i using D_j, leading to minimum χ maximum and r

Were all analogous rocks considered?

NO

YES

Is there a need to investigate another spectrum of the rock analysed?

YES

NO

Output of the results

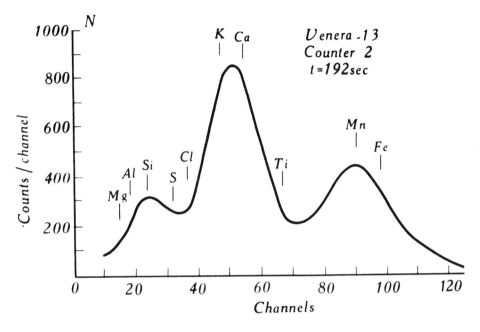

(a)

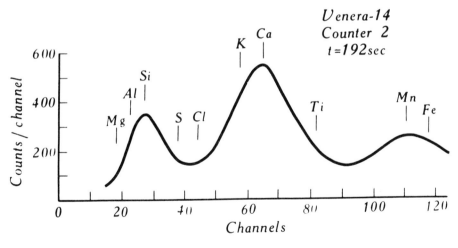

(b)

Fig. 2.2.16 — Fluorescent radiation spectra of Venusian rock measured by Venera 13 (a) and
Venera 14 (b).

laboratory analogue instrument on which the basic library of spectra was measured. The alignment criterion for these two distributions was the minimum value of χ^2.

To introduce a correction for a difference in the recording efficiency of X-radiation, the spectra of pure oxides of the elements from magnesium to iron were used of the same rocks, as measured on the laboratory analogue instrument and on flight instruments prior to setting up the latter in the spacecraft.

Furthermore, a correction for the radioactive decay of the ^{55}Fe nuclide, which has a half-life of 2.6 years, was introduced into the spectra measured at Venus' surface. Comparison of the spectra measured on Venus with the spectral library involved the introduction of only a single correction: for the decay of the ^{55}Fe radioisotope source.

The next processing stage involved a correlation analysis and a comparison of the analysed and library spectra by means of the use of Pearson's correlation criterion. Thereafter the spectra of the selected library rocks were converted by the iteration method, as a result of which the correlation coefficient reached 0.99.

The concentration of oxides in the analysed rock was determined as an average for the library rocks selected after the HICOR program and converted after the ITERA program. The overall functional diagram of the processing program for the spectra of Venusian rocks is given in Table 2.2.8 [20].

An error in determining oxide concentrations in the Venusian rock is made up of a random error, which is determined as a root-mean-square deviation, and a systematic error resulting from the presence of some random factors associated with the indeterminancy of the geometry and weight of the analysed rock, as well as with the particle size of the rock brought in by the sampler. The aforementioned methodological work conducted in the preflight period enabled this error to be determined.

By processing the spectra measured at Venus' surface the elemental composition of rocks at the landing sites of the Venera 13 and Venera 14 space probes (see Table 1.3.5.), was obtained.

It was found that the rocks at the two sites are quite similar in their content of oxides of principal rock-forming elements (Si, Al, Mg, Fe), thus giving evidence of their belonging to the same class of rocks. At the same time, a significant difference is observed in the content of Ca, K and other elements. This fact appears to be an indication of the different conditions of formation of the rocks concerned.

As is known from radar data, Venus' surface is subdivided into three main types of geomorphological terrain: high-mountainous plateaux, rolling uplands, and smooth lowlands, which occupy respectively 8%, 65% and 27% of the surface territory [22].

In this classification, rolling uplands are the most widespread type of Venusian terrain. They lie at 0.5–2 km heights above the zero level (R_o = 6051 km). The abundance of large circular structures (presumably of an impact origin) and the smoothness of the relief are an indication of the old age of these areas. It can be supposed that the rolling uplands, making up a significant part of the Venusian surface, are a preserved old crust of Venus.

Another structural–morphological type of terrain, the second most common, lying at 0.5–2 km below the zero level are lowlands with a relatively smooth relief, within the limits of which no large impact craters have been recorded. This is evidence that they are young compared with the rolling uplands, whilst an analogy with the Moon and Mars enables one to presume their basaltic composition.

Table 2.2.8

GENERAL SCHEME OF INFORMATION PROCESSING

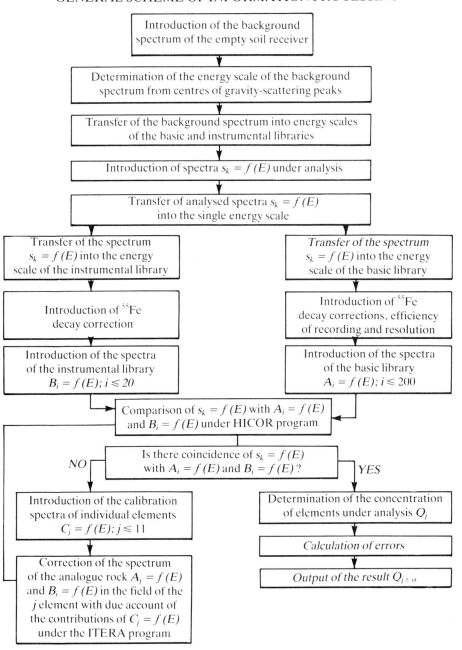

Less widespread on Venus and, supposedly, most intricately structured are the high-mountainous plateaux (Ishtar Terra and Aphrodite Terra) with a strongly broken relief and numerous mountain ranges.

The Venera 13 spaceprobe landed at an elevation lying about 1.5 km above the zero level at a point with the coordinates (psi) $\phi = -7°30$' and $\lambda = 303°11$', and Venera 14 in a lower-lying area about 0.5 km above the zero surface level, at a point with the coordinates $\emptyset = -13° 15'$ and $\lambda = 310° 09$'.

Comparison between the panoramas of the landing areas of the two space probe reveals that the surface morphology and the pattern of rocks at the landing areas are essentially different [16].

At the landing area of the Venera 13 space probe what we see is a stony desert with low outcroppings of bedrock; in the depressions between the latter there is visible a darker surface of loose, fine-grained soil. As follows from Table 1.3.5, the composition of the rock at the landing area of the space probe is represented by potassium high-magnesial alkaline basalt. On the Earth this type of igneous rock is fairly uncommon. The high contents in the rock investigated by Venera 13 of potassium, and magnesium, for a low silica content, furnish evidence of a great depth of generation of the initial melts and of the low degree of their differentiation. This rock appears to be old. This also finds support in the efforts made by the drill set, which corresponded to drilling in weathered porous basalt [23], and in the appearance of the eroded rock, as seen on the panorama.

In the panoramas photographed by the Venera 14 space probe, there is seen a relatively level stretch of a stony plain — a continuous rocky outcrop stretching towards the horizon. Here the rock has a layered structure with horizontal stratification. Its surface is observed to have tortuous fissures. In contrast to the Venera 13 space probe's landing area, no perceptible accumulations of dark soil are to be seen within the visibility limits. The composition of rock at the space probe's landing site corresponds to oceanic tholeiitic basalts which are widespread on the Earth. The efforts of the drill set were in this case less than at the Venera 13 landing area and corresponded to a compact ashy material of the volcanic tuff type [23]. As is known, such material is thrown out on the Earth as a result of explosive volcanic eruptions. However, tholeiitic basalts of the Earth's crust are not endowed with an explosive origin. They are formed as a result of lava effusions of a more viscous magma.

By comparing the Earth, Venus and the Moon it is easy to see that the main types of terrain on all these bodies are similar: the old crust (continents on the Earth, rolling uplands on Venus, and continents on the Moon) and younger formations (oceanic crust on the Earth, lowlands on Venus, and circular seas on the Moon).

Differentiation of the Earth's matter is known to have led to the formation of continental crust consisting principally of granites and metamorphosed rocks, and of the oceanic crust consisting of tholeiitic basalts. Differentiation of the Moon's matter terminated in the formation of an old continental gabbro-anorthositic crust and relatively young basaltic seas. Data obtained by the Venera 13 and Venera 14 space probes on the composition of Venusian rocks favour a conclusion that the evolutionary development of Venus is different from that of the Earth and, particularly, from that of the Moon.

It appears that on Venus the absence of water in the period of formation of rocks is responsible for the fact that we do not observe a great diversity of rocks. Possibly, the main part of Venus' surface (more than 80%), including rolling uplands and smooth lowlands, is covered only by basaltic rocks having outcropped to the surface from different depths and at different times of crust formation. Exceptions may, possibly, be only Ishtar Terra and Aphrodite Terra, which have not yet been investigated.

Such are the concepts of Venus' surface and crust that result from an analysis of data on the chemical composition of Venusian rocks at the landing sites of Venera-13 and Venera-14.

2.2.2.6. X-ray radiometric analysis of the Venusian rock from VeGa 2

The VeGa 2 space probe was launched in December 1984. In June 1985 it delivered into Venus' atmosphere a descent module designed to investigate the surface of Venus, its atmosphere and clouds. After completing its manoeuvre in the gravitational field of Venus, the space probe continued the flight to Comet Halley. The encounter with the comet took place in March 1986. One of the main tasks of the space probe was determining the chemical composition of the Venusian rock in the new geological–morphological terrain. The chemical composition of the rock was determined by an X-ray radiometric method which had been applied before on Veneras 13 and 14.

The VeGa 2 lander is similar to the Venera landers. However, due to its new set of scientific instruments, the design of the lander and its appearance were changed. Some changes were also introduced in the sampling and transportation devices.

The landing site of VeGa 2 was in equatorial eastern Aphrodite Terra. This region displays variable topopgraphy, ranging from lowland plains in the north-west through foothill mountains elevated 3–4 km above the reference datum (6051.0 km). The highest regions are in the Atla mountains to the east, or the central Aphrodite highlands to the south (see Fig. 2.2.17 facing page 47 in colour section).

All previous landing sites on the surface of Venus were in the upland rolling plains or in smooth lowlands. In contrast to them, the VeGa 2 landing site was on the slope of Aphrodite Terra. The average elevation at this point ($\phi = -7°05'$ and $= 179°08'$) is 1.8 ± 0.4 km. The average reflectivity is 0.11, with a standard deviation of 0.04. The average roughness is 2.6°, with a standard deviation of 1.87°. Such values of reflectivity and roughness generally suggest rock surfaces with some degree of soil cover.

The composition of the rock at the VeGa 2 landing site was determined by the X-ray radiometric method.

To take measurements, use was made of an instrument which was an improved version of the X-ray fluorescence spectrometer carried by Veneras 13 and 14.

The experience of working with the X-ray fluorescence spectrometer aboard Veneras 13 and 14 enabled the introduction of some modifications in the instrument structure aimed at enhancing its reliability, improving its analytical characteristics, expanding the range of elements analysed and increasing the sensitivity of measurement of these elements.

To raise the sensitivity of recording elements, the thickness of the beryllium windows of the counters was reduced and the intensity of the radioisotope sources was increased. This enabled the expansion of the range of recorded elements.

Four counters are installed in the device. Three of them have the filling of 90% Kr and 10% CH_4, and one counter has the filling of 90% Xe and 10% CH_4. The latter counter has an energy scale extending to 15–20 keV, which makes it possible to record elements heavier than iron.

The X-ray fluorescence spectrometer was operated on the surface of Venus in keeping with the given program. The device was switched on at an altitude of about 25 km above Venus' surface.

For 35 min, up to the moment of the lander's contact with the planetary surface, the spectrometer was calibrated — background spectra were collected when the soil receiver was empty. One spectrum was collected over 190 s. Simultaneously with the set of spectra, analogue parameters were recorded — the temperature of the detection unit and the pulse analyser, the pressure inside the analytical cell of the detection unit, and the total count-rate of the fluorescent quanta of each counter. The accumulated information was transmitted via telemetry channels back to the Earth.

During the first 172 s after landing of the device on the Venusian surface, the sample was selected by drilling with the soil sampler, the gas atmosphere which surrounded the sample selected was removed (i.e. the pressure was reduced to the 7.3×10^3 Pa necessary for operation of the X-ray fluorescence spectrometer) and the sample was transported inside the lander. After delivery of the Venusian rock sample into the soil receiver, the spectra of excited X-ray fluorescent radiation were measured and transmitted via telemetry channels to the Earth. According to the cyclogram of measurements after the delivery of the sample into the soil receiver, each counter carried out five measurements of the fluorescence spectrum of the Venusian rock; the duration of the data-acquisition time was 190 s.

Analysis of the Venusian rock spectra was carried out according to the following scheme.

At first the energy scale of the measured spectra was corrected to achieve correspondence to the energy scale of the preflight calibrations. Then the positions of the lines of analysed elements in the measured spectra were determined.

The next stage was the introduction of the correction for the decay of ^{55}Fe, the correlation analysis and the HICOR program [20, 52, 53].

After analysis under the HICOR program, rocks whose spectra coincided most closely with the spectra measured on VeGa 2 were singled out. Then the modification of the selected spectra of rock standards was effected under the ITERA program until they coincided with the spectra of soil analysed. This stage is in the main similar to that described in [20, 52, 53].

As a result of the processing of information obtained from the VeGa 2 lander the chemical composition of the Venusian rock was determined. Data obtained are listed in Table 1.3.5. [54, 55].

A comparison with the data on variations of the composition of igneous rocks of the Earth and the Moon combined with the experimental petrology data permits identification of the rock as a possible analogue of terrestrial olivine gabbro-norite. Such rock is distributed on the Earth both among Precambrian stratified massifs and in Mesozoic ofiolitic complexes. The heightened concentration of SiO_2 in the rock and other petrochemical peculiarities can testify that its formation occurred in the course of the differentiation of some initial melt containing approximately 1% by mass of H_2O. Such melts under terrestrial conditions separate from the mantle at temperatures of 1200–1400°C and at a depth of 10 to 60 km.

Thus, we already have the concept of the types of magmatic rocks occurring in Venus' main geological–morphological regions which correspond to different tectonic and magmatic stages of its development. These are old upland rolling plains (Venera 8 and 13 landing sites) consisting of potassium nepheline syenite; flat lowlands (Venera 14 landing site) covered with volcanic tuff of tholeiitic basalts; young shield volcanic structures (Venera 9 and 10 landing sites) and, finally, the slopes of high-mountain massifs (VeGa 2 landing site) which apparently have a composition close to olivine gabbro–norite rocks.

Knowledge of the chemical composition of rocks in these different geological–morphological regions, combined with estimates of the relative age of the terrain on the basis of the crater density, makes it possible even now to approach an understanding of the history of magmatism on Venus and the chronology of the events which formed its surface and crust.

2.2.3 X-RAY RADIOMETRIC ANALYSIS OF AEROSOLS IN VENUS' CLOUD LAYER FROM VENERAS 12 AND 14

Since the beginning of the direct probing of Venus with the aid of space vehicles (satellites, probes and landers), the main attention has been given to its atmosphere. During that period the temperature, pressure, density and gaseous composition of the atmosphere at different heights have been determined. In recent years in studying the Venusian atmosphere special interest has been shown in Venus' cloud layer. However, with the help of space vehicles it was possible to obtain only an altitudinal distribution of aerosols, i.e. the variation of particle density and sizes with height [24–27]. The nature of the aerosols remained unknown until recently, unless we take into account certain indirect indications resulting from ground observation or from general geochemical considerations. The results of investigations into Venus' atmosphere and clouds have been most fully summarized in [28–30]. The first attempt at direct determination of the elemental composition of the aerosols in Venus' cloud layer was made with the help of the equipment installed on the Venera-12 space probe [15]. That experiment was repeated by the Venera-14 space probe [31].

2.2.3.1. Equipment and method of studying aerosols

The descent vehicles of the Venera -12 and Venera -14 space probes carried an instrument used for the X-ray fluorescent analysis of the aerosol composition, as well as for determining the density and vertical structure of Venus' cloud layer [15, 31].

The elemental composition of the aerosols being collected by the instrument was determined by the X-ray radiometric method. This method is based on the excitation by a radioisotopic source of characteristic fluorescence radiation of the aerosol atoms and a subsequent registration of the spectrum of excited radiation. The vertical structure of the cloud layer was determined from the flux density of the fluorescent radiation of the aerosol atoms, reflecting the latter's accumulation the filter, as recorded during the descent of the space probe.

The aerosol analyser is composed of two units — the detection unit and the electronic unit. With respect to the performed functions and design, the detection unit can be subdivided into three main parts (Fig. 2.2.18):

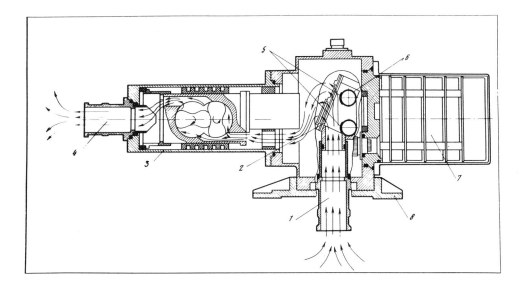

Fig. 2.2.18 — Detection unit structure of the X-ray fluorescence analyser: 1, input channel; 2, microsupercharger; 3, output channel; 4, filter; 5, ^{55}Fe radioisotope source; 6, proportional X-ray counters; 7, electronic compartment; 8, frame.

(a)   A central analytical part comprising a filter upon which the investigated aerosol atoms are precipitating; radioisotopic sources ^{109}Cd and ^{55}Fe irradiating the aerosol atoms; proportional gas-discharge counters recording fluorescent radiation.

(b)   A microbooster (microsupercharger) adjoining the central part, which secures the pumping of the atmosphere through the instrument and the collection of aerosol atoms on the filter.

(c)   The electronic compartment of the detection unit, which accommodates preamplifiers, amplifiers, and high-voltage and low-voltage supply sources.

Taking care that the parameters of the apparatus were preserved both in the on-the-ground tests and during its presence in vacuum on the flight from the Earth to Venus, the detection unit in the instrument was pressurized. There are present in the detection unit an entrance and an exit channel for pumping of the atmosphere through the instrument, which continue to be hermetically sealed until the beginning of measurements on the planet. Depressurization of the channels prior to the beginning of work by the instrument is made on command from the program-timing device on the descent vehicle.

The electronic unit of the instrument, set up in the space probe's pressurized compartment, is a multichannel analyser of pulse amplitudes. The amplitude analyser has 256 channels, the capacity of each of them being $(2^{16}-1)$ pulses. The analyser memory is divided into two parts, 128 channels in each, each part recording pulses from a separate detector. Making measurements with the aid of two spectrometers enhances the reliability of the experiment. Table 2.2.29 lists the main characteristics of the instruments.

Prior to being set up in the spacecraft, the instrument was calibrated under laboratory conditions for the content of certain constituents, the existence of which was presumed on the basis of different geochemical models and certain ground observation data.

Table 2.2.9 — Main characteristics of the aerosol composition analyser

Mass	10 kg
Power supply	34 W
Number of channels in amplitude analyser	256 (2 x 128)
Capacity of analyser channel	$2^{16}-1$
Energy range of recorded radiation	1.1 – 10 keV
Energy resolution with respect to 5.9-keV line	20–25%
Quantity of gas pumped through the instrument	0.11 m^3 min^{-1}
Filter material	Acetylcellulose
Determined chemical elements	From Al to Hg
Activity of the ^{55}Fe source	60 mCi
Activity of the ^{109}Cd source	20 mCi

Fig. 2.2.19 shows calibration spectra obtained in the precipitation at the filter of different amounts of sulphur, chlorine, and mercury, as well as under different contents of argon in the atmosphere. Fluorescent radiation of the K-series of sulphur, chlorine, and argon was excited by the radiation of the ^{55}Fe source, whilst the M- and L-series of sulphur were excited by the radiation of the ^{55}Fe and ^{109}Cd sources. Measurements were made in an atmosphere of carbon dioxide gas under normal conditions (pressure approximately 9.8×10^4 Pa (1 kg cm^{-2}), temperature approximately 20°C). Although sulphur, chlorine, and argon have fairly similar energies of fluorescent radiation and in the case of a joint presence yield a total (unresolved) peak, the contribution of each of the constituents can be determined by processing the measured spectrum in a computer with the use of a library of monoelemental

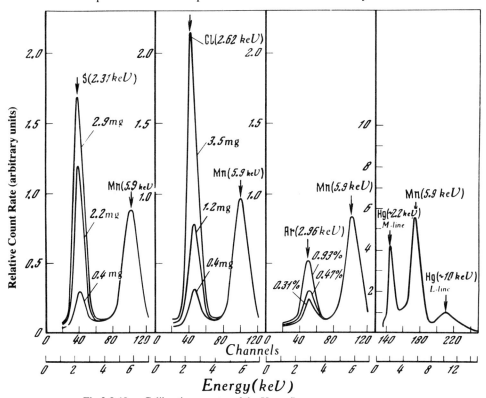

Fig.2.2.19 — Calibration spectra of the X-ray fluorescence spectrometer.

spectra. Since an increase in atmospheric pressure is accompanied by an increase in the absorption of fluorescent radiation (and moreover, the lower the energy, the higher the absorption), the intensity of the peaks shown in Fig. 2.2.19 is dependent on pressure. This dependence is shown by way of example in Fig. 2.2.20 (curve 2) for chlorine ($E_{k\alpha} \approx 2.62$ keV). As seen from the figure, within the pressure range 9.8 x $10^3 - 1.5 \times 10^5$ Pa ($0.1 - 1.5$ kg cm^{-2}), in which measurements were made, the magnitude of the peak decreased by a factor of about 2. The same figure shows the variation of the intensity of radiation of Mn ($E_{k\alpha} \approx 5.9$ keV) as dependent on pressure (curve 1). It is seen that an increase in pressure is accompanied by an increase in the number of quanta scattered by the atmosphere in a reverse direction, i.e. towards the detectors. Thus, even for the same amount of aerosol at the filter, an increase in pressure leads to an increase in count-rate in the reference peak of Mn. These factors were taken into account in the calibration of the apparatus and in processing measurement results. Account was also taken of the fact that the aerosol atoms were accumulating in quantity as the space probe descended in Venus' atmosphere. At the first stage, the authors [15, 31] proceeded from an assumption that accumulation of aerosols was proportional to the volume of gas pumped through the instrument. However, for a more correct determination of concentrations they should have proceeded from the readings of the ratemeter registering a variation of the total count-rate with the accumulation of aerosols.

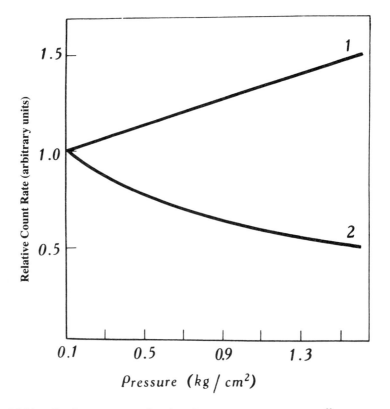

Fig. 2.2.20 — Total count-rate as a function of pressure: 1, X-quanta of the ^{55}Fe source scattered in the atmosphere; 2, X-quanta excited in chlorine.

Thus, in the calibration of the apparatus and in processing the obtained information, account was taken of the following factors subject to variation in the process of the experiment: an increasing density of the atmosphere and a variation (increase) of the quantity of aerosols collected at the filter of the instrument.

2.2.3.2 Measurements in Venus' atmosphere: the results of the experiment

Switching-on of the instruments was made on command from the program-timing device in the descent vehicle. Pumping of the atmosphere was started at the moment when the atmosphere pressure was about 9.8×10^3 Pa and the temperature about $0°C$, and continued while the space vehicle was descending, a period of about 9 min. Thereafter, when the space vehicle reached the 1.5×10^5 Pa pressure level and the temperature of the atmosphere rose to $100°C$, the instruments were switched off. During that time about 1 m^3 of atmosphere was pumped through every one of the instruments. The spectra were recorded throughout the time the atmosphere was being pumped through and the aerosol atoms were being collected. The registered spectra were stored in the analyser memories and on command were relayed to the Earth.

Fig. 2.2.21(a) shows the fluorescent radiation spectra of aerosol atoms, as measured by the Venera 12 space probe. The left-hand spectrum was obtained by irradiating the aerosols from the ^{55}Fe source, and the right-hand one from the ^{55}Fe and ^{109}Cd sources. In both spectra the right-hand peak is used as a reference. It corresponds to the energy of $Mn(E_k = 5.9\,keV)$. The left-hand peak is due to the X-ray fluorescent radiation of aerosols. Fig. 2.2.21(b) shows the aerosol spectra, as measured by the Venera 14 space probe. In this experiment ^{55}Fe sources alone were used, but their activity was twice as great.

Table 2.2.10 presents data on the elemental composition of aerosol atoms, obtained by the Venera 12 (1978) and Venera 14 (1982) space probes.

Thus, as testified by the experimental results, the main constituents of the aerosols in Venus' cloud layer at heights of 63–46 km are sulphur-containing and chlorine-containing compounds. Obviously, the ratio of sulphur and chlorine concentrations does not remain constant at different places in Venus' cloud layer. It is to be noted that no other chemical elements, the fluorescent radiation of which lies within the energy range from 1.1 to 10 keV, appear to be present in the aerosols of Venus' cloud layer in quantities commensurable with those of sulphur and chlorine. As a result of the experiments, estimations were also made of the content of argon in the atmosphere, which amounts to $0.02 \pm 0.01\%$, and the upper limit of a possible content of mercury in the aerosol of the cloud layer, which is equal to 5×10^{-8} kg m^{-3}.

During the descent of the space probe the total density of fluorescent radiation excited in the aerosols was also being recorded, thus enabling one to judge the altitudinal distribution of aerosols in Venus' cloud layer. Fig. 2.2.22 shows the altitudinal distribution of aerosols in Venus' cloud layer, as measured by the Venera 12 and Venera 14 space probes. As seen from the figure, Venusian clouds show a stratified pattern: the maximum concentration of aerosols coincides approximately with 52–56 km and 46–50 km heights. Presuming a sulphuric acid composition for the bulk of the aerosols (80% solution of H_2SO_4 in water), the total average density of the cloud aerosol at 63 km to 46 km heights will be 6×10^{-6} kg m^{-3} (6mg m^{-3}), whilst the aerosol concentration in some separate layers will be even higher.

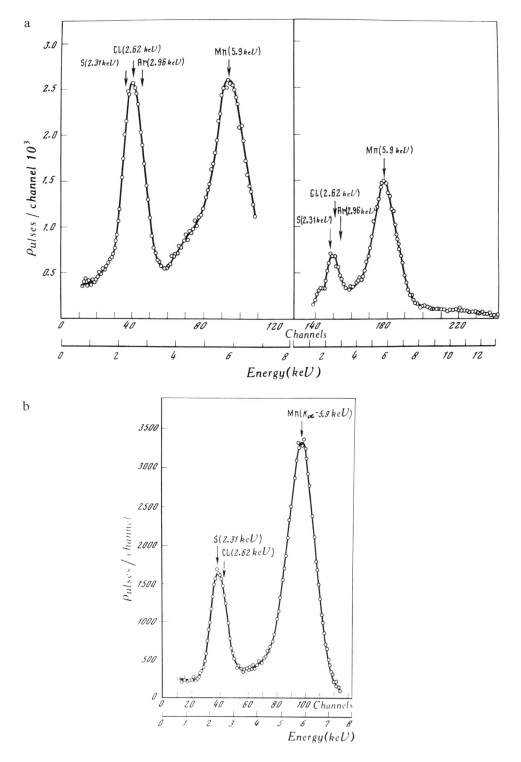

Fig. 2.2.21 – Fluorescent-radiation spectra measured from Venera 12 (a) and from Venera 14 (b)

Table 2.2.10 — Elemental composition of aerosol in Venusian clouds

Element	Content (kg m^{-3})	
	Venera 14	Venera 12
Sulphur	(1.10 ± 0.13)x10^{-6}	(0.1 ± 0.03)x10^{-6}
Chlorine	(0.16 ± 0.14)x10^{-6}	(2.1 ± 0.06)x10^{-6}
Mass of aerosol (elements with $Z\leqslant16$)	1.26x10^{-6}	2.2x10^{-6}

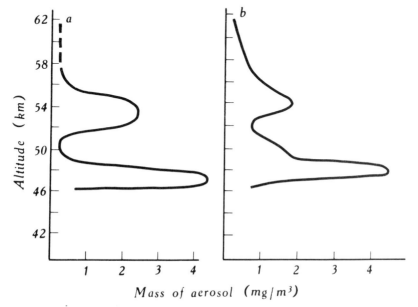

page Fig. 2.2.22 – Height distribution of aerosols in the Venusian cloud layer measured from Venera 12 (a) and from Venera 14 (b).

A general geochemical examination of the composition of the Venusian atmosphere points to the fact that the phase transformations leading to the formation of the aerosols are likely to involve numerous constituents and, in particular, S, Cl, H_2O, etc. Therefore, it can be expected that Venus' cloud layer is inhomogeneous in its composition. Evidence in favour of this assumption is also furnished by nephelometric data [25–27] pointing to the existence of a layer with a particularly high aerosol concentration in the 47–51 km altitude band. (An accurate correlation of data with height is difficult, since in different experiments use was made of different models of the Venusian atmosphere and, consequently, some lack of correspondence within 1–2 km may exist between the altitude scales.) The obtained results are in good agreement with the data in [27] on the vertical distribution of aerosols and are close to the data [25,26] on the quantity of aerosols at the indicated heights. At the same time, the composition of the aerosols turned out to be somewhat unexpected, since, apart from sulphur (or sulphuric acid, the presence of which was predicted from indirect observations), there has also been discovered a chlorine-containing constituent.

The obtained data on the composition and distribution of aerosols in Venusian clouds agree both with the results of ground measurements pointing to the presence of sulphur and chlorine in the Venusian atmosphere, and with general geochemical concepts of Venus' atmosphere attributing an important rôle to these elements in the evolution and modern structure of Venus. However, a specific construction of a geochemical model of the Venusian atmosphere with the use of obtained data meets with certain difficulties which may, possibly, be overcome in the course of further investigations of the Venusian atmosphere. At the same time, a possible geochemical interpretation of these data is to be found in [32].

2.2.4 X-RAY RADIOMETRIC ANALYSIS OF MARTIAN ROCKS FROM VIKINGS -1 AND -2

The flights of the Soviet space vehicles Mars 2, 3, 4 and 5 and the American Mariners 6 and 9 have enabled us to obtain extensive scientific information on the composition, structure and properties of the atmosphere, on seasonal and climatic variations, and on the geological structure of the Martian surface. This information has furnished evidence about the presence at the planet's surface of conditions that do not exclude the possible existence on Mars of some form of life. This has significantly intensified the long-standing interest for the search for life on Mars. The first attempt to give an answer to this question was made by the space vehicles Vikings 1 and 2 which were launched towards Mars in September 1975. Although the problem turned out to be much more complicated than it had appeared to be prior to the flight of these spacecraft and therefore could not be resolved, the results of the experiments made by Vikings 1 and 2 yielded a great deal of useful information which has significantly pushed forward our concepts of Mars.

The main purpose of experiments on the Viking 1 and 2 spacecraft was the exobiological investigation and the search for signs of the existence of life on Mars at present or in the past. One of the characteristics of the environment in which the search for signs of life was conducted was its chemical composition. Therefore, the set of scientific instruments aboard the Viking 1 and 2 space vehicles comprised X-ray fluorescent spectrometers.

As a result of an analysis of the Martian rock, it was possible to determine the content of principal rock-forming elements and rare trace elements in the fine-grained fraction of the rock lying at the planet's surface. Furthermore, the specific mass of the rock was measured, the upper limit of the thickness of iron oxide coatings on mineral grains was found, the force of cohesion of the Martian rock was estimated, and the upper limit of the argon content in the Martian atmosphere was determined [20]. Description of the measurement technique and of the instrument design had been made long before the realization of the experiment [13]. Later the instrument was perfected in accordance with the requirements of the Viking spacecraft [33].

2.2.4.1 Design of the X-ray fluorescent spectrometer

Determination of the composition of Martian rocks was made by using the X-ray radiometric method of analysis. A rock sample for analysis was taken with the aid of an automatically-controlled scoop and delivered into the measuring cell of the multichannel X-ray fluorescence spectrometer. Thereafter, it was irradiated by the radioisotopic sources ^{55}Fe and ^{109}Cd. The excited fluorescent radiation was registered by the X-ray spectrometer from which information was relayed to the Earth. Fig. 2.2.23 shows the scheme of the measuring cell into which the analysed

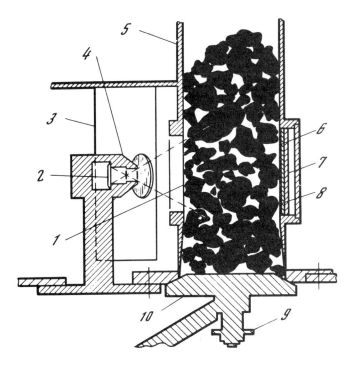

Fig. 2.2.23 – Measuring cell of the X-ray fluorescence spectrometer carried by Vikings 1 and 2: 1, reinforced thin organic film window; 2, ^{109}Cd source; 3, proportional counter; 4, source holder and radiation shield; 5, sample-analysis chamber; 6, silver calibration plaque; 7, tungsten radiation shield; 8, zinc pigment; 9, pivot assay; 10, dump valve.

rock was filled with the aid of a scoop. A grid fitted into the upper part of the measuring cell was used to prevent rock fragments in excess of 12.5 x 12.5 mm in size from getting into the cell. The measuring cell was 25 x 25 mm in cross-section (horizontally). About 25 cm^3 of rock was placed into it. The rock was irradiated by radioisotopic sources through side holes of 20 mm diameter, covered by a thin organic film. The choice of the films was made on the following considerations: (1) they should be as thin as possible, lest they should absorb weak fluorescent radiation; (2) they should be sufficiently strong, lest they collapse when rock is being inserted; (3) they should be heat-resistant under sterilization and radiation-resistant under irradiation. On this basis the choice was made of polycarbonate film of 1.5 μm thickness for penetration of ^{55}Fe radiation and polyamide film of 2.5 μm thickness for penetration of ^{109}Cd radiation.

Fig. 2.2.24 shows the scheme of analysis with the arrangement of the measured sample, radioisotopic sources and detectors, i.e. proportional counters. Positioned around the measuring cell are two sources, four detectors and two calibration targets. Detectors and sources are so located that one pair of detectors were recording fluorescent radiation excited by the ^{55}Fe source of 240 mCi activity either in the calibration target set up opposite it (when no rock is present in the cell) or in the rock sample when the latter is delivered into the cell; another pair of detectors were recording fluorescent radiation excited by the ^{109}Cd source of 55 mCi activity, likewise either in the calibration target or in the rock sample.

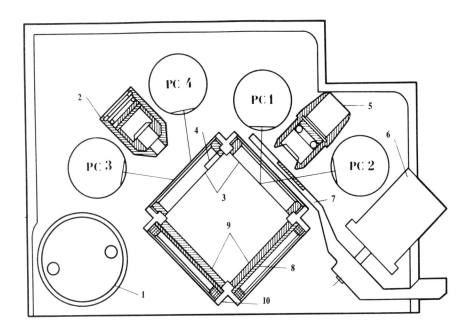

Fig. 2.2.24 — Diagram of the relative position of the measured sample, radioisotope sources and radiation detectors in the X-ray fluorescence spectrometer of Viking 1 and 2: PC1, PC2, PC3 and PC4, proportional counters; 1, dump valve solenoid; 2, ^{109}Cd source with the holder; 3, windows; 4, fixer; 5, ^{55}Fe source with the holder; 6, solenoid of the calibration plaque; 7, calibration plaque; 8, radiation shield; 9, calibration plaques; 10, sample cavity.

Proportional counters specially fabricated for the given instrument were used as detectors. The composition of the working gases and the material of the counter windows are given in Table 2.2.11. They were chosen so as to reduce to a minimum the interference from peaks due to certain elements and to have an optimal sensitivity for the group of elements under study.

Table 2.2.11 – Composition of the gas and window material of the fluorescent radiation counters

Counter No.	Composition of gas	Counter window material
1.	Ne(20%), He(75%), CO_2(5%)	Al (5 μm)
2.	Xe(10%), Ne(73%), He(10%)	Be (25 μm)
3.	Xe(40%), Ne(47%), He(10%)	Be (50 μm)
4.	Xe(40%), Ne(47%), He(10%)	Be (25 μm)

Counter 1 had a thin aluminium window (supported by an aluminium grid) intended for filtering off the fluorescent radiation of Si while recording Mg and Al radiation. The windows of the rest of the counters were made from pure beryllium. The window material was glued onto the counter frame by means of epoxy resin. All the counters were supplied from a single high-voltage source, every one having, however, a decoupling circuit of its own. The activities of the radioisotopic sources at the moment of measurement were 240 mCi for ^{55}Fe and 55 mCi for ^{109}Cd. Iron radioisotopes were deposited onto metallic substrates by the galvanic method and were sealed in capsules with a beryllium window of 5 mm diameter, The ^{109}Cd source was of the same size, but it used a filter of aluminium foil of 180 μm thickness. Its holder and collimator were made of a tungsten alloy and high-purity silver intended to secure a maximum attenuation of background gamma-radiation of 87.7 keV energy.

Calibration targets, as seen from Figs 2.2.23 and 2.2.24 are built into the remote (from the sources) walls of the measuring cell. Opposite the ^{55}Fe source there is a circular aluminium target, opposite the ^{109}Cd source a circular silver target upon which is deposited in wedge form a zinc-containing paint. As the cell was being filled, the silver peak to zinc peak relationship was changing, thus serving as a measure of filling. The position of the peaks belonging to aluminium, silver and zinc enabled the spectrometer energy scale to be calibrated.

Fluorescent radiation spectra were recorded in 128 energy channels, the channel capacity being 32 pulses. Accumulated information was stored in the memory of the onboard computer. On request it was removed in eight-channel arrays to be relayed alternately with other scientific and routine information. Data from the lander were relayed to the Earth via the Viking Orbiter spacecraft.

2.2.4.2. Method of measurement and data processing

For the purpose of processing the fluorescent radiation spectra of Martian rocks, preflight measurements were made of the spectra of 29 terrestrial rocks of known composition, as well as on standards of pure elements: Mg,Al,Si,S,K,Ca,Ti,Fe,Pb,Sr, and Zn, prepared either by mechanical processing of a pure element or by intermixing the powder with epoxy resin. The choice of the elemental concentration in the given standards was made in such a way that the total count rate in the detector was not above 1000 pulses s^{-1}. In certain cases, either aluminium or nickel powder was added to the standards to reduce backscattering. In all 225 spectra were measured before the flight. The spectra were collected in 500s each with the use of an external laboratory multichannel analyser as a substitute for an internal single-channel analyser. This instrument is endowed with a high discerning power: according to estimates, it is in principle capable of distinguishing at least 1.5×10^7 separate elemental compositions. The performance of the instrument was tested on several control specimens furnished by NASA for test purposes.

Fig. 2.2.25. shows the spectra measured by the Viking 1 lander in two energy ranges (and with different excitation sources), as well as calibration spectra particularly close to them [33]. It is seen that not a single one of the calibration spectra fits the Martian one over the entire energy range. Therefore, two independent information processing techniques were adopted for analysis of the Martian spectra obtained. Under the first method the contribution of the background is first subtracted from the measured Martian spectrum. Thereafter the latter is compared to the one constructed from multi-elemental spectra by allowing for the peak due to back-scattering. This constructed spectrum turns out to be similar only in the first approximation. Thereafter, the method of successive approximations is used to fit this spectrum to the one measured on Mars. Finally, corrections are

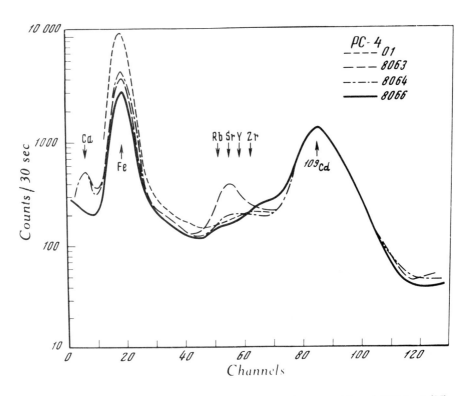

Fig. 2.2.25 — Fluorescent radiation spectra of Martian rock measured from (a) Viking 1 (S5)
and (b) Viking 2 (O1), and spectra of some terrestrial rocks (8063, 8064, and 8066) which are
the closest to Martian ones in their composition.

introduced for drifting of the threshold and amplification coefficient and, proceeding
from the obtained photon energy distribution, the elemental composition is
determined.

The second method (sample modelling) involves the choice of a particularly
similar standard spectrum and its fitting to the measured one by adding to (or
subtracting from) the given standard spectrum those elements in the energy region
of which the maximum difference between the Martian and standard spectra is
observed. In other words, an analogue of the Martian rock is artificially made after
the standard composition. Actually the processing of the Martian fluorescent
radiation spectra of rocks was more sophisticated, since there was a need to connect
separate parts of the spectrum, measured by a single-channel pulse-amplitude
analyser in different energy intervals and at different times. This was, in effect, one
of the shortcomings of the experiment. The use of a single-channel analyser called,
moreover, for exceptional thermostabilization of the electronic clock, the presence
of extra calibration devices, constancy of the resolution of detectors in time for the
measurement of external conditions, etc.

2.2.4.3. Results of experiments

The elemental composition of Martian rock specimens, as measured by the Viking 1 and 2 spacecraft, is given in Table 2.2.12 [33].

If all the discovered elements are present in the form of ordinary oxides (except for chlorine), the sum of oxides indicated in the table makes up less than 100%. The shortfall appears to be related, above all, to H_2O, Na_2O, CO_2, and NO_2.

Principal results of the experiments on the X-ray radiometric analysis of Martian rocks, conducted by the Viking 1 and 2 spacecraft, may be summarised as follows [33–35]:

— The composition of the fine-grained soil fraction (grain size below 2 mm) in both landing areas was found to be strikingly similar, though the two areas are removed from one another by 7420 km.

Table 2.2.12 – The elemental composition of Martian rock samples[a]

Elements	Viking 1			Viking 2
	Spec.1	Spec.2	Spec.3	Spec.1
Mg	5.0±2.5	—	5.2	—
Al	3.0±0.9	—	2.9	—
Si	20.0±2.5	20.8	20.5	20.0
S	3.1±0.5	3.8	3.8	2.6
Cl	0.7±0.3	0.8	0.9	0.6
K	<0.25	<0.25	<0.25	<0.25
Ca	4.0±0.8	3.8	4.0	3.6
Ti	0.51±0.2	0.51	0.51	0.61
Fe	12.7±2.0	12.6	13.1	14.2
O	50.1±4.3	49.7	—	50.4
Rb	⩽30			⩽30
Sr	60±30			100±40
Y	70±30			50±30
Zr	⩽30			30±20

[a] The contents of elements from Mg to O are given as a percentage, from Rb to Zr as parts per million.

— The fine-grained soil fraction mainly consists of one or more silicate minerals (an average content in specimens of $SiO_2 \simeq 45\pm5\%$ weight) with a high content of iron (an average content in specimens of $Fe_2O_3 \simeq 19\pm3\%$).
— The sulphur content turned out to be unexpectedly high — about 100 times as high as the average for the Earth's crust. (Its bulk is possibly formed by magnesium sulphate).
— The potassium content is less than 0.25%, thus less than one-fifth of the average for the Earth's crust. If this content reflects the average content of potassium in Mars' crust, then the low content of ^{40}Ar observed in the Martian atmosphere may either reflect the scarcity of the source material (^{40}K) or a lower degree of degassing of Mars as compared to the Earth.

— The iron oxide film covering mineral grains turns out to be very thin (less than 0.25 μm), or it is thicker, but does not completely cover each grain.

— The weight per unit volume of fine-grained soil sample, after it had filled the measuring cavity, was 1.0 ± 0.15 x 10^3 kg m^{-3} thus giving a total porosity of $60\pm15\%$.

As a result of the above-described experiment there were obtained the first data on the composition and characteristics of Martian soil, which contributed to the elaboration of certain concepts of its origin and conditions of its formation.

2.2.5. X-RAY SPECTROMETRIC ANALYSIS OF LUNAR ROCKS

The 1970s proved to be a special turning point in the study of the Moon. The despatch to the Moon of the roving vehicles Lunokhod 1 and 2 and the return of lunar soils to the Earth by the automatic sample return probes Lunas 16, 20, and 24 and the Apollo spacecraft accounted for a tremendous leap forward in the development of our concepts of the Moon. The results of lunar investigations in those years have been set forth in numerous collections and monographs [36–38 etc.]. Given in the present section is a brief description of only two experiments in the X-ray fluorescent analysis of lunar rocks, conducted by the Lunokhod 1 and 2 rovers [6,8,39,40] and the Apollo 15 and 16 spaceships [10–12]. The results of these experiments constitute and important part of the tremendous flow of new scientific information about the Moon that was acquired during the 1970s.

2.2.5.1. X-ray fluorescence radiation of the Moon

The Sun is, in effect, the main source of X-ray excited radiation emanating from the Moon's surface. Radiation from even a quiet Sun has a sufficient number of X-ray photons with an energy of several keV to be able to excite the characteristic radiation of all elements up to and including silicon. In periods of intense solar activity (flares) the X-radiation from the Sun is capable of exciting at the Moon's surface even heavier elements, including Fe and Ni. A spectral distribution of solar X-rays can be constructed by making use of a thermal mechanism at the coronal temperature of 10^6–10^7 K. Temperature variations may change the distribution of high-energy X-ray photons and, as a consequence, the number of fluorescent photons from the given element at the Moon.

The solar spectrum has a significant number of characteristic emission lines. Fig. 2.2.26 taken from the works by Adler *et al.* [10,11] illustrates the Sun's X-ray spectrum for the conditions of a quiet Sun. This figure also shows K-absorption edges for different elements. Solar X-ray photons which have an energy superior to the K-absorption edge of the element may excite the characteristic fluorescent radiation of the given element. The number of fluorescent photons is dependent on numerous factors, but is mainly determined by the fluorescent yield of the element (W_k). The energy of fluorescent lines and K-edges for principal elements present in lunar rocks is shown in Table 2.2.13.

However, a number of factors introduce complications into the problem of interpretation of a fluorescent spectrum from the viewpoint of its content of chemical elements. One of them is the matrix effect, i.e. the effect of the composition of the sample on the number of photons emitted from the surface. Another problem is the measurement geometry, comprising the angles between the directions of solar

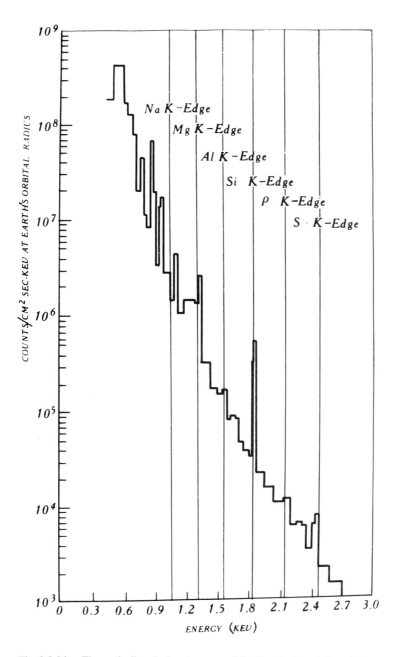

Fig. 2.2.26 — Theoretically calculated spectra of the X-radiation of the quiet Sun.

Table 2.1.13 – Magnitudes of K-edge and K-lines of fluorescent radiation from principal rock-forming elements

Element	Energy of K-edge (keV)	Energy of K-lines (keV)	Fluorescent yield (%)
O	0.53	0.52	0.5
Na	1.07	1.04	1.8
Mg	1.30	1.25	2.5
Al	1.56	1.49	3.4
Si	1.84	1.74	4.5
S	2.48	2.31	7.5
K	3.60	3.35	13.9
Ca	4.04	3.70	16.5
Ti	4.97	4.51	22.4
Fe	7.11	6.40	36.1
Ni	8.33	7.48	43.1

radiation, lunar surface and detector direction, which likewise affects the intensity of recorded radiation. A certain effect is also produced by the size of the particles of the material.

The scattering of solar X-radiation by the lunar surface material gives rise to a background spectrum superimposed on the spectrum of fluorescent photons. The background spectrum consists of a continuous distribution with an energy close to K_α-radiation of particularly widespread elements. However, this background is little dependent on the compositional variation of lunar rocks. The problem of determining a fluorescent spectrum of the lunar surface, arising as a result of its irradition by solar X-rays, was studied by Gurshtein *et al.* [42] who constructed spectra for lunar rocks of differing compositions. Calculations were made for a quiet Sun temperature $((T) \approx 4x10^6$ K) and for a solar flare $(T \approx 10^7$ K).

As shown by calculations, with the higher solar temperature the intensity of fluorescent lines from elements with a high atomic number is observed to increase. In the case of such temperature increases (up to 10^7 K) the intensity of fluorescent lines from Fe becomes an important component in the spectrum of chondritic and ultrabasic rocks.

2.2.5.2   Studying the composition of lunar rock from Lunokhods 1 and 2

The purpose of the launching of the Lunokhod 1 (1970) and Lunokhod 2 (1973) roving vehicles was the study of the geomorphological structure of the lunar surface, the nature of surface rocks and their formation conditions, as well as of physical conditions existing at the lunar surface. The choice of the areas of investigation was made so that they should be different from one another and at the same time representative of fairly typical areas of lunar surface relief. Lunokhod 1 carried out investigations in Mare Imbrium, i.e. in an area typical of the majority of lunar maria, Lunokhod 2 was in the southern part of the crater Le Monnier, at the margin of Mare Serenitatis, i.e. in a transitional zone between continental and mare areas.

Determination of the composition of lunar rocks was achieved by setting up X-ray fluorescence spectrometers with radioisotopic sources aboard the Lunokhods [7]. Fig. 2.2.27 shows the structural diagram of the instrument. It consisted of three parts — an outrigger unit with panels, radioisotopic sources placed outside the Lunokhod's pressurized compartment, and two electronic units arranged inside the pressurized compartment (an electronic unit and amplitude-to-digital converter).

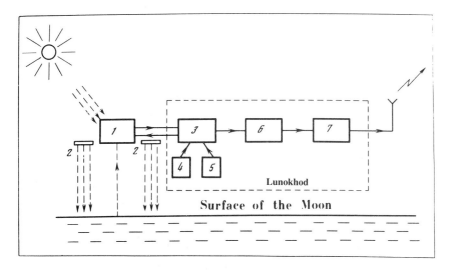

Fig. 2.2.27 — Structural diagram of the X-ray fluorescence spectrometer used on the Lunokhod 1 and 2: 1, outrigger unit; 2, panel with radioisotope sources; 3, electronic unit; 4, power source; 5, command device; 6, amplitude to digital converter; 7, onboard radio complex.

The outrigger unit carried radiation detectors and a preamplifier–commutator intended for a preliminary amplification of the pulses and changing over the detectors.

Radioisotopic sources were arranged on two panels: for Lunokhod 1 these were tritium–titanium targets set up on a molybdenum substrate; for Lunokhod 2 tritium–zirconium targets set up on a tungsten substrate. The total activity of the sources was 900 Ci in the case of Lunokhod 1 and 4000 Ci in Lunokhod 2. As fluorescent radiation detectors there were 10 proportional counters. The counters were 16 mm in diameter and 80mm in length. They were arranged in two rows, five counters in each. The counter filling was 90% Ar and 10% CH_4 at atmospheric pressure. The working voltage in the counters was 1100–1400 V. The output counter windows were made of aluminium and synthetic film about 10μm thick.

The instrument in Lunokhod 2 differed from that in Lunokhod 1 in the replacement of (T/Ti) sources by (T/Zn) sources, in having a different design of panels with the radioisotopic sources and higher activity sources, in the introduction of a standard sample, and in the addition of a temperature pickup.

Fig. 2.2.28 shows the arrangement of the outrigger unit in the X-ray fluorescence spectrometer used on Lunokhod 2.

To safeguard the outrigger unit against overheating or overcooling it is provided

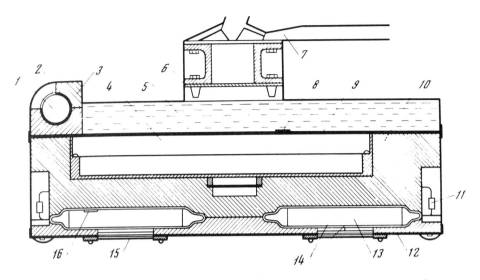

Fig. 2.2.28 — Structure of the outrigger unit of the X-ray fluorescence spectrometer used on Lunokhod 2: 1, X-ray detector of the Sun; 2, detector window; 3, detector casing; 4, preamplifier; 5, heat accumulator; 6, bracket of fixing the outrigger unit to the vehicle; 7, fixing holder; 8, temperature sensing element; 9, upper lid of the body; 10, body; 11, aligning condenser; 12, lower lid of the body; 13, detector; 14, detector window; 15, filter; 16, temperature-sensing element.

with a heat accumulator based on lithium nitrate. The phase-transition temperature of lithium nitrate (about 30°C) approximately corresponds to the average working temperature of the outrigger unit.

The outrigger unit is set up ahead of the Lunokhod at about 300 mm distance from the surface of ground. In this position the detectors were registering fluorescent radiation from a surface area confined within an ellipse having axes of about 1.2 m and 0.8 m. Measurements were made while the Lunokhods were at rest during the daytime of the lunar days.

Information from the instrument was relayed via a radio channel by binary code in real time.

Table 2.2.14 lists the main characteristics of the X-ray fluorescence spectrometers used in the Lunokhod 1 and 2 space vehicles.

2.2.5.3.   Results of the analysis of soil from Lunokhods 1 and 2

Lunokhod 1 took measurements in the western part of Mare Imbrium in an area with the coordinates 38°17'N and 35°00W. Mare Imbrium is the largest circular structure on the Moon's surface. It is observed to be quite distinctly outlined by coastal continental massifs. The surface rock in Mare Imbrium is a basalt lava outflow covered by a layer of regolith. There is observed at the Mare surface a fairly uniform distribution of craters up to several kilometers in diameter. In the area of Mare Imbrium there was discovered the largest gravitational anomaly. (The excess of mass or 'mascon' is estimated to be 5×10^{14}t).

The results of the analysis of rock along Lunokhod 1's route indicates that variations in the elemental composition at different points are insignificant and lie within the measurement accuracy. The obtained data are given in Table 2.2.15 [7].

For comparison the table also presents data on the composition of rocks in other lunar mare areas.

Table 2.2.14 — Main characteristics of the X-ray fluorescence spectrometers used on Lunokhods 1 and 2

Range of measured elements	from Al to Fe
Type of radioisotopic source, its activity	(T/Ti) 900 Ci on Lunokhod 1 (T/Zn) 4000 Ci on Lunokhod 2
Number of detectors	10
Number of energy channels	64
Energy resolution	22–26% (with respect to $E\gamma = 4.5 \text{keV}$)
Working temperature range	-70 to $+90°C$
Threshold sensitivity of elements	1–2% for Al, K, Ca; 0.5% for Fe
Measurement accuracy	10–15%

Table 2.2.15 — Composition of rocks in the lunar maria

Elements	Mare Tranquillitatis (Surveyor 5)	Oceanus Procellarum (Apollo 12)	Mare Foecunditatis (Luna 16)	Mare Imbrium (Lunokhod 1)
Al	2	7	8	7
Si	21	20	20	20
K	—	0.3	0.08	1
Ca	10	7	9	8
Fe	9	13	13	12

The results of the analysis by Lunokhod 1 indicate that the surface of Mare Imbrium is composed of rocks which are similar in their content of principal rock-forming elements to those of the other mare areas on the Moon and largely correspond to tholeiitic basalts of the Earth's crust.

Lunokhod 2 worked at the eastern margin of Mare Serenitatis in an area with the coordinates 25°51'N and 30°27'E. Mare Serenitatis is one of the youngest parts of the Moon's surface. In the process of its formation the mound at the eastern margin was partly destroyed and the bottom of the earlier existing crater Le Monnier was filled in by basaltic lava. It was the area of this crater that was investigated by Lunokhod 2.

Table 2.2.16 gives the results obtained for the composition of lunar rock along Lunokhod 2's travelling route [7]. At the part of the Moon's surface investigated by Lunokhod 2 we may identify three different regions: the plain part of the crater Le Monnier's floor, a variety of continental regions and a tectonic fault zone [42].

The results of the analysis of rocks in the plain part of the crater floor enable us to suppose that rocks here are not typically marine, since the 6% iron content in them is significantly below that in the typically mare areas, where it attains 10–12%. In the continental regions, in the uppermost regolith layer, the iron content was found to be

Table 2.2.16 — Composition of lunar rocks in continental areas and in the transition zone (percentage by mass)

Element	Appollonius C crater (Luna 20)	Tycho crater (Surveyor 7)	Crater Le Monnier area (Lunokhod 2)	
			Mare part of the route	Continental part of the route
Al	11.4	11	8.8	11.6
Si	21.4	21	24	22
K	0.08	—	1	1
Ca	10.9	13	8.0	9.1
Fe	5.5	4	6.1	4.0

even lower (4%) but close to that of the Moon's other continental regions.

Finally, in the tectonic fault zone (Straight Furrow) covered with an abundance of large stones, the iron content was found to be high.

Thus, investigation of the composition of rock in the crater Le Monnier appears to indicate an intermixing of mare and continental matter and a gradual transition from the one to the other as Lunokhod was moving forward. It is to be noted that evidence to this effect is furnished by the higher albedo (due to a higher iron content and a lower aluminium content) of mare than continental rock.

2.2.5.4. Study of the composition of lunar rock from Apollos 15 and 16

In 1971–1972 the manned space flights of Apollos 15 and 16 took place, from the orbiting command modules of which measurements were made of the fluorescent radiation from the lunar surface, excited by the Sun's X-radiation at [10–12]. Measurements were made from circular orbits around the Moon at 100–120 km altitude above its surface. The Moon's equatorial part, accounting for about 20% of its entire surface, was investigated.

The Sun's X-radiation has a maximum intensity within the 1–3 keV energy range. It is capable of effectively exciting the fluorescent radiation of only light rock-forming elements — Mg, Al and Si. However, in a period of major solar flares the X-ray spectrum becomes harder and the possibility arises of measuring heavier rock-forming elements, up to and including iron.

The elements Mg, Al and Si have close fluorescent radiation energies, and so their absolute content cannot be determined with a satisfactory precision if the resolution of the detector (particularly, a proportional counter) is not sufficiently high. In addition, determination of the absolute content of elements requires that, simultaneously with the measurement of the fluorescent radiation from lunar rocks, some analogous instruments be used to measure the X-ray spectrum of the Sun's radiation. Thereafter some sources having spectra similar to the measured solar spectrum need to be used to carry out calibration of the analogue instruments. Realization of such operations is very difficult.

Therefore, in the aforementioned experiments, the relative rather than absolute content of elements was determined.

Measurement of fluorescent radiation from the Moon's surface by Apollos 15 and 16 was done by means of small-channel X-ray spectrometers. The detectors in the spectrometers were three proportional gas counters. The counters were filled with a mixture of gases (Ar (90%), Co$_2$ (9.5%) and He (0.5%)) under 10^5 Pa pressure. Each of the counters had a beryllium window 25 mm thick and 25 cm^2 in effective area. Two of the counters were operated with filters (an Mg filter of 12.7 μm thickness and an Al filter of 5 μm thickness) and one without a filter. The angle of view of the detectors was restricted by a collimator and amounted to about 60°. For a given height and velocity of the spacecraft, and taking account of the required accuracy in determining the ratios of elements, the necessary counting statistics were collected from a lunar surface area about 100 x 150 km in size.

Fig. 2.2.29 schematically shows the arrangement of the detection unit in the instrument employed on the Apollo 15 and 16 spacecraft. The detection unit consists of three detectors — proportional counters — a collimator and a calibrating device for the instrument. It was mounted on a boom outside the spacecraft. The electronic part of the instrument, intended for the processing and codification of information, was placed inside the spacecraft. Signals from the detectors following their amplification and formation arrived at the eight-channel amplitude analyser, the information from which was relayed to Earth via telemetry channels.

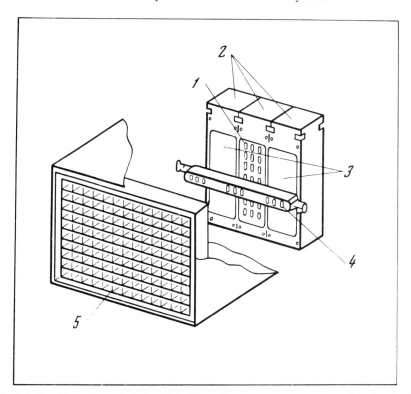

Fig. 2.2.29 — Detection unit design of the X-ray fluorescence spectrometer of the Apollo 15 and 16 orbital module: 1, counter window; 2, proportional counter; 3, filters; 4, calibration source; 5, collimator.

The spectrometer channel with a filterless detector was operated in two régimes: 0.75–2.75 keV and 1.5–5.5 keV. (A change-over was effected automatically.) The spectrometer channels with detectors having filters were operated in the 0.75–2.75

keV energy range. Information on the level of solar activity was achieved by using a special detector operating in the 1–3 keV energy range.

2.2.5.5 Results of experiments from Apollos 15 and 16

If we suppose that the Si content in all rocks along the flight paths of the Apollo 15 and 16 command modules is approximately the same, then the ratio of the flux density of X-ray quanta recorded by the counters with filters to that recorded by the filterless counter may be regarded as being approximately proportional to the ratio of the elements Mg/Si and Al/Si. Hence the measurement of these ratios along the path of the spacecraft shows variations in the content of Mg and Al. However, a variation of the Si content between different rocks and variations in the intensity and spectrum of the Sun's X-radiation at different measurement times render the determination of the absolute content of these elements practically impossible.

Fig. 2.2.30 illustrates variations in the ratios Mg/Si and Al/Si, as measured by the Apollo 15 and 16 spacecraft [10–12].

As can be seen from these data, these ratios vary by a factor of 1.5–2.0 in the transition from mare to continental rocks. In mare areas we observe a lower ratio Al/Si and a higher ratio Mg/Si as compared to continental areas. This finding correlates with the varying albedo of the rock in transition from the mare to continental areas. All these facts came to light after samples of lunar rock brought back to the Earth had been studied. It is well-known today that lunar maria are made up of basaltic rocks having a higher Al content and a lower Mg content, as well as a lower albedo compared to those from lunar continents which are made up of gabbro–anorthositic rocks.

2.2.5.6 Remote analysis of lunar rock by using gas scintillation detectors

In all the above-described experiments, the X-ray fluorescent analysis of lunar and planetary matter was made by using gas-discharge proportional counters as radiation detectors. Simplicity of manufacture and operational reliability happen to be the chief factors behind their predominant use in space research. In a standard proportional counter the maximum energy resolution is determined by the statistics of ionization processes accompanying the absorption of X-ray photons, as well as by the multiplication statistics of primary electron charges in a non-uniform electric field. Theoretically the maximum resolution of a proportional counter amounts to about 15% of the half-height of the energy peak, i.e. a resolution of 6 keV. Practically this value is attainable solely for a particularly favourable measurement geometry. However, the majority of real counters having a large surface area have an energy resolution of 20–25%.

Therefore, it is quite obvious that further progress in X-ray fluorescent analysis must involve, above all, the development of detectors with a higher energy resolution. Such detectors may, in particular, be the gas scintillation proportional counters (GSPCs). The GSPCs started to be employed in space research a relatively short time ago. Their field of application has so far been confined to astrophysical experiments associated with the measurement of spectra and locating sources of X-radiation. The greatest success in the development of GSPCs has been made by a group of workers from the European Centre for Space Research and Technology (the Netherlands). Detectors and spectrometers based on GSPCs have been

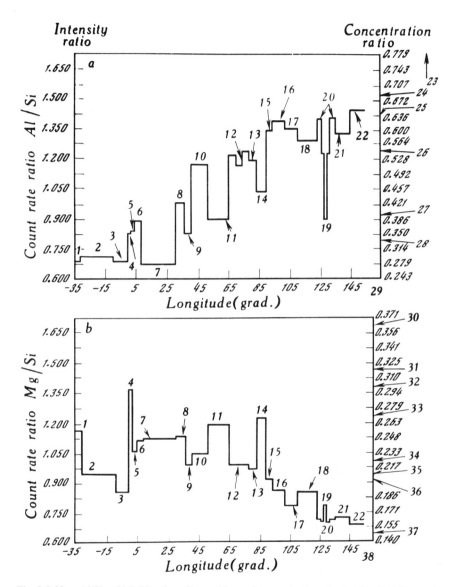

Fig. 2.2.30 — Al/Si and Mg/Si ratios of insensities and concentrations for the Apollo 15 ground northern track. The values for some reference material are shown: 1, Delisle Diophantus area; 2, Mare Imbrium; 3, Archimedes Rilles area; 4, Palus Putredinus; 5, Apennines MTS; 6, Haemus MTS; 7, Mare serenitatis; 8, Littrow area; 9, mare area around Maraldi; 10, west of Crisium; 11, Mare Crisium; 12, highlands between Smythii and Crisium; 13, west border of Smythii; 14, Mare Smythii; 15, east border of Smythii; 16, highlands east of Smythii; 17, Pasteur Hilbert area; 18, highlands west of Tsiolkovsky; 19, Tsiolkovsky; 20, highlands around Tsiolkovsky; 21, Pirquet; 22, Gagarin; 23, anorthosites (0.89–0.91); gabbroic anorthosites (0.82); 24, Rock 15418; 25, anorthositic gabbros (Apollo 11 and 12); 26, Tycho; 27, KREEP; 28, Sinus medii, Hadley Apennine soils; 29, Oceanus Procellarum, type AB rocks (0.22); 30, Oceanus Procellarum type B rocks; 31, Oceanus Procellarum type A rocks; 32, Hadley Apennine soil; 33, Hadley Appenine rocks; 34, Oceanus Procellarum type AB rocks; 35, anorthositic gabbroic, Apollo 11 and 12; 38, gabbroic anorthosites, Apollo 11 and 12 (0.074) anorthosites (0.04–0.003).

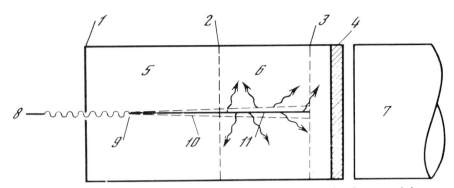

Fig. 2.2.31 — Principle of the operation of the gas scintillation proportional counter: 1, input window; 2, drift grid electrode; 3, scintillation grid electrode; 4, output window; 5, drift area; 6, scintillation area; 7, photomultiplier; 8, X-radiation; 9, photoabsorption area; 10, area of electron cloud drift; 11, photon emission area.

described by them in [43–46]. Descriptions of onboard spectrometers for astrophysical research are to be found in [47–50]. The first application of two GSPCs was on the European rocket Aries in 1980. During 500 s of work, observations of sources of X-radiation were carried out. Such counters are planned to be used in the equipment being developed for the space laboratory to be put into Earth orbit by the US Space Shuttle, and have been used on the European X-ray satellite Exosat and aboard the Soviet space station Salyut 7.

Fig. 2.2.31 illustrates the operating principle of the GSPC. In such a counter, primary electrons are accelerated by an electric field to such a degree that they are capable of exciting the atoms of the working gas but do not yet produce charge multiplication (i.e. a gas discharge). The maximum resolution of the GSPC is determined by the statistics of the primary ionization process alone. Theoretically it amounts to about 6% for an applied voltage of about 6 keV. However, the best resolution attained experimentally with small-size counters is equal to 8% [46]. Having passed through the collimator determining the field of view, X-ray quanta enter through a window into the xenon gas filler (drifting region). The uppermost energy limit of the counter is determined by the braking capacity of the drift region, which depends on the pressure and volume of the gas. Electrons formed during the photo-absorption of X-ray quanta drift towards the first grid and thereafter are accelerated towards the second grid, giving rise in their movement to a scintillation flash in the ultraviolet region, its duration being determined by the time of the passage of the electrons through the scintillation region.

X-ray quanta being absorbed in the scintillation region and charged particles passing through the detector produce scintillation flashes of different durations. Scintillation flashes are registered by a photomultiplier. Identification of the required event involves an analysis of photomultiplier pulses with respect to amplitude (energy) and duration.

To secure effective collection from a large area (regardless of the point of entry of the photon into the counter), the primary electron cloud is focused in the photoabsorption region with the aid of a spherically symmetrical electric field formed by special spherical grids and rings.

In the gas scintillator the duration of the ultraviolet flash is dependent on the detector geometry, the field in the drift and scintillation regions and the length of the electron track for an X-ray quantum or charged particle. For X-ray quanta with 6 keV energy the duration of the flash is equal to about 5 μs for the $4 \times 10^5 \text{Vm}^{-1}$ field in the scintillation region of 2 cm depth.

By selecting the energy window and the time interval in recording scintillation flashes, the gas scintillation proportional counter is capable of suppressing the background caused by charged particles and gamma-ray quanta similar to the way it is done in the gas proportional counter.

Method and apparatus

Peacock *et al* [45] have developed both the apparatus and relevant techniques for measuring the fluorescent radiation emanating from the lunar surface from a satellite orbit around the Moon. This development evolved from the experience acquired in astrophysical investigations conducted aboard rockets and Earth satellites. The apparatus is based on the use of GSPCs adapted for the measurement of fluorescent radiation within the low-energy region from 1–10 keV. Furthermore, a low count-rate and the need to obtain a maximal spatial resolution have accounted for one more characteristic of this counter — a large working surface area. Since the GSPC is still practically the only highly effective detector intended for the remote analysis of lunar rock, let us describe it in greater detail.

The schematic layout of the GSPC is shown in Fig. 2.2.32. The counter consists of a collimator, gas chamber, photomultiplier and electronic device. All these elements are set up inside an aluminium housing.

The collimator is made of porous aluminium with 85% transparency. The field of view was chosen so as to secure the required spatial resolution, measurement statistics and viewing angle of the lunar surface. The collimator is also used to give support to a thin entrance window.

The control mechanism for the calibrating source is arranged on the external side of the collimator. The calibration source has two lines: Mn_{k_α} (5.9 keV) and Al_{k_α} (1.5

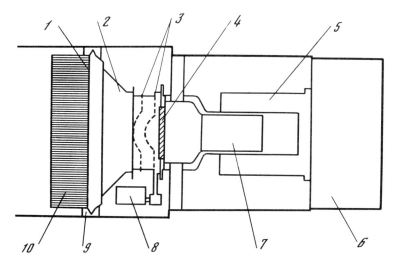

Fig. 2.2.32 — Design of the gas scintillation proportional counter: 1, beryllium window; 2, gas chamber; 3, grids; 4, quartz window; 5, gas-filled compartment of the high-voltage source; 6, electronic unit; 7, photomultiplier; 8, getter; 9, mounting flange; 10, collimator.

keV). The latter is due to the excitation of aluminium fluorescence by Mn radiation.

The gas chamber is made up of ceramic sections welded together. The entrance window for X-radiation is joined to the ceramic chamber through steel flanges. The entrance window is made of 4-mm thick quartz. It does not prevent the transmission of ultraviolet radiation.

The gilded molybdenum focusing rings form and maintain an electric field along the tapered walls of the gas chamber. A distortion of the field may result from the use of a flat rather than spherical entrance window, but it can be corrected by adjusting the focusing rings. The quasi-spherical electric field in the drift and scintillation regions is maintained with the aid of rings and grids. The optimum potentials in the drift region and in the scintillation region are 3kV and 8kV respectively.

A voltage of 11 kV is applied to the entrance window, whilst the scintillation grid (3) (right-hand) lies within the housing potential, thus removing the need for a reverse field between the scintillation grid and the exit window in the present design. This region is a source of parasitic scintillation caused by photoelectrons which arise under the effect of ultraviolet photons in the main scintillation region and are bombarding the exit window and its neighbourhood. The presence of this parasitic light impairs the energy resolution. To maintain a high level of xenon purity prior to and during the space flight, use is made of two 'getters'.

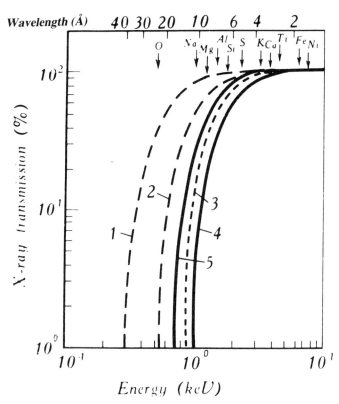

Fig. 2.2.33 — Passage of X-radiation through various materials used in detectors: (1) 1 μm of polypropylene; (2) 5 μm of polypropylene; (3) 25 μm of beryllium; (4) 10 μm of mylar; (5) 5 μm of mylar.

Fig. 2.2.33 illustrates the passage of X-radiation through a number of window materials: polypropylene (1 and 5 μm), mylar (5 and 10 μm) and beryllium (25 μm) and also shows the position of fluorescent lines of oxygen, sodium, magnesium, aluminium, silicon, etc. It is seen that oxygen lines can be measured solely by using a polypropylene window of 1 μm thickness. Manufacture of such a window with a large surface area, low gas leakage and a long service life is a problem which has not yet been solved. The sodium line can be observed with an efficiency of several per cent in the case of a beryllium window of 25 μm thickness. Such a window can be made by soldering it into the detector. In this case there is no need for a system of additional gas pumping into the GSPC under long-term operation. A high efficiency in sodium registration is attainable with a 5 μm polypropylene or mylar window.

Any kind of plastic window calls for the use of a pumping system, since, because of air diffusion through it, the xenon may get fouled during its presence on the Earth.

Given in Table 2.2.1.7 are the main characteristics of a fluorescence spectrometer based on GSPC [41]:

Table 2.2.17   Main characteristics of a GSPC-based fluorescence spectrometer

Mass (kg)	20
Overall dimensions (mm)	cylinder: $h=600$, $d=300$
Power consumption (W)	8
Energy range (keV)	1–10
Energy resolution (%)	
with respect to Fe (6.4 keV)	10
with respect to Al (1.5 keV)	20
Background noise after suppression,	
(pulse s^{-1} ke V^{-1}) 10	10
Efficiency of background suppression	
within 1–10 keV range (%)	97
Effective photoregistration area (cm^2):	
for Fe	173
for Al	93
Number of energy channels	256
Channel capacity	2^8
Collimator field of view	Depends on
Exposure time	orbital height

Interpretation of measurement results of fluorescent radiation from the lunar surface requires that the spectrum and intensity of solar radiation during the measurement period be known. This is attained by setting up a solar monitoring detector aboard the spacecraft. In an ideal case the solar detector must be similar to the lunar one. However, in the simplest case such a detector may be a conventional proportional counter directed towards the Sun.

Sensitivity of a GSPC spectrometer

The main characteristics determining the spectrometer sensitivity are the effective photon collection zone and the detector background. The effective zone is shown in Fig. 2.2.34 as a function of the energy of X-ray photons. In calculations, the

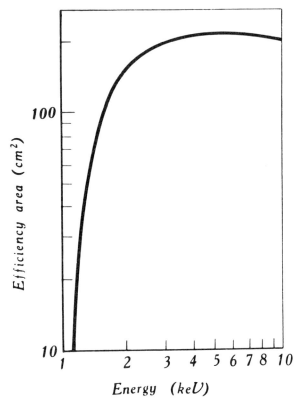

Fig. 2.2.34 — Dependence of the effective zone of a gas scintillation proportional counter on the thickness of the detector window is 25 μm of beryllium.

collimator transparency of 85% and the 25 μm thickness of the beryllium detector window were taken into account.

The level of detector background with the use of a suppression system can be determined from the space flights of rockets carrying similar detectors. However, to be able to reduce the background count-rate obtained for the conditions of a circumterrestrial orbit to those of a lunar orbit we must know the recalculation factor. Proceeding from the data obtained for X-ray counters employed on the Earth satellite COS-B and aboard the Apollo 15 command module, we may accept this factor as equal to 10. Background suppression achieved in the given GSPC amounts to 97% in the 1–10 keV energy range.

Fig. 2.2.35 shows the expected spectra of lunar rocks, as calculated for the given GSPC for the period of a quiet Sun; Fig. 2.2.36 presents similar spectra for an active Sun with solar flares [41]. The rocks significantly differ with respect to their spectra, and their principal elemental composition can be determined to within 5% accuracy for a lunar surface area of 5 km diameter. For instance, a lunar crater such as Kepler of 32 km diameter may be characterized by 40 points.

Thus, being endowed with a number of advantages over conventional proportional counters, gas scintillation counters enable us to work out a more effective solution for an urgent problem in lunar research, namely geochemical cartography of the Moon's surface. As is known, the solution of this problem paves the way for the choice of particularly promising areas of the lunar surface for future exploration and possible exploitation.

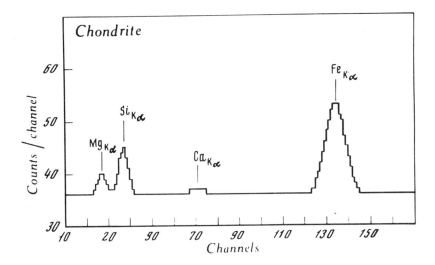

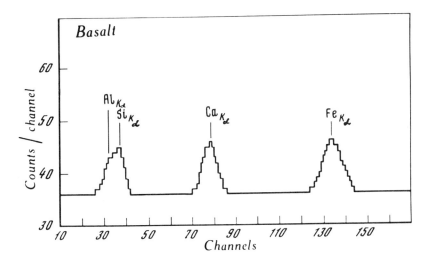

Fig. 2.2.35 — Fluorescent radiation spectra of some lunar rocks calculated by gas scintillation proportional counter in the quiet-Sun period.

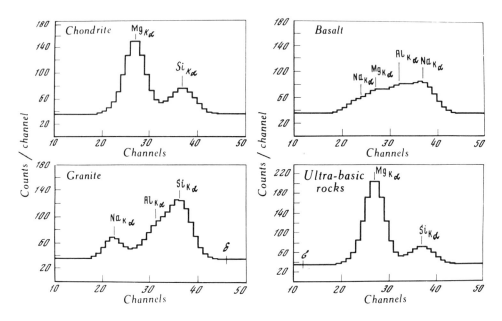

Fig. 2.2.36 — Fluorescent radiation spectra of some lunar rocks calculated by gas scintillation proportional counter for the active-Sun period.

REFERENCES

[1] N.F. Losev, In *Quantitative X-ray fluorescence analysis*. (In Russian) Moscow, Nauka, p.336 (1969).

[2] S. V. Mamikonyan, In *Instrumentation and methods of fluorescence X-ray radiometric analysis*. (In Russian) Moscow, Atomizdat, p.279 (1976).

[3] V. V. Matveyev and B. I. Khazanov, In *Instruments for measuring ionizing radiation*. (In Russian) Moscow, Atomizdat, p.695 (1972).

[4] A. L. Yakubovich, Ye. I. Zaitsev, and S. M. Przhiyalgovsky, In *Nuclear-physical methods of analysis of mineral raw materials*. (In Russian) Moscow, Atomizdat, p.415 (1969).

[5] S. L. Mandelshtam, I. P. Tindo, V. I. Karev, *Kosmich. Issled.*, **4**, 827 (In Russian) (1966).

[6] G. Ye. Kocharov, S. V. Viktorov, and N. F. Borodulin, In *The Lunokhod 1 mobile laboratory on the Moon*. (In Russian) Moscow, Nauka, Vol.1, p.89 (1971).

[7] G. Ye. Kocharov, S. V. Viktorov, and V. I. Chesnokov, In *Nuclear-physical studies of the Moon and planets*. (In Russian) Moscow, Energoizdat Publishers, p.184 (1981).

[8] G. Ye. Kocharov, and S. V. Viktorov, In *The Lunokhod 1 mobile laboratory on the Moon*. (In Russian) Moscow, Nauka, Vol 2, p.92 (1978).

[9] Yu. A. Surkov, B. M. Andreichikov, and I. K. Akhmetshin, *Kosmich. Issled.*, **10**, 930 (In Russian) (1972).

[10] I. Adler and J. Trombka, In *Geochemical exploration of the Moon and Planets*. New York, Springer Verlag, p.228 (1970).

[11] J. Adler, J. Trombka, and J. Gerard, *Science*, **177**, 256 (1972).

[12] J. Adler, J. Trombka, and R. Schmadebeck, In *Proc. 4th Lunar Sci. Conf.*, New York, Pergamon Press, Vol.3, p.2783 (1973).

[13] B. C. Clark, A. K. Baird, *Earth and Planet. Sci. Lett.*, **19**, 359, (1973).

[14] B. C. Clark, A. K. Baird, and P. Toulmin, *Science*, **94**, 1283 (1976).

[15] Yu. A. Surkov, F. F. Kirnozov, and V. I. Gugyanov, *Geokhimiya*, **1**, 3 (In Russian) (1981).

[16] V. L. Barsukov, Yu. A. Surkov, L. P. Moskalyova, O. P. Shcheglov, *Geokhimiya*, **7**, 899 (In Russian) (1982).

[17] Yu. A. Surkov, O. P. Shcheglov, and L. P. Moskalyova, *Analitich. Khimiya*, **37**, 1349 (In Russian) (1982).

[18] Yu. A. Surkov, L. P. Moskalyova, and O. P. Shcheglov, *Astron. Vestnik*, **16**, 139 (In Russian) (1982).

[19] Yu. A. Surkov, O. P. Shcheglov, and L. P. Moskalyova, *Anal. Chem.*, **54**, 957A, (1982).

[20] Yu. A. Surkov, L. P. Moskalyova, and O. P. Shcheglov, *Kosmich. Issled.*, **21**, 308 (In Russian) (1983).

[21] P. Toulmin, A. K. Baird, and B. C. Clark, *Icarus*, **20**, 153 (1973).

[22] H. Masursky, E. Eliason, and P. G. Ford, *J. Geophys. Res.*, **85**, 8232 (1980).

[23] I. V. Barmin and A. A. Shevchenko, *Kosmich, Issled.*, **21**, 171 (In Russian) (1983).

[24] V. P. Volkov, Yu. I. Sidorov, and I. L. Khodakovsky, *Geokhimiya*, **1**, 3 (In Russian) (1982).

[25] M. Ya. Marov, V. Ye. Lystsev, and V. N. Lebedev, In Report No 144, The Institute of Applied Mathematics of the USSR Academy of Sciences, (In Russian) Moscow, p.34 (1978).

[26] R. G. Knollenberg and D. M. Hunten, *Science*, **203**, 792 (1979).

[27] B. Rogent and J. Blamont, *Science*, **203**, 790 (1979).

[28] M. Ya. Marov, *Astron. Vestnik*, **13**, 3 (In Russian) (1979).

[29] V. I. Moroz, *Space Sci. Rev.*, **29**, 3 (1981).

[30] J. B. Pollack and Y. L. Young, *Annu. Rev. Earth and Planet. Sci.*, **8**, 425 (1980).

[31] Yu. A. Surkov, F. F. Kirnozov, and V. N. Glazov, *Letters to Astron. J.*, **8**, 700 (In Russian) (1982).

[32] V. L. Barsukov. I. L. Khodakovsky, and V. P. Volkov, In *Lunar and planetary science*, Houston: LPI **12**, 43 (1981).

[33] B. C. Clark, A. K. Baird, and H. J. Rose, *J. Geophys. Res.*, **82**, 4577 (1977).

[34] A. K. Baird, A. J. Castro, and B. C. Clark, *J. Geophys. Res.*, **82**, 4595 (1977).

[35] P. Toulmin, A. L. Baird, and B. C. Clark, *J. Geophys. Res.*, **82**, 4625 (1977).

[36] V. L. Barsukov, and Yu. A. Surkov, (Eds), In *Soil from the Moon's highland region.* (In Russian) Moscow, Nauka, p.359 (1979)

[37] A. P. Vinogradov, In *Lunar soil from Mare Crisium.* (In Russian) Moscow, Nauka, p.624 (1974).

[38] V. L. Barsukov, In *Lunar soil from Mare Crisium.* (In Russian) Moscow, Nauka, p.359 (1980)

[39] G. Ye. Kocharov, and S. V. Viktorov, *Dokl. AN SSSR*, **214**, 71 (In Russian) (1974).

[40] G. Ye. Kocharov, S. V. Victorov, and V. I. Chesnokov, *Space Researches B.*, **15**, 587 (1975).

[41] A. Peacock, M. Sims, B. G. Taylor, *ESA; ESTEC*, **22** (1983).

[42] K. P. Florensky, A. T. Basilevsky, and A. A. Gurshtein, *Dokl. AN USSR,* **214,** 75 (In Russian) (1974).

[43] G. Manzo, A. Peacock, and R. D. Andersen, *IEEE Trans. Nucl.Sci.*, **NS-27**, 204 (1980).

[44] G. Manzo, A. Peacock, and R. D. Andersen, *Nucl. Instrum. and Meth.*, **174**, 301 (1980)

[45] A. Peacock, R. D. Andersen, and A. Dordfecht, *IEEE Trans.Nucl. Sci.*, **NS-26**, 486 (1979).

[46] A. Peackock, R. D. Andersen, E. A. Leimann, *Nucl. Instrum. and Meth.*, 169, 619 (1980).

[47] J. Davelaar, G. Manzo, and A. Peacock, *Astron. and Astrophys.*, **87**, 276 (1980).

[48] J. Davelaar, G. Manzo, and A. Peacock, *IEEE Trans.Nucl. Sci.*, **NS-27**, 196 (1980)

[49] G. Manzo, J. Davelaar, A. Peacock, *Nucl.Instrum. and Meth.*, **177**, 595 (1980).

[50] A. Peacock, R. D. Andersen, and G. Manzo, *Space. Sci. Rev.*, **30**, 525 (1981).

[51] H. W. Head, J. B. Garvin, D. B. Campbell, G. H. Pettengill, R. S. Sanders, V. L. Barsukov, A. T. Basilevsky, and Yu. A. Surkov. In *Abstracts of XVII Lunar and Planetary Science Conference* (Houston), 327 (1986).

[52] Yu. A. Surkov, L. P. Moskalyeva, O. P. Shcheglov, V. P. Kharyukova *et al.*, *J. Geophys. Res.*, **88**, A481 (1983).

[53] Yu. A. Surkov, V.L. Barsukov, L.P. Moskalyeva *et al.*, *J. Geophys. Res.*, **89**, B393 (1984).

[54] Yu. A. Surkov, L. P. Moskalyeva, O. P. Shcheglov *et al.*, *Astronom. Vestnik*, **19**, 275 (In Russian) (1985).

[55] Yu. A. Surkov, L. P. Moskalyeva, V. P. Kharyukova *et al.*, In *Abstracts of XVII Lunar and Planetary Science Conference* (Houston), 849 (1986).

2.3 Neutronometry

2.3.1 METHOD AND INSTRUMENTATION FOR NEUTRON ACTIVATION ANALYSIS OF ROCKS

To study the lunar rock composition by space vehicles a number of instruments were created for measuring gamma-radiation excited by neutrons [1–4]. However, they have not been used up to now. This is due to the fact that the first landing modules could not carry such sophisticated instrumentation, which was fairly heavy, consumed much energy and transferred a large amount of information. Also it was preferred for the first space probes to use simpler and lighter equipment, although it was less informative, to give preliminary estimates of the lunar rock chemical composition based on recording alpha-radiation from ^{242}Cm scattered by the rock [5–8] or fluorescent radiation of the rock excited by the X-ray Ti/Zn source [9–11] and by the Sun's X-ray radiation [12].

Heavier Soviet and American spacecraft, such as Lunas 16, 20 and 24 and the Apollo spacecraft, brought lunar material back to the Earth and thus did not use equipment for analysing the composition of the lunar rock in its natural bedding. At the same time, the expediency of using such equipment is obvious for exploring material on the Moon and planets with vehicles which are not recovered to the Earth and especially from mobile stations of the Lunokhod type, when it is necessary to obtain information on the chemical composition and properties of the rock in different regions of the surface and for different geological formations. Of particular promise is the use of activation equipment for studying the rock composition on planets which possess atmospheres, where the use of other methods based on recording alpha-, beta- and X-ray-radiation is more difficult.

The collision of neutrons with nuclei leads to one of the following processes accompanied by gamma-radiation:

— inelastic scattering — (n, n');
— nuclear reactions with the escape of charged particles and neutrons — (n,p), (n,α), $(n, 2n)$, etc.;
— radiation capture of the neutron (n,γ).

The probability of each process is determined by the value of the corresponding effective cross-section. The cross-section of the process varies significantly with the change in energy of the incident neutron and also turns out to be different for nuclei with different mass numbers. In our case, the greatest interest is in the interaction of neutrons with initial energies of about 14 MeV (which according to conventional classification belong to the so-called 'fast' neutrons) and the nuclei of elements which are the most widespread in rocks; that is, elements with light ($A<25$) and medium ($25<A<80$) atomic mass numbers.

If the rock is subjected to brief irradiation by neutrons (by neutron pulse), the flux density of the gamma-radiation induced by the neutrons will vary with time in accordance with the curve shown in Fig. 2.3.1 (neither axis is to scale). Almost simultaneously with the irradiation by neutrons, gamma-ray quanta resulting from inelastic scattering are ejected. Then, in the tens of milliseconds necessary for the slowing down of the neutrons in the rock, the density of the radiation capture flux reaches a maximum. Finally, after irradiation only a few gamma-ray quanta are ejected. These quanta accompany the radioactive decay of activated nuclei.

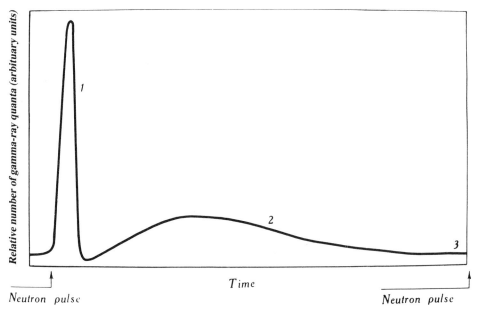

Fig. 2.3.1 — Change in the density of the gamma-radiation flu of the rock irradiated by a short-time neutron pulse: 1, inelastic scattering; 2, radiation capture; 3, activation.

The flux densities of the gamma-ray quanta produced by these three processes differ by orders of magnitude as depicted in Fig. 2.3.1. A peak short in time but large in the density of the flux (the density is of the same order as that of the neutrons) corresponds to gamma-ray quanta from inelastic scattering. A wide, gently sloping peak corresponds to gamma-ray quanta from radiation capture and is due to the relatively long duration of the slowing down of the neutrons and the fluctuation of the number of interactions of neutrons with rock nuclei. Finally, the decay of activated nuclei takes place in keeping with exponential law, and the flux of gamma-ray quanta accompanying the decay is still smaller by several orders of magnitude. It depends on the half-life of the activated nuclei.

But not only the flux density varies with time. The spectrum of gamma-radiation accompanying the above processes also varies. While the character of the change of the gamma-radiation flux with time (it is shown in Fig. 2.3.1) varies little with the rock composition, the spectral composition of gamma-radiation is determined mainly by the composition of the rock and the processes of interaction of the neutrons with it.

This section deals briefly with interaction of the fast neutrons with the basic rock-forming elements and in more detail with the structure and use of onboard equipment for studying the composition and properties of extraterrestrial material by the neutron activation method.

2.3.1.1   Onboard instrumentation for neutron activation analysis

In papers [1–4] the design features and physical characteristics of onboard equipment for neutron activation analysis of material are considered in detail. The greatest difficulty in creating such instrumentation is the design of a small and economical neutron generator possessing a high neutron flux density. Depending on the character of the recorded gamma-radiation and the corresponding modes of operation of the activation equipment, a flux of 10^7 to 10^9 neutron s^{-1} with energies of 14 MeV is the optimum one. For instance, the paper [1] deals with a version of onboard equipment based on recording gamma-radiation from inelastic scattering excited by a relatively low neutron flux of about 10^7 neutron s^{-1}. In [2] activation equipment is discussed. It is based on recording gamma-radiation from rock activated by a neutron flux of about 10^9 neutrons s^{-1}. Both versions of equipment are of undoubted interest, and the reader can get acquainted with them in above literature.

Here shall describe in detail, however, the version of universal automatic activation equipment for studying extraterrestrial material by space vehicles.

This equipment was designed by a team of researchers engaged in the gamma-ray spectrometry of the Moon and the planets [13, 14]. The equipment makes it possible to conduct the following studies on the planetary surface:

— determination of the content of the basic rock-forming elements (O,Si,Al,Mg,Fe, etc.) in the surface layer of material from gamma-radiation appearing under excitation by fast neutrons;
— determination of the water content in the rock under study from the gamma-radiation of radiation capture;
— determination of the content of natural radioactive elements (U,Th and K) from natural gamma-radiation;
— measurement of the density of the rock from the magnitude of the flux of gamma-ray quanta from inelastic scattering of neutrons;
— measurement of the flux of cosmic rays and the overall level of radiation on the planetary surface by a charged particle detector and the gamma-ray spectrometer.

These studies allow one to draw important conclusions about the character of the rock on the planetary surface and the processes which have taken part in its formation.

The principle of operation of this equipment is shown in Fig. 2.3.2.

The neutron generator creates a flux of 14-MeV neutrons emitted in short pulses having a duration of $1 - 3$ μs and with a pulse frequency of up to 10^4 Hz.

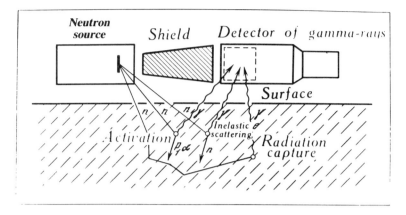

Fig. 2.3.2 — Diagram of studying the composition and properties of the rock by the neutron activation method.

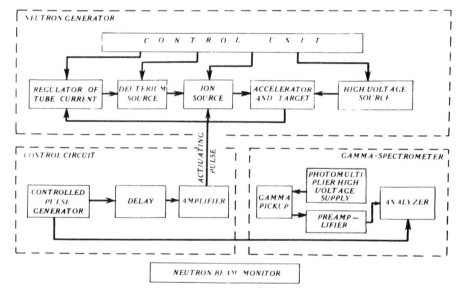

Fig. 2.3.3 — Functional diagram of instrumentation for studying the composition and properties of the rock by the neutron activation method.

Gamma-radiation generated in the irradiated rock is recorded by a scintillation gamma-ray spectrometer. Synchronization of the operation of the generator and the spectrometer by the control unit makes it possible to record separately the gamma-radiation produced as a result of inelastic scattering, radiation capture and activation.

The equipment consists of three units. The first unit (the outlying sleeve) includes a neutron generator's, scintillation detector shielded from the generator's neutron radiation and a power-supply system. The second unit consists of a multi-channel amplitude analyser and an information output system. The third unit controls and synchronizes the operation of the equipment. During the experiment the outlying sleeve is placed at the surface studied, while other units are housed inside the sealed compartment of the probe and are linked to the sleeve by a flexible cable.

The schematic diagram of the equipment is shown in Fig. 2.3.3. Its principal functional elements are the neutron pulse generator, the scintillation gamma-ray spectrometer, the control and synchronization unit, the neutron flux monitor and the power supply unit. At the same time, each of these elements contains a number of interconnected assemblies. Let us consider their structure and function in more detail.

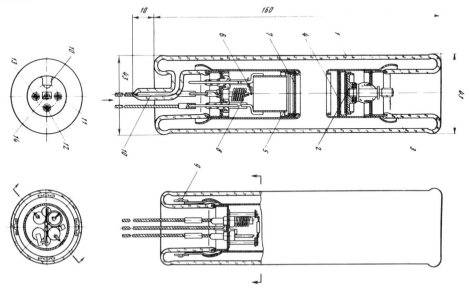

Fig. 2.3.4 — Design of the NT-7 neutron tube: 1, glass cylinder; 2, target; 3, high-voltage electrode; 4, grid; 5, anode of the ion source; 6, cathode of the ion source; 7, grid; 8, deuterium source; 9, getter; 10, exhaust tube; 11, output of the heater of the cathode of the ion source; 12, output of the anode of the ion source; 13, output of the deuterium source; 14, output of the anode of the tube. Dimensions in millimetres.

The neutron pulse generator

The small neutron pulse tube is the basis of the neutron generator. Its structure is shown in Fig. 2.3.4. The tube is a cylindrical electrovacuum device consisting of several assemblies performing different functions. Its operation is based on the nuclear reaction $T(d,n)^4He$, as a result of which neutrons with energies of about 14 MeV are produced. This reaction takes place during the interaction of deuterium ions accelerated up to 100 keV and tritium atoms absorbed on the zirconium target which serves as the cathode of the tube. On each zirconium atom of the target's surface on average about 1.5 tritium atoms are retained. The target area is about 1.5 cm^2.

Deuterium ions are obtained in an ion source of the Penning type which consists of an oxide cathode and a transparent cylindrical anode. A titanium spiral saturated with deuterium up to the atomic ratio $N_D/N_{Ti} \approx 0.2-0.4$ and placed in the ion source is the source of deuterium.

The tube operates in the following way. Being accelerated by the anode voltage of the ion source of 250 to 300 V, electrons emitted by the oxide cathode ionize deuterium which is released as a result of heating of the titanium spiral. Emerging from the ion source, ionized deuterium atoms get into the high voltage electric field, are accelerated by it to an energy of about 100 keV and get on the tritium–

zirconium target, causing the T(d,n)^{4}He reaction with the formation of neutrons with energies of about 14 MeV.

Since a change in operating conditions (for instance, temperature) causes the amount of deuterium released from the source to vary, which can change the mode of tube operation, automatic regulation of gas pressure in the tube is envisaged in the scheme for removing this dependence. In the optimum operational mode of the tube the integral flux is 5×10^7 neutron s^{-1}.

The neutron tube is supplied with high-voltage power from a special source assembled according to the multiplication scheme. At the output the high-voltage source provides a current of $20 - 40$ μA with a voltage of about 100 kV.

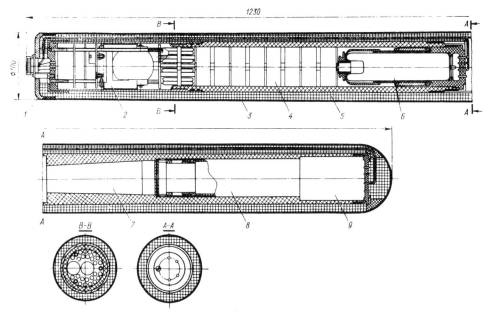

Fig. 2.3.5 — Design of the outrigger sleeve of the instrumentation for neutron activation analysis: 1, lid; 2, power-supply unit of NT-7 tube; 3, body; 4, multiplying circuit; 5, screen-vacuum insulation; 6, accelerating tube; 7, shield; 8, gamma-radiation detector; 9, power supply unit of the detector. Dimensions in millimetres.

The neutron generator is assembled in a section of the sleeve, the structure of which is given in Fig. 2.3.5. To lessen the probability of a puncture occurring the sections of the high-voltage source are assembled so that the voltage increases from the edge of the sleeve to the centre where the tube is located. In addition, the section is filled with carefully dried oil.

To stabilize the neutron flux, there is an automatic regulation scheme in the sleeve. When an increase in the current flowing through the tube occurs, this scheme accordingly reduces the current of the inlet system which leads to a reduction in the current of the tube.

The low-voltage power supply unit of the neutron generator is a transformer made according to the push–pull circuit with a common base. To maintain a constant voltage in the power-supplying circuit, a stabilizer is installed at the output of the unit. With a change in the voltage of the supply by 15%, the output voltage varies by not more than 0.1%.

The ion-source ignition pulse (this pulse is synchronized with the control pulse) is produced by the blocking generator. The high input impedance of the blocking generator is achieved through introducing an emitter follower in the circuit. The target current stabilization needed for maintaining a constant neutron flux is achieved through the automatic regulation of the gas pressure in the accelerator of the tube.

The gamma-ray spectrometer
The detection unit and the pulse-amplitude analyser are the main functional elements of the spectrometer. A special feature of the detection unit is the use of a combined scintillator in it. Pulses resulting from the passage of charged particles into the crystal are discriminated by this scintillator. The latter is an NaI (Tl) crystal 40 x 50 mm in size surrounded with scintillating plastic 3 – 4 mm thick. The crystal and the plastic are separated by a transparent glass container.

Optical contact is maintained through silicon glue. The outer sides of the plastic scintillator are covered with reflecting enamel with the exception of the side facing the photomultiplier. Pulses generated in the pickup under the effect of charged particles are discriminated by a special scheme using the difference in the time of fluorescence of the crystal and the scintillating plastic.

An FEU-81 photomultiplier is used in the detection unit. A permalloy cylinder serves as a magnetic screen for the photopultiplier. To stabilize the gain factor in different temperature conditions of detection unit operation, a thermal resistor is series-connected with the high-voltage power-supply divider for the photomultiplier. The change in the magnitude of thermal resistance compensates for the change in the magnitude of the signal.

The detection unit of the gamma-ray spectrometer, along with the high-voltage power supply (for 1800 V) and a copper screen about 150 mm long, which shields the detector from the generator neutron flux, is placed in the outer sleeve.

The gamma-radiation spectrum is recorded, analysed and memorized by the multichannel pulse-amplitude analyser. Information from the analyser is transmitted via the telemetry system.

The control and synchronization unit
The control and synchronization unit ensures the correct operation mode of the instrument depending on which method was used to analyse the elemental composition of matter (inelastic interaction, radiation capture or activation). This unit sends initiating ignition pulses to the ion source of the neutron generator, as well as signals synchronised with them which control the operation of the amplitude analyser of the gamma-ray spectrometer.

Ignition pulses have positive polarity, an amplitude of 250 – 300 V and a duration of about 2 μs. The pulse frequency depends on the type of gamma-radiation recorded.

The analyser is controlled by rectangular pulses of negative polarity with an amplitude of 5 – 10 V, a duration of 2 – 1000 μs and a frequency of 0.5 – 10 kHz. The duration of the delay of the control pulses with respect to the initiating pulses varies from 0 – 1000 μs.

Fig. 2.3.6 gives the timing diagram for the operation of the control and synchronization unit in different modes. As will be evident from the diagrams, in the

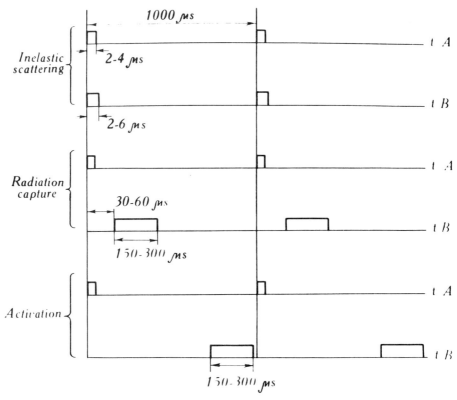

Fig. 2.3.6 — Time diagram of the operation of the control and synchronization unit: A, ignition
pulses; B, control pulses.

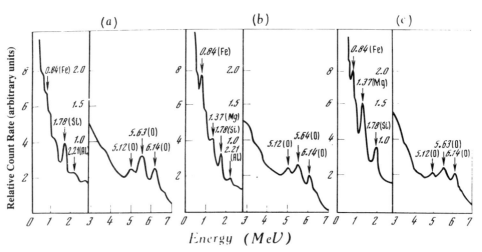

Fig. 2.3.7 — Gamma-radiation spectra induced by inelastic scattering neutrons in granite (a),
basalt (b) and dunite (c).

inelastic scattering mode the input of the pulse-amplitude anlayser is opened only during the existence of a neutron pulse, in the radiation capture mode with a delay of $30 - 60$ μs, and in the activation mode at the end of the cycle.

To choose the operation modes from the wide range of possible initial parameters, there are two wide-range pulse generators in the contol and synchronization unit. One of them gives out initiating pulses to the neutron generator and control pulses delayed with respect to them by the analyser, while the second is used to shape the ignition pulses.

2.3.1.2 Study of the composition and properties of rocks by the neutron activation method

(a) Analysis of gamma-radiation from inelastic scattering

In this instrument the spectra of gamma-radiation from the inelastic scattering of neutrons were obtained for some terrestrial rocks, as presented in Fig. 2.3.7. Some peaks, linked with the excitation of the first energy levels of different nuclei, are well displayed in these spectra. At the same time, these peaks lie on a high 'plateau' whose origin and composition will be discussed below.

The values of the cross-sections for the inelastic scattering of fast neutrons for different elements vary within rather small limits: from tenths of a barn to several barns. That is why for elements whose content in the rock does not exceed 1%, macroscopic cross-sections are too small to use the $(n,n'\gamma)$ reaction for quantitative determinations. However, if it is necessary to identify the rock type from the content of the basic rock-forming elements, the approximate equality of cross-sections is an advantage.

To estimate the effect of the irradiated rock density on the flux of gamma-ray quanta from inelastic scattering and on the shape of the recorded spectra, measurements were made on sand samples with different densities. The measurements have shown that the recorded count rate of the gamma-ray quanta from inelastic scattering increases with an increase in the density of irradiated samples. The rate of growth gradually decreases and if the density ρ is higher than about 2×10^3 kg m^{-3} the flux of the gamma-ray quanta from inelastic scattering remains approximately constant. The smoothing out of the curve, when $\rho > 2 \times 10^3$ kg m^{-3}, is accounted for by the fact that denser rocks screen the neutron flux and gamma-ray quanta formed, in this way reducing the recorded count rate.

This count rate feature enables one to determine the density of the irradiated rock from the recorded count rate of the gamma-ray quanta from the inelastic scattering of neutrons. The absolute error of determing the density is roughly 1×10^2 kg m^{-3}.

The 'plateau' in the spectrum of the gamma-radiation from inelastic scattering is mainly accounted for by the following processes: (1) the passage of neutrons through the shielding and the formation of gamma-ray quanta in it; (2) the scattering of neutrons from the sample measured; (3) the scattering of neutrons from surrounding objects and the generation of gamma-ray quanta in them, especially if measurements are taken indoors.

The use of a significant amount of shielding makes it possible to shield the detector from the neutron flux almost completely and thus to record the spectrum resulting only from the scattering of neutrons from surrounding objects and the appearance of gamma-ray quanta in them. For instance, for a copper filter 25 cm thick, the direct passage of neutrons accounts for 2% of the initial flux.

From tabular data and the above-mentioned spectra for gamma-radiation from inelastic scattering, it is evident that elements which are the most widespread in rocks have sufficiently typical and well-displayed gamma-ray lines for measurement. For example, in oxygen in the course of the inelastic scattering of fast neutrons, the level with an energy of 6.14 MeV is excited with the largest cross-section. In the instrumental spectrum the gamma-radiation of oxygen manifests itself in the form of three peaks caused by the absorption of one or two annihilation gamma-ray quanta, or by the escape of both of them from the crystal. In carbon the level with an energy of 4.43 MeV is excited while gamma-radiation corresponding to it also produces a triad of peaks in the instrumental spectrum. In the gamma-ray spectrum of silicon a peak with an energy of 1.78 MeV is the most intense, in the spectrum of aluminium a 2.21-MeV peak, in the spectrum of magnesium a 1.37-MeV peak while iron is marked by a peak an energy of 0.84 MeV.

On the basis of the above-mentioned gamma-ray lines the quantitative processing of the spectra of gamma-radiation from the inelastic scattering of fast neutrons is carried out. With this aim in view use is made of a method [15] in which the content of elements or their ratios are determined from the areas of peaks belonging to the same elements. The corresponding calibration curves are plotted on the basis of measuring the spectra of the gamma-radiation from inelastic scattering for rock samples having a known composition. The content of oxygen in rocks of different types varies within relatively small limits and the average oxygen content for a number of rocks can be assumed to be the known value. In addition, the sum of the contents of the five above-mentioned elements represents for most rocks a value close to 90%. Consequently it becomes possible to find the absolute contents of elements, although their ratios are sufficiently indicative of the type of rock which is being studied.

This method of processing the spectra of the gamma-radiation from inelastic scattering has certain positive aspects. In the first place, there is no need to normalize strictly the recorded gamma-ray spectra on the basis of the neutron flux since during the processing of spectra it is not the absolute numbers of pulses in the peaks of the determining elements which are used, but their ratios within the same spectrum. Secondly, the change in the density of the sample does not introduce noticeable distortions in the results obtained because in this case only the flux of recorded gamma-radiation varies while the shape of the gamma-ray spectrum, as noted above, remains unchanged. The errors in the ratios of peak areas found in this way enable one to assess the sensitivity of the method; that is, to find the contents of elements which can be determined with an error of 100%. For instance, for iron, magnesium, aluminium and oxygen these values are 0.6, 1.2, 0.6 and 2.0%, respectively.

(b) Analysis of gamma-radiation generated during the activation

Knowledge of the half-life periods of radioisotopes and the energies of gamma-ray quanta emitted during their disintegration makes it possible to prepare a rather simple (from the point of view of the final aim of the experiment) programme for irradiating the samples which are being studied and of recording the induced activity. Fig. 2.3.8 gives the spectra of the gamma-radiation generated during the the activation. The spectra were obtained 12 min after the end of the irradiation. The

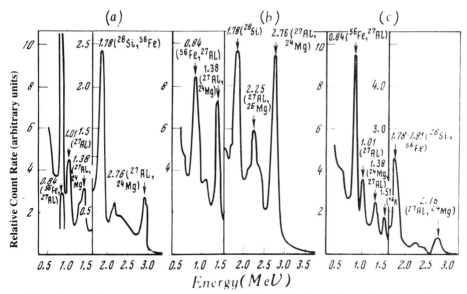

Fig. 2.3.8 — Activation gamma-spectra recorded 12 min after the end of the irradiation of the rock by neutrons: (a) basalt, (b) dunite, (c) granite.

irradiation took 45 min and the recording 30 min. The neutron flux was 5 x 10^7 neutron s^{-1}.

Recording of the activation gamma-radiation in the process of irradiation of the rock using the same measurement geometry as during the analysis from inelastic scattering enables one, despite the background resulting from activation of material in the detection unit, to obtain a spectrum containing a number of peaks caused by the activation of Mg,Si,Al,Fe and O (the latter is in the harder region of the spectrum), and thus to determine their content in the irradiated rock.

Similar spectra of the activation gamma-radiation, in which the same lines are displayed, can be obtained with the use of another programme of measurements when the irradiation and recording are carried out consistently with short (about 20s duration) exposures. In this case, use can be made of a rotating [2] or similar geometry of measurements which enables one to remove the background caused by the activation of material in the detection unit.

Gamma-radiation resulting from the activation of oxygen can also be recorded by means of a channel of the analyser tuned in such a way as to record gamma-ray quanta having an energy higher then 4.5 MeV. Such a method of recording gamma-radiation during the activation of oxygen is applicable to the above-mentioned irradiation and measuring programmes.

After a 12-minute exposure, during which ^{16}N generated from oxygen disintegrates almost fully and the amount of ^{28}Al formed mainly from ^{28}Si is significantly reduced, the spectrum of the gamma-radiation from activation products is recorded in which peaks with energies of 0.84; 1.01, 1.28 and 1.78 MeV are displayed. This spectrum is used to determine the content of aluminium and silicon.

By 120 min after the end of the irradiation ^{27}Mg and ^{28}Al have disintegrated too. In the activation gamma-radiation spectrum recorded after such exposure, a peak with an energy of 0.84 MeV, resulting from the decay of ^{56}Mn formed from ^{56}Fe, and peaks with energies of 1.37 and 2.75 MeV, resulting from the decay of ^{24}Na, appear. As far as ^{24}Na is concerned, it is formed from both ^{24}Mg and ^{27}Al, due to (n,p) and (n,α) reactions, respectively. The contribution from the activation of ^{27}Al which hinders the determination of magnesium is taken into account by measuring magnesium boring samples. Thus, magnesium is determined from the area of peaks with energies of 1.37 and 2.75 MeV, and iron from the peak having an energy of 0.84 MeV.

Activation gamma-radiation spectra are processed in the same way as when using inelastic scattering. The accuracy of the determination is approximately the same. For instance, the sensitivity of the determination is 1.0% for oxygen, and magnesium, and 0.4% for aluminium and iron.

(c) Analysis of the gamma-ray spectra from radiation capture.

The gamma-ray quanta from radiation capture are recorded during intervals between neutron pulses. Along with this radiation the gamma-ray quanta appearing due to the activation of the rock and the material of the detection unit and also due to natural radioactivity are recorded. Due to the mutual interposition of a large number of gamma-ray lines, such a spectrum, even after the deduction of gamma-ray radiation resulting from the activation of material of the detection unit and natural radioactivity, represents a distribution in which one sees only the triad of peaks (6.14, 5.63 and 5.12 MeV) due to the activation of oxygen, a peak with an energy of 1.78 MeV due to the activation of silicon, and a peak with an energy of 2.23 MeV due

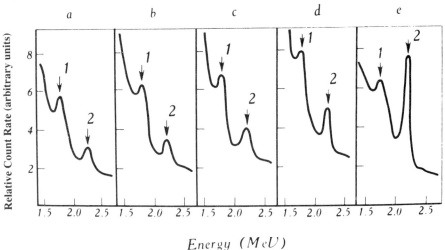

Fig. 2.3.9 — Spectra of the radiation capture and activation obtained during the irradiation of sand of different humidity by neutrons (1) 6%; (2) 8%; (3) 10.5%; (4) 13%; (5) 50%.

to the radiation capture of hydrogen. The last two peaks are used for plotting a curve of the ratios of the areas of the peaks belonging to hydrogen and silicon as a function of the ratios of the contents of these elements in the rock. With this aim in view, the spectra of the gamma-ray quanta from radiation capture and the activation of quartz sand of different water saturation (Fig. 2.3.9) can be used. In addition to the relationship between hydrogen and silicon, when silicon content is known, water content in the rock, which is being studied, can be determined from the calibration curve. The sensitivity of the determination is approximately 0.5% from H_2O.

2.3.2 REMOTE STUDIES OF THE COMPOSITION OF ROCKS FROM THE NEUTRON FIELD

2.3.2.1 Neutrons appearing in the rock under the effect of cosmic rays

The nuclear-physical methods considered above make it possible to determine remotely the content of the basic rock-forming elements or natural radioactive elements in the rock. However, there are some elements for which determination by the neutron method is more convenient. These are, above all, hydrogen, the rare earths and some other elements having a large neutron-capture cross-section in the thermal or resonance energy ranges. That is why the neutron method efficiently complements other methods of analysis. Specifically, it is reasonable to apply this method to search for water (ice) on the surface or under the layer of regolith on Mars [16], for detecting frozen water in the Moon's polar regions [17] and for finding rocks with high rare earth content on the lunar surface [18]. Neutron methods can be used for such purposes when studying any celestial bodies deprived of an atmosphere or possessing an atmosphere which is not dense.

As mentioned above, celestial bodies deprived of atmospheres are irradiated by galactic or solar cosmic rays leading to the formation of neutrons whose quantity and spectral composition depend on the elemental composition of the rock. If we ignore solar flares which occur rarely, it can be said that the surface of the body is irradiated only by galactic cosmic rays which are isotropically distributed in space, and with a constant flux density. Since the formation rate of secondary neutrons at different depths is almost independent of the rock composition, we have a three-dimensional neutron source which is fairly constant in time and distribution over the depth. However, the flux density of neutrons in different energy groups (thermal, epithermal and fast) near the surface can be calculated theoretically, proceeding from the spectral composition and the flux density of galactic cosmic rays. In [19–22] the formation rates of fast neutrons at different depths in the rock were calculated. It was determined that the maximum occurs at a depth of about 4×10^2 kg m^{-2}, and that the neutron formation rate integrated over the depth is about 1.8×10^5 neutrons m^{-2}.

Knowing the distribution of fast neutrons over the depth, one can calculate the flux densities of neutrons in different energy groups on the surface, or measure them in model experiments.

Fig. 2.3.10 gives the flux densities of neutrons in different energy groups (thermal, epithermal and fast) over the surface of waterless rock from a layer of unit thickness (this layer is at different depths) with the formation rate of fast neutrons equal to the formation rate of neutrons at the given depth under the effect of cosmic rays. For the sake of comparison, the same figure shows the flux densities of neutrons for the same rock containing a water layer 5 cm thick lying on the surface. (The position of the water layer at different depths of $0 – 5 \times 10^2$ kg m^{-2} (50 g cm^{-2}) of the rock does not significantly alter the character of these curves.)

As will be evident from Fig. 2.3.10, the flux density of fast neutrons near the surface of the dry rock is much higher than that of thermal and epithermal neutrons, and exponentially decreases with depth. At first the flux density of thermal and epithermal neutrons increases, reaching a maximum at a depth of $(4–5) \times 10^2$ kg m^{-2} $(40 – 50$ g cm$^{-2})$, and then slowly falls, becoming an order of magnitude lower at a depth of about 2×10^3 kg m^{-2} (200 g cm^{-2}). The addition of water to the rock sharply

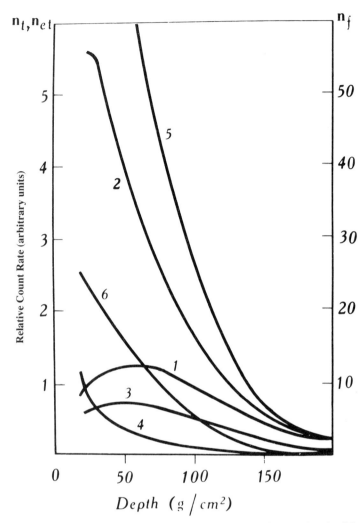

Fig. 2.3.10 — Density of the neutron flux of different energy groups ($\underline{n}_t$, $\underline{n}_e$, $\underline{n}_f$) at the different depth of the rock. ($\underline{n}_t$, $\underline{n}_e$, $\underline{n}_f$-fluxes of thermal, epithermmal and fast neutrons respectively). (a) Dry rock; 1, thermal neutrons; 3, epithermal neutrons; 5, fast neutrons. (b) The same rock with the addition of the water layer of $50 \text{Kgm}^{-2} (5 \text{gcm}^{-2})$; 2, thermal neutrons; 4, epithermal neutrons; 6, fast neutrons.

increases the flux of thermal and epithermal neutrons and reduces the flux of fast neutrons, especially near the surface; that is, at low depths. (The ratio of the fluxes of thermal and fast neutrons varies by a factor of 2 to 3.)

Model experiments show that a hydrogen-containing layer (water, polyethylene and plexiglass) 5–10 kg m^{-2} thick significantly varies the count rates of neutrons in different energy groups if it is at the depth of 0–5 x 10^2 kg m^{-2}. The ratios of the fluxes of neutrons of different energy groups will definitely also vary with the presence of other elements which slow down or capture neutrons.

2.3.2.2 Structure of the neutron detector for remote studies of rocks

Fig. 2.3.11 shows the structure of the device for remote studies of rocks from the neutron flux. This onboard device has a sealed cylindrical body in which the detectors and electronics are mounted. The device houses 16 neutron counters filled with helium-3 at a pressure of 7×10^3Pa.

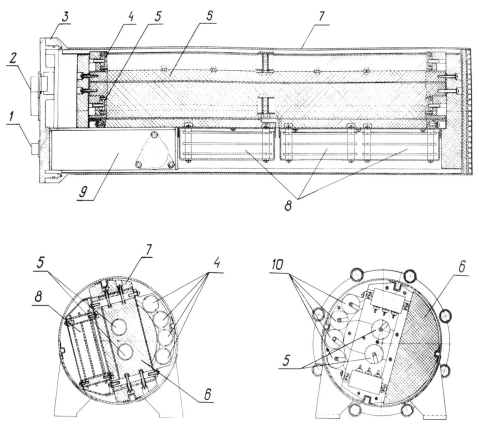

Fig. 2.3.11 — Arrangement of the instrument for remote measurements of the neutron flux: 1, filling valve; 2, plug; 3, instrument body; 4, thermal neutron detectors; 5, fast neutron detectors; 6 and 7, moderator; 8, electronic device; 9, power-supply source; 10, epithermal neutron detectors.

The first group of four counters is installed close to the axis of the device. The counters shielded from all sides by a 5 cm layer of a moderator (polyethylene) and protected by a cadmium shield from outside are used to measure the flux of fast neutrons which are slowed down in polyethylene.

The second four-counter group is installed near the cylinder wall facing the neutron flux. From the neutron flux side the counters are shielded only by a thin wall which barely influences the neutron flux. These counters record the thermal and epithermal neutron flux. Finally, the third four-counter group is located within the same geometry as the second group, but is surrounded with a cadmium shield. This third group records only the epithermal neutron flux.

The instrument body also contains all the electronic devices used to record and analyse signals from the detectors: preamplifiers, amplifiers, upper – and lower-level discriminators, counting devices, a voltage converter, and a high-voltage source.

The whole volume of the instrument is filled with helium up to a pressure of 7×10^5 Pa. This filling serves as an additional fast-neutron moderator and guarantees adequate performance of the detectors in the event of leakage of the working fluid from them. The basic characteristics of the instrument are as follows: mass 12 kg, power consumption 8 W, overall dimensions 200 mm in diameter and 500 mm in height, overall working area 500 cm^2, efficiency about 80% for slow neutrons and 3 – 5% for fast neutrons, the number of energy channels – three, the capacity of each energy channel 10^5, and the working temperature range lies between – 50°C and + 70°C.

The instrument was designed with due account taken of corresponding requirements made of onboard instrumentation (minimum mass, energy consumption and dimensions, etc.). That is why it does not represent the optimum version from the point of view of nuclear-physical characteristics. However, such a dense packing of the detector makes it possible to measure the flux of neutrons in different energy groups actually at one point. (The placing of three types of detectors at large distances from each other would lead to different effects of the probe's body on the neutron flux).

Using this instrument, it is possible to carry out neutron mapping of the surface of a celestial body with respect to the different moisture content or the content of elements with a large neutron-capture cross-section in the rock.

REFERENCES

[1] R. L. Caldwell, W. R. Mills and L. S. Allen, *Science*, **152**, 457 (1966).

[2] J. A. Hislop, and R. E. Wainardi, *Anal. Chem.*, **39**, 29A (1967).

[3] C. D. Schrader, J. A. Waggoner and A. E. Metzger, *Nucleonics*, **20**, 67 (1962).

[4] C. D. Schrader and R. J. Stinner, *J. Geophys. Res.*, **66**, 1951 (1965).

[5] T. E. Economov and A. L. Turkevich, *J. Geophys. Res.*, **78**, 781 (1973).

[6] J. H. Patterson, E. J. Franzgrote and A. L. Turkevich, *J. Geophys. Res.*, **74**, 6120 (1969).

[7] A. L. Turkevich, K. Knolle, and R. A. Emmert, *Rev. Sci. Instrum.*, **37**, 1681 (1966).

[8] A. L. Turkevich, K. Knolle and E. Franzgrote, *J. Geophys. Res*, **72**, 831 (1967).

[9] G. Ye. Kocharov, S. V. Viktorov and N. F. Borodulin. In *The Lunokhod 1 mobile laboratory on the Moon*. (In Russian.) Moscow, Nauka, Vol. 1, p.89 (1971).

[10] G. Ye. Kocharov, and S. V. Viktorov, *Dokl. AN SSSR*, **214**, 71 (In Russian.) (1974).

[11] G. Ye. Kocharov, and S. V. Viktorov, In *Space research. B.*, **12** 13 (1972).

[12] J. Adler, J. Trombka and J. Gerrard. In *Proc. 3rd Lunar Sci. Conf.* New York, Pergamon Press, vol. 3, p.2157 (1972).

[13] B. G. Yegiazarov, B. N. Kononov and S. S. Kurochkin, *Kosmich. Issled.*, **4**, 265 (In Russian.) (1968).

[14] Yu. A. Surkov, F. F. Kirnozov and O. P. Sobornov, *Kosmich Issled.*, **11**, 781 (In Russian.) (1973).

[15] D. F. Covell, *Anal. Chem.*, **31**, 1785 (1959).

[16] T. A. Mutch, R. E. Arvidson and J. W. Head. *In The geology of Mars.* Princeton University Press. p.262 (1976).

[17] K. Watson, B. C. Murray and K. Brawn. *J. Geophys. Res.,* **66**, 3033 (1961).

[18] H. J. Hubbard, C. Meyer and P. W. Gast, *Earth and Planet. Sci. Lett.,* **10**, 341 (1971).

[19] T. W. Armstrong and R. G. Alsmiller, In *Proc.2nd Lunar Sci. Conf.* New York, Pergamon Press, Vol. 2, p.1729 (1971).

[20] J. J. Kornblum, E. L. Fireman and M. Levine, In *Proc.4th Lunar Sci. Conf.,* New York, Pergamon Press, Vol. 2, p.2171 (1973).

[21] R. E. Lingenfelter, E. N. Canfield and V. E. Hampel, *Earth and Planet. Sci. Lett.,* **16**, 353 (1972).

[22] R. C. Reedy and J. R. Arnold, *J. Geophys. Res.,* **77**, 537 (1972).

2.4 Alpha-spectrometry

2.4.1 ANALYSIS OF LUNAR ROCK FROM SURVEYORS 5, 6 AND 7 BY THE METHOD OF ALPHA-PARTICLE SCATTERING

2.4.1.1 Method and instrumentation

The method of scattering alpha-particles in analysing lunar material was used by the US Surveyor spacecraft in the period 1967–1968. The chemical composition of the rocks in two mare regions and one highland region of the Moon's surface was determined. The instrument used in these experiments was described in detail in papers [1, 2], the method of analysis in papers [3, 4] and the results of the experiments in [5–8].

This method of analysis is based on the irradiation of the rock by alpha-particles from a radioisotope source and the measurement of the spectra of back-scattered alpha-particles or protons produced in reactions with light nuclei.

Alpha-particles back-scattered at an angle close to 180° have the energy $E'_\alpha = [E^\circ_\alpha (A - 4)^2/(A - 4)^2]$ where E°_α and E'_α are energies of the incident and the scattered alpha-particle, respectively, A is the mass number of the irradiated element. Due to the weak dependence of the energy of the scattered alpha-particle on A the measurements of the spectrum of E'_α and the determination of the content of the element call for the use of a detector with high energy resolution. The measuring technique used in the experiments on Surveyors 5, 6 and 7 makes it possible to determine with good accuracy the elements up to about $A \leqslant 40$. Heavier elements can also be determined if they differ in A by more than unity.

The determination of elements from the spectrum of protons generated as a result of the (α, p) reaction has certain limitations. For instance, light elements, such as C and O, cannot be determined due to the insufficiency of the energy of alpha-particles of radioisotope sources to excite the reaction (α, p). On heavier elements the (α, p) reaction gives a higher yield. However, beginning with $A \approx 30$–40 the proton yield becomes insignificant because of the high coulomb barrier in heavy nuclei. Therefore, determination of the content of elements from the (α, p) reaction is possible only within limits ranging roughly from Na to K.

By way of example, Fig. 2.4.1 shows the spectra of alpha-particles scattered by lunar rock and the spectra of protons generated in (α, p) reactions on the same rock. Spectra of alpha-particles and protons (these spectra were obtained from the

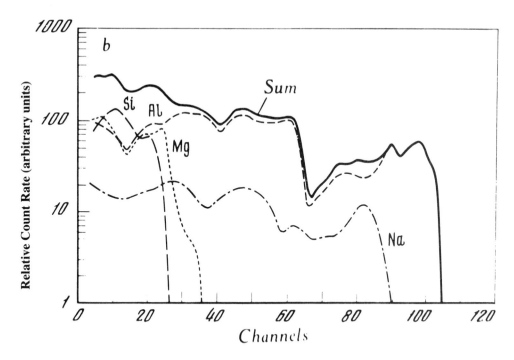

Fig. 2.4.1 — Spectra of alpha-particles scattered by lunar rock (a) and by protons generated in (n,p)-reactions on the same rock (b).

individual elements composing this rock) are also given. Knowing the spectra of individual elements (or their oxides), it is possible to decompose the spectrum of the rock into its components. For instance, the decomposition can be made by the method of least squares. However, it seems that use of the method [9] described in Chapter 2.2 would be more efficient.

The analytical potentials of this method were discussed in [1–4]. They boil down to the following:

— the method has good sensitivity for elements heavier than He, but its sensitivity sharply decreases with increase in the mass number of the element;
— the method does not allow the determination of hydrogen, since alpha-particles are not back-scattered from hydrogen;
— the sensitivity and accuracy for determining light elements are approximately the same as for oxygen, but they are somewhat lower for heavier elements, e.g. for iron;
— due to the low penetrating power of alpha-particles, this method gives the composition of only the uppermost layer of the analysed sample-several micrometres thick;
— with the intensity actually used of the radioisotope source of ^{242}Cm (about 200 Ci), a weak flux of alpha-particles and protons is recorded which requires a long measurement period. For instance, spectra were recorded for 10 hours by Surveyors, 5, 6 and 7 to obtain the appropriate statistics.

Methodological papers [8] show that this method enables one to determine the content of basic rock-forming elements in rocks with an accuracy of up to 0.5% by mass (1σ). Lower accuracy is achieved only for neighbouring elements — K and Ca — if both of them are present in commensurable quantities.

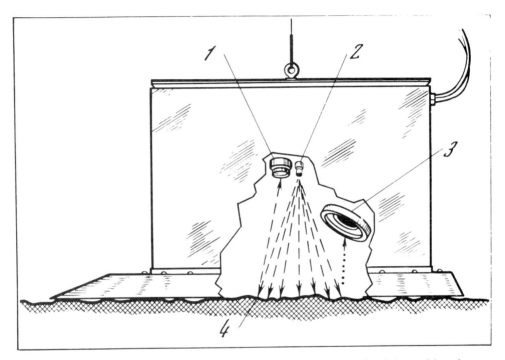

Fig. 2.4.2 — Diagram of the detector action of the instrument for measuring alpha-particle and proton spectra used on the Surveyor spacecraft: 1, scattered alpha-particle detector; 2, alpha-particle source; 3, proton detector; 4, surface of the rock analysed.

Fig. 2.4.2 presents a diagram of the detector portion of the instrument used on Surveyors 5, 6 and 7. The diagram shows the mutual position of the radioisotope sources, radiation detectors and the sample to be analysed. The device uses six radioisotope sources of ^{242}Cm (with a total activity of 200 mCi) which irradiate the surface of the sample; two alpha-particle detectors measure the spectrum of scattered alpha-particles, and four proton detectors measure the spectrum of protons generated in the target as a result of the (α, p) reaction.

To record and measure the energy of alpha-particles, use is made of silicon surface-barrier detectors. The detectors' sensitive layer is 50 μm thick. This thickness ensures a high efficiency for recording alpha-particles and is almost transparent to protons. The outer surface of the detectors is covered with a thin gold-covered organic film protecting them from pollution and the penetration of light. Collimators with a window area of 0.25 cm^2 are installed in front of the detector.

To measure the energy of protons, use is made of Li-drift silicon detectors with a sensitive layer 350 μm thick. From the side of the working surface the detectors are shielded by gold leaf 11 μm thick (about 0.21 kg m⁻²). This gold leaf fully absorbs alpha-particles, but allows through protons with energies greater than about 1.5 MeV. In front of the detectors, collimators are installed. They restrict the detectors' working area to about 1.2 cm².

Since the cross-section of the (α, p) reaction is small and, as a consequence, the number of generated protons is small, the contribution of protons from cosmic rays becomes considerable. To eliminate this contribution, alpha-particle detectors are shielded from the outer (upper) side by protective silicon Li-drift detectors. These detectors have a working area of about 3 cm² and a sensitive layer 400 μm thick. The basic and protective proton detectors operate according to the scheme of anticoincidence, which enables one to record only protons produced in the course of (α, p) reactions and to exclude the protons of cosmic rays. The count rate of alpha-particles on the Moon's surface from Surveyors 5, 6 and 7 was about 2 s⁻¹ while the count rate of protons was about 2 min⁻¹.

All sources and detectors in the instrument are mounted within a single outlying unit whose lower side has no wall. This unit was lowered on to the Moon's surface by means of a special device. The instrument's electronics were housed inside the device and operated under thermostatically-controlled conditions. The mass of the entire instrument is about 13 kg, and its power consumption is 2 W.

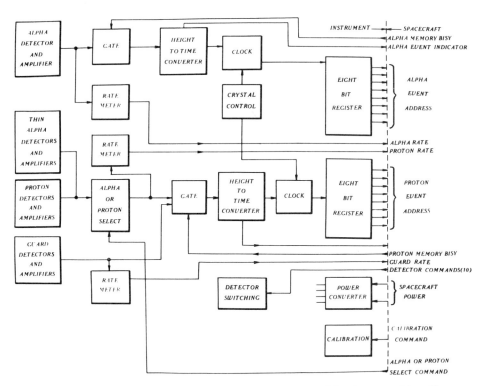

Fig. 2.4.3 — Structural electronic circuit of the instrument for studying the composition of lunar rocks used on Surveyors: A, alpha-detectors with preamplifiers; P-proton detectors with preamplifiers; CR, cosmic-ray detectors with preamplifiers.

Due to the absence of an atmosphere on the Moon, alpha-particles reach without hindrance the rock to be analysed and, after scattering, the appropriate detectors. The interaction of alpha-particles with the atoms of the rock takes place at a depth of just a few micrometres. In the course of elaborating this method, some problems associated with the interaction of alpha-particles and the thick target were considered both theoretically and experimentally. The spectra of alpha-particles scattered by the thick target; the resonance nuclear scattering of alpha-particles on light elements, such as C and O (this scattering increases the scattering cross-section by an order or magnitude with alpha-particle energies of about 6 MeV as compared with Rutherford scattering); nuclear (α, p) reactions with Na, Mg, Al and Si from the point of view of the quantitative determination of these elements, etc., were all considered.

Fig. 2.4.3 shows the instrument structural diagram [2]. The signals from the detectors come through the preamplifiers, mixers and amplifiers to analogue-to-digital converters, and then in digital form to the telemetry system. To calibrate its energy scales the device has a calibration generator controlled from earth which produces calibration pulses corresponding to alpha-particle energies of 2.5 and 3.5 MeV.

Table 2.4.1 – The content of the basic rock-forming elements measured from Surveyors 5,6 and 7 (percentage of atoms)

Element	Surveyor 5	Surveyor 6	Surveyor 7
O	61.1±10	59.3±1.6	61.8±1.0
Na	0.47±0.15	0.6±0.24	0.5±0.2
Mg	2.8±1.5	3.7±1.6	3.6±1.6
Al	6.4±0.4	6.5±0.4	9.2±0.4
Si	17.1±1.2	18.5±1.4	16.3±1.2
Ca	5.5±0.7	5.2±0.9	6.9±0.6
Ti	2.0±0.5	1.0±0.8	1.0±0.4
Fe	3.8±0.4	3.9±0.6	1.6±0.4

2.4.1.2 Results of the experiments

Table 2.4.1 summarizes the results of measuring the elemental composition of lunar rocks from Surveyors 5,6 and 7. The measurement errors are given with a 90% confidence level. Both statistical and instrumental errors have been taken into account.

Assuming that Surveyor 5 (Mare Tranquillitatis) and Surveyor 6 (Sinus Medii) explored typical mare regions while Surveyor 7 (the vicinity of the crater Tycho) a typical highland region of the Moon's surface, the following conclusions have been drawn [8]:

— Rocks lying in maria are close in composition to basalts of the Earth's crust. (Specifically, the rock explored by Surveyor 5 has proved to be very similar in composition to basalts of ocean ridges.) The content of the basic rock-forming elements in mare rocks is within the limits of their contents in terrestrial basalts. This testifies to the past heating of the Moon and, as a consequence, to the differentiation of its material, which has led to the fusion of basaltic rocks. The comparison of the composition of the rocks of three lunar regions with the composition of granites of the Earth's crust shows that in lunar rocks there is no enrichment of Si and Na and depletion of Mg, Fe and Ca as on the Earth's granite continents. Although the mare basically consist of basaltic rocks, their elemental composition has significant differences from terrestrial basalts.

For instance, Na content (about 0.5%) is much lower than in terrestrial basalts (in ocean ridges it is about 1.5%). Mare Tranquillitatis is also marked for having a higher Ti content (about 2%) than terrestrial basalts. If these two elements are considered important, the Earth apparently has no rocks whose composition accurately corresponds to the composition of lunar regolith.

— The composition of lunar rocks shows that their origin differs from that of meteorites which fall on the Earth. (The exception is the recently discovered meteorite Alha 81005.2 which has apparently fallen to the Earth from the Moon.)

— There is a great difference between the rock composition in maria and on the highlands. For example, mare rocks contain three times more Ti and Fe and much less Al and Ca. At the same time, as far as the amount of Si,Na and Mg are concerned, the two types of rocks differ insignificantly.

— The mare regions of the Moon's surface have a higher albedo, apparently due to the large proportion of minerals which contain iron and titanium.

— The lower content of elements heavier than Ca on the Moon's highlands indicates the lower density of the rock in highland areas. This fact has been noticed by Finney *et al.* [10] who have calculated on the basis of the preliminary analysis of the data obtained from Surveyors 5, 6 and 7 that the bedrock of maria and highland regions on the Moon must have densities of 3.15×10^3 and 2.95×10^3 kg m^{-3}, respectively.

— If we consider that the data obtained by Surveyor 7 are representative for lunar highlands, which account for over 80% of the Moon's entire surface, and that the density of 2.95×10^3 kg m^{-3} corresponds to the density of highland rocks, the difference of their density from the average density of the Moon (3.36×10^3 kg m^{-3}) is indicative of the great depth of the distribution of differentiated material.

— Finally, the lower density of lunar highlands correlates with their higher uplift as compared with lunar maria. This shows that highlands are not primary accumulated material, but a chemically segregated fraction which, due to its lower density and isostatic equilibrium, is more uplifted than mare regions formed by denser rocks.

After the experiments carried out from Surveyors 5, 6 and 7, the lunar samples brought back to the Earth have been studied thoroughly in many world laboratories. Almost all elements which are encountered in terrestrial rocks have been identified. Within the framework of these large-scale and long studies of lunar material, the experiments performed by the Surveyor spacecraft should be regarded as the initial stage on the road which has led now to understanding the history of the formation of lunar material.

2.4.2 INSTRUMENTATION FOR ANALYSING THE COMPOSITION OF THE MARTIAN ATMOSPHERE AND SURFACE BY THE ALPHA-PARTICLE SCATTERING METHOD

An analytical instrument slightly modified from the device carried by Surveyors 5, 6 and 7 was suggested [11] for studying the composition of Mars' rock and atmosphere.

Despite the fact that Mars' has a thin atmosphere, the accuracy of determining chemical elements there is approximately the same as on the Moon. In addition, the device can measure the density of the atmosphere with an accuracy not worse than 5% and determine nitrogen, neon and argon content in amounts of over 1%. The sensitivity in determining carbon and oxygen has been improved, which makes it possible to detect several per cent of water or carbonates in the rock.

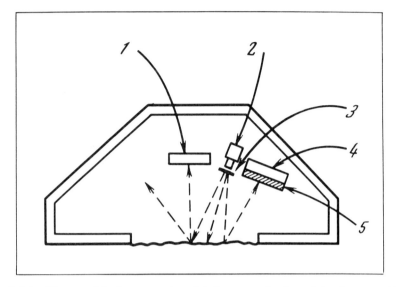

Fig. 2.4.4 — Diagram of the detector section of the instrument for determining the composition of the atmosphere and surface of Mars: 1, alpha-particle detector; 2, alpha-particle source; 3, movable shutter; 4, proton detector; 5, screen alpha-detector.

The principle of the instrument's operation is shown in Fig. 2.4.4. It uses an alpha-particle detector, four proton detectors and six radioisotope sources. Like the lunar device this instrument makes use of the radioisotope source ^{242}Cm with an activity of 60 mCi. (The source emits mainly alpha-particles with energies of 6.1 MeV.) The main differences between this instrument and the device used earlier in the Surveyor spacecraft may be summarised as follows:

— The distance from the source to the sample and from the alpha-particle detector to the sample as been reduced from 7 to 2.5 cm to reduce the effect of the Martian atmosphere on the spectra of alpha-particles and protons. This has led also to the reduction of the irradiated area of the sample from 100 to 10 cm^2 and has increased the count rate of alpha-particles and protons with the same activity of the source.
— Due to the increase in the count rate one of the two alpha-particle detectors has been removed because experience of the operation has shown that the surface-barrier silicon detector is reliable in operation.
— The thin gold leaf above the proton detector has been replaced by a thin silicon detector about 35 μm thick. Under this detector the main proton detector is mounted as on the Surveyor craft, and still lower is the third detector which is switched on the anticoincidence with two upper detectors. The second and third detectors are drift Si (Li) detectors like those on the Surveyor spacecraft. Only

those particles are recorded which lose the appropriate portion of their energy simultaneously in the two upper detectors. The upper detector operates as an absorber of alpha-particles. The portion of the proton energy absorbed in it is added by means of an electronic circuit to the energy absorbed in the main proton detector.

—In front of the sources a mechanical shutter is mounted which reduces the probability of instrument pollution during the radiation destruction of the coating of the sources, and makes it possible to measure the background before the opening of the sources.

—The number of channels in the analyser (for alpha-particles and protons) has been increased from 128 and 256 which has raised the instrument's resolution.

As on the Surveyors, the device has two spectrometric sections which record the spectra of alpha-particles scattered by the rocks, and protons produced as a result of the (α, p) reaction with the nuclei of light elements.

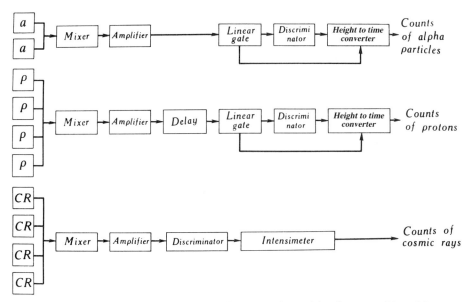

Fig. 2.4.5 — Structural electronic circuit of the instrument for studying the composition of the Martian atmosphere and surface.

Fig. 2.4.5 shows the block diagram of the device's electronic section. The latter enables one to record simultaneously two spectra (of alpha-particles and protons) in 256 channels of the analyser with a capacity of 2^{16} pulses per channel. The components of this circuit were used earlier in onboard equipment installed on some spacecraft and showed their ability to operate reliably.

This instrument can be used not only for analysing Mars' surface, but also for determining the composition and density of the Martian atmosphere.

When this experiment was prepared, the data on the Martian atmosphere were only of a preliminary character. They were obtained from the Mariner 9 orbiter vehicle. It followed from these estimates that the overall pressure of the atmosphere near the planetary surface was about 6.3 x 10^2Pa and that CO_2 is the main component. That is why the technique of determining the most probable admixtures – N_2, Ar and others – was worked out on the device under these conditions.

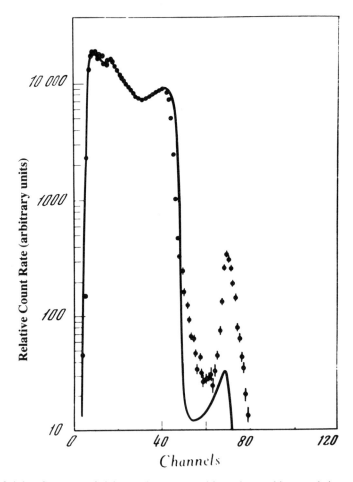

Fig. 2.4.6 — Spectrum of alpha-particles scattered from the graphite sample in vacuum (solid line) and in the CO_2 atmosphere at the a pressure of 5mm Hg (dots.)

Fig. 2.4.6 shows the spectrum of alpha-particles scattered from a graphite sample in a vacuum and in a CO_2 atmosphere with a pressure of 6.3 x 10^2Pa. The main region of the spectrum is due to the scattering of alpha-particles from graphite, while the peak in about the 70th channel is due to the scattering from oxygen which is part of CO_2. (This peak in the vacuum medium appears from the upper oxidized graphite layer.) From the magnitude of the oxygen peak belonging to CO_2 one can determine the density of the atmosphere to an accuracy of about 5%.

Nitrogen in the atmosphere can be determined from the proton spectrum because alpha-particles with energies of 6.1 MeV give rise to the (α, p) reaction only with nitrogen. The proton spectrum from pure nitrogen is presented in Fig. 2.4.7. The results of the measurements show that nitrogen can be determined at amounts of 1% and higher, at an overall pressure of CO_2 equal to 6.3 x 10^2 Pa.

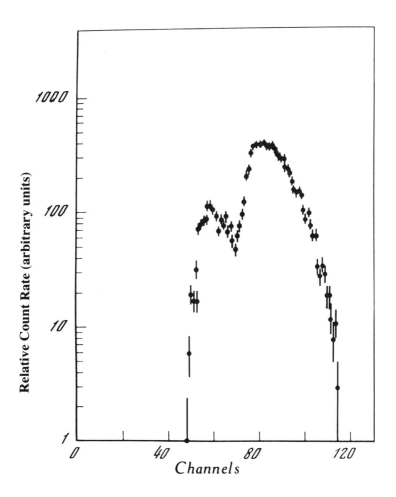

Fig. 2.4.7 — Spectrum of protons generated in the (n,p) reaction in pure nitrogen.

Fig. 2.4.8 gives the spectrum of a mixture of argon and CO_2. The designed technique enables one to determine in 6.3 x 10^2 Pa of CO_2, the Ar content from 1% and neon content from 3% with good statistics.

Thus, the design modifications introduced in devices used by the Surveyors and the further development of the methodology have enabled the authors [11] to create a device for exploring not only the rock, but also the atmosphere of Mars.

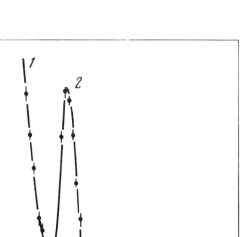

Fig. 2.4.8 — Alpha-particle spectrum from 5.1% of argon (balance CO_2) at a pressure of 5mm Hg.

As far as the analysis of Martian rock is concerned, this device makes it possible to measure carbon and oxygen with high accuracy in addition to measurement of the basic rock-forming elements. In turn, this makes it possible to detect several per cent of water or carbonates in the Martian rock.

The main analytical opportunities of this device are as follows:

(1) The basic rock-forming elements are determined in amounts of 1% and higher.

(2) Light rock-forming elements (which are not determined by gamma- and X-ray spectrometric methods) are detected with an accuracy of about 20% for carbon and sodium and of about 2 – 3% for oxygen.

(3) The density of the rock and the atmosphere is determined with an accuracy of about 5%.

(4) The main atmospheric component (CO_2) is determined with an accuracy of about 5%. The lower limit for measuring the minor components is 1% for N_2 and Ar and 3% for Ne and other inert gases.

Vikings 1 and 2 which explored Mars's atmosphere and surface in 1975/76 carried X-ray spectrometers. The X-ray radiometric method has some advantages over the alpha-particle scattering method. In particular, since X-ray radiation has a higher penetrating power than alpha-particles, X-ray radiometry gives a more representative analysis. This is especially important for the exploration of Mars where rock may have an oxidized film. Besides, X-ray radiometry allows one to determine heavier elements. However, for exploring small bodies devoid of an atmosphere may be reasonable to use the alpa-particle scattering method, since this method makes it possible to determine light elements (C, N, O and Na).

REFERENCES

[1] J.H. Patterson, E.J. Franzgrote and A.L. Turkevich, *J. Geophys. Res.*, **74**, 6120 (1969).

[2] A.L. Turkevich, K. Knolle and R.A. Emmert, *Rev. Sci. Instrum.*, **37**, 1681 (1966).

[3] J.H. Patterson, A.L. Turkevich and E. Franzgrote, *J. Geophys. Res.*, **70**, 1311 (1965).

[4] A.L. Turkevich, K. Knolle and E. Franzgrote, *J. Geophys, Res.*, **72**, 831 (1967).

[5] E. Franzgrote, J.H. Patterson and A.L. Turkevich, *Science*, **167**, 376 (1970).

[6] J.H. Patterson, A.L. Turkevich and E. Franzgrote, *Science*, **168**, 825 (1970).

[7] A.L. Turkevich, E. Franzgrote and J.H. Patterson, *Science*, **165**, 277 (1969).

[8] A.L. Turkevich, *Accounts Chem. Res.*, **6**, 81 (1973).

[9] Yu. A. Surkov, L.P. Moskalyova and O.P. Shcheglov, *Kosmich. Issled.*, **21**, 308 (In Russian.) (1983).

[10] W.C. Phinney, J.A. O'Keefe and J.B. Adams, *J. Geophys. Res.*, **74**, 6053 (1969).

[11] T.E. Economov and A.L. Turkevich, *J. Geophys. Res.*, **78**, 781, (1973).

2.5 Mass-spectrometric studies

The use of mass spectrometers in space exploration began in the early 1950s. By the late 1960s dozens of mass spectrometers were carried annually by space probes and Earth satellites. During the first decade of the 'Space Age' all space vehicles were fitted with radio-frequency mass spectrometers. These mass spectrometers are the simplest in design, although they are somewhat inferior in their physical characteristics to mass spectrometers of other types.

Since the early 1960s, along with radio-frequency mass spectrometers, other types have been in use — magnetic (single-focusing or double-focusing) mass spectrometers, quadrupole and single-field mass filters, omegatrons and time-of-flight mass spectrometers. All of them have been used mainly for exploring the Earth's upper atmosphere (at altitudes above 100 km). In such instruments there is no need to have an injection and pumping-out system and, therefore, they are of relatively simple construction. These devices have enabled important scientific results to be obtained which have been presented in many papers.

The exploration of planetary and satellite atmospheres makes specific requirements of mass spectrometric equipment. Some of them are incompatible in a single instrument. It is impossible to make a single device suitable for solving a wide range of problems or applicable on different planets. For example, the exploration of the Moon which has a very rarefied atmosphere calls for a device with a particularly high sensitivity. For exploring the Martian atmosphere, one needs a device to measure the atmospheric composition both at high altitudes in order to obtain information about the planet's history (this requires a mass spectrometer with an open source) and at low altitudes for understanding the interaction of the atmosphere and the planetary surface (this calls for a mass spectrometer with a closed source). To measure the dense Venusian atmosphere, it is important to use the pressure-reduction system during the injection of gas into the instrument and also to use absorption of the main component (CO_2) in order to have the instrument sensitivity sufficient for determining minor admixtures. Finally, special requirements are made of ion-excitation sources in mass spectrometers designed for analysing the solid phase of extraterrestrial material. While considering particular devices we will draw the attention of readers to some of these specific features.

The basic parameters of the mass spectrometers used for exploring Solar System bodies are summarized in Table 2.5.1. These parameters are not the best attainable for the devices of these types since to a large extent they depend on the particular space vehicle on which they were installed and on the character of scientific problems which they were designed to investigate. At the same time, taken as a whole, they enable one to assess the potential of mass-spectrometric studies of planets and satellites.

Table 2.5.1 — The main characteristics of mass spectrometers for exploring planets and satellites

No.	Object of study	Spacecraft (launch year)	Type of mass spectrometer	a.m.u. range	Resolution	Sensitivity, (percentage by vol.)	Dynamic range	Reference
1	Lunar atmosphere	Apollo 17 (1972)	Magnetic	1–4 12–48 27–110				[8]
2	Martian atmosphere	Mars 6 (1974)	Radio frequency	12–48	20–25 at the 0.5 level	0.5 for N_2 0.1 for O_2 0.05 for Ar	10^4	[5]
3	Martian atmosphere	Viking 1,2 (1975)	Magnetic	12–200	200 at the 0.1 level	0.2 for C	10^2	[6]
4	Venusian atmosphere	Veneras 9,10 (1975)	Single-field mass filter	10–55	>55 at the 0.1 level		10^5	[1]
5	Venusian atmosphere	Veneras 11,12 (1978)	Radio frequency	11–105	25–35 at the 0.1 level	0.2 for N_2 5×10^{-4} for Ne	10^5	[2]
6	Venusian atmosphere	Pioneer Venus (1978)	Magnetic	1–208	>440 at the 0.1 level	10^{-4} for Ar,K	10^6	[3,4]
7	Venus clouds	VeGa (1984)	Hyperboloidal radio frequency	10–150	150 at the 0.1 level	$\sim 10^{-4}$ for N_2	10^6	[22]
8	Surface rock	—	Magnetic	2–200	>250 at the 0.1 level	$\sim 10^{-3}$	10^6	[21]

As will be evident from the table, all mass spectrometers have similar analytical characteristics despite the fundamental differences in excitation sources, mass analysers, pumping-out systems, etc. The mass numbers all range below 200; this is mainly due to the composition of the planetary atmospheres. The dynamic ranges of mass spectrometers (10^4 to 10^6) provide the opportunity for determining minor constituents with a concentration that is only a few millionths of the main component. Finally, their small mass and low power consumption make mass spectrometers competitive against other onboard devices used for analysis of the composition of extraterrestrial material. Up to now mass spectrometers have been used mainly for exploring the atmospheres of Venus, Mars and the Moon. Mass spectrometric equipment for exploring the surface rocks of planets and satellites is currently being designed. One of these devices will be considered below.

2.5.1 MASS SPECTROMETRY OF VENUS' ATMOSPHERE AND CLOUDS

Mass spectrometry has played a special rôle in exploration of the Venusian atmosphere. It seems paradoxical that on a planet where the conditions for the application of mass spectrometers are particularly unsuitable (e.g. high pressures and temperatures) they have found a broader application than any other analytical device. The difficulty in employing mass spectrometers for exploring Venus' atmosphere is accounted for primarily by the necessity to select gas for analysis at a pressure which is millions of times the pressure which is required in the analyser of the mass spectrometer. Besides, these measurements are usually made in dynamic conditions; that is, at constantly varying pressures and temperatures during the descent of the spaceprobe through the planetary atmosphere. This calls for the use of special gas-injection and pumping-out systems that have strictly the same throughput, as a result of which a constant low pressure (about 1.3×10^{-3} Pa) is maintained in the mass analyser with a continuously renewing analysed gas sample.

2.5.1.1 Exploration of the Venusian atmosphere by Veneras 9 and 10

The first mass spectrometer for exploring Venus' dense atmosphere was used aboard the Venera 9 and 10 spaceprobes by Surkov *et al.* [1]. The functional diagram of this mass spectrometer is given in Fig. 2.5.1. The analytical portion of the mass spectrometer consists of a device for the intake of atmospheric gas (A), a system for filling the ion source (B), with gas mixture, an analyser (C), and a magnetoionization pump (D). An electronic unit (E) controls the operating mode of the mass spectrometer, processes and encodes information transmitted to the TM system, and ensures power supply for the mass-analyser. A separate unit (F) supplies the vacuum pump with high-voltage (HV) power.

All parts of the apparatus, except for the sampler, were installed on the mounting plate in the scientific instrumentation compartment of the descent modules of Veneras 9 and 10. The sampler, placed outside the instrumentation compartment, is mounted on to the probe by a sealed flange. The instruments record mass spectra within the range of 10 – 55 a.m.u. with a resolving power of not less than 55 at the level of 10% of the height of the peak in the mass area of 55. The spectrum scanning time is 50 s, the instrument's weight 9.5 kg, and the power consumed 35 W.

During the storage period and the probe's flight to Venus, the sampler (see Fig. 2.5.1.) selecting samples for analysis is sealed by a glass cap (1) which is broken by a device (2) at the moment of the beginning of measurements. A porous inlet system (4), limiting the entry of gas into the injection system, is installed in the bulge of a capillary tube (3). The inlet system is surrounded with a heating spiral (5) for removing probable condensation within it. The open end of the capillary is in the input slit of the sampler. The slit is located in such a way that it is blown through by atmospheric gas during the probe's descent. This ensures analysis of the atmosphere, layer by layer, and prevents products from the possible outgassing of the skin of the probe body from getting into the sampler.

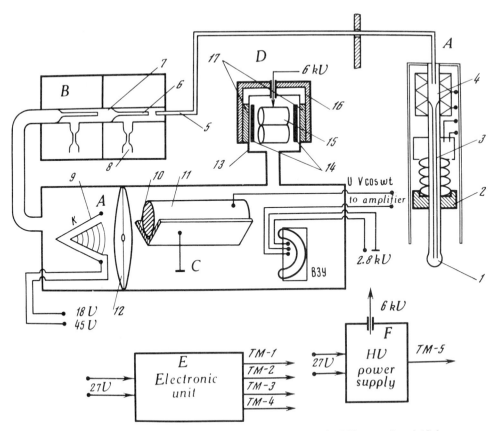

Fig. 2.5.1 — Functional diagram of the mass spectrometer used of Veneras 9 and 10 for exploring the Venusian atmosphere: A, sampler; B, inlet device; C, mass analyser; D, magnetodischarge pump; E, electronic device; F, high-voltages supplier; 1, protective cap; 2, opening device; 3, input capillary; 4, porous inlet device; 5, 6 and 8, capillaries; 7, porous inlet device; 9, ion source; 10 and 11, electrodes of the analyser; 12, diaphragm; 13, pump body; 14, cathodes; 15, anode; 16 and 17, magnetoconductor.

The injection system ensures the entry of the correct amount of gas into the ion source such that the working pressure in the analyser (about 1.3×10^{-3} Pa) is preserved when the pressure at the entry into the sampler varies from 10^4 to 10^6 Pa.

In designing the injection system, the principle of the dependence of the conductivity of capillaries and inlet systems on the character of the molecular (or viscous) flow is used. Porous inlet systems (6) located in the path of gas to the source ensure the molecular mode of the flow, due to which the amount of gas passing through them varies proportionally to the first degree of pressure, while the amount of gas passing through the pumping-out capillaries (7) into evacuated volumes in the viscous mode of the flow varies proportionally to the square of the pressure. The conductivities of porous inlet systems and capillary tubes are chosen so that with the above-mentioned change in the pressure at the entry into the sampler, the pressure in the ion source of the mass spectrometer varies by less than an order of magnitude.

The values of the time constant of the injection system (τ is 5 s) and persistence (J is 10 s) enable one to record the concentration of the components of the Venusian atmosphere during the descent. The design of the system envisaged the removal of the fractionation in the gas flow. The fractionation is accounted for by the dependence of the passage rate of gas molecules on their mass.

The sensor of the mass spectrometer incorporates an ion source, a single-field mass filter and a secondary electron multiplier mounted on a rigid frame and housed in the thin-walled cylindrical body. The ion source anode (9) is made of a tungsten net with high transparency in the form of a truncated cone extended between two parallel frames so that the cone axis passes though the centre of the input diaphragm. An iridium thread 0.05 mm in diameter covered with yttrium oxide serves as a cathode (14). A focusing field is produced between the anode and the input diaphragm for increasing the resolution with the preservation of a sufficiently high sensitivity. To increase reliability a reserve cathode is placed in the ion source. This cathode can be automatically switched on by the electronic device.

As far as the design is concerned, the analyser represents a unit consisting of two electrodes: an earthed 'corner' electrode (10) consisting of two rectangular places connected along their longer edge and butting at right angles to one another, and a cylindrical electrode (11) which lies along the bisectrix plane of the 'corner' electrode, to which direct voltage U and high-frequency $V = V_o \cos \omega t$ is supplied.

The channel-type secondary electron multiplier with a gain factor of about 10^7 is an ion collector.

A magnetoionization vacuum pump is employed in the mass spectrometer. It is similar in design to the standard types of such pumps but is miniature in size. The pumping-out rate for nitrogen at a pressure 1.3×10^{-4} Pa torr is 4 lires per second.

The mass spectra were measured during the vehicle's descent through the Venusian atmosphere at altitudes of 50 to 30 km from the surface. By way of example Fig. 2.5.2 presents one of the mass spectra recorded at an altitude of 47 km (Venera 9). Curves 1 and 2 correspond to different gain factors (different scales). The character of other spectra is similar. It is determined by the presence of large amounts of carbon dioxide which make contributions of fragmentary CO_2^{2+} ions to the intensity of many mass lines. The amplitudes of the signals corresponding to masses 44, 28 and some others are limited by the electronics and, therefore, are trapezium-shaped (i.e 'chopped').

The concentrations of minor components were determined with respect to carbon dioxide whose content was evaluated, from the mass 22 (CO_2^{2+}) specified, for every value of the pressure from the curve based on the spectra, and which showed the dependence of the intensity of the line corresponding to this mass on the descent time. (The descent time was correlated with the pressure value).

The contribution by fragmentary CO_2^{2+} ions was taken into account on the basis of studying their distribution in the calibration mass spectrum of chemically pure CO_2.

Nitrogen was determined from the peak of fragmentary N^+ and N_2^{2+} ions.

An analysis of the character of the change in the relative value of the mass 32 line in spectra of Venus' atmosphere has shown that the intensity of this line exceeds the intensity resulting from the contribution by fragmentary O_2^+ ions from CO_2 and that the value of the excess intensity decreases with altitude above the surface. Apparently this is accounted for by the presence of oxygen or sulphur in the Venusian atmosphere. Laboratory investigations made on the instrument analogue into the conditions of passage through the filling system of oxygen, pure sulphur and

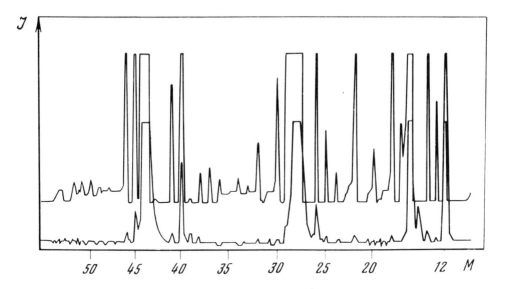

Fig. 2.5.2 — Mass spectrum of the Venus atmosphere measured from Venera 9.

some of its compounds (COS, CS_2, SO_2, H_2S and SO_3), the presence of which in Venus' atmosphere can be expected on the basis of geochemical concepts, have led the authors to the assumption that the excess intensity of the line corresponding to a mass of 32 is linked most probably with the presence of COS in the Venusian atmosphere.

The limits of the ammonia and argon contents were also estimated.

As a result of these first mass-spectrometric studies of Venus' atmosphere (and in general the first use of the mass spectrometer in studying dense planetary atmospheres) the following composition of Venus' atmosphere (in percentage by volume) was obtained [1]:

CO_2	~97
N_2	2 ± 0.5
Ar	2×10^{-2}
COS (?)	10^{-3}
NH_3	$<5\times10^{-4}$

The limited possibilities for transmission of a large volume of information during the module descent in Venus' atmosphere have placed certain limitations on the characteristics of this device. That is why the device operated within a small mass range (10 – 55) and in a small dynamic range (about 10^4) as compared with the mass range of 10 – 150 and the dynamic range of about 10^5 which are in principle attainable with this instrument. The reason for the limitation is that the device was placed in the probe's sealed thermostatically-controlled compartment which could function until the temperature of the atmosphere reached about 200°C.

The tabulated data have shown that CO_2 and N_2 are the principal components of the Venusian atmopshere. A comparison of the amount of these components on Venus and on the Earth has led the authors [1] to an important conclusion. It has turned out that despite a quite different content of these components in the atmospheres of Venus and the Earth, their total amount on the planets is roughly equal (within a factor of 2). However, on the Earth, probably due to the lower surface temperature, elemental carbon is in a bound state in the carbonates of sedimentary rocks. If the Earth's surface is heated to 500°C (as is the case on Venus), carbonates will be decomposed with the formation of wollastonite and carbon dioxide according to a reaction of the type

$$CaCO_3 + SiO_2 \qquad CaSiO_3 + CO_2$$

Thus, carbon will enter the Earth's atmosphere in the form of CO_2 and its amount in the atmosphere will be approximately the same as on Venus. Since the amount of nitrogen on the Earth will be preserved, its concentration will decrease and will roughly correspond to that which is maintained now in the Venusian atmosphere. Such a striking difference between the atmospheres of two planets so close in their physical characteristics is due to the difference in the temperatures of their surfaces, which in turn is accounted for by the different distances of Venus and the Earth from the Sun.

2.5.1.2 Exploration of the Venusian atmosphere by Veneras 11 and 12

After the mass spectrometric studies from Veneras 9 and 10, all Venus-bound spacecraft carried mass spectrometers. The next mass-spectrometric experiment was conducted on Veneras 11 and 12 by Istomin *et al* [2]. As a result of this experiment the content of inert gases in Venus' atmosphere was determined.

To measure the inert gas content, use was made of the radio frequency mass spectrometer whose functional diagram is given in Fig. 2.5.3. The device consisted of five basic functional units: the injection system, the ion source, the radio-frequency analyser, the magnetodischarge pump and the electrometer.

The mass spectrometer was mounted inside the thermostatically-controlled compartment of the descent module. Atmospheric gas was taken through a sampler which consisted of a pipeline with a bell mouth at its lower end. During the module's descent, the atmosphere under study was blown through the pipeline due to the natural thrust of the gas. The gas which passed through the pipeline was taken to the mass spectrometer for analysis via a controllable valve. The bell mouth was outside the module in the direction of its descent to prevent the products of outgassing from getting into the mass spectrometer.

The sample of the atmospheric gas from the sampler (18) entered, via the injection valve (13), initially the prechamber and then the analyser (14), through the diaphragm (17). The ion current which passed through the analyser was measured by the charge amplifier (1), the signals from which were encoded before entering the telemetry system.

The measuring cycle of the mass spectrometer consisted of four stages: (1) the search, (2) measurement of the full chemical composition, (3) the search and (4) measurement of the content of inert gases. The whole measuring cycle lasted 6 min 40 s. The cycle was repeated during the entire descent almost as far as the surface.

To select a gas sample, an injection system with closed feedback was used. The

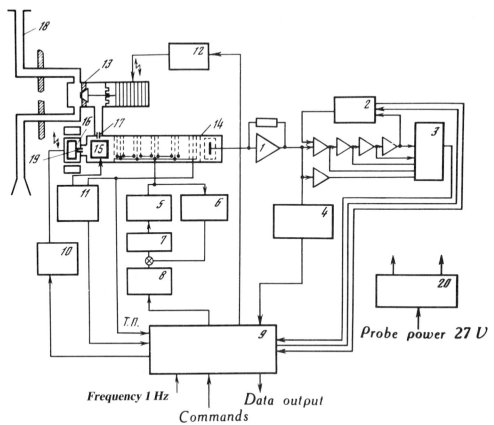

Fig. 2.5.3 — Functional diagram of the mass spectrometer used on Veneras 11 and 12 for exploring Venus' atmosphere: 1, electrometer; 2, automatic frequency control circuit; 3, automatic scale-selection circuit; 4, injection-level discriminator; 5, controllable high-frequency generator; 6, frequency meter; 7, integrator; 8, circuit for shaping the HF variation law; 9, programmer; 10, power supply unit of the magnetodischarge pump; 11, circuit of stabilization and emission-current measuring; 12, injection-valve control circuit; 13, injection-system valve; 14, radiofrequency analyser; 15, ion source; 16, magnetodischarge pump; 17, injection-system diaphragm; 18, sampler; 19, pump diaphragm; 20, power-supply source.

injection valve with piezo-striction drive was controlled by a high-voltage pulse. The pulse amplitude range was divided into 64 levels. The transition from one level to the next highest level raised the sample volume two-fold. The system ensured the given pressure value in the prechamber could be maintained with high accuracy irrespective of the outside pressure.

Gas from the prechamber flowed into the analyser through the diaphragm with a slit of about 20 μm. The pressure in the prechamber dropped and the flux diminished. The diaphragm was chosen so that during the scanning of two consecutive 7–second spectra the gas flow to the analyser decreased approximately two-fold. By the moment of selection of the next sample, the gas pressure in the analyser had diminished practically to the initial value.

The analyser had four selection cascades separated by three drift spaces. The mass spectrum was scanned by varying the HF voltage frequency. The generator frequency was altered by changing the permeability of the ferrite core of a loop placed in the field of the electromagnet. The frequency of the HF voltage was altered in such a way as to ensure the maximum sensitivity of the measuring channel. For this purpose the HF voltage varied according to the exponential law from 7.5 to 2 MHz.

The ion current which had passed through the selection system was measured by the electrometer. The required accuracy for measuring the ion current in the dynamic range from 5×10^{-14} to 5×10^{-9}A was attained due to the presence of a chain of four series-connected DC amplifiers at the electrometer input. Their transfer ratios were 0.1, 1, 10, 10^2 and 10^3. So, five measuring scales were obtained. During measurements the scale was chosen automatically, which gave a signal in the 0.6- to 6-V range at the electrometer output. The signal entered the telemetry system through the commutator of the control unit.

The device had the following main characteristics: a mass number range of 11 to 105; a resolution at the level of 10% of the amplitude of the peak $M/\Delta M = 35 \pm 5$; a scanning time of 1 s (in the search mode) and 7 s (in the measurement mode); a time for transmitting control parameters of 1 s; a gas-sample selection time of about 5×10^{-3} sec; a sensitivity of 0.2% for N_2, 5 parts per million for Ne and NH_3 and 1 part per million for Ar and Kr; a mass of 9.5 kg and a power consumption of 17 W.

The mass spectrometer was mounted on Veneras 11 and 12 and operated during their descent through the planetary atmosphere. Samples for analysis were taken from an altitude of 23Km down almost to the surface. Eleven samples were taken and 176 spectra were transmitted back to Earth. These spectra characterize the elemental, isotopic and chemical composition of Venus' atmosphere.

Fig. 2.5.4 gives a fragment of a spectrum measured by the spectrometer described above.

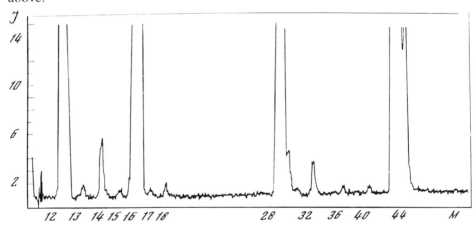

Fig. 2.5.4 — Fragment of the mass spectrum of the Venusian atmosphere measured by Venera 11.

As a result of the experiments conducted by Veneras 11 and 12, the following values for the content of the components (excluding CO_2) in Venus' atmosphere (in percentage by volume) were obtained [2]:

Nitrogen	$4.5 \pm 0.5\%$
Argon	1.5×10^{-2}
Neon	$(10-15) \times 10^{-4}$
Krypton	$(0.5-0.8) \times 10^{-4}$ (as a percentage by volume of CO_2).

The relative frequency of the argon isotopes was also determined:

^{36}Ar	42±2%
^{38}Ar	8±2%
^{40}Ar	50±2%

Mass-spectrometric experiments carried out on Veneras 11 and 12 were repeated by the same authors on Veneras 13 and 14, although the instrumentation was slightly improved. As a result of new experiments the above contents were determined more precisely and the upper limits of the probable contents of other components were assessed [23].

The data obtained show that Venus' atmosphere is mainly primary, i.e. it consists of components which appeared on the planet as a result of the accretion of gas from the protoplanetary nebula.

2.5.1.3 Exploration of the Venusian atmosphere by the Pioneer Venus probe

The US Pioneer Venus spacecraft sent to Venus in 1978 carried, among other scientific instruments, mass spectrometers for exploring the Venusian upper ($H>100$ km) and lower ($H<100$ km) atmosphere. The mass spectrometer for determining the composition of the neutral components of the lower atmosphere was designed by Hoffman *et al.* [3]. It was installed on the Large Sonde (i.e. on one of the four sondes dropped into the planetary atmosphere). The sonde began taking measurements at an altitude of 62 km and continued until it reached the planetary surface.

The device measured the composition of gases relative to CO_2, the main component of the Venusian atmosphere. The mass range of the instrument was 1 to 208 a.m.u. and its sensitivity was of the order of 10^{-6}.

The mass spectrometer consisted of a sector magnetic analyser, a gas inlet system, a pumping-out system and an electronic unit which controlled the device. All the spectrometer components were mounted on a common frame 31 by 36 cm in size. The instrument volume was 10.6 litres and mass 11 kg.

A functional diagram of the device is presented in Fig. 2.5.5. The inlet systems, closed by a sealed lid, and the depressurization mechanism were located outside the spherical sealed compartment of the spacecraft. This input portion of the mass spectrometer was positioned below the 'equator' of the craft's spherical body, and, therefore, the inlet systems (metallic capillaries) which were about 6 cm long were outside the zone of possible pollution by outgassing of the spacecraft material.

The atmospheric sample was taken through two micro-inlet systems made of passivated tantalum at a flow rate of around 10^{-12} m^3 s^{-1} for the inlet system used at altitudes of 62 – 46 km and about 10^{-13} m^3 s^{-1} for the flow regulator used at altitudes below 46 km.

The analysed gas sample flows through the inlet system, the ion source and the magnetic analyser and is absorbed by a getter (zirconium–aluminium alloy). To maintain a relatively constant pressure in the ion source during the entire descent of the spacecraft, a controlling valve is used. It is located in the path from the ion source to the getter. (The valve gradually opens when atmospheric pressure increases in the analyser.) In this case the dynamic range is preserved at the level of over 10^6, while the pressure of the outside atmosphere changes by three orders of magnitude.

The mass analyser is pumped out by the getter pump and by another chemical

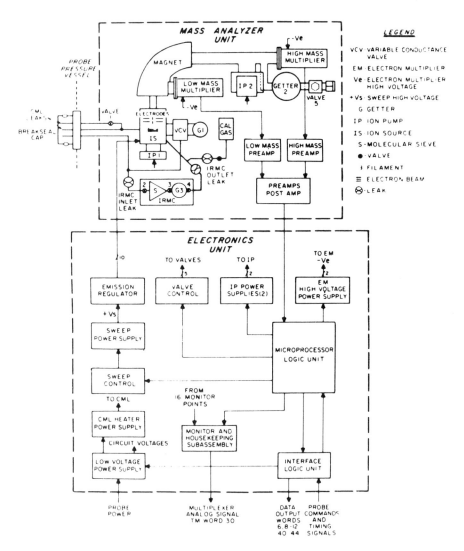

Fig. 2.5.5 — Functional diagram of the mass spectrometer used on Pioneer Venus for studying
the Venusian atmosphere.

getter. The pumping-out rate of this system from the ion source region is limited by
the diaphragm to a maximum of 5×10^{-6} m^3 s^{-1}. This pumping-out of ions is the only
one for inert gases. Its rate remains constant during the descent to the surface.
However, since the rate of the leak-in rises with increase in outside pressure as the
spacecraft is descending, the ratio of inert gas content to CO_2 also increases.

The main parts of the mass analyser are the ion source (produced by electron
bombardment of molecules), the sector analyser for the magnetic moments and two
ion detectors (for small and large masses separately).

The energy of the ionizing electrons varies three times as the craft is descending and has values of 70, 30 and 22 eV. (The change in this energy provides additional information for the identification of parent molecules.) Cathodes with double tungsten filaments serve as electron sources.

Ions accelerated in the ion source enter the analyser for magnetic moments, are separated according to m/e values and are recorded by detectors. Two channels simultaneously record ions in the ranges 1–16 and 15–208 a.m.u. The resolution in the large mass region is $M/\Delta M \leqslant 440$ at the level of 10% of the peak height.

The mass spectrum is scanned by the stepwise change in high voltage which accelerates ions. It takes 59 s to scan the total spectrum consisting of 236 positions of mass peaks. Then it takes 5 s to measure the background and to calibrate the device. For calibration, use is made of a mixture of gases — methane and xenon – which produces peaks at 15 (CH_3^+), 68 ($^{136}Xe^{2+}$) and 136 ($^{136}Xe^+$). The peaks of the calibration scale serve as reference points for the microprocessor which controls the ion accelerating voltage. The microprocessor enables one to control the mass scale and to scan not all mass peaks, but only those which are put into the program. By way of example Fig. 2.5.6 gives a spectrum measured by this mass spectrometer under laboratory conditions.

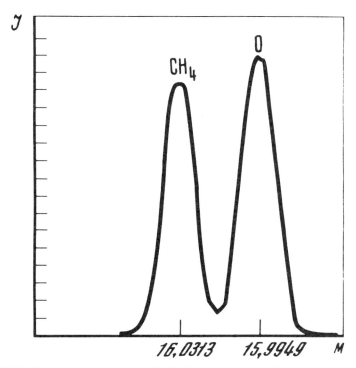

Fig. 2.5.6 — Spectrum of the mass doublet for 16 a.m.u. measured in laboratory conditions by the mass spectrometer of the Pioneer–Venus spacecraft. (Mass difference of 1/440. Dip between the peaks makes up 9% of the oxygen peak.)

Information transmitted via the Pioneer Venus telemetry channel made it possible to obtain 2% accuracy in determining components throughout the dynamic range. In addition to the measured mass spectra, information on the modes of instrument operation was transmitted: the mass scale, electron energies, the amplification of electron multipliers and the filament used in the ion source.

The mass spectrometer is controlled mainly by the micro processor according to the given program, except for the depressurization of input capillaries and the operation of the cell for enriching the inert gas sample.

The device operated in the descent section from an altitude of 62 km to the surface. However, at altitudes of approximately 50–28 km the inlet systems were clogged by aerosol particles of the cloud layer and in this section only background spectra were measured. Below 30 km the flow regulators opened again and the measurements of atmospheric spectra continued.

Table 2.5.2 sums up the results of studying the composition of the atmosphere in the experiment conducted by Hoffman *et al.* [4]. Data on nitrogen and inert gases are in agreement (within a factor of 2) with the data obtained in [1, 2] considered in the previous sections of this book. Of interest amidst the data obtained by this mass spectrometer are the estimates of the concentrations of minor active components (O_2, SO_2 and COS), whose content varies with height since the components themselves undergo phase transformations. One of the important conclusions drawn by the authors is that primary gases are widespread on Venus. As far as oxygen is concerned, its content is apparently very low since it has not been detected in this experiment or in other experiments.

Table 2.5.2 — The composition of Venus atmosphere as measured by Pioneer Venus [4]

Element	Content (10^{-6})	Isotope ratios
Ne	9^{+20}_{-6}	$^{22}Ne/^{20}Ne = 0.07\pm0.02$
Ar	70^{+50}_{-30}	$^{40}Ar/^{36}Ar = 1.03\pm0.04$
Kr	<0.2	$^{38}Ar/^{36}Ar = 0.18\pm0.02$
N_2[a]	4 ± 2	
O_2	$<30\,(H=52\text{–}22\,\text{km})$	
COS	$<3\,(H=22\,\text{km})$	
SO_2	$<300\,(H=22\,\text{km})$	
H_2O	$<1000\,(H=52\text{–}0\,\text{km})$	

[a]N_2 content is given as a percentage.

Judging from the results of the experiment, on the whole, the lower atmosphere (below the clouds) is of a reducing character, unlike the upper atmosphere (above the clouds) which exhibits oxidizing properties.

2.5.2 MASS SPECTROMETRY OF THE MARTIAN ATMOSPHERE FROM VIKINGS 1 AND 2

The first attempt to measure the composition of the Martian atmosphere was made in 1974 from the Mars 6 spacecraft [5]. The authors of the experiment used a simple mass spectrometer whose main components were a gas-injection system, a radio frequency mass analyser of the Bennett type and a magnetoionization pump. However, mass spectra were not transmitted, since after the vehicle landing on the planetary surface radio communications stopped. Only one parameter of the device

— the pump current — was measured, from the value of which the authors drew the erroneous conclusion of high argon content in the Martian atmosphere.

A similar mass spectrometer but with improved performance was successfully used by the same authors [2] on Veneras 11 and 12. (This mass spectrometer was considered in the previous section.)

The composition of the Martian atmosphere was measured in 1975 by Vikings 1 and 2. The landers of these spacecraft carried two mass spectrometers. One of them was designed for measuring the neutral component in the upper atmoshpere at altitudes of 100 – 200 km from the surface, while the other was for measuring the composition of the lower atmosphere and the surface of the planet. (The second mass spectrometer, along with the gas chromatograph, was used also for analysing organic compounds in the Martian rock.)

The making of mass spectrometers for exploring the Martian atmosphere began many years before the launch of Vikings 1 and 2 (1975), and designs were published in 1972. In designing mass spectrometers for the upper atmosphere the following considerations were taken into account. (1) Measurements must begin with entry into the atmosphere at a pressure of 1.3×10^{-4} Pa, which requires a device of high sensitivity; (2) samples for analysis must be taken at the high speed of spacecraft entry into the atmosphere; and (3) analysis must be performed every few seconds in order to obtain the profile of the atmosphere. To study Mars' upper atmosphere the

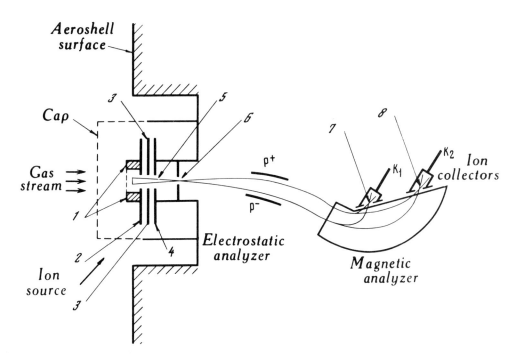

Fig. 2.5.7 — Functional diagram of the mass spectrometer used for studying the Martian upper atmosphere from Viking 1 and 2: 1, magnets; 2,3,4, focusing plates; 5,6,7,8, slits; L,H, detectors.

authors [6] used a mass spectrometer with double focusing whose schematic structure is presented in Fig. 2.5.7. The device is an evacuated system. During the flight to Mars the mass spectrometer was in a 'pumped-out' state. After the lander's separation from the orbital module, the device was pressurized (the protective lid was opened) and the flux of the gas under analysis got into the mass spectrometer, directly into the ion source. (During entry into the atmosphere the axis of the mass spectrometer was directed along the velocity vector.)

Since measurements were made at a speed of about 4×10^3 ms^{-1}, gas entered the mass spectrometer with the same speed. During entry the gas jet is ionized by an electron beam (the beam is directed along the normal to the diagram), is collimated by the magnetic field produced by permanent magnets (1), passes through the slit, is focused by the electrostatic field of plates (3) on the slit (4) and then onto the earthed slit (6). The ion beam collimated in this way escapes the ion source and gets into the electrostatic analyser whose field is generated by plates P$^+$ and P$^-$. After the electrostatic analyser, the ion beam gets into the magnetic analyser where the ions move in a circular orbit and are collected by the collector C_1 (or C_2).

The mass analyser's focusing properties are chosen in such a way that the output beam of ions which have a definite mass range is focused into a line. The position of an ion along the line is proportional to $m^{1/2}$ (where m is the ion mass). If only one ion collector is used, the mass of collected ions must be proportional to the accelerating voltage. This leads to the necessity of having an undesirably high or low voltage. That is why the device has two collectors (C_1 and C_2). These collectors cover two ranges from 1 to 7 and from 7 to 49 a.m.u. at a time. The mass spectrum is scanned for 5 s by altering the accelerating voltage.

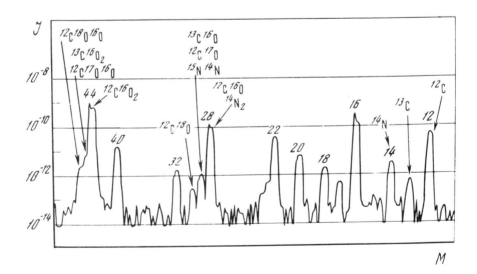

Fig. 2.5.8 — Mass-spectrum of the Martian upper atmosphere measured by Viking 1.

Fig. 2.5.8 shows a spectrum measured by the spectrometer described above [6]. The intensities of the peaks corresponding to different a.m.u.s are shown on the spectrum. They were measured during the scanning, which took 5 s. Since during the probe's descent through the atmosphere the pressure increased, the peaks at the right-hand side rose. Specifically, the carbon contribution to 12 a.m.u. (^{12}C) is 0.7 times that to 44 a.m.u. ($^{12}C^{16}O_2$). The measurements were taken at altitudes of 111 – 157 km.

As a result of the experiment, the presence of NO in Mars' upper atmosphere was detected. It is shown that the isotopic composition of carbon and oxygen is the same as in the Earth's upper atmosphere. However, the Martian atmosphere has turned out to be enriched with the heavy nitrogen isotope ^{15}N (a 75% enrichment as compared with the Earth's atmosphere). Apparently, this is accounted for by the partial loss of the lighter ^{14}N isotope on Mars. If the assumption is made that during the early stage of Mars's existence the isotopic ratio $^{15}N/^{14}N$ was the same as on the Earth, the partial pressure of nitrogen on Mars at that time was not less than $2x10^2$ Pa. The amount of oxygen which could be on Mars in CO_2 and H_2O was also assessed. Initially its partial pressure could have reached $2x10^5$ Pa [6].

We have considered above the mass spectrometry of Mars' upper atmsphere for which the mass spectrometer with an open source and without a pumping-out system was used. Quite different requirements were made of the mass spectrometer which was also operated on Pioneer Venus and used jointly with the gas chromatograph on Mars' surface.

This mass spectrometer was designed for (1) the qualitative or semi-quantative determination of organic components which are present in the rock surface layer, (2) the qualititative or quantitative determination of the composition (including the isotopic one) of the atmosphere near the surface, and (3) the semi-quantitative determination of water (and, if possible, its physical state in the surface rock). The appropriate technical requirements appeared as a consequence of these scientific tasks. The technical requirements comprised the following: (1) measurements must be taken within a wide a.m.u. range, (2) the sample of the atmosphere for analysis must be taken at a pressure of about $5x10^2$ Pa (i.e., exceeding the pressure used in the mass spectrometer by five orders of magnitude), and (3) the mass spectrometer must have a pumping-out system ensuring multiple analysis of the atmosphere and organic elements contained in the rock.

To solve these tasks, use was made of a mass-spectrometer based on the same principle as that described above. The neutral components of the atmosphere or evaporated volatile components of the rock entered the ion source, were irradiated by an electron beam, were accelerated and collimated by the electric field and were analysed by the magnetic mass analyser. To remove the analysed gas sample from the mass spectrometer and to maintain a constant low pressure (about $1.3x10^{-3}$ Pa), a magneto-discharge pump was used. This pump was periodically switched on during the flight path to Mars to maintain the necessary vacuum in the device. For the dosed selection of the sample a filling system was used which limited the flow of analysed gas into the device up to the value equal to the pumping-out speed. The mass spectrometer took measurements in the 12–200 a.m.u. range. Its sensitivity ensured the determination of minor components to a level below $5x10^{-6}$ of the amount of CO_2.

Using this mass spectrometer, Vikings 1 and 2 analysed the Martian atmosphere [7]. As a result of the analysis, isotopic ratios of carbon, nitrogen, oxygen and argon, as listed in Table 2.5.3, were determined. The following limits of the content in the

Martian atmosphere (in parts per million) were also determined: CH_4 <120; Ne <10; Kr <0.3 and Xe <1.5.

As evident from the table, the differences in the isotopic ratios of carbon and oxygen on Mars lie within 10%. The $^{15}N/^{14}N$ ratio is higher on Mars. The argon isotopic ratios for Mars and the Earth are approximately the same.

From the data obtained the following dilemma appeared. The relatively low abundance of ^{36}Ar on Mars shows that Mars' total outgassing apparently comprised only about one per cent of that which took place on the Earth. However, the excess of ^{15}N over ^{14}N points to the opposite: that a considerable amount of nitrogen was dissipated, and thus the initial outgassing must be more intensive while the atmosphere must be denser. The conclusion was made on the assumption that the initial amount of volatile matter on both planets was the same. However, if one assumes that the content of volatile matter Mars was closer to the composition of CI chondrites, then it would be concluded that the initial amount of nitrogen must be 30 times and the amount of carbon dioxide 10 times greater than their present amounts. This conclusion [7] is in agreement with the model of the initial low outgassing when the maximum pressure near the Martian surface was about 10^4 Pa.

As far as the analysis of organic compounds is concerned, they have not been detected in the Martian rock within the level of sensitivity of the method used.

Table 2.5.3 — Isotopic ratios of some components in the atmospheres of Mars and the Earth [7]

Isotopes	Mars	Earth
$^{15}N/^{14}N$	0.0064–0.0050	0.00368
$^{13}C/^{12}C$	0.0118±0.0012	0.0112
$^{18}O/^{16}O$	0.00189±0.0002	0.00204
$^{26}Ar/^{38}Ar$	4–7	5.3

2.5.3   MASS SPECTROMETRY OF THE LUNAR ATMOSPHERE FROM APOLLO 17

The measurements conducted by Apollos 14 and 15 have shown that the density of the Moon's atmosphere is 10^7 atoms cm^{-3} on the day side and 2×10^5 on the night side. To determine the composition of an atmosphere which has such a low density, a magnetic mass spectrometer with high sensitivity (up to about 100 molecules cm^{-3} for such gases as nitrogen and argon) was created. This spectrometer was used in measurements carried out from the command service module of Apollo 17.

The structure of the mass spectrometer is described in [8]. The principle of its operation is the same as in laboratory magnetic spectrometers. Gas molecules which enter through the diaphragm are bombarded by electrons, are accelerated by the electric field, are collimated into the beam, pass through the magnetic field, and are recorded by the detector of the mass spectrometer. The mass range recorded is determined by the value of the voltage which accelerates the ions of the gas analysed. In this device the mass spectra were recorded simultaneously in three a.m.u ranges: 1–4, 12–48 and 27–100 (the small, medium and large mass ranges, respectively). The medium and large mass ranges are chosen so that masses 28 and 64 are recorded simultaneously. This makes it possible to measure simultaneously CO and SO_2 (the presence of which may result from volcanic activity), by changing ion accelerating voltage and choosing appropriate conditions of the focusing for these masses. For every mass range, standard recording facilities were used — electron multipliers, pulse amplifiers, discriminators and counting devices. Information accumulated during a voltage scan (0.6 s) entered the memory unit with a capacity of 21 bits and was stored before interrogation by the telemetry system. Information was transmitted via the telemetry channel by a 7-bit code, i.e. with an error of about one per cent.

During preparation of the experiment the calibration of the mass spectrometer presented a particular difficulty. For the calibration a cryochamber was used. It was cooled by liquid helium, and a molecular beam of known flux density was produced there. The mass spectrometer was connected with the chamber so that the beam could enter the input diaphragm of the device. The calibration coefficients of the mass spectrometer were determined with a known ion flux and a known temperature for the ion source. A change of the gas pressure in the chamber of the molecular beam source altered the beam density and this allowed confirmation of the device's linearity. The highest count-rate of 5×10^5 pulses s^{-1} was reached, after which saturation of the detector began.

The calibration exercise was carried out for Ar, CO_2, CO, Kr, Ne, N_2 and H_2. There was no calibration for helium because it was impossible to pump helium out of the chamber. The calibration coefficient for helium was calculated from the ratio of the known ionization cross-sections for He and Ar.

Table 2.5.4 sums up the results of determining the composition of the Moon's atmosphere [8]. They point to the existence of mainly four gases — hydrogen, helium, neon and argon — in the lunar atmosphere. Their content, except for the argon content, is close to the equilibrium value which is maintained by two oppositely directed processes — the solar wind and dissipation. These gases are not condensed on the lunar surface, even at night time, due to the insufficiently low temperature. Argon isotopes are condensed on the surface at night and are evaporated in the daytime. It is worth noting that ^{36}Ar can also be of solar origin and that ^{40}Ar can be evolved from the rock due to the disintegration of ^{40}K. Thus, the studies have shown that the Moon has only the traces of an atmosphere, mainly of solar origin.

Table 2.5.4 — Gas contents in the lunar atmosphere [8]

Gas	Concentration (molecules cm^{-3})	
	Day side of the Moon	Night side of the Moon
H_2	—	6.5×10^4
^4He	2×10^3	4×10^4
^{20}Ne	—	8×10^4
^{36}Ar	—	$3 \times 10^{3(a)}$
		$3.5 \times 10^{4(a)}$
^{40}Ar	—	$(7-8) \times 10^{3(b)}$
O_2	—	$<2 \times 10^2$
CO_2	—	$<3 \times 10^3$

[a] The morning terminator.
[b] The evening terminator.

2.5.4 MASS SPECTROMETER FOR STUDYING AEROSOLS IN CLOUDS

Many Soviet and American spacecraft which headed for Venus took nephelometric measurements which permitted scientists to study the cloud layer structure and to obtain indirect information (from the light-refraction properties of the aerosols) that concentrated sulphuric acid droplets are the probable component of Venusian clouds [9–14]. Direct measurements by the X-ray-radiometric method [15–17] described in Chapter 2 have shown that in addition to the sulphur-bearing component a chlorine-bearing component is also present in the aerosols of Venusian clouds. However, up to now the detailed chemical composition of Venusian clouds has not been determined, despite the fact that spacecraft have regularly been sent to Venus over the past two decades. It is hard to study the composition of Venus' clouds, not only because of the difficulties in creating appropriate analytical equipment, but also due to the low aerosol content, which calls for preliminary concentration of the aerosol. Besides, Venusian clouds are heterogeneous in structure and apparently in composition. In all probability, particle groups differing in size (three size groups have been detected) have different compositions. That is why measurements at different levels of the atmosphere and of different particle groups are needed.

The mass spectrometric equipment which will be considered below is designed for the selection, the fractional separation (correspondingly to the particle size), and the mass spectrometric analysis of the composition of each aerosol fraction of Venus' cloud layer. The equipment was designed jointly by French and Soviet scientists [19, 22].

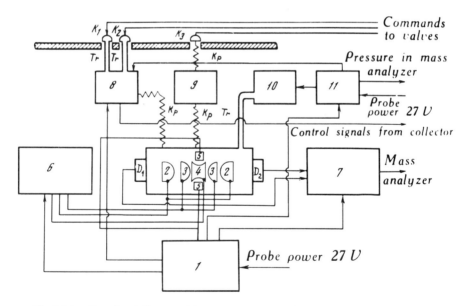

Fig. 2.5.9 — Functional diagram of the mass spectrometer for studying cloud aerosol: 1, power supply source; 2, optical system; 3, butt-end electrodes; 4, ring electrode; 5, electron sources; 6, HF-generator; 7, count-coding device; 8, collector–pyrolyser of aerosol; 9, gas-inlet device; 10, pump; 11, HV-supply source for pump. D_1 and D_2 – ion detectors; K_1, K_2 and K_3, injection valves; P, pipelines; Tr, capillary tubes.

Fig. 2.5.9 presents a simplified functional diagram of this equipment. It operates as follows. On command from the programmer–timer (PT) of the descent module, the valve V_1 (or V_2) is opened and the atmosphere together with any aerosol is pumped via the pipeline through the collector–pyrolyser (CP). In the inertia separator of the collecter–pyrolyser, the aerosol is separated into two groups of particles (diameter $<3\mu m$ and diameter $<3\mu m$). Each group of particles is pyrolysed separately in pyrolytic chambers, and the gas products of pyrolysis enter the mass analyser (MA) through the injection system. In the mass analyser, which is of an hyperboloidal type, molecules are ionized by an electron beam, the ions formed are separated according to m/e values by a high-frequency electric field, and are focused and injected onto detectors D_1 and D_2. In the detectors the ion flux is turned into current pulses (whose frequency characterizes the ion flux intensity) and then into voltage pulses with normalized characteristics. From the detectors the pulses come to the counter–encoder where they are counted and encoded for transmission to the telemetry system.

To analyse the gas component of the atmosphere the valve V_3 is opened and gas passes via the capillary tube through the gas-injection device (ID) where the main component of Venus' atmosphere — CO_2 — is absorbed, directly to the mass-analyser, and is then analysed in the same way as the products of the pyrolysis of the aerosol.

In this device an hyperboloidal mass analyser is used [20]. Its operating principle is based on the capacity of the high-frequency (with a constant component) electric field to separate ions according to their specific charges. The charge separation takes place in the sensor of the mass analyser. The sensor is a system of three field-forming electrodes — a middle cylindrical one and two extreme butt-end electrodes. These electrodes, which have the shape of hyperboloids of revolution, form a closed volume in which the molecules of gas under investigation are ionized, separated and injected onto the detectors. Between the cylindrical and butt-end electrodes a voltage of the form $U = +U \sim \varphi$ (t) is applied, where φ (t) is a square-shaped pulse signal.

The operating cycle of the mass analyser consists of three stages: T_1, T_2 and T_3. Electrons formed in the electron source are put through channels in the cylindrical electrode into the working volume of the sensor during time T_1. At the end of this time the introduction of electrons stops. The ions formed move in the high-frequency (HF) field. Depending on their specific charge, the amplitude of oscillation of the ions either increases continuously and the ions, getting onto the electrodes, are neutralized, or remains within the limits of the analyser working volume. By selecting the values of voltages on the electrodes and the frequency of the HF signal such conditions are created that only ions with a definite specific m/e charge remain within the analyser working volume. The degree of scattering of all the remaining ions is determined by the sorting time T_2. Upon completion of the sorting the output signal is applied to the electrodes and during time T_3 the ions are put through the ion-optical system into secondary electron multipliers. Thus, the ion flux which is transformed in the detectors into electric pulses comes to the input of the amplifer. The amplified signals enter the integral discriminator with regulated threshold. Any signals below the control level determined by noise is removed by means of the discriminator.

Since two similar detectors are used in the analyser, the signals from the outputs of the two discriminators enter, via shapers, the mixing circuit, which is located in the counter–encoder. The maximum count-rate of pulses is 2×10^6 pulses s^{-1}.

The HF generator is designed for scanning the mass spectrum. The scanning is carried out by varying the frequency of the HF signal. For scanning the range from 10 to 150 a.m.u. the frequency varies from 400 to 86 kHz during a period of 50 s.

The counter–encoder is designed for counting, encoding, memorizing and transmitting mass spectra to the telemetry system.

The counter-encoder operates as follows. At the moment of commencement of the scanning of the mass spectrum, the transmission circuit opens and pulses from detectors D_1 and D_2 enter the mixer, and after mixing are counted in the 19-bit register. Then the information is encoded and in the transformed 12-bit code (10-bits for the number and 2 bits for the sign) is recorded in the electronic memory. Information accumulated in the memory is taken at the request of the telemetry system.

To create the necessary vacuum in the analytical part of the device (namely 1.3×10^{-4} to 1.3×10^{-5} Pa) a magnetoionization pump is used. Two types of pumping are employed in the pump: ion pumping based on the injection of ions into the cathode material, and adsorption pumping based on the binding of the gas molecules by a titanium (or tantalum) film. The pump has a sealed stainless steel body placed into a magnetic field. There is an electrode system inside the body. The system consists of two plane-parallel cathodes and a cellular anode placed between them. A high voltage ($+ 5$ kV) is supplied to the anode. The electric field is directed along the normal to the magnetic field. When high voltage is applied on the anode, a gas discharge appears between the electrodes, as a result of which ionic bombardment sputters the titanium cathode and titanium microparticles settle on the walls of the pump body, forming an active film which adsorbs gases. In these conditions chemically active gas molecules can also form compounds with sputtered titanium and can be covered with subsequent titanium layers. The discharge current of the pump depends on the pressure of the gas in it, while the magnitude of the current is an indicator of the pressure in the working volume of the mass analyser.

The intensity of the magnetic field in the centre of the pump is 90000 Am^{-1}; the voltage between the electrodes is 6 kV; the maximum working pressure 6.7×10^{-6} Pa; and the pumping-out rate 3 litre s^{-1}.

The power unit is designed to transform the onboard network voltage of ± 27 V into voltages required for supplying power to the units of the collector-pyrolyser, the HF generator, the mass analyser and the counter-encoder and for the stablization of these voltages. A separate unit gives high voltage of $+ 6$ kV for supplying the pump with power and a command for closing the channels through which the analysed gas enters the mass analyser, if the pressure in the mass analyser working volume has exceeded the permissible value (4×10^{-7} Pa).

Fig. 2.5.10 presents a calibration spectrum measured by this device.

Fig. 2.5.11 gives a simplified cyclogram of the operation of the device described above. The device is designed for the selection and analysis (with the separation into fractions and with pyrolysis) of aerosol samples and multiple (or continuous) analysis of the gas phase of the atmosphere.

The mass spectrometer described above was installed on the lander of the VeGa 1

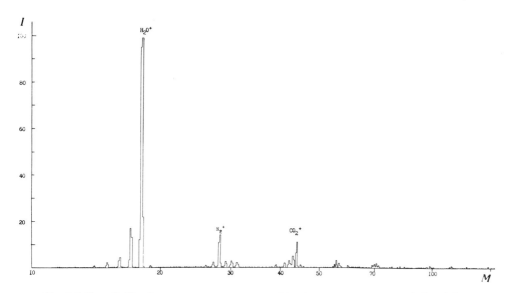

Fig. 2.5.10 — Calibration mass spectrum measured by the mass spectrometer designed for studying cloud aerosol.

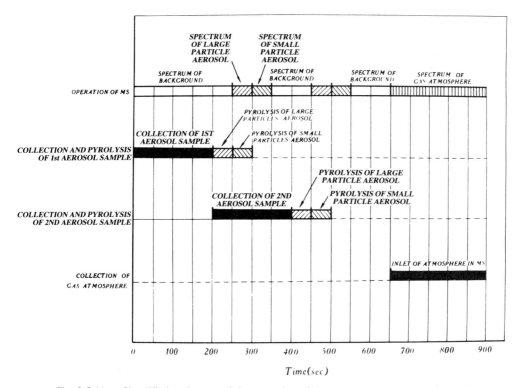

Fig. 2.5.11 — Simplified cyclogram of the operation of the mass spectrometer designed for studying cloud aerosol.

space probe and was used for the study of Venus' clouds [22]. The instrument was hermetically sealed before the flight. To maintain a vacuum in the instrument it was pumped out throughout the flight from the Earth to Venus. Upon entry of the lander into the planetary atmosphere and the opening of the parachute at an altitude of 64 km above the surface, the sampler was depressurised by a pyrotechnical device and access of gas with aerosol to the collector-pyrolyzer allowed. The atmosphere was pumped by a fan through the separator chamber where the intertial separation of particles into the light and heavy fractions was effected. Both groups of particles were collected on separate filters which were subject to pyrolytic heating (at a temperature of 400°C). The products of pyrolysis entered the mass anlyser through the injection system. A gas flow of not more than 1.3×10^{-7} litre Pa s^{-2} was secured through the inlet system.

During analysis of the mass spectra of the particles assembled in the upper layer of clouds at an altitude of 62–54 km, a peak at 64 a.m.u. was detected which can be accounted for by the presence of sulphur dioxide in the products of pyrolysis. The relative magnitude of the peak of SO_2^+/CO_2 is $(3-4) \times 10^{-3}$. Taking into account the losses during the collection of aerosol on the filter, during the transformation into the gaseous phase in the course of pyrolysis, and during the absorption in the system of the introduction of gas the lower boundary of the H_2SO_4 content in the aerosol was estimated as 2.0×10^{-6} kg m^{-3}. The value obtained is in good agreement with the estimate of the mass density of aerosol from H_2SO_4 drops in the upper layer of the clouds from the results of the measurements by the Pioneer Venus spacecraft [4]. The spectrum also contains the 35 and 37 a.m.u. lines which belong to chlorine. The value of the peak of the basic ^{35}Cl isotope is $(0.8-1.0) \times 10^3$ mg m^{-3} and of the ^{37}Cl isotope 3×10^{-4} mg m^{-3}, which corresponds to the lower boundary of chlorine content $— 3 \times 10^{-7}$ kg m^{-3}.

So, the mass-spectrometric determination of the chemical composition of aerosol by the VeGa 1 lander has shown that the predominant component of heavy cloud particles is sulphur. Apparently the latter is present in the form of liquid H_2SO_4 aerosol or other condensate which is decomposed during the heating with the release of sulphur dioxide.

2.5.5 MASS SPECTROMETERS FOR ROCK STUDIES

Mass spectrometers have not yet been used for exploring the solid phase of planets and satellites by spacecraft.

Apparently this is accounted for by the fact that they are more sophisticated than alpha-particle, X-ray and gamma-ray spectrometers, and can be used only on landing modules, while spectrometers of radioactive radiations can also make remote measurements. At the same time, the mass spectrometer enables one not only to expand the range of determined chemical elements, but also to gather additional information about the isotopic composition of elements, which provides an opportunity to understand the processes which occurred on planets and satellites long ago.

At the time of writing, work is under way on the first onboard solid–body mass spectrometers designed for studying the solid matter composition from spacecraft. One such mass spectrometer has been designed by Cherepin *et al.* [21] for studying the composition of the material of bodies devoid of atmospheres. The two-channel

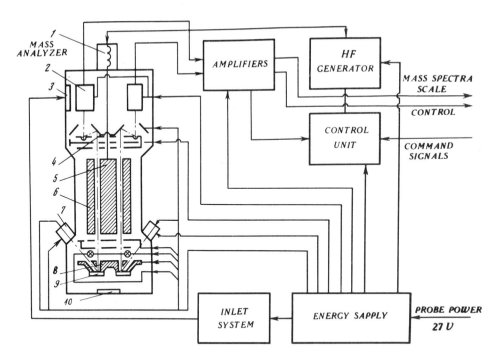

Fig. 2.5.12 — Functional diagram of the mass spectrometer for studying the solid phase of extraterrestrial material: 1, HF pulse bobbin; 2, secondary electron multipliers; 3, decompression device; 4, ion–electron converter with the energy analyser; 5, cylindrical electrode; 6, corner electrode; 7, ion source; 8, immersion objective; 9, sample analysed; 10, input window-opening; device.

device makes it possible to take simultaneously the mass spectra of two solid-body samples (or the mass spectra of the sample under study and a reference sample).

A functional diagram of this mass spectrometer is given in Fig. 2.5.12. The device consists of the following principal functional units: a sensor, control electronics, an inlet system, a power unit, amplifiers and an HF generator.

The sensor is the analytical part of the device. Its cylindrical body houses a two-channel radio-frequency mass analyser, a two-channel immersion objective, a two-channel ion–electron converter, two ion sources with flow regulators and two secondary electron multipliers.

The mass analyser of the sensor consists of two field-forming electrodes (one is angular and the other cylindrical). The angular electrode is a square cross-section pipe. The cylindrical electrode is installed inside it coaxially. Such a design of the electrodes makes it possible to use two diametrically opposite quadrants of the quadrupole field. The electron-optical axes of the channels lie at two opposite angles of the angular electrode and are directed parallel to the axis of the cylindrical electrode.

The electric field is generated in the mass analyser when alternate HF and direct voltages are applied to the electrodes. Ions which get into the space between the electrodes perform oscillations which depend on the parameters of the field and on the m/e ratio. With preset parameters of the field, ions of only one m/e value have a stable trajectory. Such ions can pass through the mass analyser only along this trajectory because their oscillations will not go beyond the limits of the mass analyser. All the remaining ions with other mass values will have unstable trajectories and will get onto the electrodes.

The immersion objective of the sensor is designed for the collection, acceleration and focusing of secondary ions knocked out from the sample under analysis by the ion beam. The immersion objective consists of three (upper, middle and lower) electrodes. To accelerate the ions a potential difference of about 700 V is applied between the upper and lower electrodes; the middle electrode is linked with the body. All electrodes have two openings located along the electron-optical axes of the device.

The ion–electron converter of the sensor is designed for transforming the ion current into an electron current which is then amplified by the secondary electron multiplier. The converter consists of a single electrostatic lens (whose outer electrode is simultaneously an electron emitter) and a reflecting electrode which reflects ions with energies lower than a defined level while remaining ions are neutralized on its surface. Signals from the secondary electron multiplier enter the amplifier unit.

To produce the ion beam of the working gas, use is made of the ion source with a cold cathode on the basis of Penning's electric discharge in the magnetic field. The ion source is supplied by a constant voltage of 6 kV. In the 1.3×10^{-6} to 1.3×10^{-7} Pa pressure range the ion source with the Penning discharge shows an almost linear dependence of the discharge current on the gas pressure in the discharge chamber. Hydrogen is used as the working gas.

For the dosed supply of working gas to the discharge chamber of the ion source, use is made of the flow regulator of hydrogen based on the palladium alloy heated to a high temperature.

HF voltage is supplied to the mass analyser from the HF generator through the outlying coil located in the sensor. The generator delivers a voltage consisting of direct (U) and alternating (V) components. The components U and V vary smoothly from the minimum value to the maximum value. The U/V ratio always remains constant. The oscillation frequency of the voltage varies within $2.0 - 2.2$ MHz while the amplitude varies from $0 - 3000$ V. The direct voltage varies from $0 - 450$ V.

To transform the electron current, which comes from the sensor, into voltage pulses transmitted via the communication channel, a recording system is used. It consists of two secondary electron multipliers, an amplifier unit, an automatic control unit and an electron commutator located in the power supply unit.

Due to the wide range of input currents and the limited dynamic range of the transmission system, the recording system has three-scale with an automatic switch between the scales, with the transmission of the intensity and the working scale number occurring via the communication channel.

In the recording unit, secondary electron multipliers with $K=10^5$ are used. The value of the current measured by the electrometer amplifier is 10^{-11} to 10^{-5} A. The amplifier operates in a non-linear functional conversion mode. Every two orders of magnitude of the variation in the input current are transformed into a variation in the voltage of 6.2 V.

The automatic control unit is designed for receiving external commands and for performing the following functions: control of the sample-supply mechanism; delivery of the control voltage for the HF generator; changing of the channels of the mass spectrometer; sending commands to the power-supply unit; and stabilization of the discharge current of the ion sources.

The power-supply unit transforms the onboard voltage of 27 V into high voltages for the immersion objective, the ion–electron converter and secondary electron multipliers, as well as a low-voltage supply for the amplifier unit, the HF generator and the automatic control unit. The main characteristics of the solid-body mass spectrometer described above [21] are: range of measurement in a.m.u. is 2 – 220; resolution at the 0.1 level not lower than 1.2 M; threshold of sensitivity with pure aluminium not less than 10^{-11} A; dynamic range of measurement for ion currents is 10^6 and the instrument mass is not more than 15 kg.

Fig. 2.5.13 presents a basalt spectrum obtained using this device under laboratory conditions.

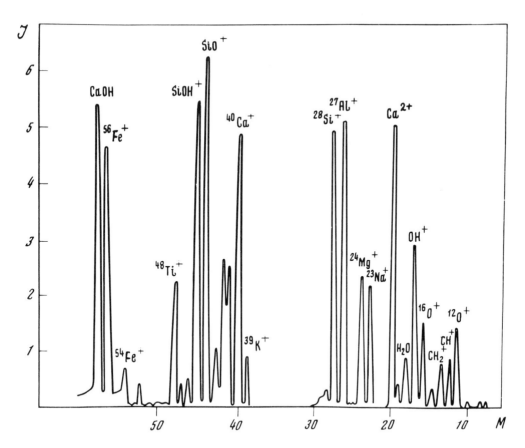

Fig. 2.5.13 — Basalt mass spectrum measured by the instrument designed for the study of rock composition. (The vertical scale is increased with respect to the a.m.u. reference base range of 21 to 40 by a factor of 30 in the a.m.u. range of 41 to 50 and by a factor of 10 in the a.m.u. 50 range.)

The mass spectrometer described above can be used for determining the elemental and isotopic composition of solid material on planets and satellites devoid of an atmosphere. It has no pumping-out system and, therefore, cannot by used for exploring the rocks on bodies which have atmospheres. However, celestial 'bodies which have no atmospheres are more numerous in the Solar System. These include most planetary satellites and the countless number of asteroids.

REFERENCES

[1] Yu. A. Surkov and V. F. Ivanova, *Geokhimiya*, **4**, 506 (In Russian) (1977).

[2] V. G. Istomin, K. V. Grechnev, and V. A. Kochnev, *Kosmich. Issled.*, **17**, 703 (In Russian) (1979).

[3] J. H. Hoffman, R. R. Hodger, and W. W. Wright, *IEEE Trans. Geosci. Electron*, **GE-18**, 80 (1980).

[4] J. H. Hoffman, R. R. Jr. Hodges, T. M. Donohue, and M. B. McElroy, *J. Geophys. Res.*, **85**, 7882 (1980).

[5] V. G. Istomin, K. V. Grechnev, and L. N. Ozerov, *Kosmich. Issled.*, **8**, 16 (In Russian) (1975).

[6] A. O. Nier, W. B. Hanson, and W. B. Mc Elroy, *Icarus*, **16**, 74 (1975).

[7] K. Beiman, T. Owen, and D. R. Rushneck, *Science*, **149**, 76 (1976).

[8] J. H. Hoffman, R, R. Hodger, and F. S. Johnson, In *Proc. 4th Lunar sci.conf.*, Pergamon Press, New York, **3**, 2865 (1973).

[9] M. Ya. Marov, V. Ye. Lystsev, and V. N. Lebedev, (In Russian) Preprint No 144, the Institute of Applied Mathematics of the USSR Academy of Sciences, Moscow, p.34 (1978).

[10] M. Ya. Marov, *Astron. Vestnik*, **13**, 3 (In Russian) (1979).

[11] R. G. Knollenberg, J. Hansen, and B. Ragent, *Space Sci. Rev.*, **20**, 329 (1977).

[12] R. G. Knollenberg and D. M. Hanten, *Science*, **203**, 792 (1979).

[13] M. Ya. Marov, V. N. Lebedev, and V. E. Lysetev, Report presented to the 19th COSPAR meeting, USA (1976).

[14] B. Rogent and J. Blamont, *Science*, **203**, 790 (1979).

[15] Yu. A. Surkov, Paper presented at the COSPAR 22nd meeting, Bangalore, India, 15 (1979).

[16] Yu. A. Surkov, F. F. Kirnozov, and V. I. Guryanov, *Geokhimiya*, **1**, 3 (In Russian) (1981).

[17] Yu. A. Surkov, F. F. Kirnozov, and V. N. Glazov, *Letters to Astron. J.*, **8**, 700 (In Russian) (1982).

[18] J. H. Hoffman, R. R. Hodges, and W. W. Wright, *IEEE Trans. Geosci, Electron.*, **GE-18**, 80 (1980).

[19] G. Israel, D. Imbauer, and C. Hantz, Report presented at International Astronaut's Federation session (Lausanne, October 1984), 16.

[20] E. P. Sheretov, *Measurement, Control, Automatization,* **11**, 29 (In Russian) (1980)

[21] V. T. Cherepin, and M. A. Vasilyev, In *The secondary ion–ion emission of metals and alloys.* (In Russian) Kiev, Naukova dumka, p.240 (1975).

[22] Yu. A. Surkov, V. F. Ivanova, E. P. Scheretov *et al.*, *Letters to Astron. Zh.*, **12**, 110 (In Russian) (1986).

[23] V. G. Istomin, K. V. Grechnev, and V. A. Kochnev, *Pisma Astron. Zh.*, **8**, 391 (In Russian) (1982).

2.6 The exploration of Mars and Phobos (Phobos mission)

In section 1.5.2 we considered Mars' two small satellites Phobos and Deimos. The interest in these bodies stems not only from their enigmatic origin, but also from the close links which exist between their own history and that of the Solar System as a whole. This interest led to the planning of the ambitious international Phobos project [1, 2, 3]. Thirteen nations and scientific organisations participated in the project with the Soviet Union which, if it had gone according to plan, would have culminated in the landing of two small probes on the surface of Mars' larger statellite, Phobos, and the application of laser and ion beams to analyse the composition of its surface layers.

Two Phobos space probes were launched from the Baikonur Cosmodrome in July 1988. Communcation with the first of these, Phobos 1, was lost in late-August, when an erroneous message was uploaded to the spacecraft from mission control. Despite a number of technical problems *en route* to Mars, including loss of its main radio transmitter, the sister craft Phobos 2 was successfully injected in to an elliptical orbit around Mars on January 29 1989. This orbit covered the near-equatorial part of the Martian surface, the main exploration sessions of the planet being conducted in the periapsis section of the trajectory several hundreds of kilometres above the surface. The orbit was changed several times as the controllers moved the spacecraft steadily closer to its main target. The aim was to put the probe into a near-circular orbit close to that of Phobos, with a revolution period about Mars of around 7 hours 40 minutes.

The first of nine TV sessions devoted to Phobos took place on February 21, and later observations, made after carefully aligning the camera and verifying the orientation of the spacecraft, were used to improve the accuracy of Phobos' orbit. When the spacecraft were launched, the orbit of the moon had been uncertain by hundreds of kilometres. By early March, this error had been reduced to only 20 to 30 km, and as the probe continued to close in on the moon over the next few weeks, its orbit was refined to within just two or three kilometres.

This accuracy was required so that the probe could approach Phobos, and slowly pass above its surface at a height of only about 50 metres. The fly-by speed was to be of the order of 2 to 5 m s^{-1}, so the probe would remain in close proximity to the moon for around 20 minutes, allowing it to drop two descent probes on to the surface and perform analyses of the soil. The constant tri-axial orientation of the spacecraft was ensured by aligning one axis with the Sun and another towards the bright star

Canopus. The accuracy of the spacecraft's stabilization using this tri-axial orientation system was $\pm 1°$, the angular speed of the drift in this mode being less than $0.005°\,s^{-1}$.

By the third week of March, the probe was approaching within 100 km of Phobos, and it was planned to make the final close approach to the moon on April 9 or 10. By the last week of March, it had already successfully acquired many good quality optical and infra-red images of both Phobos and the Martian surface; a detailed thermal chart of part of Mars had been made, and the shadow of Phobos on the planet's surface had been detected. In fact, the inclusion of the infrared scanning device on the spacecraft had been a 'last-minute' decision, and in spite of this it functioned extremely well.

The Phobos 2 spacecraft also took important measurements of the interaction between Mars and the solar wind. These data showed that although Mars has only a weak magnetic field, it does appear to possess radiation belts containing electrically-charged particles, similar to those of the Earth. X-ray images of the Sun had also revealed major solar flares whose peak intensity approached record-breaking levels. As well as photographing Phobos, the spacecraft had also studied Mars' smaller satellite, Deimos, and had been able to fix its orbit with an accuracy of a few tens of kilometres.

Against this background of many successful achievements, there had been a few minor problems including some malfunctioning of the probe's on-board auxiliary radio transmitter. On March 27, the spacecraft was turned to take another series of TV images of Phobos to further improve the parameters of its orbit, and the auxiliary transmitter was shut down, exactly as planned, while the photographic session took place. After the operations were completed, the information was to be downloaded to Earth, but mission control failed to re-establish immediate contact with the probe. After four hours of attempts to regain communication with the spacecraft, a weak response signal was received, but after a period of less than fifteen minutes, it finally disappeared.

On March 29, Alexander Dunayev, Chief of Glavkosmos, announced that an expert commission had been set up, and had been given a week to investigate the causes of failure. At that time, efforts to restore links with Phobos 2 were still continuing around the clock. Eventually, on April 15, it was announced that the expert commission had recommended that attempts to re-establish contact with the spacecraft be discontinued. This was confirmed by Roald Kremnev, Chief Designer at the Babakin Research and Test Centre, who was quoted as saying that, "judging by the parameters of the signal, Phobos 2 lost its bearings and is rotating. Its solar cells have stopped supplying energy, while the capacity of the (on-board storage) electric batteries is enough for only five hours of work. Further attempts to establish communications were futile. By April 13, the temperature on board the spacecraft would go down to a critical point, below which the instruments cannot function. This is why it was decided to discontinue the attempts to regain contact with the vehicle."

In spite of the spacecraft's failure to achieve the main mission objectives, Phobos was an interesting design of multi-objective spacecraft and, in keeping with the subject matter of this book (the study of extraterrestrial material from spacecraft), I shall describe its main characteristics and the set of on-board scientific instruments designed for exploring the material of Mars and Phobos.

The Phobos spacecraft carried two decent modules, which were to be dropped on to the surface of the Martian satellite. One of these, the long-term automated lander, was designed to continue operating on the surface of Phobos for a long time (more than three months), while the other, nicknamed 'the hopper' would operate for only a short time (just a few hours), but was designed to move across the surface of Phobos to extend its range of operations.

The spacecraft carried about 30 scientific instruments for the exploration of Mars, Phobos and the Sun. In particular, at least five instruments were designed to study the chemical composition of these bodies: a gamma-ray spectrometer, a neutron detector, a laser mass spectrometer and an ion mass spectrometer installed on main spacecraft, as well as an X-ray spectrometer mounted on each of the descent modules.

2.61   THE EXPLORATION OF MARS
During the Phobos 2 probe's orbital motion around Mars, remote sensing of the surface in the visible, infrared and gamma-ray wavelength bands was performed. The most intensive remote sensing was carried out during the spacecraft's closest approaches to Mars. The thermal and reflecting properties of the planetary surface were also studied.

The aim of this exploration of Mars from the spacecraft was to compile a thermal map of the surface, to study the planet's diurnal and seasonal temperature variations, to measure the thermal inertia of the soil, and to identify areas where there is release of endogenic heat and permafrost regions.

Experiments for determining the chemical composition of rocks on Mars are of special importance. The spacecraft carried two scientific instruments for such studies: a gamma-ray spectrometer and a neutron detector. Additional information on the character of Martian rocks was provided by studies using optical methods.

To study Martian surface material the following experiments were performed by the Phobos 2 space probe:
  — acquisition of pictures and mapping of the surface by a television camera and an infrared spectrometer within the $0.4 - 1.1$ μm band.
  — study of the mineralogical composition, the thermal and reflecting properties of the surface, and preparation of a temperature map (using a spectrophotometer for $0.3 - 0.9$ μm, a spectrometer for $0.8 - 3.5$ μm and a radiometer for $8 - 13$ μm);
  — gamma-ray spectrometry of the planetary surface;
  — neutronmetry of the planetary surface;
  — optical spectrometry of the planet's atmosphere.
Since the methods used for study of the composition of extraterrestrial material is the main aim of this book, I shall describe the experiments in gamma-ray spectrometry and neutronmetry [3, 5] in more detail.

2.6.1.1. Gamma-ray spectrometry of the Martian surface
In Chapter 1.4 it was noted that Mars has been explored by remote methods from the probes Mars 2, 3, 4 and 5, Mariners 6, 7 and 9 and Vikings 1 and 2. So, some information on the Martian surface rocks is already available. However, the data on the composition of rocks relate only to a very limited part of the Martian surface. Specifically, the content of natural radioactive elements and some rock-forming elements has been determined in the Tharsis–Thaumasia–Sinus region, and the composition of rocks was analysed at the two Viking landing sites (Chryse Planitia and Utopia Planitia).

The aim of the gamma-ray spectrometry experiment on the Phobos 2 spacecraft was to continue the study of the composition of rocks in other regions of Mars that began with Mars 5.

The gamma-ray spectrometer consisted of three units: an outrigger hermetically-sealed detection unit, a multi-channel pulse analyser and a unit for analysing gamma-ray bursts. A functional diagram of the device is presented in Fig. 2.6.1. The detection unit incorporated a scintillation detector (a CsI (Tl) monocrystal optically fused with the photomultiplier), a spectrometric amplifier, a circuit separating the pulses from gamma-ray quanta and charged particles, count-rate meters, and a power supply unit. To lessen the contribution to the recorded background gamma-ray spectrum due to the natural and induced radioactivity in the spacecraft's structural materials, the detection unit was installed on the edge of the solar panel more than 3 m away from the spacecraft's main body. It had a self-contained temperature control system.

The pulse analyser separated pulses according to their amplitudes, accumulated and stored information, encoded it and ensured its output to the telemetry system. The analyser had 1024 channels. The capacity of each channel was 16 binary digits. Accumulated digital information was retrieved in a sequential binary code on receipt of request pulses from the spacecraft. The data transmission speed was 16 kHz. The analyser was mounted inside the spacecraft's thermostatically- controlled compartment.

The same compartment housed a unit for analysing gamma-ray bursts, which made it possible to record the energy and time distribution of gamma-ray quanta during the burst.

The main characteristics of the gamma-ray spectrometer were as follows: total mass 14 kg, power consumption 18 W, number of analyser channels 1024 (2 x 512), volume of information transmitted 35 kbits, number of burst analyser channels 128, volume of information transmitted 2.5 kbits, range of the measured energies of gamma-ray quanta 0.1 – 10.0 MeV, detector's energy resolution about 11% ($E\gamma = 0.662$ MeV), and type of crystal CsI (Tl), 100 x 100 mm in size. The range of the elements determined varies from carbon to nickel, and includes uranium and thorium.

In keeping with the planned flight programme, the following operating mode of the gamma-ray spectrometer was envisaged. It was switched on immediately after putting the spacecraft into the transfer trajectory for its flight to Mars. During the mission, the gamma-ray bursts were registered, and the background spectrum periodically recorded for an hour. Upon the spacecraft's entry into an elliptical orbit about Mars', the background at apoapsis and the gamma-radiation of Mars at perapsis were measured for an hour and four hours, respectively (See also section 2.7 of this volume).

With the spectrometer, measurements were possible with a 'switched on' and 'switched off' circuit separating the signals of gamma-ray quanta from those of charged particles. In the first case, information was accumulated separately in two sections of the pulse analyser with 512 channels each, and in the second case the total spectrum was accumulated. The efficiency of operation of the separation circuit was controlled by a radioisotope source of alpha-particles, namely [241]Am ($E\alpha = 5.46$ MeV), which was introduced in the scintillation crystal.

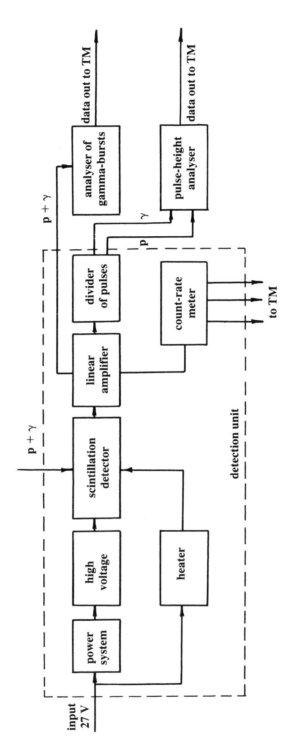

Fig. 2.6.1 — Functional diagram of the gamma-ray spectrometer carried by the Phobos spacecraft.

In addition to recording the gamma-radiation spectrum within the entire energy range from 0.1 – 10.0 MeV (which is accumulated in the pulse analyser), the spectrometer memorized and sent to a telemetry channel the counting rate in three energy ranges: 0.1 – 3.0; 3.0 – 6.0; and 6.0 – 10 MeV. This control information was output in analogue form.

The optimum temperature conditions for operation of the outrigger detection unit of the gamma-ray spectrometer were achieved through a heater with a thermoregulator. Additionally, temperature control was achieved in different units by thermosensors, the readings from which, in analogue form, were also output via a telemetry channel.

The analysis of the nature of Mars' gamma-radiation and the description of data-processing methods were given briefly in Chapter 1.2. Here I would like only to add that in this case the gamma-ray spectrometer's background was measured in a low-background building as a component of the entire spacecraft. The instrument, together with the whole spacecraft, was calibrated on rocks (with a known average content of radioactive elements) in their natural bedding.

2.6.1.2. The neutron detector

The second instrument designed to obtain information on the character of Martian rocks was a three-channel neutron detector [3]. As pointed out in Chapter 2.3, the neutrons coming from the planet's surface are of secondary origin. They are formed by the interaction between cosmic rays and the rock. Their flux density and energy composition depend on the content of elements, the nuclei of which have great scattering cross-sections or capture cross-sections. These rock elements are, first of all, hydrogen and some rare-earth elements.

As far as Mars is concerned, determination of the water (ice) content in the rock's surface layer is of particular importance. This enables one to identify regions with enhanced humidity, favourable soil cover, and possessing moderate climatic conditions which can be chosen for promising research (including exobiological studies) and for selecting soil samples to be returned to Earth for analysis.

Measurements of the neutron flux make it possible also to spot the regions possessing igneous rocks resembling lunar KREEP basalts (which have an increased content of rare-earth elements) and rocks with an anomalously high content of iron and other elements.

Fig. 2.6.2 gives a diagram of a neutron detector, like that flown on Phobos 2. It has three groups of counters (four counters in a group) which record neutrons. The counters are filled with the gas ^{3}He. The detector registers neutrons in three energy intervals (thermal, epithermal and fast neutrons) in the 0.025 – 2.0 MeV range.

Since the counters record with high efficiency only thermal neutrons, the latter enter the counters directly (without any screening); epithermal neutrons get onto the counters through a cadmium screen, and fast neutrons after a hydrogen-bearing moderator.

The instrument's main characteristicss are: energy range 0.025 – 2.0 MeV, time resolution 50 to 100 μs, mass 10 kg, size 100 x 600 mm, and power consumption 5 W.

The neutron detector on Phobos 2 operated periodically during the flight to Mars and when the spacecraft was in a similar orbit to the Martian satellite Phobos. Its operational programme is similar to that of the gamma-ray spectrometer described above. Information on the neutron flux in each channel was recorded by an 8-bit

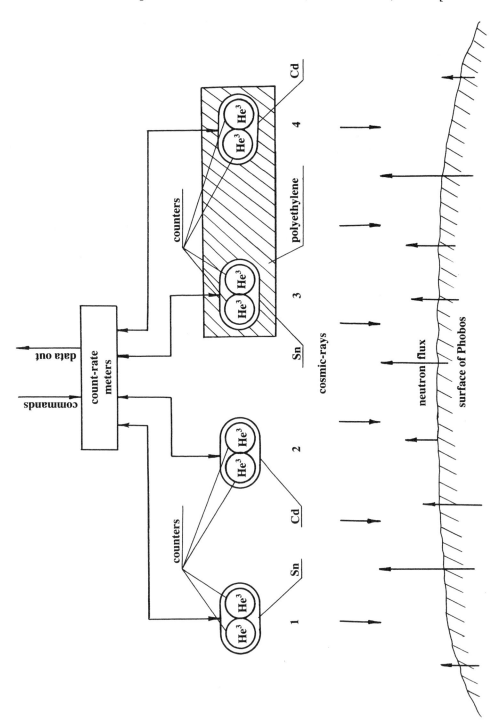

Fig.2.6.2 — Diagram of the neutron detector installed on the Phobos Spacecraft.

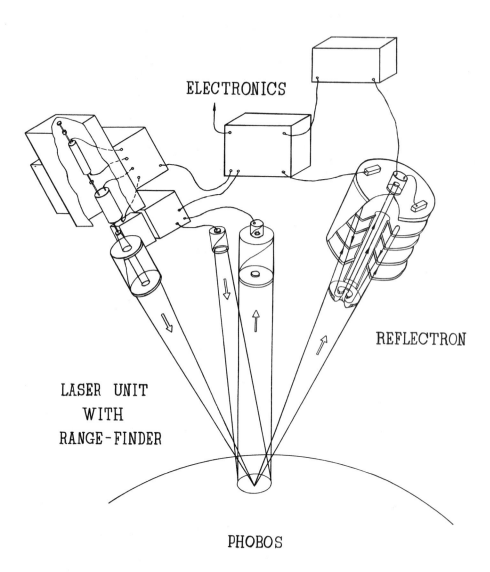

ELECTRONICS

REFLECTRON

LASER UNIT
WITH
RANGE-FINDER

PHOBOS

Fig.2.6.3 — Diagram of the experiment in the laser mass spectrometry on the Phobos
spacecraft.

digital counter. The interrogation frequency of analogue channels was 1 min.

Before the mission, the instrument was calibrated on rocks in their natural bedding having a different content of hydrogen, rare-earth elements, iron, etc.

Thus, the data obtained by these two instruments, along with the results from optical studies of the Martian surface, enable one to judge the character of rocks, their chemical composition, and, hence, the degree of differentiation of rocks in the process of their formation. The data on the concentration of uranium, thorium and potassium can also be used for studying the thermal history of Mars.

2.6.2. THE EXPLORATION OF PHOBOS

In section 1.5.2. it was noted that the exploration of Mars' satellites is of particular interest. According to modern concepts Phobos and Deimos are, in all likelihood, captured asteroidal bodies. Spectral observations of the variations in these satellites' reflectivities have shown that they have the same characteristics as carbonaceous chondrites. The low density (1.5 to 2.5 x 10^3 kgm^{-3}) of these satellites also testifies to this.

If the satellites are indeed C-type asteroids, they must be preserved in close to their original state. In other words, their material must contain a large amount of lightweight elements (in particular, carbon) and of volatile components (primarily water). Therefore, the methods of analysis of the material of Phobos were selected with due account of its expected composition. However, it was also taken into account that the surface soil layer (regolith) of Phobos has been transformed under the effect of bombardment by meteorites, the solar wind, cosmic rays, etc. That is why exploration of the surface soil layer provides information not only on the nature of Phobos and its origin, but also on the conditions of formation of other Solar System bodies and their subsequent evolution.

To carry out a comprehensive study of Phobos, the flight programme envisaged the approach of the space probe close to the surface of Phobos to a minimum height of about 50 m, and a flight over it at low speed. The following studies were planned:

— gamma-ray spectrometry of natural gamma radiation and gamma radiation induced by cosmic rays;
— neutronmetry of secondary neutrons generated by cosmic rays;
— laser mass spectrometry of soil;
— ion mass spectrometry of soil;
— X-ray radiometry of soil from the descent modules.

The first two experiments were described above as applied to the study of rocks on the surface Mars. The next three experiments will be considered below.

2.6.2.1. Laser mass spectrometry (LIMA-D)

The laser mass spectrometer was designed to determine the elemental and isotopic composition of the soil. Analysis is carried out to a depth of 1–2 μm, with the area analysed being 1–2 mm in diameter. The principle of the instrument's operation is expounded in [2, 3].

Upon reaching the prescribed height of 50 m (determined by an altimeter) a focused laser beam was to have been directed towards the surface of Phobos. Upon interaction of the laser pulses with the soil, the ions would be evaporated and scattered into the space above. Some ions in the cloud of vapour that rises from the spot would enter a reflectron on the spacecraft which has a retarding electric field.

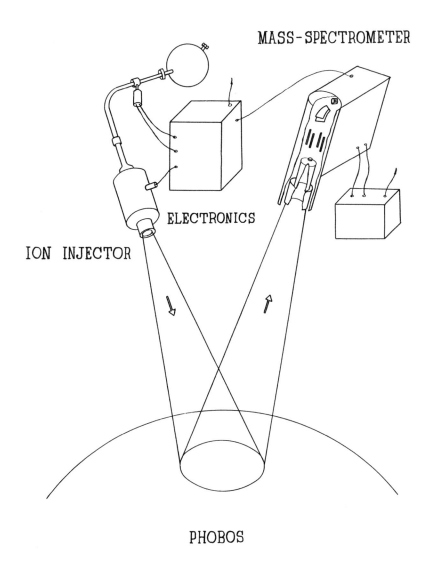

MASS-SPECTROMETER

ELECTRONICS

ION INJECTOR

PHOBOS

Fig.2.6.4 — Diagram of the experiment in the mass analysis of secondary ions on the Phobos spacecraft.

The reflectron analyses the ions on the basis of the time of their flight from the spot on the surface under study to the spacecraft. It was supposed that about 10^6 ions would be recorded per laser beam pulse.

The diagram of the experiment is presented in Fig, 2.6.3.

The device had the following characteristics:

range of masses explored	1–200 a.m.u.
resolution with respect to masses $M/\triangle M$	150
wavelength of the laser beam	1.06 μm
energy in a pulse	0.5 J
duration of a pulse	10 ns
frequency of laser pulses	0.1–0.2 Hz
mass of instrumentation	70 kg

The instrument was designed in cooperation with scientists and engineers from Austria, Bulgaria, the German Democratic Republic, the Soviet Union, West Germany, and Czechoslovakia.

2.6.2.2. Mass spectrometry of secondary ions (DION)

The aim of this experiment was also to determine the elemental and isotopic composition of the soil on Phobos. The principle of the instrument's operation is set forth in [2, 3]. The surface of Phobos, from a distance of about 50 m, was to be irradiated by an accelerated krypton ion beam. The energetic ions would impinge on the surface of Phobos and knock out the secondary ions of rock-forming elements. The secondary ions would then be scattered into the hemispherical space above, and some of them would enter a mass analyser of the quadrupole type. Since the energy of primary ions is not very high, the secondary ions would be knocked out of the soil from a depth of only about 1 nm. Since this thin surface layer has been subjected to the greatest extent to the effect of various cosmogenic factors, its composition must be the most modified as compared to the satellite's primary composition. Thus, the data on this layer would provide detailed information on the processes which have taken place on the surface of Phobos during the long period of its existence.

The diagram of the experiment for the mass analysis of the secondary ions is given in Fig. 2.6.4.

The instrument possessed the following main characteristics:

range of ion masses recorded	1–60 a.m.u.
resolution with respect to masses $M/\triangle M$	100–150
maximum counting rate of ions	$10^6 s^{-1}$
duration of the injection pulse	1 s
frequency of pulse repetition	0.2 Hz
beam current	about 2 mA
energy of ion beam	2–3 keV
working medium	krypton
mass of instrumentation	18 kg

This experiment was designed in cooperation with scientists and engineers from the Soviet Union, France, West Germany and Hungary.

2.6.3. EXPLORATION OF THE SURFACE OF PHOBOS FROM LANDERS

Within the framework of the Phobos project two types of descent probes were designed to land on the surface of Mars' satellite Phobos. One of them — the long term automated lander — was designed to carry out exploration at one point of the surface. Due to the possibility of sending information from the lander directly back to the Earth, prolonged measurements of the evolution of Phobos' orbit would have been carried out. The other vehicle — the hopping rover (the hopper or 'frog') — for studying the surface was to have a relatively short lifetime, but with the ability to move and conduct measurements at several points on the surface. The landers had approximately the same size and weight, and therefore, were interchangeable aboard the Phobos spacecraft. The Phobos 2 spacecraft carried one each of the two different landers — the long term automated lander and the hopper.

2.6.3.1. The hopping rover (hopper)

Due to the small size of Phobos (an ellipsoid with semi-axes 13.5 x 10.8 x 9.4 km) the acceleration due to gravity near the surface has the small value of about 5×10^{-3} m s^{-2} (roughly 2000 times smaller than on the Earth). That is why the hopping mode of the rover's motion across the surface of Phobos was chosen. The basis of this method of movement is that a certain initial speed is imparted to the rover, and it then moves along a ballistic trajectory. By this means it is possible to overcome obstacles considerably exceeding the rover in size.

The diagram of the hopper along with the mounting unit and the damper is shown in Fig. 2.6.5. The hopper was connected to the main spacecraft by the mounting unit, which would also have controlled the direction and speed of the hopper's separation from the spacecraft. The damper was designed to reduce the path and time taken to settle on to the surface after the hopper's initial impact on the surface. (The damper prevents the probe from rolling down slopes and protects the hopper during its first impacts on the surface).

The hopping rover is a self-contained space station and consists of a spherical body with a protective envelope, auxiliary systems (a power supply unit, a radiotelemetry complex, a programme timer, and automatic control unit, etc.), a hopping propulsive device, an orientation device and a set of scientific instruments.

The planned sequence of the hopper's operation on the surface of Phobos is presented in Fig. 2.6.6, and is described briefly here.

Upon separation from the base of the main spacecraft, the rover falls to the surface of Phobos under the effect of the force of gravity. Upon reaching the surface, several consistently damping impacts and a roll of the rover take place. After completion of this process, the damper separates and the rover is orientated in the correct position. In the correct position the rover rests on the surface soil supported by the hopping propulsive device. Then the scientific instruments are switched on. Upon completion of the operation of the scientific instruments and the transmission of information via a telemetry channel at that spot, the hopping propulsive device operates, and the rover hops as much as 20 metres sideways to another point on the surface, and all operations are repeated. This was planned to continue until the available power resources were exhausted.

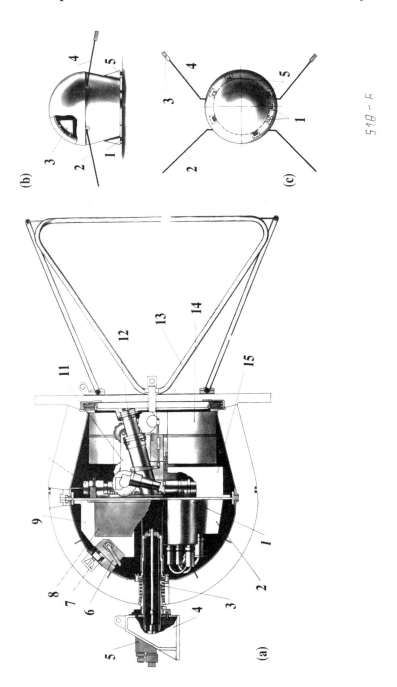

Fig.2.6.5 — Diagrammatic representation of the hopping rover studying the surface of Phobos. (a) Section through hopper: 1, switching device; 2, measuring unit; 3, separation device; 4, mounting arm; 5, pyropin; 6, radio transmitter; 7, antenna; 8, power source; 9, accelerometer; 10, orientation unit; 11, penetrometer; 12, repulsion device; 13, damper; 14, X-ray spectrometer; 15, automatics unit. (b) Hopper's position on the surface: 1, magnetic susceptibility sensor, 2, active supports, 3, gravimeter, 4, passive supports, 5, thermistor. (c) View of the hopper (plan): 1, magnetic susceptibility sensor; 2, active supports; 3, magnetometer's sensor; 4, passive supports; 5, thermistors.

The main characteristics of the hopping rover were:

mass of the rover	50 kg
mass of scientific instruments	7 kg
capacity of the power source	30 A h
radio transmitter power and frequency	0.3 W and 224 bit s^{-1}
memory size	8.2 kbits
dimensions	a sphere of diameter 500 mm
operation time at each point on the surface	20 min
total operation time on the surface	$\geqslant 4$ hours
distance between extreme points on path	< 1 km.

The hopping rover was designed to solve the following scientific tasks:

(a) The determination of the chemical composition of soil

To determine the composition of soil the X-ray radiometric method was to be used. The sample under study would have been irradiated by a radioisotope source, while the excited fluorescence radiation of chemical elements present in soil was recorded by an X-ray spectrometer. The device was located in the lower part of the rover. The rover's lower wall had two windows through which the rock was irradiated by radioisotope sources and excited fluorescence radiation was received by the detectors.

A diagram showing the method of measurement is presented in Fig. 2.6.7. The instrument had two radioisotope sources (^{55}Fe with an activity of 120 mCi and ^{109}Cd with an activity of 40 mCi) and four detectors (gas proportional counters). The signals from the detectors enter — through appropriate linear amplifiers — the 512 (128 x 4)-channel pulse-height analyser in whose four sections information is accumulated, encoded and memorized. The accumulated data would then be transmitted via a telemetry channel to the main spacecraft.

The main characteristics were as follows: mass 3.5 kg, power consumption 5 W, number of analyser channels 4 x 128, capacity of each channel 2^{16} pulses, volume of information per cycle 19.2 kbits, energy ranges 0.9 to 7.0 keV and from 3.0 to 24 keV, and energy resolution of the detectors 20%.

The results of measurements would have been processed on the basis of the preliminary calibration of the instrumentation on reference rocks. The sensitivity of determining the content of the elements was about 0.01%.

(b) Measurements of soil temperature

The soil temperature was to be measured by two methods. The first method consisted of using four flat thermistors located on the rover's lower surface. However, due to the expected ruggedness of the surface of the soil, the thermistors' contact with the soil was unreliable. To increase reliability a second method was also used. This entailed measuring the temperature of the thermal flux by point thermistors located inside spherical cavities in the rover's lower surface operating in the mode of a bolometer.

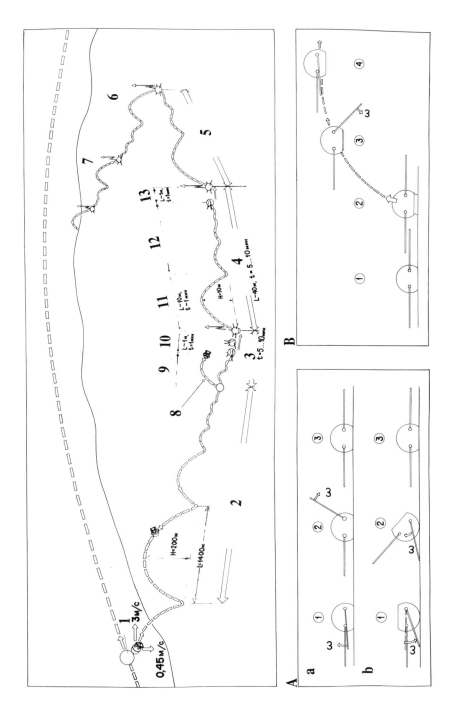

Fig.2.6.6 — Diagram of the landing and motion of the hopping rover on the surface of Phobos. 1, delivery vehicle; 2, damping after the ejection from the delivery vehicle; 3, 1st operation cycle; 4, 2nd operation cycle, 5, 3rd operation cycle; 6, 4th operation cycle; 7, 5th operation cycle; 8, separation of the damper; 9, damping, 10, orientation; 11, jump; 12, damping; 13, orientation. A Orientation. (a) normal landing, (b) landing with the support directed upwards. B Jump.

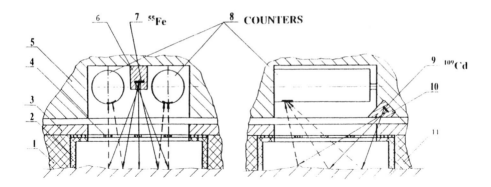

Fig.2.6.7 — Functional diagram of the X-ray fluorescence analysis of soil on Phobos.

(c) Measurements of free-fall acceleration

This task was to be solved by measuring the time taken for a small metal ball to free-fall in the gravitational field. The ball, which was inside a spherical cone, would first be raised into its upper position by an electromagnet, and then, after the electromagnet was de-energized, would fall onto the cone's base, which was in contact with a piezo-sensor. The time of fall was to be measured by the number of clock pulses (having a frequency of 500 Hz) counted during the ball's descent.

(d) Magnetic measurements

To measure any magnetic field on Phobos use was made of a two component ferroprobe magnetometer whose principle of operation was based on the emergence of an e.m.f. (even harmonics) during magnetization of the magnetosensitive element by the sum of the measured field H_o and the exciting field H_M namely $+ H_M \sin \omega t$.

The measuring range is $0 - 120$ nT, resolution 1 nT, and sensitivity 1 nT.

The magnetic susceptibility of the rock was to be measured by a device based on the change in the phase of sine-wave oscillations as compared with the reference frequency of oscillations when the sensor was placed directly on the rock. Power consumption was $30 - 65$ mA, and the measuring range was ± 120 nT.

(e) The assessment of the physical and mechanical properties of soil

One of the methods would be to measure the parameters of the dynamics of the rover's collision with the soil during its initial fall onto the surface, its damping impacts and hopping. The method has been used for all space vehicles which have landed on the surfaces of planets. For this purpose a triaxial accelerometer was installed on the rover.

The second method of estimating the physical and mechanical properties of the soil would be to analyse the forces exerted by the support of the hopping propulsive device on the soil. This enables one to use the support as a 'stamp' for the classical determinations of the deformation properties of soil (the modulus of strain, bearing strength, etc.). To implement this possibility a motion sensor was installed on the extensible support.

Another possibility for assessing the properties of soil was to be provided by a dynamic penetrometer installed on the rover. The mechanical properties would have been determined from the parameters of the stamp's penetration into soil (bearing strength) and also from the selected soil sample (the modulus of strain, the internal resistance angle, cohesion, and the granulometric class).

Measurements to be conducted from the rover would have given not only the detailed characteristics of the limited region at the rover's landing sites, but also reference values for fixing and interpreting the results of the remote measurements which were to be performed from the main spacecraft.

2.6.3.2. The stationary long-tem automated lander

When the Phobos spacecraft was at its closest to Mars' satellite, the long-term automated lander was to be separated from it so that it would slowly move towards the surface of Phobos. Upon touchdown, its protruding contact sensors would give a command for the operation of the mechanism for fixing the station on the surface. Since the force of gravity on the the surface of Phobos is low, it was necessary to fix the station mechanically in the correct position. This was to be ensured by the 'berthing mechanism' which consisted of a device firing a harpoon penetrator. In soft soil this device could reach a depth of up to 10 m, but in sandstone a depth of less than a metre. The penetrator was connected to the long-term automated lander by a flexible rope which made it possible to pull the station down on to the surface. It was supposed that the station would operate on the surface of Phobos for serveral months. The station is briefly described in [2, 3].

The main objective of the long-term automated lander was to conduct scientific experiments which required measurements over long time periods. They included:

(a) experiments in celestial mechanics carried out by the station's radio system and ground-based receiving–transmitting stations;
(b) registration of seismic noise by a seismometer (this noise is caused by the gravitational field of Mars and by thermal expansion during the transition from day to night).

As a result of long-term studies in the field of celestial mechanics it would have been possible to specify the position of Phobos in the standard coordinate system linked with the Earth and with respect to quasars — the most distant radio sources in the Universe. This is necessary for specifying the astronomical unit, and for accurate determination of the value of the secular acceleration of Phobos' orbit, etc.

The optical sensor used to determine the exact direction of the Sun would have yielded information on the libration of Phobos — its oscillations back and forth with respect to its own centre of mass.

Another group of experiments carried out by the lander were designed to study the elemental composition of the surface layer, its structure and physical and mechanical characteristics.

The following instruments were mounted on the long-term automated lander:
— alpha particle back-scattering and X-ray fluorescence spectrometer;
— optical sensor of the Sun's angular position;
— seismometer;

Fig.2.6.8 — General view of the long-service lander designed for the exploration on the surface of Phobos. 1, scientific instruments; 2, solar panels (3), 3, antenna of the transmitter; 4, solar sensor, 5, antenna of the receiver.

— penetrating probe (penetrator);
— TV camera.

Fig. 2.6.8 presents a general view of the long-term automated lander. It consisted of a platform with scientific and auxiliary equipment mounted on three supports about 80 cm above the base. The opening solar panels, an aerial, a radio complex and the solar optical sensor were mounted on this platform. The solar panels were to be orientated towards the Sun by the optical sensor. The station was to maintain communications with the Earth every day (a day on Phobos lasts for 7 h 40 min). In the lower part of the station there was a base on which the supports for the equipment platform rested. Scientific instruments (a penetrator with temperature sensors and an accelerometer, sensors for alpha particle back-scattering, an X-ray fluorescence spectrometer and a seismometer) were also mounted on the base.

To control all the instruments the station had a microprocessor, which would also have carried out the preliminary processing of the accumulated scientific information before its transmission to the Earth.

REFERENCES

[1] R. Z. Sagdeyev, V. M. Balebanov, A. V. Zakharov, V. M. Kovtuneko, R. S. Kremnev, L. V. Ksanfomaliti and G. N. Rogovsky. *The Phobos Project. Scientific Objectives*, Reports to the 26th COSPAR Session, June 1986, Toulouse, France.

[2] V. M. Balebanov, A. V. Zakharov and V. M. Linkin. *Mars' enigmatic moons, Nauka v SSSR (Science in the USSR)*, No. 4, p. 3, 1986.

[3] *The Phobos Project*. Publication by the Institute of Space Research, USSR Academy of Sciences, p. 52, 1986.

[4] A. L. Kemurdzhian, Yu. A. Surkov, V. V. Gromov, P. S. Sologub and F. F. Kirnozov. *Exploring the surface of Phobos from a rover*. Abstract from the 24th Lunar–Planetary Conference. Houston, USA, March 14–18, 1988.

[5] Yu. A. Surkov, L. P. Moskalyova, O. S. Manvelyan and V. P. Kharyukova. *Remote gamma-ray spectrometry of Mars and Phobos*. Abstract from the 24th Lunar-Planetary Conference, Houston, USA, March 14–18, 1988.

2.7 First results of gamma-ray measurements of Mars from Phobos 2 spacecraft

The abundance of television pictures of the Martian surface taken from space probes in the 1960s and 1970s enabled great progress to be made in developing ideas of the surface and crust of Mars.

To explore Mars further in July 1988 the Phobos 2 spacecraft was launched. It carried a set of scientific instruments, in particular, a scintillation gamma-ray spectrometer. In January 1989 the spacecraft entered a satellite orbit around Mars. For about two weeks the spacecraft was in a three-day elliptic orbit with minimum and maximum distances from the planet of 870 and about 80,000 km, respectively. (The inclination of the satellite orbit to the planet's equator was 1.0°.) While in this orbit, the spacecraft made four circuits around the planet, approaching it in the equatorial region. Then in February 1989 the spacecraft was transferred to a nearly circular orbit with an average radius of 9760 km and a period of revolution of about eight hours. During the stay in this orbit observations of Mars and Phobos were conducted using a television system.

2.7.1 MEASUREMENTS OF GAMMA RADIATION [1]

During the flight from the Earth to Mars the gamma-ray spectrometer operated in two modes:

(1) on commands from the Earth the gamma radiation background was periodically (one or two times a month) measured. During the flight, 10 spectra were measured. The time of collecting each spectrum was 60 min.

(2) According to the signals from the gamma-ray detector the corresponding functional channel recorded gamma-ray-bursts. During the flight to Mars more than 20 gamma-ray-bursts were recorded. The energy of gamma-ray quanta and their temporal distributions were measured.

Measurements of Mars' gamma radiation were conducted during the spacecraft's stay in the elliptic orbit. With the approach to the surface (in the periapse region) the planet's gamma radiation was measured and at the maximum distance (in the apoapse region) the measurements of the background were carried out.

Fig. 2.7.1 gives a map of the Martian surface on which regions of measuring gamma radiation are indicated. Points PC-1, PC-2, PC-3 and PC-4 correspond to

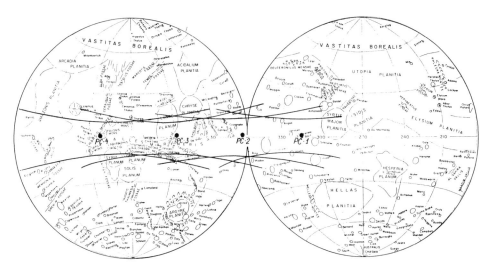

Fig. 2.7.1 —   Map of Mars with regions of measured gamma radiation.

places of the spacecraft's closest approach to the Martian surface.   Lines indicate
how the area scanned by the detector varies during the passage of the pericentre by
the spacecraft. As evident from the figure, measurements were performed only in
the equatorial part in a band roughly 1000 km wide. However, this investigated part
of the surface includes also the ancient greatly cratered surface (the planet's ancient
crust) embraced by trajectories PC-1, PC-2 and partly PC-3, and the younger
volcanogenic region Tharsis explored during the flight along the PC-4 trajectory.

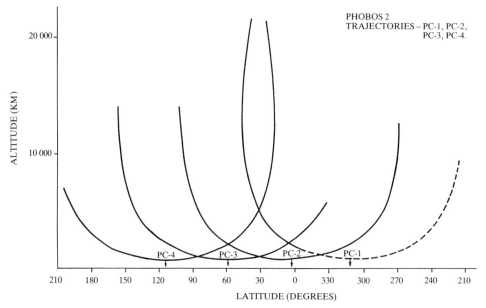

Fig. 2.7.2 —   Trajectories of the approach of Phobos 2 to the surface of Mars in
which gamma radiation was measured.

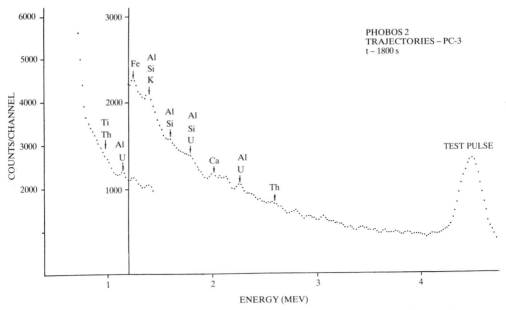

Fig. 2.7.3— Spectrum of gamma radiation measured in the PC-3 trajectory in the period of the closest rendezvous with Mars.

Fig. 2.7.2 shows trajectory sections in which measurements were made. As can be seen from the figure, measurements of gamma radiation began from distances of over 3000 km from the surface, then they continued at closer distances and, finally, were completed when the spacecraft again moved away from the surface at a distance of over 3000 km. The duration of each session of measurements was about 10 min.

In Fig. 2.7.3 a measured gamma radiation spectrum is given as an example. In the spectrum one can see peaks belonging to natural radioactive elements (U, Th and K) and some rock-forming elements (Mg, Si, Al, Fe, etc.). The peak in the right part of the spectrum belongs to alpha radiation of ^{241}Am used as a reference point for the calibration of the energy scale of the gamma spectrum.

At present, only preliminary results of processing the gamma-ray spectrum measured on the PC-3 trajectory have been obtained.

2.7.2 PROCESSING OF GAMMA-RADIATION SPECTRA

A gamma-radiation spectrum represents a continous distribution with slightly pronounced characteristics radiation peaks. It consists of the following components: (1) gamma radiation of natural radioactive elements contained in the rock, (2) gamma radiation induced by the interaction of cosmic rays with the atmosphere and the surface and (3) gamma radiation generated during the interaction of cosmic rays with the material of the spacecraft (and the instrument itself).

The first component makes it possible to determine the U, Th and K content in the Martian rock. For this purpose the gamma-ray spectrometer was calibrated on terrestrial rocks with different contents of these elements.

The second component gives information on the content of basic rock-forming elements in the Martian rock. To determine these elements we used theoretical calculations of the processes of the interaction between cosmic rays and nuclei of chemical elements contained in the rock and carried out experiments on accelerators and balloons in simulating these processes.

The third component in this case does not carry scientific information but is a background from the measured spectrum: (2) the breaking down of the spectrum the spacecraft's stay in satellite orbit (at the apoapse).

The basic stages of processing gamma-ray spectra are: (1) the subtraction of the background from the measured spectrum: (2) the breaking down of the spectrum into the continuous component and characteristic radiation (3) the breaking down of the spectrum of characteristic radiation into the monoelement spectra of rock-forming elements and (4) the determination of the concentration of rock-forming elements.

Table 2.7.1 – Elemental composition of Mars' rocks measured by gamma-ray spectrometers (percentage by mass)

Element	Phobos 2	Mars 5
O	48 ± 5	44 ± 5
Mg	6 ± 3	—
Al	5 ± 2	5 ± 2
Si	19 ± 4	14 ± 3
K	0.3 ± 0.1	0.3 ± 0.1
Ca	6 ± 3	—
Ti	1 ± 0.7	—
Fe	9 ± 3	14 ± 4
U	$(0.5 \pm 0.1) \times 10^{-4}$	$(0.6 \pm 0.1) \times 10^{-4}$
Th	$(1.9 \pm 0.6) \times 10^{-4}$	$(2.1 \pm 0.5) \times 10^{-4}$

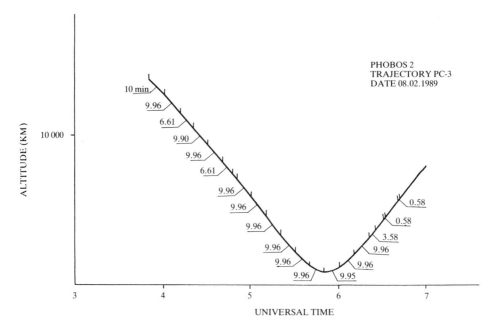

Fig. 2.7.4—   The PC-3 trajectory in which gamma radiation measurement sessions
are indicated.

Table 2.7.1 summarizes the preliminary results of processing one of the gamma-ray spectra measured on the PC-3 trajectory (see Fig. 2.7.4) . They made it possible to average composition of the Martian rock in a complex region, the western part of which is ancient highly cratered upland, while the eastern part forms a flat Lunar plateau. The giant Valles Marineris is adjacent to this region to the south. The elemental composition of the Martian rock listed in Table 2.7.1 relates to a rather vast area. Therefore, it is hard to refer it to a definite type of the geomorphological province. This gamma radiation spectrum was measured roughly in the region where we conducted measurements of gamma radiation of Mars in 1974 from Mars 5 spacecraft. The fact that the data were obtained in the same region of the Martian surface enables us to consider the data from the Mars 5 and Phobos 2 spacecraft together.

2.7.3 DISCUSSION OF THE RESULTS
It is evident from Table 2.7.1 that the contents of rock-forming and natural radioactive elements measured by both spacecraft are rather close to each other. The difference is contents do not exceed 20% in mass, which lies within the limits of the accuracy of their determination. The differences could be still greater because the conditions of measurement are not identical (different altitude of measurement and variation in the location of sites beneath the apoapse, etc.).

The results of this experiment can be regarded as the confirmation of data obtained earlier from Mars 5 spacecraft. At the same time, they show that perhaps vast territories of the Martian surface are to a large extent covered with a surface layer of aeolian depositions (fine-grained material). The results of determing the composition of the rock from Vikings 1 and 2 (see Table 1.4.3) testify to these considerations. Such compositions are also rather close to the compositions measured from Mars 5 and Phobos 2 spacecraft, despite the fact that these regions lie far from each other.

However an analysis of these data in more detail allows us to see some differences in compositions of the Martian rocks investigated from Phobos 2 and Vikings 1 and 2. It gives the basis for some conclusions about the composition of the underlying bedrock. The data obtained by Vikings 1 and 2 give us the composition of a thin surface layer of soil, the thickness of which is several centimetres (the depth of sampling by Viking arm), and data obtained from Phobos 2 spacecraft pertain to a surface layer of about 2 m thickness.

It can be supposed that as a result of aeolian process the layer of fine grained material is on the surface of Mars. The composition of the material is changes with depth from the average composition on the surface to the composition of the underlaying bedrock.

To make the conclusion about the underlying bedrock, the content of sodium was estimated first of all using known correlations between K_2O, Al_2O_3 and Na_2O in magmatic rocks of basic composition.

It is seen in Table 2.7.2 that concentrations of SiO_2 and FeO are lower and concentrations of other oxides are higher in the Phobos 2 rock than in the Vikings 1 and 2 rocks. It testifies that the Phobos 2 rock composition is a mixture of the surface fine grained material and underlaying bedrock.

Proceeding from the rock composition determined at the Phobos 2 landing site and assuming different amounts of fine grained material in it (presumably 10 to 50%

Table 2.7.2 – Chemical composition of the rocks on Mars and Reunion (percentage by mass)

Oxide	Phobos 2	Viking 1	% V	Reunion
SiO_2	48.6	52.9	46.7	46.5
TiO_2	2.0	1.1	2.4	2.4
Al_2O_3	11.3	7.0	13.1	12.5
FeO	13.8	20.2	11.1	11.8
MgO	11.9	10.3	12.6	13.3
CaO	10.0	6.9	11.4	11.0
Na_2O	1.9	1.2	2.2	2.1
K_2O	0.4	0.4	0.5	0.4
SiO_2/MgO	4.1	5.2	3.7	3.6
Na_2O+K_2O	2.4	1.6	2.7	2.8

because an upper limit of approximately 60% is determined by the content of FeO) the composition of underlaying bedrock was estimated.

The consideration of this bedrock's composition in the framework of the systematic ($Na_2O + K_2O$ as a function of SiO_2 content) of magmatic rocks of the Earth's crust shows that the closest analogue in the Earth's crust is probably subalkaline picritobasalts. This kind of the rock occurs on the oceanic islands.

As an example the composition of Reunion picritobasalt is given in Table 2.7.2. Perhaps further processing of information obtained from Phobos 2 will reveal noticeable differences in the composition of the bedrocks lying in other regions of the Martian surface. In this sense, spectra obtained from the PC-4 trajectory can be of particular interest because they correspond to the vast volcanogenic massif Tharsis. However, the processing of gamma-ray spectrometric information obtained from the Phobos 2 spacecraft will take a relatively long time.

REFERENCE

[1] Surkov, Yu. A., Barsukov, V.L., Moskaleva L. P., *et al*. Measurements of gamma-radiation of Mars from Phobos 2 spacecraft. Report at 20th Lunar and Planetary Sciences Conference, Houston USA, March 1989.

2.8 Conclusion

Completing the book, I would like to look back once again at past progress in the investigation of the cosmochemistry of planets and satellites and to touch upon its prospects for further development.

In the Soviet Union these studies were initiated under the guidance of Academician Alexander Vinogradov with the most vigorous support by Academician Mstislav Keldysh, President of the USSR Academy of Sciences. Realizing the paramount importance of the development of the concepts of the Solar System bodies, and especially the Earth, they exercised decisive influence on the development of these studies in the USSR.

In this book only the cosmochemical area of the exploration of Solar System bodies is considered. Almost every space flight and every experiment described in this book were of a pioneering nature and actually led to discoveries.

Today, reviewing the past, one can see how far we have advanced in developing our concepts of the planets and their satellites. It was a path of countless surprises and justified expectations, a path of sophisticated experiments and wonderful discoveries. During this short period of time new concepts of the planets and satellites have been formulated.

Two decades ago, while preparing the first experiments, we often proceeded just from suppositions and surmises. For instance, when the first space probe was being prepared for the flight to Venus, we did not know the composition of the Venusian atmosphere (N_2 or CO_2) and its thickness, and even the possible existence of oceans of organic or inorganic liquids on the planetary surface was not ruled out. Among the scientific instruments carried out by the first space probe was one to identify the type of liquid.

When preparing the first spacecraft which was tō land on the Moon's surface, researchers were greatly concerned over the possibility that the lander would sink into a thick layer of dust. Today, recalling the suppositions about oceans on Venus and the dust layer on the Moon, we can appreciate how little was our knowledge of the Moon and the planets before exploration by spacecraft. However, despite the giant leap in the development of our concepts of the Solar System, we find ourselves at the very beginning of the endless process of understanding its nature.

Considering planets and satellites, I have mentioned the main problems of their exploration. The solution of these problems will take a long time. The complexity of constructing space vehicles, their high cost, and the long intervals between launchings (they are determined by astronomical 'windows') are factors determining the rate of exploration of Solar System bodies.

As we have seen, over the past two decades, attention has focused on the Moon and terrestrial planets. No doubt in the near future this line of research will retain its priority.

The exploration of terrestrial planets — bodies whose origin and the history of formation are similar to those of the Earth — will remain a basis for development of the concepts of our planet.

The Moon, as the body closest to the Earth, as a space detector which has retained an imprint of the early history of the Solar System bodies, as a natural platform for exploring far-out space, and a potential source of raw materials for the use and colonization of adjacent space is an object of particular attention in the scientific and applied respects.

The Pioneer and Voyager flights to the giant planets have opened the road to the satellites of Jupiter and Saturn. The size of these satellites is commensurable with the Moon and Mercury. Their exploration is of particular importance for understanding the process of the formation of Solar System bodies and the early stages of planetary evolution. Our first acquaintance with these satellites has already revealed many interesting phenomena. In particular, it has turned out that Jupiter's satellite Io and Neptune's satellite Triton are the only bodies on which present-day volcanic activity has been detected with certainty, similar to that taking place on the Earth, while Saturn's satellite Titan has proved to be the only body having a dense atmosphere consisting mainly of nitrogen like the Earth's atmosphere. The exploration of Io will make an important contribution to the understanding of the Earth's early history (the first 1000 to 1500 million years), in particular, the process of the differentiation of its material. Studies of Titan's atmosphere composed of nitrogen, methane, ammonia and complex hydrocarbons will perhaps advance us in understanding the origin of life on the Earth. At present we know very little about the planetary satellites. However, it is quite obvious that their further study will open up to us a host of so-far unpredictable phenomena.

In this book we have summed up the main results of cosmochemical studies of planets and satellites. Further development of studies along this line will eventually make it possible to evolve a consistent theory of the origin, evolution and modern structure of planets and satellites from their formation to the present time. However, the interests of science are extended also to the more remote (pre-planetary) period of the existence of the Solar System, to its origins. In this connection, more and more attention is being given to small bodies — asteroids, comets and meteoric dust. These bodies have changed little during their lifetime and up to now have retained the traces of events which took place in the early Solar System.

Such priority of studies is confirmed, specifically, by the projects which are being worked out by the USSR Academy of Sciences, the US National Aeronautics and Space Administration (NASA), the European Space Agency (ESA) and other countries within the framework of national space programmes.

Despite the striving of countries elaborating space projects to conduct studies under programmes distinct for their novelty and originality, scientific interests focus their attention on the most topical problems.

For instance, attaching particular importance to obtaining the Moon's global characteristics (its geological mapping, the preparation of maps of magnetic, gravitational, thermal and radiation fields, the chemical and mineral composition), Soviet and foreign scientists independently consider the problems of creating lunar polar satellites. The obtaining of these global characteristics is necessary for choosing the areas which are most promising for future research and for working out a long-term programme of the exploration and use of the Moon.

The flights of Soviet and American spacecraft to Mars made it possible to obtain only the first information about the Martian atmosphere and its surface. The main problem — whether any life form exists (or existed) on this planet — has remained unsolved. To study Mars' atmosphere, surface and interior, the ESA is elaborating the project of Mars' polar satellite — Kepler. A similar project for a Mars satellite designed to determine the global composition of surface rocks and the role of water in the Martian climate is being discussed by American scientists (Project Mars Observer).

In the space era great attention has been given to Venus. The planet has been explored by about 20 Soviet and American space probes. We have learnt much about its atmosphere, surface and history of formation. At present, of great interest is study of the geological structure and the history of the formation of the planetary surface and crust. Veneras 13 and 14 (arrived March 1982) Pioneer Venus (arrived December 1978) and Veneras 15 and 16 (arrived October 1983) made a particularly great contribution in this respect. Finally, in 1985 Vegas 1 and 2 conducted very interesting studies of Venus. Now NASA's Magellan probe will explore the topography of the surface by using SAR (synthetic aperture radar) methods.

In 1986 Halley's comet attracted scientists' closest attention. This comet returns to perihelion every 76 years or so. In 1986, the circumstances for Earth-based observations of the comet were not particularly favourable; the closest approach was 63 million km in April 1986. The comet reached its descending mode in early March and in this connection Soviet space probes Vegas 1 and 2, the European Space Agency's Giotto spacecraft and the Japanese craft Suisei and Sakigake were sent to encounter Halley's comet. Such intensive exploration of the comet yielded much new information about these hard-to-access minor bodies of the Solar System.

At last, problems are being discussed which are linked with the exploration of far-off planets and their satellites.

Evidently not all projects planned at the present time will be implemented, but their orientation testifies to the most topical trends and main scientific problems which are of interest to researchers at the present time.

With the development of space technology, the rate of the penetration into space will grow. Apparently, before the end of this century fundamental concepts of the origin and evolution of the Solar System will be solved, and the next century will open up an era of manned flights to planets and satellites, which until recently represented the world of mysteries and exotica.

As Konstantin Tsiolkovsky, the man who was the inspiration for the Soviet space programme, once put it, 'mankind will not remain for ever on the Earth, at first it will timidly penetrate beyond the limits of the atmosphere and then will conquer for itself entire circumsolar space'.

Index